PROLOG FOR PROGRAMMERS

This is volume 24 in A.P.I.C. Studies in Data Processing
General Editors: Fraser Duncan *and* M. J. R. Shave
A complete list of titles in this series appears at the end of this volume

PROLOG FOR PROGRAMMERS

Feliks Kluźniak

Stanisław Szpakowicz

Institute of Informatics
Warsaw University
Warsaw, Poland

With a contribution by Janusz S. Bień

1985

ACADEMIC PRESS, INC.

Harcourt Brace Jovanovich, Publishers
London   Orlando   San Diego
New York   Austin   Montreal   Sydney
Tokyo   Toronto

ACADEMIC PRESS INC. (LONDON) LTD.
24–28 Oval Road
LONDON NW1 7DX

United States Edition published by
ACADEMIC PRESS, INC.
Orlando, Florida 32887

British Library Cataloguing in Publication Data

Kluźniak, Feliks

    Prolog for programmers.
    1. Programming languages (Electronic computers)
    2. Electronic digital computers––Programming
    I. Title   II. Szpakowicz, Stanisław
    000.64'24   QA76.7

Library of Congress Cataloging in Publication Data

Kluźniak, Feliks.
    Prolog for programmers.

    Includes index.
    1. Prolog (Computer program language) I. Szpakowicz,
Stanisław. II. Bień, Janusz St. III. Title.
QA76.73.P76K58 1985   001.64'24   84-14520
ISBN 0–12–416520–6 (alk. paper)

PRINTED IN THE UNITED STATES OF AMERICA

86 87 88 89   9 8 7 6 5 4 3 2

Agacie Sarze, i jej mamie—F. K.

Pakowi, Mikołajowi, Błażejowi i Gumce—Szp.

Zosi i Basi—J. S. B.

CONTENTS

PREFACE

Prolog is a non-conventional programming language for a wide spectrum of applications, including language processing, data base modelling and implementation, symbolic computing, expert systems, computer-aided design, simulation, software prototyping and planning. A version of Prolog has been chosen as a systems programming language for so-called fifth-generation computers; experiments with systems programming and concurrent programming are in progress.

Prolog, devised by Alain Colmerauer, is a logic programming language. Logic programming is a new discipline which lends a unifying view to many domains of computer science. Prolog can be classified as a descriptive programming language, as opposed to prescriptive (or imperative) languages such as Pascal, C and Ada. In principle, the programmer is only supposed to specify *what* is to be done by his or her program, without bothering with *how* this should be achieved. Robert A. Kowalski has coined the "equation"

Algorithm = Logic + Control,

which emphasizes the distinction between the *what* (logic) and the *how* (control). The programmer need not always specify the control component. In practice, however, Prolog can be treated as a procedural language.

Prolog is not standardized, and it comes in many different flavours. The most widespread dialect of Prolog is Prolog-10, originally implemented by David H. D. Warren for DEC-10 computers. We describe a variant of this dialect, based on an interpreter written in Pascal especially for this book.

The main part of the book is Chapters 1–5. Chapters 1 and 3 are an introduction to Prolog, intended for those who use prescriptive languages in their everyday practice. Both intuitions and the presentation are "practically" biased, but we assume the reader has a certain amount of programming experience and sophistication. Chapter 2 explains Prolog in terms of logic. It requires no deep knowledge of mathematics and is intended as a counterpoint to Chapter 1, but can be skipped on a first reading. Chapter 4 contains some useful programming techniques and hints. Chapter 5 is a reference manual for the version of Prolog described in this book. In addition, Chapter 8 is a discussion of two rather illuminating applications.

For those who wish to gain more insight into the language and its inner workings, Chapter 6 introduces basic principles of Prolog implementations. An implementation of the dialect described in this book is presented in Chapter 7 and in the appendices (which contain complete listings). We used this implementation to test our examples, including the case studies of Chapter 8.

Chapter 9, written by Janusz S. Bień (who also did most of the bibliography), briefly outlines the most characteristic features of several other Prolog dialects.

The material in this book, supplemented by some additional reading and a programming assignment, can be used for a two-semester course at the level of third-year computer science majors. Re-implementation of or extensions to the interpreter of Chapter 7 might make interesting assignments for a translator-writing course.

While working on this book, we used the computing facilities of the Institute of Informatics, Warsaw University. We would like to thank Pawel Gburzynski and Krzysztof Kimbler, who helped us switch almost painlessly to a different machine when the one we originally used broke down for a protracted period of time. We thank David H. D. Warren for permitting us to include the listings of WARPLAN. We are also grateful to all those who have provided us with logic programming literature for the past 10 years.

PROLOG FOR PROGRAMMERS

1 AN INTRODUCTION TO PROLOG

Prolog is an unconventional language. In particular, its data structures are quite different from those found in other programming languages. As it is difficult to talk about a computation without understanding the sort of data that can be processed, we shall discuss data structures at some length before coming to the question of how to do anything with them. Have patience.

1.1. DATA STRUCTURES

1.1.1. Constants

Constants are the primitive building blocks of data structures. Constants have no structure, so they are often called "atoms." They represent only themselves—they can be thought of as identical with their names.

In Basic or Fortran, 1951 is a constant. The integer variable **J** is not, because it represents both a memory cell and—in certain contexts—a value. The value is something quite different from the variable itself.

One is accustomed to treating 1951 as a number greater than 1948, but this is because in programming languages constants usually belong to certain types. The usual properties of integer constants (their ordering, ability to be used in arithmetic operations, etc.) are taken for granted by virtue of their belonging to the type **integer**, just as in Pascal blue is a successor of red when one writes

colour = (red, blue, green)

1

Such type definitions impose a certain structure on the otherwise undifferentiated universe of individual symbolic constants, each of which has only one attribute: its name.

The interpretation of a constant rests solely with the programmer. 1951 can be the price of a computer, the weight of a truck, the time of day or a year of birth. One can always multiply it by 4, but this seldom makes sense when it represents a car's registration number. The constant blue is less burdened with inadequate interpretations, but one might wish not to have the colours ordered. Constants are the primitives, and collecting them into types should only be done when necessary.

In Prolog, as in other symbolic languages (such as Lisp) there is no need to declare constants or group them into types. One can use them freely, simply by writing down their names.

A legal constant name is one of the following:

—A sequence of digits, possibly prefixed by a minus sign; by convention, such constants are called **integers** (e.g. 0, -7, 1951);
—An **identifier**, which may contain letters, digits and underscores but must begin with a lower case letter (e.g. q, aName, number_9);
—A symbol which is a nonempty sequence of any of the following characters:

    + $-$ * / < = > . : ? $ & @ # \ ¬

—Any one of the characters

    , or ; or !

—The symbol [] (pronounced "nil");
—A **quoted name**, written according to the Pascal convention for strings: an arbitrary sequence of characters enclosed in apostrophes, an apostrophe being represented by two consecutive apostrophes (e.g. 'Can''t do this.' consists of 14 characters).

All of these constants are purely symbolic and have no inherent interpretation. However, some primitive operations in Prolog do treat them in a special way:

—Arithmetic operations interpret integers as representations of integer values (they can also create new integers);
—Comparison operations interpret integers as integer values, and all other constants as representations of the sequences of characters forming their names (these are lexicographically ordered by the underlying collating sequence);
—Input/output operations interpret all symbols as sequences of characters forming their names.

Each occurrence of a constant's description (name) is treated as referring to *the same* constant, but of course we are free to interpret each separately.

1.1.2. Compound Objects

An important aspect of the expressive power of a programming language is its ability to *directly* describe various data structures. Of the popular and widely used languages, Pascal is the most powerful in this respect, but it has several shortcomings. (This is *not* a criticism of Pascal: our point of view does not take into account important design objectives such as a safe type mechanism.)

Firstly, type definitions in Pascal are overspecified. It is impossible to program general algorithms which process stacks or trees regardless of the type of their elements. (Records with variants are only a rough approximation to generic data types found in some more recent programming languages.)

Secondly, those data structures which change their form dynamically can only be built with pointers. One must therefore deal with the structures at a very low level: the level of representation rather than the conceptual level at which many other things are done in Pascal. Programs using pointers are error-prone and hard to understand, because operations on such data structures are *encoded* rather than directly *expressed.*

The third shortcoming has a similar effect. Ironically, Pascal types are also *under* specified, in that there is no way to directly express certain quite natural constraints on the arguments of operations. One cannot say that the function POP can only be applied to a non-empty stack; one can only write a piece of code (hopefully correct) which checks the argument.

It is interesting that these shortcomings are not shared by Prolog data types (or rather by their counterparts, since "type" is not really a Prolog concept). And yet Prolog data structures are very simple. Let us look at the details.

Functors

To describe a compound object, it is not enough to list its components. The ordered pair (19, 24) can be an object of the type

rectangle = **record**
height, width : integer
end

as well as an object of the type

>timeofday = **record**
>>hour, minute : integer
>
>**end**

The complete description of a compound object must include a definition of its structure. Structure is defined principally by describing the way in which the object and its components are interrelated. Describing these interrelationships often consists in simply giving a **type name** to an aggregate of components (as in the example above). It is the programmer's responsibility to interpret this name in terms of real-world relations between entities being modelled by the program.

In conventional programming languages, the structure of a compound object is usually described in a declaration associating the object with a type definition. The type definition lists the name of the object–component relationship (type name) and, possibly, additional information about the structure (types) of the components. The object is described by its name (or the name of a pointer). The name's definition is textually remote from its occurrences.

A different approach is taken in Prolog. Here, the type name is an integral part of all the occurrences of the object's description. The notation is very simple: a description of a compound object is the type name followed by a parenthesized sequence of descriptions of its components, separated by commas. We write either

>rectangle(19, 24)

or

>timeofday(19, 24).

The notation is similar to that used for writing functions in mathematics. Terminology reflects this similarity. The type's name is called a **functor**, and the components are called **arguments**. There is more to it than superficial similarity of two simple syntactic conventions. One can certainly regard a type such as *rectangle* as a function mapping components into compound objects. From this point of view it is not surprising that we can have functors with no arguments: these are simply constants. Sometimes it is also useful to have one-argument functors. For example, the integer 2 can be represented by the object successor(successor(zero)) (the fact that $2 > 1 > 0$ is evident from its structure).

From the discussion above, it should be obvious that the important attributes of a functor are both its name and its **arity** (i.e. the number of arguments it takes). In Prolog, we can use both

>timeofday(17, 13)

and

timeofday(1713)

in the same program. Even if the intended interpretation is the same, these are two different objects: one has two components, and the other has one. There are also two different functors, both named timeofday. Whenever we speak of a functor in a context which gives no indication about its arity, the arity must be given explicitly. The conventional notation is to write it after a slash: timeofday/2 or timeofday/1.

The lexical rules for forming functor names are the same for all arities, but integers can only be constants. Thus

123(a, b)

is incorrect, but

'123'(a, b)

is perfectly all right. Also, [] is only a constant.

OBJECT DESCRIPTIONS

Descriptions of constants and compound objects are referred to as **terms**. Usually, the objects themselves are also called terms: this causes no confusion in practice, but in this chapter we shall try to distinguish between the two meanings.

The arguments of a term are arbitrary terms. For example, one can write a term describing a "record":

customer(name(john, smith),
              address(street(north_ave), number (173))).

Of the various functors in this example, the outermost, customer/2, can be said to define the general structure of the term. It is called the **main functor**, or **principal functor**. Similarly, name/2 is the main functor of the first argument.

Here is another example of a common data structure. A list can be defined as either the empty list, or a list constructed of any object (a head) and a list (a tail). A list of the first three letters in the alphabet could then be described by the term

cons(a, cons(b, cons(c, emptylist))).

The following term would be a description of the two-element list constructed of the above list and a list containing the integer zero:

cons(cons(a,cons(b,cons(c,emptylist))),cons(0,emptylist))

Even this small example demonstrates that nested parentheses can be difficult to read. Prolog therefore provides syntactic sugar to hide this **standard** or **canonic form** of terms. Instead of writing

successor(successor(zero))

one can choose to use *successor* as a **prefix functor** and write

successor successor zero.

Alternatively, *successor* can be made a **postfix functor**:

zero successor successor.

Functors with two arguments can be declared as **infix functors**, e.g.

&(a, b)

can be written as

a & b.

The term

a & b & c

would be ambiguous, so an infix functor is either **left-associative** or **right-associative** (or non-associative, in which case the term is incorrect). If & is right associative, the term's standard form is

&(a, &(b, c)) ;

if & is left-associative, then the term stands for

&(&(a, b), c).

We can use parentheses to stress or override associativity. If & is right-associative, then

a & b & c

is equivalent to

a & (b & c)

but not to

(a & b) & c,

which stands for

&(&(a, b), c)

regardless of associativity.

To make parentheses even less frequent, prefix, postfix and infix functors are given **priorities**. Functors with lower priority take precedence over those with a higher priority (a Prolog-10 convention, different from that used in other programming languages and mathematics). For example, if the priority of * is lower than that of +, then

    3 * 4 + 5   and   5 + 3 * 4

denote

    +(*(3, 4), 5)   and   +(5, *(3, 4))

We can use parentheses to stress or override priorities, by writing

    (3 * 4) + 5   or   3 * (4 + 5).

Prefix, postfix and infix functors are usually referred to by the generic name **operators**. Remember that these are not operators in any conventional sense: they are only a syntactic convenience.

Operator names may not be quoted. If an operator is to be written in standard form or with a different number of arguments, it must be quoted. If + is an infix functor,

    a + b,   '+'(a, b)   and   '+'(a, b, c)

are correct terms, but

    +   and   +(a, b)

are not.

It is also possible to declare **mixed operators**, i.e. functors such as the minus sign, which is both prefix and infix in ordinary arithmetic. Details about declaring prefix, postfix and infix functors can be found in Sections 5.1 and 5.7.3.

For the time being, we shall only use infix functors to write terms representing lists. However, instead of

    a cons b cons c cons emptylist

we shall use a more concise notation, modelled after Lisp. The empty list will be denoted by the constant [] (pronounced "nil"), and the constructing functor − by the right-associative infix functor ./2. Our two lists are then written as

    a.b.c.[]

and

    (a.b.c.[]).0.[]

The convention is arbitrary, in that any constant and two-argument functor would do in place of [] and the dot. It is more convenient than others, because these are the symbols expected by several built-in procedures.
(You can write such terms after feeding Prolog with

:- op(800, xfy, '.').

However, a minor technical difficulty makes it impossible to use the period as a functor when it is immediately followed by a white space character, such as blank, tab or new line. This is a nuisance, and Prolog provides special syntactic sugar for lists: it is somewhat confusing, so we will put it off until Chapter 4.)

STRINGS

Characters are constants whose names consist of single characters. One can use quoted names for characters which are not correct identifiers (e.g. '', '(', '3'; and 'x' is equivalent to x).

Strings are lists of characters. One can also write them in double quotes. For example

"string"   and   " ''''''

stand for

s.t.r.i.n.g.[]   and   ' '.''''.[]

(Actually, the convention adopted in this book is different from that of Prolog-10. There, a string denotes a list of ASCII codes and not a list of characters, so "string" stands for

115.116.114.105.110.103.[].

Similarly, in Prolog-10 operations for reading and writing characters deal directly with ASCII codes. We refuse to accept these conventions.)

1.1.3. Variables

Objects discussed so far are all, in a sense, constant. Their structure is fixed, we know everything about them and cannot learn anything new. A programming language in which one could specify only such fully defined objects would hardly be interesting. One must be able to use objects whose complete form is defined dynamically during a computation.

In Prolog, the simplest such as-yet-unknown objects are called **variables** (do not confuse them even for a moment with the variables of conventional programming languages!). The term denoting a variable is called a **variable name** (this is also usually called a variable: as with terms and objects, we shall try to maintain the distinction throughout chapter 1). A variable name is written as an identifier starting with an upper case letter or an underscore (e.g. Q, Number_9, _nnn).

A variable is an object whose structure is totally unknown. As a computation progresses, the variable may become **instantiated**, i.e. a more precise description of the object may be determined. The term embodying this description is called the variable's **instantiation**. An instantiated variable is identical with the object described by its instantiation, so it ceases to be a variable, although the object can still be referred to through the variable's name. (In general, a variable may be instantiated also to another variable—we shall soon see the meaning of this.)

There is also an alternative terminology. One says that a **free** (or **unbound**) variable becomes **bound** to another term and is henceforth indistinguishable from that term (which is called its **binding**). The variable becomes **ground** if its binding contains no variables. This terminology brings to mind the process of binding formal parameters to actual parameters. If the formal parameters were not allowed to change their value (as in pure Lisp, say), the similarity would be very close indeed, except that a binding need not be ground.

Intuitively, Prolog variables are somewhat like the variables used in mathematics. When we say that

$$f(x) = e^x + 3x$$

is a function of one variable, we mean that the equation allows us to determine the function's value for any (one) given argument. The variable denotes a single (albeit arbitrary) substitution and is not in itself an object to which values can be assigned.

You can also regard a Prolog variable as an "invisible" pointer. When not free, the pointer is automatically dereferenced in all contexts, so it is impossible to distinguish it from the referenced object: in particular, it is impossible to exchange the object for something else.

1.1.4. Terms

If one thinks of a type as a set of objects, then a term is also a definition of a type. The term Variable3 describes the set of all objects, because a variable can be instantiated to anything. On the other hand, one can have a very precise type specification. For example, the term a.b.c.[] describes a set containing only one object: the list of length 3, whose first element is a, whose second element is b and whose third element is c. There is a wide range of choices between these extremes.

We describe objects by defining those of their properties which we find interesting in a given context. We do so by using variable names to denote objects (in particular: components of other objects) whose exact form is either unknown or unimportant. Our descriptions thus denote sets of objects satisfying the explicitly formulated properties.

A few examples should make it clear:

1. painting(Painter, 'Saskia')
                                    —all 'Saskia's of an unknown artist
2. painting(rembrandt, Picture)
                                    —all pictures by Rembrandt
3. painting(rembrandt, picture(Title,1646))
                                    —all pictures painted by Rembrandt in 1646
4. Head.Tail
                                    —all non-empty lists
5. One.Two.Three.[]
                                    —all lists of three elements
6. One.Two.13.Tail
    —all lists containing at least three elements, such that the third element is the number 13.

Actually, our comments in examples 4 and 6 are somewhat imprecise, as they reflect an intended interpretation. Since a variable name denotes an arbitrary object, the type Head.Tail contains more than true lists: the object one.two also answers this description. Similarly, the term in example 1 describes objects such as painting(59, 'Saskia'). Term notation does not allow us to express directly our wish to consider only paintings whose first arguments are the names of painters. This is in keeping with the principle that the type of a compound object is defined primarily by the interrelationship between the object and its components, rather than by the types of the components. The restriction is not necessarily a bad thing: we shall see that a procedure popping an element off a stack is most naturally written so that it can handle all stacks, whatever the types of their elements. If one considers it important to restrict the types of components, one can do it easily enough (we shall see how), but only consciously and only when needed.

As a computation progresses, variables in various terms may become instantiated. As a result, more is known about the objects described by these terms. We extend our terminology so that we can talk about **instantiating terms** and terms which are **instantiations of other terms**. For example, f(X).Tail is an instantiation of Head.Tail; and it may, in due course, be further instantiated to a yet more precise description. As we shall see, such a multi-step approximation to a desired description is very characteristic of Prolog.

We have proposed to regard a term as a type definition, i.e. a description of a class of objects, or alternatively as a description of a single, as yet undefined object. These are two sides of the same coin. A single object whose form is known only in general outline can be thought of as a representative of the class of all objects having that form. A term denotes a set by virtue of denoting any one of its possible instantiations.

A comment on the role of variable names. They are used as handles on the objects they denote. Through a name we can, at any moment, look at what we have actually learned about the shape of the object. For example, no matter what the instantiation of Head.Tail, the variable name Head denotes the first element of this list. The term X.X.Tail is also quite legal in Prolog and denotes a list whose first and second elements are the same object.

Notice that we said "the same object," not "identical objects." It is important to note that different compound objects can **share** components. In general, Prolog terms describe data structures which can be represented as directed acyclic graphs (DAGs). If we use an arrow to denote the relation of "being built of" (X → Y means that Y is a component of X), then Fig. 1.1 illustrates the object denoted by

one(two(A.B), three(A.B, C), B).

Sometimes one is not interested in certain objects and needs no name to refer to them. Such terms can be denoted by **anonymous variables**, each of which is written as an underscore. For example

a._._.b.[]

describes a list of length four whose first and last elements are a and b. The second and third elements can be any two different objects, or the same object: we don't care.

1.2. OPERATIONS

The majority of operations in a Prolog program are calls to procedures defined by the user. Standard operations—addition, comparisons, input/output etc.—are used relatively infrequently. For uniformity, **every** operation is written as if it were a procedure call, and the principal property of all standard operations is only that they need not (and must not) be de-

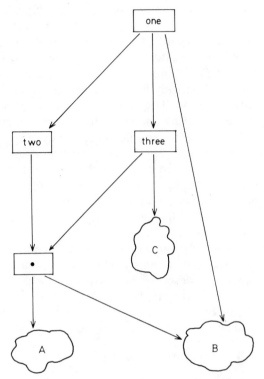

FIG. 1.1   Recurring components of an object.

fined by the user. Standard operations are accordingly called **built-in procedures** (or **system procedures**).

Procedure calls are written according to the usual practice. The procedure name is followed by an optional list of terms—actual parameters, enclosed in parentheses and separated by commas, e.g.

show(painting(rembrandt,X), etching(rembrandt,X)).

The "procedure name" is often called a **predicate symbol** (sometimes shortened to **predicate**). Like functors, a predicate symbol has two attributes: a name and an arity. Two distinct procedures can share the same name, provided one has a different number of parameters than the other.

Procedure calls (and, as we shall see, procedure definitions) have the same syntax as terms. This notational uniformity is useful when programs are dynamically modified (as is normally the case during an interactive session), but it may be confusing for the uninitiated. We shall try to help by reserving the word "argument" for components of terms: procedures will be said to have parameters.

Some versions of Prolog—including those described in this book—carry this uniformity to the point of allowing the user to use prefix, postfix and infix notation for predicate symbols (such symbols are also called "operators"). This is achieved exactly as for functors, but a number of frequently used symbols are usually predeclared to give the language a more conventional flavour. A case in point is the built-in procedure *is*, whose name is written in infix notation. It expects its second parameter to be an "expression": a term representing the abstract syntax tree of an integer arithmetic expression; the tree is evaluated and the result is returned through the first parameter. The two-argument functors $+$, $-$, $*$, $/$ and mod are predeclared as infix functors with conventional priorities and associativity, so one can write

V is X $-$ 7 $-$ Y $*$ Z mod (2 $+$ X)

to instantiate V to an integer (provided the instantiations of X, Y and Z are integers or "expressions").

Sequences of procedure calls use commas for separators, for example:

... buy(picture(rembrandt,Title), Price),
   NewPrice is Price $*$ 135/100,
     sell(picture(rembrandt,Title), NewPrice),
      drink(beer) ...

(We shall enlarge on this in Sections 1.2.2 and 1.3.1.)

We shall need two built-in procedures for our examples:

— nl/0 terminates an output line;
— write/1 outputs a term (variables are written as X1, X2, etc.); for example, if A and B are uninstantiated, then

write(f('an id',g(A,B),7,A)), nl

writes

f(an id, g(X1, X2), 7, X1).

More precise descriptions of system procedures can be found in Chapter 5. We shall now see how to define user procedures.

1.2.1. The Simplest Form of a Procedure

Try to think of a procedure which computes the head and the tail of a list: we shall call it carcdr. What should its specification be like?

Let the list be the first parameter and let the second and third parameters return its head and its tail. Head and tail are defined only for non-empty lists, so the first parameter's type is described by the term Head.Tail (Q1.Q2 would do just as well, but it is better to use meaningful names). This type specification is most naturally written in the procedure heading, thus

carcdr(Head.Tail, ..., ...) ...

If a list is denoted by Head.Tail, then Head denotes its head and Tail denotes its tail. We can therefore write

carcdr(Head.Tail, Head, Tail).

The fullstop terminates the specification. It is rather concise, but it contains all the necessary information; the procedure is called carcdr and has three parameters; the first parameter must be a non-empty list, the second parameter is to become the head, and the third is to become the tail of this list.

It turns out that what we have written is also the complete definition of this procedure in Prolog. The call

carcdr(1.2.3.[], H, T)

instantiates H to 1 and T to 2.3.[]. (Recall that 1.2.3.[] is really .(1,.(2,.(3,[])))   .)

Actually, our definition is somewhat more general, because—as we have already pointed out—Head.Tail need not be a list, as no conditions are imposed on the form of its tail. But this does not matter: there is no misunderstanding about the desired effect of, say

carcdr(timeofday(12, 30).any(Object,"at all"), F, S).

What we have here is a general procedure for getting at the first and second arguments of a term whose main functor is ./2.

We shall now specify the reverse of carcdr: a procedure which returns, via its third parameter, a list constructed of its first and second parameters. We shall call it cons.

We do not really mind if the first two parameters are not lists, so there are no restrictions on their types:

cons(Object, Another, ...) ...

If Object describes an object and Another describes an object, then applying the list constructor to the two gives us a third object, whose description is Object.Another. This term is sufficient as a specification of the third parameter, so we get

cons(Object, Another, Object.Another).

Here, again, we have a complete definition of this procedure. But notice that the order of parameters has no meaning in itself, so we might as well have decided to pass the constructed list through the first parameter:

cons(Object.Another, Object, Another).

Variable names have no inherent meaning either, so cons is really the same as carcdr. Indeed, when we read out the specification of carcdr, we cheated a little: "the parameter must be," or "the parameter is to become"—these distinctions were not present in the specification.

While both carcdr and cons could be so named to reflect their intended use, they are both really a single procedure

conscarcdr(Head.Tail, Head, Tail).

This is not very surprising, as cons is the reverse of the coin of which carcdr is the face.

Now the call

conscarcdr(1.2.3.[], H, T)

instantiates H to 1 and T to 2.3.[] and the call

conscarcdr(L, a, b.[])

instantiates L to a.b.[]. But how is it done? We shall come to that, as soon as we have cleared up a point of syntax.

1.2.2. Directives

In versions of Prolog deriving from Prolog-10, the syntax of a simple procedure definition such as our conscarcdr example need not necessarily differ from that of a procedure call. The meaning is defined by context.

Such Prolog systems function in two modes: the command mode and the definition mode. Command mode is the default.

In command mode, the system reads and executes **directives**. The directives are read in from the user's terminal or from a file. Each directive is terminated by a fullstop (the character., immediately followed by a white space character, including newline), and is either a **query** or a **command**. A query is a procedure call or a sequence of procedure calls separated by commas. Roughly, its execution consists of executing its call and printing the resulting variable instantiations (see the end of Section 1.2.3 for a more precise description). For example, if conscarcdr has been defined, then after reading the query

    conscarcdr(1.2.3.[], H, T).

the system writes

    H = 1
    T = 2.3.[]

(The actual printout might be in the special syntax used for lists; see Section 4.2.1.)

A command has the form of a query prefixed by the symbol :-. Its calls are executed but the variable instantiations are not written out automatically. To get the same printout with a command, one would write

    :- conscarcdr(1.2.3.[], H, T),
        write('H = '), write(H), nl,
        write('T = '), write(T), nl.

The terminology is somewhat fluid: directives are often called **goal statements**, while queries and commands are not always recognized under those names. (Sometimes there are also slight syntactic differences. We try to follow the original definition of Prolog-10, but in this book the standard is set by the version of Prolog described in Chapter 7.)

Definition mode is entered upon executing the system procedure consult/1 or reconsult/1. (The argument is the name of the file from which procedure definitions are to be read; *user* is the name of the user's terminal. The details are in Section 5.11.) In this mode, the system accepts procedure definitions, which are also terminated by fullstops. Our definition of conscarcdr is an example, but see Section 1.3.1 for the complete syntax. Commands are allowed and properly executed in this mode, but queries are not. Definition mode is exited when the system encounters the definition

    end.

A note about comments in Prolog. A comment starts with a % character (not contained in a string or quoted name) and extends till the end of line. Be careful not to place a comment immediately after a dot that terminates a clause: a fullstop is required.

As a point of interest, all directives and the basic building blocks of procedures (called clauses—we will describe them in due time) are simply single terms. Standard operator declarations include the infix functor , (comma) and the prefix functor :-, so the directive

    :- p(2, X), write(X), nl.

is really the term

    ':-'(','(p(2, X), ','(write(X), nl))).

This data structure is interpreted as a directive, so you need not worry about these things unless you are an advanced Prolog hacker.

There is one important point, though probably you will find it obvious. The actual parameters of procedure calls are the current instantiations of terms directly written in the call. Thus

```
:- conscarcdr( a.b.[], H, T ), conscarcdr( L, H, T ), write( L ), nl.
```

will print out

```
a.b.[]
```

1.2.3. Unification

Since we succeeded in packing the whole definition of conscarcdr into its heading—the part specifying its name and formal parameters—we can expect that its execution boils down to applying a sufficiently powerful and general parameter-passing mechanism. This mechanism is imple-mented by a term-matching operation called **unification**.

We will describe this operation as a pidgin–Pascal algorithm. The function UNIFY is applied in turn to each formal and actual parameter pair. If it returns true for all such pairs of terms, we say that unification **is successful** (or **succeeds**); otherwise unification **fails**. Unification fails when the terms describing the parameters do not match. In a very general sense this means that the types of actual parameters are incompatible with those of the formal parameters. A concrete implementation of the algorithm can be found in Appendix A.1.

```
function UNIFY ( var Actual, Formal : term ) : boolean;
var success : boolean;
begin success:= true;
    if Formal is a variable then
        Formal is instantiated to Actual
    else
        if Actual is a variable then
            Actual is instantiated to Formal
        else
            if the main functors of Formal and Actual have
                different names or arities then success:= false
            else
                while success and unmatched arguments remain do
                    success:= UNIFY( next argument of Actual,
                            next argument of Formal );
    UNIFY:= success
end;
```

Notice that if we treat both the call and the procedure heading as terms, then the process of matching successive pairs of parameters is subsumed by the loop in UNIFY. We extend our terminology accordingly, and say that—like a pair of terms—a call and a procedure heading do or do not **match**. Alternatively, we say that they do or do not **unify** (are or are not **unifiable**). The algorithm **unifies** matching terms. Unified terms are indistinguishable, so they describe the same object.

If both Formal and Actual describe variables, then unification **binds them together.** Variables which are bound together also represent the same object: both their names refer to the same variable. (It is pointless to ask whether the formal becomes an instantiation of the actual or the other way round. Our algorithm implements the latter case, but this is not observable from the outside. You can envisage a set of bound-together variables as a chain of invisible pointers.)

Time for a very detailed analysis of a simple example: the procedure

p(A, b(c, A))

called with the query

p(X, b(X, Y)).

Figure 1.2 shows the situation immediately before unification. The horizontal line separates objects local to the directive and objects local to

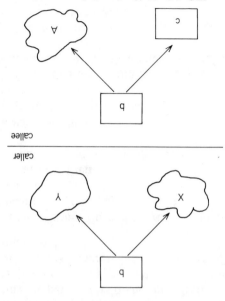

FIG. 1.2   Unification: before matching.

the procedure. Note that objects—including variables—are accessible both directly through their names and as components of other objects. The first pair of parameters is matched by binding X and A together. The variables will behave as if they had merged into a simple object (somewhat like two drops of water). This object is accessible under two different names (Fig.1.3).

The second pair of parameters is unified in two phases. First, c be-comes the instantiation of the "amalgamated" variables X and A. They cease to exist as variables, but c is now also accessible through the name A inside the procedure and through the name X outside (Fig. 1.4).

In the second phase Y is instantiated to the instantiation of A. The object c is now accessible as c, A, X and Y (Fig. 1.5).

The procedure p now terminates, but its local object c remains, being accessible from the outside as X or Y. The instantiation of b(X, Y) is b(c, c) (Fig. 1.6).

It is convenient to use a special notation for showing the effects of unification. We shall write

A → B.[]

instead of "A is instantiated to B.[]"; and

A ↔ B

instead of "A and B are bound together."

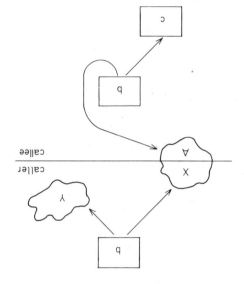

FIG. 1.3 Unification: the first pair of parameters is matched.

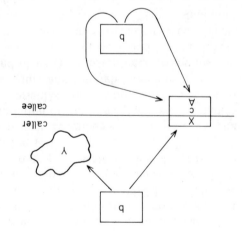

FIG. 1.4   Unification: the first pair of b's arguments is matched.

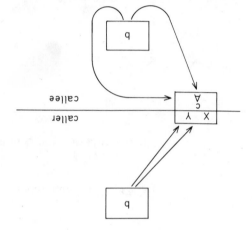

FIG. 1.5   Unification: matching was successful.

FIG. 1.6   Unification: the callee is terminated.

Here are some example calls to our procedure

conscarcdr(Head.Tail, Head, Tail).

1. conscarcdr(element.[], Car, Cdr)
   Head ← element, Tail ← [],
   Car ← element, Cdr ← [].
2. conscarcdr(L, one.two.[], 3.4.5.[])
   L ← Head.Tail, Head ← one.two.[],
   Tail ← 3.4.5.[].
   Hence the instantiation of L is
   (one.two.[]).3.4.5.[]
3. conscarcdr(A.B, 2, 2.[])
   A ↔ Head, B ↔ Tail,
   Head ← 2 (and hence also A ← 2),
   Tail ← 2.[] (and hence also B ← 2.[]).
   The instantiation of A.B is now
   2.2.[].
4. conscarcdr(A.B.C, 10, [])
   A ↔ Head, Tail ← B.C,
   Head ← 10, *failure*.
   Unification fails. This is not surprising, as the first actual parameter
   describes a list of at least two elements, while the list constructed of
   the second and third actual parameters would have only one element.

We shall wind this up with four general remarks.

First, we want to stress that the unification algorithm treats actual and
formal parameters absolutely symmetrically. This results in a very characteristic property of Prolog: there is no difference between formal parameters used to bring information into a procedure and those used to
carry information out of a procedure. The direction of information flow
changes from call to call, as in examples 1 and 2 above. We can even
make a parameter serve both for input and for output. An example is the
call

conscarcdr(A.2.[], 1, B) .

Here, Head ← A and Tail ← 2.[];
then Head ← 1 (and therefore A ← 1)
and B ← 2.[] .
The result is that the first formal parameter was used both for obtaining
information (that 2.[]) and for yielding information (that 1).

This multi-way functioning of procedure parameters sometimes
makes it possible to use procedures in unexpected ways. Whenever we

shall say that a procedure does this and this, we shall not worry about what it does after an "unreasonable" call. But you might find thinking about these things a useful exercise.

The second remark: effects of unification such as merging two variables are quite consistent with the interpretation of terms as descriptions of types. We shall illustrate this with a very simple example. The following two procedures accept only three-field records whose neighbouring fields are identical:

```
first2( record( Field12, Field12, Field3 ) ).
last2( record( Field1, Field23, Field23 ) ).
```

Each of these procedures can be thought of as imposing a constraint on a description of the record type. The constraints are not mutually inconsistent, so the directive

```
:- first2( record( F1,F2,F3 ) ),
   last2( record( F1,F2,F3 ) ),
   write( record( F1,F2,F3 ) ), nl.
```

writes out the description of a record whose three fields are identical:

```
record( X1, X1, X1 ).
```

Similarly, the query

```
first2( record( F1,F2,field ) ), last2( record( F1,F2,field ) ).
```

is answered with

```
F1 = field
F2 = field
```

Third, the convention that only the most interesting aspects of an object are captured in a type description turned out to be quite useful. Example 3 would not have worked if the type of the first formal parameter had specified that the tail must be a proper list. The term A.B would not have been accepted.

The fourth, and last, remark. If you follow the unification algorithm carefully, you will notice that it can create cyclic data structures. For example, if the procedure

```
same( X, X ).
```

is invoked with

```
same( f( V ), V ), write( V ), nl.
```

then we are in trouble. First, $X \leftarrow f(V)$; then $V \leftarrow X$, that is to say $V \leftarrow f(V)$. As a result, f becomes its own component and the printout will be potentially infinite:

f(f(f(f(f(f(f(f(f(f(f(f(....

Such cyclic structures can also cause trouble during unification. If we write

same(f(V), V), same(f(W), W), same(V, W),...

then the unification algorithm will not terminate for the third procedure call (this will probably manifest itself as recursion stack overflow): f matches f, their first arguments are both f, and *their* first arguments are both f, and so on. ·

All this could be avoided if a variable were not unifiable with a term in which that variable occurs. The unification algorithm is borrowed from automatic theorem proving (see Chapter 2). The original algorithm contains this **occur check**, but most versions of Prolog do not, as it considerably increases the algorithm's running time. Fortunately, cyclic structures seldom occur in practice, and one learns to live with the knowledge that terms are not always DAGs if one blunders badly. One version of Prolog (Prolog II; see Section 9.2) is built to take advantage of cyclic data structures. They are called **infinite trees** and are treated as bona fide representations of graphs arising in the real world. If one is careful, one can use such structures even in more conventional Prolog systems: an example is the calltree program listed in Appendix A.5.

1.2.4. Clauses

If we want a procedure which computes the fourth element of a list, we can write

fourth(_._._.E4._, E4).

But this method is useless if we want the n-th (or even the hundredth) element.

After parameters are passed, a procedure can—just as in other languages—execute a sequence of operations. For example, a procedure which prints the fourth element of a list would be:

fourth(_._._.E4._) :- write(E4), nl.

Its body is a sequence of calls, separated by commas and prefixed by a :-. As you see, a command is like a procedure without a heading.

A procedure heading, possibly followed by a body, is called a **clause**. We shall now see how to use clauses for less trivial tasks.

1.3. CONTROL

1.3.1. The General Form of a Procedure

What happens when unification fails?

Part of the answer is that a procedure can consist of a number of clauses. All these clauses must have headings with the same predicate symbol, but the parameter specifications may differ. When unification of a call with the first clause's heading is successful, the first clause executes its body (if any). When unification fails, its effects are **undone**: all variables which were instantiated by the attempt at unification are restored to their original, unbound state. The call is then matched against the heading of the second clause. If this is successful, the second clause is executed; otherwise the third clause is attempted and so on. To execute a procedure is thus to execute the first of its clauses whose head matches the call (but see the next section for a refinement of this statement). Roughly, the matching clause contains code for that particular combination of parameter types.

An elementary example is provided by an extended version of the procedure carcdr of Section 1.2.1.

    carcdr(Head.Tail, Head, Tail).
    carcdr([], _, _) :- write('can''t crack empty list'), nl.

Here is a somewhat less trivial example, an immortal classic of introductory Prolog courses. It is a procedure which appends a list at the end of another list:

    append(Hd.Tl, List, Hd.TlAndList) :-
                            append(Tl, List, TlAndList).
    append([], List, List).

All terms written in a clause are **local to that clause**. Both occurrences of List in the first clause refer to the same variable, which has nothing to do with the variable named List in the second clause. The second clause might as well have been

    append([], Q14, Q14).

As in other programming languages with recursion, activation of a clause is accompanied by creation of new instances of all its local objects.

The terms appearing in the clause describe these instances. Before an attempt to unify a call with a clause heading can be made, a new instance of the clause is created. When unification fails, the instance is destroyed.

Armed with this knowledge, we can now watch the effects of calling append in the query

append(a.b.[], c.d.[], Result).

For clarity, we shall use X', X'', etc., to denote different instances of a variable named X.

The original call will successfully activate the first clause, after the following instantiations:

Hd' ← a, Tl' ← b.[], List' ← c.d.[],
Result ← a.TlAndList' (because Hd' is now a).

This clause will execute the call

append(b.[], c.d.[], TlAndList'),

activating a second instance of the first clause:

Hd'' ← b, Tl'' ← [], List'' ← c.d.[],
TlAndList' ← b.TlAndList'' .

In this instance, the body is

append([], c.d.[], TlAndList'') .

This call does not match the first clause's heading, so the second clause is used:

List''' ← c.d.[], TlAndList'' ← c.d.[] .

The third instance of append has no calls to execute, so it returns to the second instance. The second instance is done with its body, so it returns to the first instance, which also terminates. The variable Result was instantiated to a.TlAndList', and TlAndList' to b.TlAndList'', and TlAndList'' to c.d.[]. Therefore, the query can be answered with

Result = a.b.c.d.[]

It is sometimes useful to represent the state of a computation by the sequence of calls which must be executed. The sequence is often called the current **resolvent** (see Section 2.4). If we use our procedure in the directive

:- append(a.b.[], c.d.[], Result), write(Result), nl.

then the successive resolvents are as follows:

1. append(a.b.[],c.d.[],Result), write(Result), nl.
2. append(b.[],c.d.[],TlAndList'), write(a.TlAndList'), nl.
3. append([],c.d.[],TlAndList''), write(a.b.TlAndList''), nl.
4. write(a.b.c.d.[]), nl.
5. nl.

When no calls remain, the directive is terminated.

Here is the procedure to find the n-th element of a list. Its first parameter is n and the second a list. The third parameter returns the n-th element of the list; if the element does not exist, the constant **?** is returned and an error message is printed. It is assumed that the first parameter is not negative (we will learn how to check this in the next section). The procedure is

    nth(0, _, ?) :- write('nth(0,...,..)??'), nl.
    nth(N, [], ?) :- write('nth(..,too short,..)??'), nl.
    nth(1, El._, El).
    nth(N, _.Tail, El) :- M is N − 1, nth(M, Tail, El).

Do trace its execution for a few examples.

1.3.2. Backtracking

But what if a call matches none of the clause headings? An example is the call

    conscarcdr(notalist, something, other)

This suggests the answer. If none of the clauses fits the call, then evidently the call is wrong: its set of actual parameters does not conform to any of the type specifications describing parameters acceptable to the procedure.

As in other modern programming languages, such an erroneous call does not abnormally terminate a program's execution but activates an error-handling mechanism. In contrast to other languages, however, the error is not necessarily handled by an active procedure present on the activation stack. Prolog uses a more general method and takes into account even those procedures which returned to their caller after successful termination. Procedure instances are looked at, one by one, in reverse order of their activation. The nearest such procedure instance—call it p— which contains as-yet-unactivated clauses matching its call is assumed to be able to handle the situation. The computation is **undone**: its state is made to appear as if the heading of p's most recently activated clause did **not** match its call, and p is given a chance to execute other clauses.

This process is called **backtracking**, and a call which does not match any clause heading is said to **fail**. Backtracking closely resembles our behaviour in systematically searching for a solution to a problem. If we end up in a blind alley, we get back to the nearest point at which we could have applied another approach, and apply it. If no approach seems to be working at that point, we return to the previous point in which we apparently made a wrong choice, and so on.

In implementation terms, each time a selected clause is not the last in its procedure, a record is pushed onto a special stack of **fail points** (also called **choice points**). The record contains all information necessary to restore the state of the computation. When a procedure fails, the topmost fail point is popped off the stack, the state described by it is restored and the computation proceeds with the next clause.

It is important to note that not all effects of a computation are obliterated on backtracking. Some system procedures do things which cannot be undone, such as writing information on a terminal screen. We say that these procedures have **side-effects**.

Using our description of backtracking, try to follow the execution of procedure p in the following example:

```
p :- q( X ), write ( trying( X ) ), nl.
      female( X ), write( ok ), nl.
p :- write( 'Sorry!' ), nl.

q( X ) :- writer( X ).
q( ? ) :- write( 'No more writers.' ), nl.

writer( hesse ).
writer( mann ).
writer( grass ).

female( austen ).
female( sand ).
```

You should get the following printout:

```
trying( hesse )
trying( mann )
trying( grass )
No more writers.
trying( ? )
Sorry!
```

You may have noticed from this example that error handling is somewhat inadequate as a metaphor for backtracking. This is the subject of the next section.

1.3.3. How to Use Backtracking

When a procedure instance is backtracked to, it behaves as if its most recently activated clause did not match its call. We can therefore use backtracking to implement extended type checking.

Recall from Section 1.1.4 that we found it impossible to write terms which could describe properties such as "the object is a painter's name" or "the tail is a properly constructed list." In other words, while rather powerful in certain respects, this kind of type specification is weak in others. This can be remedied by using procedures which do additional type checking and either fail or successfully terminate, depending on the outcome. If we want procedure q to accept only properly constructed representations of paintings, we can write

```
q( painting( Painter, Name ) ):-
    ispainter( Painter ), process( painting( Painter,Name ) ).

ispainter( rembrandt ).
ispainter( velasquez ).
......
```

Here, the role of ispainter is similar to the declaration of an enumeration type in Pascal.

Prolog has several built-in procedures which can be used to check properties of objects. For example, one can check whether the object denoted by Something is an integer, by seeing whether the call

```
integer( Something )
```

succeeds or fails.

A number of built-in procedures implement comparison operations. Like *is*, procedures for comparing integer values "evaluate" terms resembling conventional arithmetic expressions. The procedures are $<$, $=<$, $=:=$ (equality), $=\backslash=$ (inequality), $>=$ and $>$. Their names are predeclared as infix predicate symbols. For example the call

$$7 * 2 + 5 =:= 1 + 3 * 6$$

will be successful. There are also procedures comparing non-integer constants according to their lexicographic ordering: $@<$, $@=<$, $@>=$, $@>$. For example,

alpha $@>$ beta

is a failing call.

Equality of constants can be determined by means of the procedure $=$

(= is predeclared as infix). The procedure is most easily expressed in Prolog

    X = X.

It can be used for any two terms, but of course it does more than checking equality. It may cause its parameters to *become* equal, as it attempts to unify them. For example,

    a(b, X) = a(Y, c)

will succeed after instantiating

    X ← c, Y ← b .

Note that 7=7 succeeds, but 5+2=2+5 fails, as these are different terms.

Remember that all these procedures do not yield a Boolean result: they only succeed or fail.

When we are interested in the structure of a compound object, we can use a recursive procedure which does nothing but "accepting" the object. Here is a version of carcdr which works only for true lists and fails for objects such as a.b.c (but not for objects with variable tails, which match []).

    carcdr(Head.Tail, Head, Tail) :- islist(Tail).

    islist([]).
    islist(_.L) :- islist(L).

Such type checking can be quite general. For example, we can process objects differently according to whether they are or are not members of a set represented by a list:

    process(Obj, Set) :- member(Obj, Set),
                           yes_action(Obj).
    process(Obj, _) :- no_action(Obj).

    member(El, El.Tail).
    member(El, _.Tail) :- member(El, Tail).

Try to trace the execution of *process* for a couple of simple calls, and notice how *member* is called with successively shorter tails of the list, until it finds a tail whose head is unifiable with the first parameter.

The fact that the first clause of member expresses unifiability rather than equality has very interesting consequences. The most obvious is that the procedure can be used to retrieve information from a dictionary represented by a list. The call

member(phone(krull, Number),
        phone(mann,11).phone(hesse,5).phone(krull,11).[])

instantiates Number to 11.

When this information-retrieving effect is coupled with backtracking, the result is rather striking. Consider the procedure

intersect(L1, L2) :- member(E, L1), member(E, L2).

When given two sets represented by lists, the procedure terminates successfully if the sets intersect and fails if they are disjoint. Here is a trace of what happens when we call it with

intersect(a.b.c.d.[], c.d.[]), write(ok), nl.

1. intersect(a.b.c.d.[],c.d.[]), write(ok), nl.
   (this activates the procedure:

   $$L1 \leftarrow a.b.c.d.[], \quad L2 \leftarrow c.d.[]$$

2. member(E,a.b.c.d.[]), member(E,c.d.[]), write(ok), nl.
   (activates the first clause of member:

   $$E \leftrightarrow El', \quad El' \leftarrow a)$$

3. member(a,c.d.[]), write(ok), nl.
   (only the second clause matches the call)

4. member(a,d.[]), write(ok), nl.
   (only the second clause matches the call)

5. member(a,[]), write(ok), nl.
   (the call to member fails, nearest "handler" is in the procedure activated in step 2, so we backtrack to that situation)

6. member(E,a.b.c.d.[]), member(E,c.d.[]), write(ok), nl.
   (the second clause now:

   $$E \leftrightarrow El', \quad Tail' \leftarrow b.c.d.[])$$

7. member(E,b.c.d.[]), member(E,c.d.[]), write(ok), nl.
   (the first clause:

   $$E \leftrightarrow El'', \quad El'' \leftarrow b)$$

8. member(b,c.d.[]), write(ok), nl.

9. member(b,d.[]), write(ok), nl.

10. member(b,[]), write(ok), nl.
    (failure, backtracking to step 7)

11. member(E,b.c.d.[]), member(E,c.d.[]), write(ok), nl.
    (the second clause now:

    $$E \leftrightarrow El''', \quad Tail''' \leftarrow c.d.[])$$

12. member(E,c.d.[]),member(E,c.d.[]), write(ok), nl.
    (the first clause:

    $$E \leftrightarrow El'''', \quad El'''' \leftarrow c)$$

13. member(c,c.d.[]), write(ok), nl.
    (the first clause)
14. write(ok), nl.
15. nl.
Success.

Notice how the first call to member in intersect is used as a "back-track driven" **generator** of successive elements on the list. A terminated procedure can be reactivated if the effects of its execution prove unsatis-factory. It can return several results—or behave in several ways—and its final effect is determined not only by its actual parameters, but also by what happens to the computation later on. It is this multiplicity of possible behaviours that we have in mind when we say that, in general, a Prolog procedure is **nondeterministic**. (This does not mean that its behaviour cannot be predicted to the smallest detail.)

If one wants to see all the results produced by a nondeterministic procedure, one can force Prolog to backtrack by calling an undefined procedure (the call will fail, because there is no matching clause). It is customary to use the name *fail*, both for readability and because Prolog makes it impossible to declare a procedure with this name. To print the elements of a list, one can write

    :- member(E, a.b.c.[]), write(E), nl, fail.

Alternatively, one can use a query. After answering a query, the system accepts a single printing character from the terminal. If the char-acter is a semicolon, it backtracks; otherwise it terminates the query. When all the possibilities are exhausted, the word *no* is printed and the system reads another directive. For example,

    user: female(W).
    system: W = austen
    user: ;
    system: W = sand
    user: ;
    system: no

If a successful query contains no non-anonymous variables (i.e. no instan-tiations to show), the answer is *yes*.

Our *intersect* example does more than check for common elements. If the elements are not ground, the sets are modified. For example,

    intersect(one.X.three.[], 1.Y.[])

succeeds after binding Y to one. This has a natural explanation. Since Y is unknown, we cannot say that the sets do not intersect, but by binding Y we ensure that the computation will fail if the supposition that Y is one will turn out to be unacceptable. We shall then assume that X is 1, that X and Y are the same object, etc., etc.

1.3.4. Static Interpretation of Procedures

Detailed simulation of a program is not a very attractive way of learning its meaning. We insisted on doing it to help you understand what happens inside the computer and to introduce techniques which can sometimes be useful for debugging, when things are not happening the way they should. But it is often quite clear what should happen, as many Prolog procedures can be read without giving a thought to details of execution.

A clause which has no body is called a **unit clause**. It is a direct definition of a relation between its parameters. The clause

    phone(hermann, 5).

says that hermann and 5 are in the relation *phone*. Other clauses can extend the relation to other objects:

    phone(mann, 11).
    phone(hesse, 5).
    phone(krull, 11).

Unary relations can be thought of as expressing properties of objects:

    red(herring).
    red(square).

Nullary relations can denote general facts:

    tired.
    debugging.

A look at the clauses of *phone* tells that the call

    phone(siddhartha, N)

will fail, and the call

    phone(Who, 5)

will nondeterministically produce hermann and (after a failure) hesse. Note that the calls can be read as "establish whether the actual parameters are in the relation phone, i.e. succeed if they are in the relation, or instantiate them so that they will be in the relation and succeed, or fail."

Somewhat less trivially, the unit clause

conscarcdr(Head.Tail, Head, Tail).

can be used to establish whether the first parameter is a list formed of the second and third parameters. It is self-evident that

1. conscarcdr(a, b, c) fails, because the objects are certainly not in the relation;
2. conscarcdr(A.2.B, 1, C.[]) succeeds, because there does exist a list of at least two elements whose second element is 2, such that its head is 1 and its tail is a one-element list—the list is 1.2.[] and the tail is 2.[];
3. conscarcdr(A, B, B.[]) succeeds, because there do exist objects A and B such that A is a list constructed of B and B.[]—A is B.B.[] and B can be any object.

Nonunit clauses are indirect definitions of relations. Thus

append([], L, L).
append(H.T, L, H.TL) :- append(T, L, TL).

can be read as

"L is L appended to []," and
"H.TL is L appended to H.T *if* TL is L appended to T."

It is usually convenient to flavour this a little with the intended meaning, as in

"a list L appended to an empty list is L itself," and
"a list L appended to a non-empty list H.T is formed of the head of that list, H, and the result of appending L to its tail, T."

And, most spectacularly,

intersect(L1, L2) :- member(E,L1), member(E,L2).

reads:

"L1 and L2 intersect *if* an object E is a member of L1 *and* a member of L2",

in other words

"two lists intersect if they have a common member."

You will find more about this in Chapter 2. But note here that this interpretation does not fully explain procedures such as *process* of Section 1.3.3—this is further discussed in Section 4.3.1.

1.3.5. The Order of Calls and Clauses

In practice, static interpretation is not always sufficient to explain a program's behaviour. It cannot account for the order of calls in a clause and the order of clauses in a procedure, because "x and y" means the same as "y and x." Yet this order is important, for three principal reasons.

The first reason is that some procedures, such as write and nl, have side-effects, i.e. their results are not only variable instantiations. The order in which several things are written has an obvious effect on the form of the printout.

Another important reason is efficiency. Here is a famous example (Kowalski 1974) of a naive naive sort:

    sort(List, Sorted) :- permute(List, Sorted),
                            ordered(Sorted).

The procedure generates successive permutations of a list until it finds one that is ordered. If *permute* and *ordered* can be used both to check their parameters and as generators, then this could also be expressed as

    sort(List, Sorted) :- ordered(Sorted),
                            permute(List, Sorted).

Here, successive ordered lists are generated until a permutation of the first parameter is found. Both procedures express the same definition of a sorted list, but while the first is only very costly, the second is absolutely useless.

A third reason is that all computations should be finite. We will illustrate this point with the procedure *append*, which can be written either as

    append(H.T, L, H.TL) :- append(T, L, TL).
    append([], L, L).

or, apparently equivalently, as

    append([], L, L).
    append(H.T, L, H.TL) :- append(T, L, TL).

Both versions are equivalent when *append* is used for appending. But note that its precise reading from section 1.3.4 allows for other uses. For example the second clause, "H.TL is L appended to H.T if TL is L appended to T," defines H.TL in terms of H.T and L, but also H.T and L in terms of H.TL. Indeed, *append* is often used for splitting a list. If one executes

```
:- append( Front, End, a.b.c.[] ),
      write( Front ), write( ' & ' ),
      write( End ), nl, fail.
```

then the first version of *append* will produce

```
a.b.c.[] & []
a.b.[] & c.[]
a.[] & b.c.[]
[] & a.b.c.[]
```

and the second version

```
[] & a.b.c.[]
a.[] & b.c.[]
a.b.[] & c.[]
a.b.c.[] & [].
```

This difference is not very important. But when we write

append(L1, a.[], L3)

we expect that *append* will succeed, after instantiating the terms so that L3 is a.[] appended to L1. The second version does just this: L1 ← [] and L3 ← a.[]; then, if we backtrack, L1 ← X1.[] and L3 ← X1.a.[]; then, if we backtrack again, L1 ← X1.X2.[] and L3 ← X1.X2.a.[]; and so on— there are infinitely many such solutions.

The first procedure, however, first looks for the *last* solution in this infinite set, and this causes endless recursion.

Nevertheless, with careful programming, considerations of this sort are needed only to obtain refinements of the general meaning of procedures given by their static interpretation. Moreover, the order of calls and clauses is usually a local thing, seldom requiring looking beyond a single procedure.

1.3.6. The Cut

We shall now pass on to so-called **extralogical features** of Prolog. These are simple and powerful mechanisms which play a large part in making Prolog a practical programming language, but cannot be understood in terms of static interpretation, as outlined in Section 1.3.4.

Since we have generators, we must be able to stop them. Suppose that we have two methods for finding the solution of a problem described in terms of two sets. Assume one of these methods is significantly cheaper than the other, but a necessary—though not sufficient!—condition for its applicability is that the problem-defining sets intersect. We might write something like

        try(Set1, Set2, Solution) :-
            intersect(Set1, Set2),
            method1(Set1, Set2, Solution).
        try(Set1, Set2, Solution) :-
            method2(Set1, Set2, Solution).

Now if method1 fails, we want to try method2. But if the sets are large and have many elements in common, we are effectively stopped by a generator. Backtracking from method1 will cause *intersect* to find another way of showing that the sets do indeed intersect: this changes nothing, so method1 will be attempted again and again until *intersect* enumerates all the elements in the intersection of Set1 and Set2. In terms of processing time, this might be a disaster. And note that we are lucky: the generator is not infinite.

To help in such cases, Prolog provides a commit operation, written as ! and called the **cut** procedure (old Prolog hands tend to call it the **slash**, after the character /, which was its name in the original Marseilles Prolog). When procedure p executes a cut, everything that was done by p up to that moment—including its choice of current clause—is taken as fixed and not to be reconsidered on backtracking. In implementation terms, ! cuts away the top section of the fail point stack, leaving only fail points created before p was called.

Our problem can be solved by modifying *intersect*:

        intersect(L1, L2) :- member(E, L1),
                               member(E, L2), !.

The cut kills the generator of elements from L1.

A more involved example might be useful in clearing up doubts about the effects of a cut. We will try to move a single cut around in our example of section 1.3.2:

        p :- q(X), write(trying(X)), nl,
             female(X), write(ok), nl.
        p :- write('Sorry!'), nl.

        q(X) :- writer(X).
        q(?) :- write('No more writers.'), nl.

        writer(hesse).
        writer(mann).
        writer(grass).

```
female( austen ).
female( sand ).
```

If we insert a cut into the first clause of writer:

```
writer( hesse ) :- !.
```

the printout will be

```
trying( hesse )
No more writers.
trying( ? )
Sorry!
```

If we insert it into q instead:

```
q( X ) :- !, writer( X ).
```

we will get

```
trying( hesse )
trying( mann )
trying( grass )
Sorry!
```

But if we choose to insert it at the end of this clause:

```
q( X ) :- writer( X ), !.
```

the program will write

```
trying( hesse )
Sorry!
```

By inserting the cut after the call to q in the first clause of p, we would obtain only

```
trying( hesse )
```

As evidenced by these examples, the cut is a powerful tool. A single cut can drastically alter the behaviour of a program. It must be used very carefully: Section 4.3.1 contains some useful hints.

An important property of the cut is that it can be used to implement a sort of negation. When we want to list all male writers, we can write

```
:- writer( X ), male( X ), write( X ), nl, fail.
```

If, however, the program contains only descriptions of female persons (as in our example), we must define *male* in terms of *female*:

```
male( X ) :-female( X ), !, fail.
male( _ ).
```

When X is such that *female* succeeds, the second clause of *male* is cut off and the whole procedure fails. When *female* fails, the second clause takes over and the procedure succeeds. The trick is dirty, but very useful. One must be careful, however: if the constant *christie* is not listed among the females, male(christie) will succeed. (More on this in Section 4.3.2.)

1.3.7. Variable Calls

The negation schema shown in the previous section is of quite general utility. For example, we could write a procedure for checking that two sets (represented as lists) do not intersect:

    disjoint(S1, S2) :- intersect(S1, S2), !, fail.
    disjoint(_, _).

Prolog provides a very convenient extension which allows us to use such schemas without going to the trouble of rewriting them again and again. A **variable call** is a variable occupying the position of a call in a clause or directive. When the turn comes to execute the call occupying this position, the variable's current instantiation is taken as the call, by treating its main functor as a predicate symbol and its arguments as parameters. If we define

    do(X) :- X

then the call

    carcdr(el.[], A, B)

is exactly equivalent to

    do(carcdr(el.[], A, B))

as well as to

    do(do(carcdr(el.[], A, B))) .

We can use this feature to define

    not(X) :- X, !, fail.
    not(_).

and write

    male(X) :- not(female(X)).
    disjoint(S1, S2) :- not(intersect(S1, S2)).

The dirty trick is now nicely packaged.

In versions of Prolog described here, **not** is predefined and the predicate symbol is predeclared as a prefix symbol. Expanding **male** in-line, we would write the directive of Section 1.3.6 as

:- writer(X), not female(X), write(X), nl, fail.

Variable calls can be used to define many useful procedures. We shall end by showing two companions of "not": "and" and "or." The first is written as a comma and the second as a semicolon; the first succeeds when both its parameters—taken as calls—succeed, and the second succeeds when either of its parameters succeeds (but establishes a fail point if it is the first one). Their definitions are

',''(A, B) :- A, B.

';'(A, _) :- A.
';'(_, B) :- B.

Comma and semicolon are predeclared as infix symbols. After defining *do*, we could write the directive above as

:- do((writer(X), not female(X), write(X), nl, fail)).

The extra parentheses are needed to avoid confusion with a call to do/5. Priorities are chosen so that

artwork(X, Y) :- painting(X, Y), oil(Y);
                etching(X, Y), brass(Y).

is equivalent to

artwork(X, Y) :- ';'(','(printing(X,Y),oil(Y)),
                  ','(etching(X,Y),brass(Y))).

To make the comma and semicolon appear a part of Prolog's syntax, Prolog-10 and some of its offsprings made the cut behave somewhat differently for these procedures: they are "transparent" to it. Thus

artwork(X, Y) :- painting(X, Y), oil(Y), ! ;
                etching(X, Y), brass(Y).

avoids checking the second alternative if the first succeeds.

A similar exception applies to variable calls. If the procedure

a(X) :- b, X.
a(_) :- c.

is called with

a((d, !, fail))

then the cut will commit all choices made by d and b and a—the procedure will fail without executing c.

One should avoid taking advantage of this peculiar property of the cut. It is doubtful whether it is necessary.

2 PROLOG AND LOGIC

2.1. INTRODUCTION

"Prolog" stands for "**Pro**grammation en **lo**gique" (programming in logic). Static interpretation of procedures (see Section 1.3.4) is possible because Prolog can also be viewed as a system for proving theorems expressed in logic. Adopting this viewpoint can provide the programmer with new insights about the nature of his task.

In this chapter we attempt to introduce the fundamentals of this aspect of Prolog in an intuitive manner. Full appreciation of the subject is possible only for people with a solid background in mathematical logic, and we assume the reader's knowledge of logic is very elementary. Consequently, the presentation is often not sufficiently precise, and sometimes the terminology is a little unconventional: we are interested in Prolog rather than logic. The chapter is a shortcut, so in some places you will find it heavy going. A more detailed, but still non-technical treatment can be found in Kowalski (1979b). Another relevant book is Robinson (1979). See also van Emden and Kowalski (1979).

2.2. FORMULAE AND THEIR INTERPRETATIONS

Below is a pair of formulae written in the language of predicate logic (also known as first-order logic or predicate calculus):

(2.1) $\forall x \, D(Z, x, x)$

(2.2) $\forall x \, \forall y \, \forall z \, D(x, y, z) \Rightarrow D(S(x), y, S(z)).$

The basic building blocks of such formulae are **predicates**. A predicate consists of a **predicate symbol** (e.g. D), optionally followed by arguments—a list of **terms** in parentheses, separated by commas. A term is a variable (e.g. x, y, z), or a functor (e.g. Z, S) with an optional list of arguments, which are terms. Terms denote objects in some universe (more on this presently) and predicates stand for relations between these objects.

A single predicate is a formula. A larger formula can be built from simpler ones by means of **logical connectives**. The commonly used connectives, listed in order of decreasing priority, are

—the **negation** ("not"), written as ¬
—the **conjunction** ("and"), written as ∧
—the **disjunction** ("or"), written as ∨
—the **implication**, written as ⇒

Parentheses can be used to increase clarity or override priority.

A formula (i.e. also a subformula) can be prefixed by a number of quantifiers, whose priority is lower than that of the connectives. A quantifier can be

—the **existential quantifier,** written as ∃x and read as "there exists an x".
—the **universal quantifier,** written as ∀x and read as "for all x", or "for any x".

The formula prefixed by a quantifier is called its **scope**, and the quantified variable is local to this scope (an occurrence of its name outside the scope does not denote the same object). In this chapter we shall deal only with **fully quantified** formulae; i.e. our formulae will not contain unquantified variables.

Our example formulae can be read as

"for any object—call it x—the object Z is in relation D with x and x"

and

"for any three (not necessarily distinct) objects—call them x, y and z—if x, y and z are in relation D, then so are objects S(x), y and S(z)".

In practice, it is more convenient to use a slightly abbreviated reading, in which the second formula is

"for all x, y and z, D(x, y, z) implies D(S(x), y, S(z))".

Formulae of this kind are purely formal statements. One cannot discuss whether they are true or false, because no particular meaning is attributed to the functors and predicate symbols. To talk about a formula's meaning, we must give it an **interpretation.** An interpretation is a definition of a **universe** (the set of objects which can be denoted by terms) and a decision to let predicate symbols and functors denote particular relations and functions defined in this universe.

A concrete interpretation maps a (fully quantified) formula to a statement which is true or false, depending on what it says about relations between objects. Somewhat imprecisely, we shall say that a formula is **true (or false) in an interpretation**. Of course, some formulae are true in all interpretations (the formula *true* is a trivial example, and A $\lor \neg$ A is another); others are false in all interpretations (e.g. *false*, A $\land \neg$ A). The first kind of formulae are called tautologies; formulae of the second kind are called **inconsistent**.

As an example, consider the following two interpretations of formulae (2.1) and (2.2). The first interpretation is the following:

—the universe is the set of natural numbers (positive integers);
—Z stands for the number 1 (one);
—S stands for the function $S(x) = 2x$;
—D(x, y, z) is true if and only if $xy = z$.

Our formulae now become the true statements

"for any natural number x, $1x = x$"

and

"for all natural numbers x, y and z, $xy = z$ implies $2xy = 2z$".

Another interpretation is:

—the universe is the set of non-negative integers;
—Z stands for the number 0 (zero);
—S stands for the successor function $S(x) = x+1$;
—D(x,y,z) is true if and only if $x+y = z$.

The formulae are now

"for any non-negative integer x, $0+x = x$"

and

"for all integers x, y and z, $x+y = z$ implies $(x+1)+y = z+1$".

If an interpretation maps a formula into a true statement, then it is called a **model** of this formula. We can also speak about a model of a **set** of formulae—an interpretation in which all of them are true.

Our two interpretations are models of the example formulae. If Z stood for 1 in the second interpretation, then it would not be a model. When an interpretation interests us as a model, formulae which are true (or false) in that interpretation will be referred to as true (or false) **in the model**.

All interpretations are models of tautologies. Inconsistent formulae have no models.

When we want to talk about a particular model, we prefer to use symbols which have some mnemonic value. The formula

(2.3) $\forall$h $\forall$t conscarcdr(.(h,t), h, t)

can be interpreted as

"for all integers h and t, the difference between h+t and h is t",

but this is better written as

$\forall$h $\forall$t difference(+(h,t), h, t).

The similarity is interesting, though: looking for other models of our statement of a problem often provides illuminating insights into its nature.

Notice that the "natural" interpretation of formula (2.3) is very down-to-earth. A list constructor can be thought of as a function mapping two objects (a head and a tail) into a third object: the universe can be a set of data structures.

2.3. FORMAL REASONING

The notion of **logical consequence** allows us to perform **formal** reasoning, i.e. reasoning which takes into account only the syntactic form of formulae and disregards their interpretations. We say that formula α is a logical consequence of a set of formulae $\beta, \beta', \beta'' \ldots$ if all models of the set $\beta, \beta', \beta'' \ldots$ are also models of α. It is a fundamental fact of logic that there exist **inference rules**, which are correct recipes for deriving logical consequences (conclusions) of other formulae (premises), provided the latter have a certain form. The inference rules are usually quite simple, but we can use them as elementary steps in long derivations. This is the backbone of mathematics: a set of formulae (**axioms**) defines a **theory**, which is the set of all formulae (called **theorems**) true in all models of the axioms; a formal derivation of a new theorem is called its **proof**. (The name **axioms** is often reserved for a **minimal** set of theorems specifying the theory of interest. We find it more convenient to use the name for any "given" set of theorems accepted without proofs.)

Some inference rules are relatively trivial applications of the definitions of logical connectives. A well-known example is the **modus ponens**:

"from any formula α and from any formula of the form $\alpha \Rightarrow \beta$, derive the formula β".

Now the definition of implication can be stated as follows: if α and β are arbitrary formulae, then, *in any interpretation*, $\alpha \Rightarrow \beta$ is false if and only if α is true and β is false in that interpretation. Hence, any model of both α and $\alpha \Rightarrow \beta$ must also be a model of β.

Two other simple rules are

"$\alpha \Rightarrow \beta$ is equivalent to $\neg \alpha \vee \beta$,
(i.e. one can be derived from the other)"

and one of the De Morgan laws

"$\neg (\alpha \wedge \beta)$ is equivalent to $\neg \alpha \vee \neg \beta$".

Do check their validity—we will need them presently!

Armed with a number of inference rules, we can attempt to derive a formula directly or by means of a technique known as **reductio ad absurdum**. To derive formula α from a set of axioms, assume that $\neg \alpha$ is a theorem: if the resulting theory is inconsistent, then α is a theorem. A theory is inconsistent if it contains an inconsistent formula. In this method of proof we often show inconsistency by finding a formula β such that we can derive

$$\beta \wedge \neg \beta.$$

It is worth noting that all formulae are theorems of an inconsistent theory. This is because, there being no models of the theory, no formula is false in any of the models. (This might not have sounded too convincing, but notice that if we can derive *false*, then we can derive any formula α using **modus ponens** and *false* $\Rightarrow \alpha$. For any α, the formula *false* $\Rightarrow \alpha$ is a tautology, because it is equivalent to $\neg$ *false* $\vee \alpha$, that is to say *true* $\vee \alpha$.) Consequently, if the set of formulae

$\neg \alpha$
β
β'
...

is inconsistent, then α is certainly a theorem, regardless of whether the set $\beta, \beta', \ldots$ is consistent or not.

2.4. RESOLUTION AND HORN CLAUSES

We shall be interested in an inference rule which we shall call the **rule of resolution** (Robinson 1965). It says

"from $\neg \alpha \vee \beta$ and from $\alpha \vee \gamma$ derive $\beta \vee \gamma$".

Its validity is not hard to explain. In any model of $\neg\,\alpha \vee \beta$ and $\alpha \vee \gamma$, either $\neg\,\alpha$ is false or α is false. In the first case β must be true (or else $\neg\,\alpha \vee \beta$ would not be true), in the second γ must be true. If a model of $\neg\,\alpha \vee \beta$ and $\alpha \vee \gamma$ must also be a model of β or a model of γ, then—by definition of disjunction—it is a model of $\beta \vee \gamma$.

There are two interesting special cases of this rule. One is

"from $\neg\,\alpha \vee \beta$ and from α derive β",

and the other is

"from $\neg\,\alpha$ and from α derive $\square$".

Here $\square$ stands for the empty formula, which must be treated as equivalent to *false* if this form of the rule is to be valid.

The rule of resolution is useful for reductio ad absurdum proofs when our formulae are written in a restricted form called clausal form. A **clause** is a disjunction of **literals**. A literal is either a predicate (called **positive literal**) or a negated predicate (called **negative literal**). All clauses are prefixed by universal quantifiers, one for each variable in the clause.

We shall limit our attention to **Horn clauses**, which have at most one positive literal each. Here is a set of four Horn clauses (the predicates are all nullary):

$A \vee \neg\,B \vee \neg\,C$
$B \vee \neg\,D$
C
D

Now, if we want to prove that A can be derived from these clauses, we can use the rule of resolution to show that by adding the Horn clause

$\neg\,A$

to our set of formulae, we obtain an inconsistent set of clauses. The proof can be carried out in the following four steps (we use parentheses to make things more clear):

1. from $\neg\,A$ and from $A \vee (\,\neg\,B \vee \neg\,C\,)$ derive $\neg\,B \vee \neg\,C$
2. from $\neg\,B \vee \neg\,C$ and from $B \vee \neg\,D$ derive $\neg\,C \vee \neg\,D$
3. from $\neg\,C \vee \neg\,D$ and from C derive $\neg\,D$
4. from $\neg\,D$ and from D derive $\square$

Notice that this type of reductio ad absurdum proof is successful when we derive the empty clause $\square$ (i.e. **false**). The special cases of the resolution rule are used to shorten formulae, while the general rule is used to generate formulae which can be shortened. Now, if in an application of the resolution rule both the premises have one positive literal each, then the conclusion must also have one positive literal (do you see why?). Hence, the proof cannot be successful unless at least one of the clauses has only negative literals. However, if one of the premises has only negative literals, then so has the conclusion. If only one of the initial clauses has this form, then the proof can be made particularly simple (Kowalski and Kuehner 1971; Hill 1974). One of the premises in the first step is the clause without positive literals. If this step cannot derive the empty clause, then the second step must use the only other clause without positive literals, i.e. the conclusion of the preceding step, and so on. If—as in the example—all our axioms have positive literals, then the negated theorem must have none and the final proof has the form of an orderly chain, in which each step provides a premise for the immediately succeeding one. In each step, we shall call the premise without positive literals the **current resolvent**.

Each step consists in **cancelling** a negative literal $\neg\lambda$ in the current resolvent, by replacing it with the negative literals of a clause having λ as its only positive literal. The resolvent shrinks when one of its literals is cancelled with a **unit clause**, which has only a single positive literal.

Because a clause is a disjunction of literals, it can be written as an implication. By the De Morgan law (see Section 2.3) $A \vee (\neg B \vee \neg C)$ is equivalent to $A \vee \neg (B \wedge C)$. This, in turn, is equivalent to $B \wedge C \Rightarrow A$.

By analogy, we can write

$$B \wedge C \Rightarrow$$

to denote $\neg B \wedge \neg C$ (i.e. a Horn clause with no positive literals). The empty consequent represents *false*, since *false* (or its equivalent) is the only formula α such that $\alpha \vee (\neg B \vee \neg C)$ is equivalent to $\neg B \vee \neg C$, for all B and C.

Similarly, we shall denote A, a Horn clause with no negative literals, by

$$\Rightarrow A$$

Here, the empty premise represents *true*: A is equivalent to *true* $\Rightarrow$ A. An empty clause has no literals and can be written

$$\Rightarrow$$

i.e. *true* $\Rightarrow$ *false*, which is equivalent to *false*.

It is preferable to write the implication from right to left:

$$A \Leftarrow B \wedge C$$

to suggest the reading

"to prove A, prove B and C".

Recalling that our resolvents have no positive literals, we can now write the resolution rule as

"from $\Leftarrow \alpha \wedge \beta$ and from $\alpha \Leftarrow \gamma$ derive $\Leftarrow \gamma \wedge \beta$"

where β, γ or both may be empty (in that case we do not write a $\wedge$). This is a rather mechanical prescription: to get rid of α, find an implication whose consequent is α and replace α with its premises. This is clearly justified: since α can be proven by proving γ, then $\alpha \wedge \beta$ can be proved by proving $\gamma \wedge \beta$.

A clause being always prefixed with universal quantifiers for each of its variables, it is convenient not to write the quantifiers. Our formulae from Section 2.2 are two Horn clauses, written as

D(Z, x, x) $\Leftarrow$
D(S(x), y, S(z)) $\Leftarrow$ D(x, y, z)

Let us see whether these clauses are consistent with

$\Leftarrow$ D(S(Z), x, S(S(Z)))

The clause can be thought of as a query whether there exists an x which is in relation D with S(Z) and S(S(Z)). It is equivalent to

$\forall$x $\neg$ D(S(Z), x, S(S(Z))),

and since this is the *negation* of what we are trying to prove, our derived formula—if we succeed—will be

$\exists$x D(S(Z), x, S(S(Z)))

(if α is not false for all x, then there must be at least one x for which α is true).

The rule of resolution, in the form presented above, is useless for this example. In fact, it could only be used for nullary predicates, because the argument for its validity does not apply to premises such as

$\forall$x $\neg$ A(x) $\vee$ $\neg$ B(x)   and $\forall$y A(Z) $\vee$ $\neg$ C(y).

Fortunately, we can also employ a simple inference rule called the **substitution rule**. It says

"from $\forall$x α(x) derive $\alpha(\tau)$, where τ is an arbitrary term".

Here, $\alpha(x)$ means that the formula α contains occurrences of variable x. $\alpha(\tau)$ stands for a formula which looks exactly like α, except that all occur-

rences of x have been replaced by occurrences of term τ. An example of
the rule's application is

''from **∀**x D(S(Z), x, S(x)) derive

D(S(Z), S(S(Z)), S(Z), S(S(Z)))''

The substitution rule is valid, of course. In every model of **∀**x α(x), α is
true for any object x (that is what the quantifier says!): hence, it is true for
any particular object.

It should now be clear that

''from **∀**x α(x) and **∀**y β(y) derive **∀**z α(z) ∧ β(z)''

is also a valid inference rule. It can be looked on as an application of the
substitution rule: in all models of **∀**x α(x) and **∀**y β(y), α(τ) and β(τ) are
true for any τ, hence (by the definition of conjunction) α(τ) ∧ β(τ) is true
for any τ, and therefore **∀**z α(z) ∧ β(z) is true.

The substitution rule allows us to **match** different formulae by using
appropriate variable substitutions. For example, we can easily show that
¬ D(x, y, z) is inconsistent with D(Z, Z, Z), because we can derive
¬ D(Z, Z, Z) from the first formula by substituting Z for x, y and z. We
shall denote such substitutions by

$$x \rightarrow Z, \ y \rightarrow Z, \ z \rightarrow Z.$$

Our ability to match formulae allows us to apply to the problem at
hand implications which express general rules. This is best illustrated
with our running example. (We use apostrophes to distinguish between
variables similarly named, but quantified in different scopes or used in
different applications of a formula.)

1. Match ⇐ D(S(Z), x, S(S(Z)))
   and D(S(x'), y', S(z')) ⇒ D(x', y', z')
   by substituting x' → x, y' → Z, z' → S(Z).

2. From ⇐ (D(S(Z)), x, S(S(Z)))
   and D(S(Z), x, S(Z)) ⇒ D(Z, x, S(Z))
   derive ⇐ D(Z, x, S(Z)) by the rule of resolution.

3. Match ⇐ D(Z, x, S(Z)) and D(Z, x', x'')
   by substituting x'' → x, x → S(Z).

4. From ⇐ D(Z, S(Z), S(Z)) and D(Z, S(Z), S(Z))
   derive □ (the empty resolvent) by the rule of resolution.

A noteworthy feature of this example is that the term S(Z), finally
substituted for the x in

⇐ D(S(Z), x, S(S(Z)))

can be thought of as a **counterexample** to the disproved hypothesis that this formula is consistent with the others. We learned in effect that, in any model of the two clauses playing the role of axioms,

''it is not true that **∀x** ¬ D(S(Z), x, S(S(Z))), because ¬ D(S(Z), x, S(S(Z))) is false when x is S(Z)''.

But this is the same as saying that our question

''does there exist an x such that D(S(Z), x, S(S(Z)))?''

is answered with

''yes, S(Z) is such an x''.

Recall our two interpretations from Section 2.2. In the first we asked whether there is an x such that 2x = 4, and the answer is that 2 is such an x. In the second interpretation, the question whether there is an x such that 1 + x = 2 was answered by 1.

The various substitutions were used to narrow the set of interesting objects to those objects for which the formula being disproved is not true. Indeed, it is evident that for all x other than S(Z), the formula ¬ D(S(Z), x, S(S(Z))) is true in both interpretations. It is so in all models of the two original formulae, but we shall not attempt to justify it directly. Our example would be an ''indirect'' justification if we could be certain that the substitutions did not ''lose'' other objects satisfying the disproved formula. Such certainty would be of practical value, because the answer to our query (i.e. our counterexample) can be a term containing variables. We want it to be as general as possible, in the sense that the set of all terms obtainable by substituting something for its variables should be the set of all answers.

It is a fundamental fact of resolution theory that the algorithm of unification (as presented in Section 1.2.3, but extended with the occur check) finds the most general set of substitutions needed to match two literals. ''Most general'' means that it is contained by all sets of substitutions which make the literals match. When we match A(x) and ¬ A(y), both x ← y and y ← x are possible—we treat them as indistinguishable. In a sense, this is the minimal necessary set of substitutions.

We used unification in our example, so we did not lose any solutions. Notice, however, that our discussion is concerned with the effects of the substitution rule; as we shall see, different proofs can come up with different solutions. Try the *consecadr* and *append* examples from Chapter 1 to get a feeling for this kind of proof. You may use infix notation for functors—it does not matter. The *intersection* example might be a little more difficult: read on.

2.5. STRATEGY

Disjunction being commutative, we can apply the rule of resolution to any literal in the current resolvent: in our examples, we always chose the leftmost one. The choice does not affect our ability to finish the proof, as we must be able to cancel all the literals before obtaining the empty resolvent. As it turns out, the desirable properties of unification mentioned in the previous section ensure that the order in which the cancelling of literals is performed does not influence the final outcome of the proof. The *length* of a proof, however, can be affected by the choice of literals very strongly indeed. We shall discuss this matter at the end of this section.

In our examples, at most one clause could be used to cancel a literal in each step. In general, a number of clauses can be applicable (after suitable matching) to a given literal. Choosing the right clause could be important, because some of them can lead into ''blind alleys''. After many steps, we may turn up with a resolvent to which the rule of resolution cannot be applied (because there are no matching clauses for its literals), even though another choice of clause at an earlier step might have speedily led to the empty resolvent.

The situation is illustrated by Fig. 2.1b, which shows part of the **search space** for the problem listed in Fig. 2.1a. The space is tree-shaped: each path from the root to a leaf represents a possible derivation sequence; its nodes are labelled with the successive resolvents. Some of the paths are successful, some end in failure.

Notice that several subtrees occur more than once. This effect would be less pronounced if the resolvents reflected the history of substitutions, but we did not feel up to creating such a drawing for predicates with variables for arguments. Try it for the application of *intersect* traced in Section 1.3.3. (Figure 2.5 will show you how to do it.)

Prolog always tries to use the leftmost literal, so its search space is considerably smaller, as illustrated in Fig. 2.1c. Whenever it is presented with a number of applicable clauses, the system always attempts the first one first. When it encounters failure, it backtracks and tries another path. In effect, it executes an orderly preorder search of the search space tree.

Figure 2.1c also illustrates the effect of a cut: a part of the search space is shorn off, but one must be aware that this part may contain solutions! While this is not important in the example (if we expect a yes/ no answer), in general different solutions may represent essentially differ- ent instantiations (i.e. substitutions) of variables in the root of the tree. This is not in contradiction to our earlier statements about ''the desir- able properties of unification''. As evidenced by Fig. 2.2, by choosing different literals we change only the order in which things are proved, but the general structure of the proof is not changed. It is convenient to represent the structure of a proof by means of a **proof tree** (do not confuse it with the search space), as illustrated in Fig. 2.3. The first tree shows the proofs of the preceding figure, which all used B and C to prove A, and F to prove B. The other proof trees represent classes of proofs obtained through a different choice of clauses: the proofs are carried out quite differently.

Structurally different proofs use different subsets of the available clauses for performing various subproofs, so the "counterexamples" of Section 2.4—which are descriptions of sets of objects for which the clauses cannot all be true—may turn out to be different. Therefore, not all solutions are the same.

Proof trees are interesting also because they reflect the invocation tree when clauses are treated as procedures. As long as there are no failures, the conventional procedure activations stack can be regarded as an equally conventional stack used for preorder traversal of the proof tree, or—if failure is imminent—of a quasi-proof tree which has a failure

(a)   A ⇐ B ∧ C

       A ⇐ D

       B ⇐ D ∧ E

       B ⇐ F

       C ⇐

       C ⇐ F ∧ D

       D ⇐

       F ⇐   ⇐ A

       The axioms   The (negated) theorem

FIG. 2.1   (a) A search space: the source formulae. (b) A search space: an initial part of the complete space. (Choice of literals denoted by an arc, choice of clauses by a dot.) (c) A search space: Prolog search space has no choices for literals. (Solution one is found, the others could be found on backtracking. ! marks the subspaces made unreachable by executing a cut at the end of A's first clause.) (*continued*)

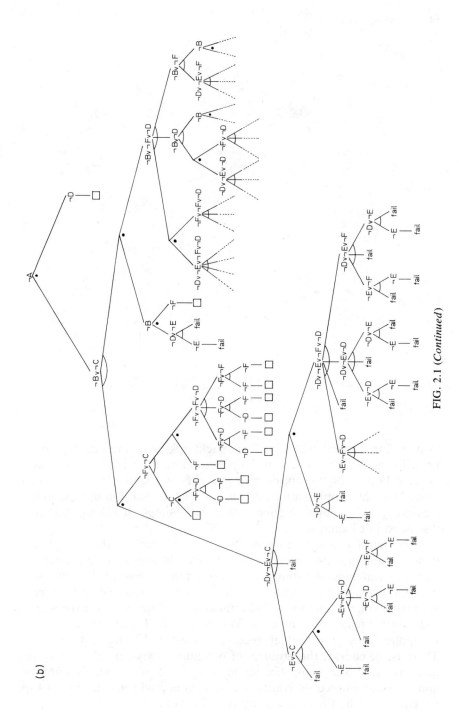

FIG. 2.1 (*Continued*)

(b)

(c)

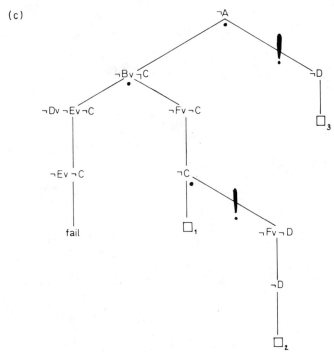

FIG. 2.1 (*Continued*)

in its rightmost leaf (see Fig. 2.4). Backtracking to the nearest choice point in the search space may reopen an attempt to prove a node in a finished branch of the quasi-proof tree, i.e. to reactivate a terminated procedure (this would happen if D had a second clause in our example). Obviously, this cannot be done with a single simple stack: the matter is discussed in Chapter 6.

The word **strategy** refers to the way in which a theorem-prover (whether automatic or human) finds its way through a search space. In logic programming literature the preferred term is **control**. It is not all a question of choosing the order of clauses and literals. Some logic programming systems employ no backtracking, choosing to cover the search space in a breadth-first manner. This helps avoid problems caused by misapplied generators and left recursion (see Fig. 2.5 and Section 3.5.2). There is, of course, the problem of potentially exponential memory requirements. Prolog's appetite for memory is at most roughly linear in number of attempted derivation steps. This is paid for with the cost of backtracking: the time complexity is still exponential.

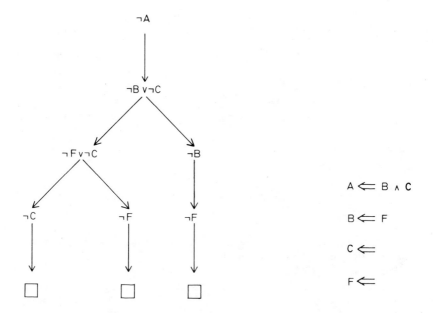

The tree   of   possible proof   paths

The clauses   used
in   these proofs

FIG. 2.2   Choice of literals with fixed choice of clauses from Fig. 2.1. (Prolog would choose the leftmost path, but only after some backtracking caused by choosing the first clause of B.)

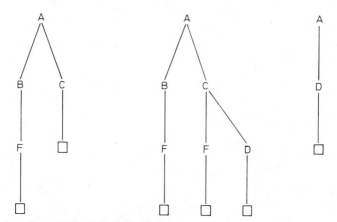

FIG. 2.3   Proof trees for the example of Fig. 2.1. (The leftmost tree represents the proofs of Fig. 2.2. Backtracking would cause Prolog to build each tree in turn, from left to right.)

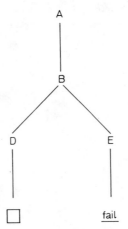

FIG. 2.4   A quasi-proof tree, representing a failing attempt to prove B by using its first clause. (The right son of A was not generated.)

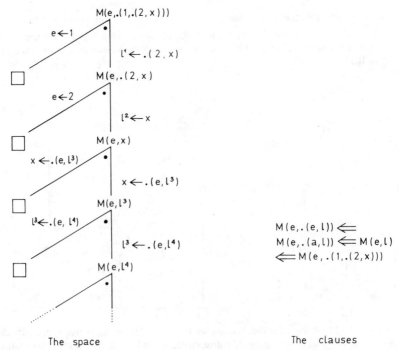

The space   The clauses

FIG. 2.5   Prolog search space for an infinite generator. (The example is *member*.)

There have been attempts to decrease this cost by means of a more sophisticated backtracking strategy (Bruynooghe 1978, Pereira and Porto 1980b, 1982, Bruynooghe and Pereira 1981).

The more ambitious scheme, appropriately called "intelligent backtracking", attempts to retain subproofs (which would otherwise have been discarded) in order to avoid recomputing them again and again. In other words, it attempts to take advantage of the multiplicity of identical subtrees in a search space (compare Fig. 2.1b).

A simpler approach, called "selective backtracking", consists in analysing which variable instantiations caused the failure. It is then possible to backtrack directly to the nearest point where one of these instantiations was made or where the computation would take an entirely different course. In some cases this can save us a lot of thrashing about in a failure-infested region of the tree's crown.

Unfortunately, these interesting ideas have not influenced Prolog implementations. They require a further complication of the already complex runtime data structures and they do not mesh well with side-effects of system procedures. The fact that Prolog can be used as a practical language is still largely due to our dexterity in fighting exponential complexity with the cut.

Attempts to modify Prolog's strategy so that it would incorporate parallelism or coroutining have been a little more successful. Parallelism consists in growing various branches of a proof tree (or even several trees) simultaneously. It is difficult, not only because it raises tricky technical problems, but because we still lack sufficient understanding of its effects on both time/space complexity and the number of solutions gained or lost. Several very different approaches have been documented, but none of them seems to answer all pertinent questions. Some of the references are (Clark and Gregory 1983, Shapiro 1983b, Conery and Kibler 1983, Wise 1984, Eisinger *et al.* 1982).

Coroutining is just that: switching control between several active procedures. In terms of our drawings, coroutining is a non-trivial traversal of a proof tree. Roughly, it is a matter of choosing a different order of literals (a different path in Fig. 2.2). It is possible to demonstrate spectacular improvements in the performance of some programs when they are executed in coroutining fashion. A simple example is the naive naive sort (see Section 1.3.5):

```
sort( List, Sorted ) :- permute( List, Sorted ),
                        ordered( Sorted ).
```

When the execution of *permute* is interleaved with that of *ordered* so that the latter can cause failure as soon as the first out-of-order element is produced by the former, the program's behaviour compares very favourably with that shown when each permutation must be completed before *ordered* is called. When the initial sequence of a permutation is rejected, all other permutations starting with the same sequence can at once be rejected as well, resulting in a significant reduction of the search space.

Section 9.2 contains two short examples of coroutining Prolog programs. Coroutining comes in many flavours: some of the references are (Clark *et al.* 1979, Clark *et al.* 1982, Porto 1982, Colmerauer *et al.* 1983). Unfortunately, most of these schemes are of restricted utility (Kluźniak 1981). The problem is that coroutines do not mesh well with backtracking. We comment on this at greater length in (Kluźniak and Szpakowicz 1984).

3 METAMORPHOSIS GRAMMARS: A POWERFUL EXTENSION

3.1. PROLOG REPRESENTATION OF THE PARSING PROBLEM

We shall begin with a very simple formulation of the parsing problem: given a sequence of items, find out whether it has some presupposed structure. The problem appears e.g. in programming languages when we want to make sure that some text is a syntactically valid statement. Admissible structures are usually described by a context-free grammar. As an example we shall consider the following small grammar in Backus–Naur–Form, which describes simple list expressions:

$$
\begin{aligned}
&< \text{list} > ::= () \mid (< \text{items} >) \\
&< \text{items} > ::= < \text{item} > \mid < \text{item} >, < \text{items} > \\
(3.1) \quad &< \text{item} > ::= < \text{atom} > \mid < \text{list} > \\
&< \text{atom} > ::= < \text{letter} > \mid < \text{letter} > < \text{atom} > \\
&< \text{letter} > ::= a \mid b \mid c \mid d \mid e \mid f \mid g \mid h \mid i \mid j \mid k \mid l \mid m \mid \\
&\qquad\qquad\qquad n \mid o \mid p \mid q \mid r \mid s \mid t \mid u \mid v \mid w \mid x \mid y \mid z
\end{aligned}
$$

Terminal symbols of this grammar are small letters, round brackets, and a comma. For example, the list

(a,(big,ox))

consists of 12 terminal symbols.

There are several commonly used methods of describing the structure of a list (or, more generally, of a valid sequence of terminal symbols). The method we adopt here leads to an elegant formulation of the parsing problem in Prolog[1].

We shall depict a sequence of terminal symbols in a graph (3.2):

(3.2)

Every node in this graph corresponds to a boundary between two consecutive terminal symbols; every edge connecting two nodes corresponds to the terminal symbol it is labelled with. Two edges are *contiguous* if they share a node; a sequence $e_1, ..., e_m$ of edges is *contiguous* if e_i and e_{i+1} are contiguous for $i = 1, 2, ..., m - 1$. For example, the edges labelled b, i, g are contiguous. The labels of contiguous edges are also *contiguous*.

A sequence of contiguous labels may constitute a whole which is meaningful in that it corresponds to the right-hand side of a production. For example, the (only) label of the one-element sequence of edges

constitutes a letter; the labels of the sequence

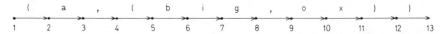

constitute an atom.

We shall describe such meaningful combinations by connecting the extreme nodes of a contiguous sequence by an edge. The edge will be labelled with the name of an appropriate non-terminal symbol, as for example in Fig. 3.1.

To be able to represent graphs in a program, we must give each node a unique name. For example, we can name nodes with numbers:

(	a	,	(	b	i	g	,	o	x	)	)
1	2	3	4	5	6	7	8	9	10	11	12	13

We can represent such a graph as a set of edges, every edge expressed by a unit clause[2] that specifies the label of the edge and the names of the nodes it connects. Perhaps the most compact way is to use the label as the clause name, e.g.

    atom(9, 11).
    letter(9, 10).
    o(9, 10).

[1] This manner of presentation is due to Colmerauer; it was also used by Kowalski (1979b).

[2] For other ways of representing graphs in Prolog, see Sections 4.2.4 and 4.4.3.

FIG. 3.1   Meaningful combinations of edges.

We now observe that clauses which represent edges labelled with non-terminal symbols might be derived from those corresponding to terminal symbols, by virtue of general structural relationships inherent in the grammar. The reasoning would be roughly as follows:

letter(9, 10) because o(9, 10): o̲ is a letter;
letter(10, 11) because x(10, 11): x̲ is a letter;
atom(10, 11) because letter(10, 1͞1): a letter makes an atom;
atom(9, 11) because letter(9, 10) and atom(10, 11): a letter and an atom make an atom.

Relationships of this kind can be generalized in a straightforward manner, e.g.

(3.3)
letter(K, L) :- o(K, L).
letter(K, L) :- x(K, L).
atom(K, L) :- letter(K, L).
atom(K, M) :- letter(K, L), atom(L, M).

Contiguity of edges is assured by using the same term (variable name) to denote every intermediate node: once at the end of an edge and once at the beginning of the next one.

Given the clauses that describe edges with terminal symbols, e.g.

(3.4)
o(9, 10).
x(10, 11).

we might now derive all the remaining relevant edges. Strictly speaking, they would be present only implicitly. For example, to confirm the presence of the edge

atom(9, 11)

we would issue the command

:- atom(9, 11).

from which the following computation might ensue:

atom(9, 11).
letter(9, L), atom(L, 11).
o(9, L), atom(L, 11).

(3.5) $L \leftarrow 10$

atom(10, 11).
letter(10, 11).
x(10, 11).
success

The method of specifying the initial graph is rather awkward, even for this small example. Moreover, it requires that terminal symbols be only identifiers (nullary functors)—the restriction is unnatural but, fortunately, unnecessary. We shall now describe a slightly different and much handier notation.

Names of nodes need not be consecutive integers. On the contrary, it is much better to derive (unique) names from the original sequence of terminal symbols than to introduce another, completely independent nomenclature. We shall exploit the one–one correspondence between a node and the sequence of (contiguous) edges following it. As the name of a node we shall take the *list* of terminal symbols labelling the corresponding sequence. For example, the leftmost node of the graph (3.2) will be named

'('.a.','.'('.b.i.g.','.o.x.')'.')'.[]

and the name of the rightmost one—corresponding to the empty sequence of nodes—will be

[]

With this notation, the (implicit) clause describing the atom <u>ox</u> becomes

atom(o.x.')'.')'.[], ')'.')'.[]).

Notice how the underlying sequence of terminal symbols can be seen without resorting to separate clauses for <u>o</u> and <u>x</u>: it is simply the "difference" of the first and the second node names, <u>o</u> and <u>x</u> in our case. For a terminal symbol this difference is guaranteed to consist of the symbol itself, as, say, in

In other words, if an edge connects the nodes X, Y and is labelled with the terminal symbol T, then

X = T.Y

In order to allow arbitrary terms as terminal symbols, we can write, e.g.

terminal(o, K, L)

instead of o(K, L). Moreover, rather than writing

......
terminal(o, o.x.')'.')'.[], x.')'.')'.[]).
terminal(x, x.')'.')'.[], ')'.')'.[]).
......

we shall use the general-purpose, one-clause auxiliary procedure

terminal(T, T.Y, Y).

However, now we need some other way of specifying the initial sequence of terminal symbols, which in the previous formulation could be read from the assertions (3.4). Before we explain this, we shall rewrite (3.3):

letter(K, L) :- terminal(o, K, L).
letter(K, L) :- terminal(x, K, L).
atom(K, L) :- letter(K, L).
atom(K, M) :- letter(K, L), atom(L, M).
terminal(T, T.Y, Y).

The computation analogous to that shown in (3.5) would now look as follows:

(3.6)
$\quad$ atom(o.x.')'.')'.[], ')'.')'.[]).
$\quad$ letter(o.x.')'.')'.[], L), atom(L, ')'.')'.[]).
$\quad$ terminal(o, o.x.')'.')'.[], L), atom(L, ')'.')'.[]).
$\quad$ atom(x.')'.')'.[], ')'.')'.[]).
$\qquad\qquad\qquad\qquad$ L ← x.')'.')'.[]
$\quad$ letter(x.')'.')'.[], ')'.')'.[]).
$\quad$ terminal(x, x.')'.')'.[], ')'.')'.[]).
$\quad$ success

All the necessary information about the initial graph was supplied by the first call. What is more, the graph itself is now implicit: we only get—and manipulate—the two sequences of terminal symbols.

We are now in a good position to restate each instance of the parsing problem in terms of Prolog. A grammar is given in the form of Prolog clauses, each clause corresponding to some structural relationship between a unit and its immediate components (in particular, to a BNF rule). For example,

items(K, N) :-
$\quad$ item(K, L), terminal(',', L, M), items(M, N).

A call on one of these clauses (or, to be more precise, on the procedure to which it belongs) fully specifies two lists of terminal symbols, the second being the tail of the first. As a matter of convention, the clause name will also be the name of a nonterminal symbol, i.e. it will tell us what structure we want to attribute to the underlying sequence of terminal symbols. For example, the call

> :- items(b.i.g.',','.o.x.')'.')'.[], ')'.')'.[]).

can be interpreted as the question: In the graph determined by the parameters, can an edge labelled with *items* be validly drawn between the extreme nodes? Or briefly: Is *items* the valid structure of a given sequence of terminal symbols, big,ox in our case?

The answer to this question is YES if the call succeeds, and NO otherwise. Examples of unsuccessful attempts to parse are;

> :- items(','.o.x.')'.')'.[], ')'.')'.[]).
> /*items* cannot begin with a comma/
> :- atom(o.x.')'.')'.[], ')'.[]).
> /*atom* cannot end with a bracket/

Procedural interpretation can be expressed in terms of the successive augmentation of the original graph. Every *successful* call implicitly adds an edge. Parsing succeeds if we can connect the extreme nodes with a single edge. This construction proceeds bottom-up: we can imagine an edge being added only after the successful *termination* of a corresponding call.

We shall illustrate this by a complete program for parsing lists.

$$
\begin{aligned}
&\text{list(K, M) :- terminal('(', K, L), terminal(')', L, M).}\\
&\text{list(K, N) :-}\\
&\quad\text{terminal('(', K, L), items(L, M), terminal(')', M, N).}\\
&\text{items(K, L) :- item(K, L).}\\
&\text{items(K, N) :-}\\
&\quad\text{item(K, L), terminal(',', L, M), items(M, N).}\\
&\text{item(K, L) :- atom(K, L).}\\
&\text{item(K, L) :- list(K, L).}\\
&\text{atom(K, L) :- letter(K, L).}\\
&\text{atom(K, M) :- letter(K, L), atom(L, M).}\\
&\text{letter(K, L) :- terminal(a, K, L).}\\
&\quad\ldots\ldots\\
&\text{letter(K, L) :- terminal(z, K, L).}\\
&\text{terminal(T, T.Y, Y).}
\end{aligned}
$$

(3.7)

The call on *list* in the command

:- list('('.a.')'.'.'.'('.b.i.g.',',.o.x.')'.')'.[], []).

results in the implicit construction of the graph shown in Fig. 3.2. Notice the similarity of this graph to a conventional parse tree (Fig. 3.3).

The parameters of a call that initiates the parsing serve as an input and an output parameter. The former contains a given list of terminal symbols. Some initial segment of this list is supposed to constitute the unit under consideration. For example, in

atom(o.x.')'.'.')'.[], ')'.'.')'.[])

we expect that some initial part of the list

o.x.')'.'.')'.[]

constitutes an atom. Should that be the case, the computation succeeds provided the second parameter matches the tail of the list which remains after "chopping off" the initial segment. For example, ')'.'.')'.[] remains after chopping o and x off the list o.x.')'.'.')'.[]. In most cases the second parameter is a variable, so that it actually behaves like an output parameter. As an example, the call

(3.8)   atom(o.x.')'.'.')'.[], Tail)

instantiates Tail as ')'.'.')'.[]—compare this with (3.6).

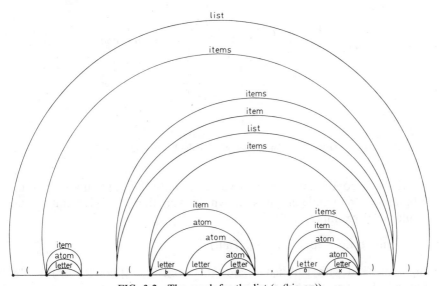

FIG. 3.2   The graph for the list (a,(big,ox)).

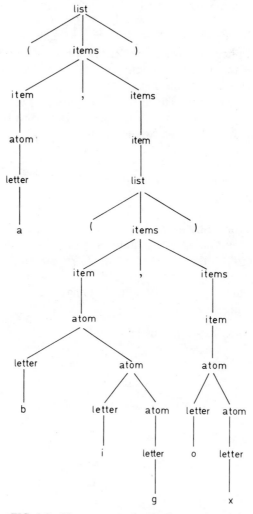

FIG. 3.3   The parse tree for the list (a,(big,ox)).

If the second parameter is a variable, only the entry node of some subgraph of the whole graph is known. Parsing then may give ambiguous results. For example, the call

items(b.i.g.',','.o.x.')'.')'.[], Tail)

might succeed with Tail instantiated to ',','.o.x.')'.')'.[] or to ')'.')'.[]. In general, the results depend on how the clauses of a parsing program are ordered. In the program above, the recursive clause for *items* would only

be activated because of forced failure coming after a successful parsing
of big as *items*.

Recall now that the parameter of a Prolog procedure can, in principle,
be bi-directional, the direction—input or output—depending on the form
of the corresponding actual parameter. This also applies to calls that
initiate parsing. If the first parameter is a variable, what we ask is whether
there exists a sequence of terminal symbols that has a particular structure. For example, the call

list(AList, [])

should instantiate AList to *any* valid list of terminal symbols; in other
words, some list should be constructed, or synthesized. One example of
such a list is the empty list.

However, the situation is not fully symmetric. For any given sequence of terminal symbols, a call on *list* either succeeds or fails, i.e.
every sequence can be classified as a list or a non-list—can be syntactically analysed. Not so with synthesis. It is easy to see that the two calls

list(AList, []), fail

will act as a generator of one-element lists:

()   (a)(b) ... (z)(aa)(ab) ... (az)(aaa)(aab) ...

Moreover, if we reorder the two clauses for *item,* the call on *item* with a
variable first parameter would result in infinite recursion.

3.2. THE SIMPLEST FORM
OF GRAMMAR RULES

The input and output parameters of the clauses that constitute a parsing program, such as (3.7), are the basis of yet another interpretation of
those clauses: in terms of operations on sequences of terminal symbols.
Take the clause

items(K, N) :- item(K, L), terminal(',', L, M), items(M, N).

It can be read as follows: (an instance of) *items* can be "chopped off"
(recognized at the beginning of) K, leaving N, if (an instance of) *item* can
be chopped off K, leaving L, and then a comma can be chopped off L,
leaving M, and finally (another instance of) *items* can be chopped off M,
leaving N. Now the essence of all this is that *items* consist of an *item*, a
comma, and *items*. The other information can be routinely added to this
fundamental fact. All we need is four variables to stand for successive
remainders of the initial sequence of terminal symbols.

In the notation we shall use henceforth, this routine information is suppressed. The notation resembles BNF productions. The lefthand side of a **Prolog grammar rule** names the construction, and the righthand side enumerates its constituents. For example:

atom → letter, atom.

The symbol → is rendered in Prolog as --> (it must be written without intervening blanks). There is a simple convention to distinguish nonterminal and terminal symbols: the latter are enclosed in square brackets, e.g.

items → item, [','], items.

Contiguous terminal symbols can be enclosed in a single pair of brackets. For example, the rule for empty lists can be written as

list → ['(', ')'].

If all terminal symbols are characters (one-character nullary functors), we can use string notation:

list → ''()''.

Such grammar rules are merely syntactic sugar for the underlying clauses. The translation is fairly straightforward, the gain in clarity significant. However, some Prolog implementations, especially on small computers, do not support grammar rule notation. Even then it seems worthwhile to write a preprocessor in Prolog (we shall describe such a preprocessor in Section 7.4.4).

The counterpart of a parsing program, written down as a collection of grammar rules, will be called a **metamorphosis grammar**[3], or grammar in short. Here is the grammar of lists, corresponding to the program (3.7).

list → ['(', ')'].
list → ['('], items, [')'].
items → item.
items → item, [','], items.
item → atom.
item → list.
atom → letter.
atom → letter, atom.
letter → [a].
......
letter → [z].

---

[3] This is the name invented by Colmerauer (1975, 1978). The name "definite clause grammars" was later introduced by Pereira and Warren (1980) for metamorphosis grammars in normal form (as defined by Colmerauer).

The procedure *terminal* need not be explicitly given (it ought to be provided by the implementation).

This grammar deserves its name. It is best understood independently of the Prolog program it has been used to conceal. Every rule reflects the "consist of" relationship between a whole and its constituents, exactly as the original BNF grammar does. However, it should be remembered that the grammar is also a program in disguise, and is executable *immediately*, without any additional effort on the programmer's part!

Parsing can be initiated in two ways. First, we can simply call one of the underlying procedures, e.g.

:- list('('.a.',','.'('.b.i.g.',','.o.x.')'.')'.[], []).

Second, we can use the build-in procedure *phrase* with two parameters: the nonterminal symbol and the sequence of terminal symbols (which is supposed to be an instance of the nonterminal). For example:

:- phrase(list, '('.a.',','.'('.b.i.g.',','.o.x.')'.')'.[]).

It should be pointed out that the first way brings out the routine information we just managed to hide. On the other hand, the second way is less flexible, e.g. we cannot use *phrase* to perform calls such as (3.8).

3.3. PARAMETERS OF NON-TERMINAL SYMBOLS

Grammars of the kind described so far are of little practical use. We seldom parse anything just to accept or reject it. More often than not, we need to compute the representation of its structure or to transform it somehow, and we must do this while accepting the input. The representation of the structure will be built step by step, with the terminal symbols taken into account in succession.

We shall give an example. Suppose we want to build a parse tree—a Prolog term—for every valid sequence of terminal symbols that constitute a list; see Fig. 3.3. To this end, we shall give each of the procedures in (3.7) an additional parameter to hold the representation (of a structure) to be constructed upon exit from the procedure. We must not meddle with input and output parameters: their role remains the same as before. Here is the program.

```
list( list( '(', ')' ), K, M ) :-
    terminal( '(', K, L ), terminal( ')', L, M ).
```

```
list( list( '(', ITEMS, ')' ), K, N ) :-
    terminal( '(', K, L ), items( ITEMS, L, M ),
    terminal( ')', M, N ).
items( items( ITEM ), K, L ) :- item( ITEM, K, L ).
items( items( ITEM, ',', ITEMS ), K, N ) :-
    item( ITEM, K, L ), terminal( ',', L, M ),
    items( ITEMS, M, N ).
item( item( ATOM ), K, L ) :- atom( ATOM, K, L ).
item( item( LIST ), K, L ) :- list( LIST, K, L ).
atom( atom( LETTER ), K, L ) :- letter( LETTER, K, L ).
atom( atom( LETTER, ATOM ), K, M ) :-
    letter( LETTER, K, L ), atom( ATOM, L, M ).
letter( letter( a ), K, L ) :- terminal( a, K, L ).
......
letter( letter( z ), K, L ) :- terminal( z, K, L ).
```

Again, we shall suppress the routine information, i.e. leave out the input and output parameters. The resulting grammar will be as follows:

```
list( list( '(', ')' ) ) → [ '(', ')' ].
list( list( '(', ITEMS, ')' ) ) →
    [ '(' ], items( ITEMS ), [ ')' ].
items( items( ITEM ) ) → item( ITEM ).
items( items( ITEM, ',', ITEMS ) ) →
    item( ITEM ), [ ',' ], items( ITEMS ).
item( item( ATOM ) ) → atom( ATOM ).
item( item( LIST ) ) → list( LIST ).
atom( atom( LETTER ) ) → letter( LETTER ).
atom( atom( LETTER, ATOM ) ) → letter( LETTER ),
    atom( ATOM ).
letter( letter( a ) ) → [ a ].
......
letter( letter( z ) ) → [ z ].
```

To compute the parse tree of Fig. 3.3, call:

```
:- phrase( list( T ), '('.a.','.'('.b.i.g.','.o.x.')'.')'.[] ).
```

The conciseness and power of metamorphosis grammars can hardly be appreciated in this tiny example. We shall show a grammar that describes (and parses) sequences of statements of a simple programming language. The admissible statements are: assignment, if–then–else–fi,

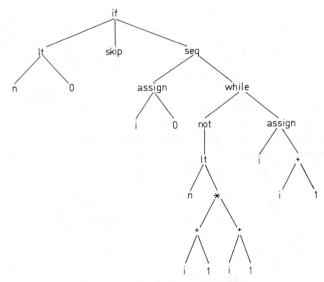

FIG. 3.4   An abstract syntax tree.

while–do–od, and skip. The sequencing operator is the semicolon. The condition is either an arithmetic relation (= or <) or a relation negated[4].

The intended meaning of a sequence of statements is the term that shows its structure. We shall not go into details; instead, we shall give an example which ought to explain the idea. Given the (one-element) sequence of statements:

if n < 0 **then** skip **else**
    i := 0 ;
    while not n < (i + 1)∗(i + 1) **do**
        i := i + 1
    od
fi

we should obtain the abstract syntax tree (a Prolog term):

(3.9)
    if(lt(n, 0), skip, seq(assign(i, 0),
    while(not(lt(n, '∗'('+'(i, 1), '+'(i, 1)))),
    assign(i, '+'(i, 1)))))

The same tree is shown in Fig. 3.4.

---

[4] Both parts of this example, here and in Section 3.4.1, are modelled on the illustration in Colmerauer's original paper (1975).

Terminal symbols of our grammar are tokens (lexical units of the language), e.g. if, n, +, (. Variables and expressions are intentionally left undefined: we want to avoid too many details. A grammar for expressions will be discussed in Section 3.5.2. The following ten rules take care of the rest of language constructions.

```
statements( S ) → statement( S ).
statements( seq( S, OtherS ) ) →
    statement( S ), [ ';' ], statements( OtherS ).
statement( assign( V, E ) ) →
    variable( V ), [ := ], expression( E ).
statement( if( C, S1, S2 ) ) →
    [ if ], condition( C ), [ then ], statements( S1 ),
                        [ else ], statements( S2 ), [ fi ].
statement( while( C, S ) ) →
    [ while ], condition( C ), [ do ], statements( S ), [ od ].
statement( skip ) → [ skip ].
condition( R ) → relation( R ).
condition( not( R ) ) → [ 'not' ], relation( R ).
relation( eq( E1, E2 ) ) →
    expression( E1 ), [ '=' ], expression( E2 ).
relation( lt( E1, E2 ) ) →
    expression( E1 ), [ '<' ], expression( E2 ).
```

This grammar would probably be activated by calls such as

```
... read_a_list_of_tokens( LisT ),
    phrase( statements( Structure ), LisT ) ...
```

which analyse LisT and instantiate Structure appropriately, or fail if LisT is not a valid sequence of statements. Another possibility (not always practical, though) is to build—synthesize, if you prefer—a list of Tokens starting from a given structure:

```
... take_a_structure( S ), phrase( statements( S ), Tokens ) ...
```

Here, Tokens will be instantiated if only S is a proper structure. The grammar establishes one–one correspondence between structures and lists of tokens, and provides transformation both ways.

A more realistic example of synthesis based on a metamorphosis grammar will be given in the next section. Here we only observe that in both cases (analysis and synthesis) similar computations ensue. They differ because, on analysis, the sequence of terminal symbols "controls" the computation (i.e. determines the choice of rules) whereas, on synthesis, it is "controlled" by the initial non-terminal symbol's parameter.

3.4. EXTENSIONS

3.4.1. Conditions

Grammar rules described so far correspond to clauses in which every call manipulates the sequence of terminal symbols, i.e. every call has an input and an output parameter. Other calls could be inserted in between without affecting the transfer of terminal symbols. The question is: Would it be useful, and how could it be interpreted?

As a simple possibility, consider the cut in the first clause of *list*:

    list(list('(', ')'), K, M) :-
        terminal('(', K, L), terminal(')', L, M), !.

The cut turns the computation based on the *list* procedure into a "deterministic" process: it handles either the empty list or non-empty lists. It does not matter when we want to recognize a list. However, it is now impossible to generate lists. The command

    :- list(L, T, []), write(L), write(T), nL, fail.

will only write one instance of L and T, namely

    list('(', ')')   and   '('.')'.[]

The gain from the cut is small in this case, anyway. Cuts would be of much greater use, say, in the program that parses statements (see the previous section), where long and deep computations may occur.

Another example: suppose we want to change the program for parsing lists so that for an atom it produces a Prolog atom instead of a parse tree, e.g. returns

    list('(', items(item(big), ',', items(item(ox))), ')')

for the list (big,ox). One way to do so is to make the procedure for atoms return a Prolog list of letters, and apply the built-in procedure *pname* (see Section 5.10) to this list

    item(item(ATOM), K, L) :-
        atom(LETTERS, K, L), pname(ATOM, LETTERS).
    item(item(LIST), K, L) :- list(LIST, K, L).
    atom(LETTER.[], K, L) :- letter(LETTER, K, L).

atom(LETTER.LETTERS, K, M) :-
    letter(LETTER, K, L), atom(LETTERS, L, M).
letter(a, K, L) :- terminal(a, K, L).
......
letter(z, K, L) :- terminal(z, K, L).

One final example: in the program above we shall replace the 26 clauses that define letters by a single clause:

letter(LETTER, K, L) :-
    terminal(LETTER, K, L), isletter(LETTER).

with *isletter* defined, say, as

isletter(LETT) :- a $@=<$ LETT, LETT $@=<$ z.

This new clause can be used as follows:

letter(Lett, x.')'.')'.[], Tail).
terminal(Lett, x.')'.')'.[], Tail), isletter(Lett).
  Lett ← x,   Tail ← ')'.')'.[]
isletter(x).
etc.

The variable in the call on *terminal* matches *every* terminal symbol. If the terminal symbol is *not* a letter, a call on *isletter* will fail and a letter will not be recognized. We call such terminal symbols **variable terminals**: the first (still unprocessed) symbol is selected and is then either accepted or rejected, e.g. according to the result of a test such as *isletter*.

Extra calls that do not comprise input and output parameters have been known as *conditions*, but the name is slightly misleading. Only in the last example *isletter(Lett)* can be interpreted as a condition: the clause will only be applied if *isletter* succeeds. The call on *pname* in the second example is rather an action performed on the parameters of non-terminal symbols. Finally, the cut can be reasonably interpreted exactly as in any other clause, as pragmatic information on the future use of the clause.

Conditions in metamorphosis grammars are enclosed in curly brackets, so that they will not be confused with terminal and non-terminal symbols. Examples:

list(list('(', ')')) → ['(', ')'], {!}.
item(item(ATOM)) → atom(LETTERS),
    { pname(ATOM, LETTERS) }.
letter(LETTER) → [LETTER], { isletter(LETTER) }.

As an exception, the cut need not be placed within curly brackets, e.g.

list(list('(', ')')) → ['(', ')'], !.

Contiguous conditions can be combined in a single pair of brackets, and in general a condition can also contain alternatives conjoined by semicolons, e.g.

alphanum(Char) → [Char], { isletter(Char) ; isdigit(Char) }.

We shall now present a small fragment of a metamorphosis grammar, meant primarily for synthesis (but applicable both ways, although not without reservations). We want to take a structure computed by the grammar for statements (see the previous section) and produce its translation into a machine-oriented symbolic language. We shall only give a hint of the target language by showing schematic translations of while(C, S) and if(C, S1, S2).

Let $\overline{C}$ and $\overline{S}$ be the translations of C and S. The evaluation of $\overline{C}$ sets a flag used implicitly by a conditional jump instruction. Let $\ell 1, \ell 2$ be unique labels. The translation of while(C, S) will be

label($\ell 1$)
$\overline{\text{not(C)}}$
jumpiftrue($\ell 2$)
$\overline{S}$
jump($\ell 1$)
label($\ell 2$)

The translation of if(C, S1, S2) will be

$\overline{C}$
jumpiftrue($\ell 1$)
$\overline{S2}$
jump($\ell 2$)
label($\ell 1$)
$\overline{S1}$
label($\ell 2$)

The "code generator" can be written as a grammar of the target language. By way of explanation, we shall show three of the rules that belong to the uppermost level of the definition:

code(seq(S, OtherS)) → code(S), code(OtherS).
code(while(C, S)) →
    { newlabel(L1) }, [label(L1)], codecond(not(C)),
    { newlabel(L2) }, [jumpiftrue(L2)], code(S),
    [jump(L1), label(L2)].
code(skip) → [].

The action *newlabel* can generate a new, unique label. The definition of *codecond* will be given below. The third rule illustrates a new feature of grammar rules. If the righthand side contains no terminal and non-terminal symbols, nothing will be produced during synthesis and nothing will be "chopped off" during analysis. The underlying clause is

code(skip, K, K).

Try to trace the execution of

:- code(seq(skip, skip), Translation, []).

Assuming that *coderel* defines the grammar of codes for relations eq and lt, the definition of *codecond* can be as follows:

codecond(not(not(C))) → codecond(C).
codecond(not(Rel)) → coderel(Rel), [revert(_)].
codecond(Rel) → coderel(Rel).

where "revert" is an instruction of the target language that resets the "condition flag".

The example would be completed after specifying the translation of expressions and of assignments, in particular the handling of variables.

The code generator together with the grammar of statements might constitute the core of a simple compiler. Its overall structure might be:

compile :- read_tokens(Token_list),
            parse(Token_list, Syntax_tree),
            generate_code(Syntax_tree, Object_code),
            write_code(Object_code).

with *parse* and *generate_code* defined as

parse(T, S) :- phrase(statements(S), T).
generate_code(S, O) :- phrase(code(S), O).

The procedure read_tokens, reading the source program in and performing lexical analysis, might also be (partly) written as a metamorphosis grammar—see Colmerauer (1975, 1978).

3.4.2. Context

Another feature of grammar rules in Prolog is a mechanism for modifying the sequence of terminal symbols during the computation. In general, this would require explicit manipulations on input and output parameters, but such general mechanisms seem only necessary in natural language processing (an important application of Prolog). A very restricted mechanism, so-called context grammar rules, is quite sufficient, though, in most of the other applications.

In a context grammar rule, the lefthand side is supplemented by a so-called **context**[5]: terminal symbols, preceding the arrow →. For example:

    otherst(S, S), [Delim] → [Delim], { stsdelim(Delim) }.
    do, ['not'] → dont.

The output parameter in the head of an underlying clause is appended to the context. As clauses, the above rules are:

    otherst(S, S, K, Delim.L) :-
        terminal(Delim, K, L), stsdelim(Delim).
    do(K, 'not'.L) :- dont(K, L).

The first rule can be interpreted without resorting to the corresponding clause; we shall give the interpretation below. The second rule, however, can only be explained in terms of manipulations on sequences of terminal symbols: a *new* terminal symbol appears after recognizing an instance of *dont*, and only then is an instance of *do* recognized as well. We shall elaborate on this example a little, too.

First we come back to the grammar for statements. In its present shape it performs rather poorly on incorrect inputs. It fails without giving any message or diagnostics. We shall try to improve the definition of *statements*, leaving the other rules as an exercise. We observe that a statement (other than the last) may be delimited by a semicolon (it indicates that there are other statements in this sequence), by **else**, **fi**, or **od**. Other delimiters are erroneous. In case of errors, no meaningful structure may be found for the whole sequence of statements, but we elect to continue the analysis, after skipping a portion of input up to the nearest semicolon. Here are some rules of a grammar that implements these ideas.

    statements(Sts) → statement(St), otherst(St, Sts).
    otherst(St1, seq(St1, Sts)) →
        [';'], statement(St2), otherst(St2, Sts).
    otherst(St, St), [Delim] →
        [Delim], { stsdelim(Delim) }.
    otherst(_, _) → [T], erroneous(T).
    otherst(St, St) → [].   % this for the last statement
    erroneous(T) → { write(bad(T)), nl }, skipped.
    skipped, [';'] → [';'].

---

[5] Readers familiar with context-sensitive grammars will notice that neither rule is a proper context-sensitive rule. Even if we disregard parameters and conditions, the rules will only belong to Chomskian type 0.

skipped → [_], skipped.
skipped → [].   % if we are skipping the last statement
stsdelim(else).   stsdelim(fi).   stsdelim(od).

The context rule can be interpreted in the following manner: "the remainder of a sequence of statements is empty if we have encountered a proper delimiter; this delimiter is retained". Notice that we have actually effected one-item lookahead on a list of terminal symbols. In general, we can have lookahead for any *fixed* number of terminal symbols, for example

p, [T1, T2] → [T1, T2], { test(T1, T2) }.

This translates into

p(K, T1.T2.M) :-
     terminal(T1, K, L), terminal(T2, L, M), test(T1, T2).

We can use *p* to make the *test*; e.g. in

a → p, b, c.

p consumes no input, so that the rule is structurally equivalent to

a → b, c.

but it will only be applied if two leftmost terminal symbols of the current sequence pass the test.

The second example is a very simplified little grammar that recognizes auxiliary "do not", "don't", does not", "doesn't". This particular problem can easily be solved differently; the way we have chosen is intended as an illustration of context grammar rules:

aux → do, ['not'].
do, ['not'] → dont.
do → [do].
do → [does].
dont → ['don''t'].   %i.e. don't
dont → ['doesn''t'].   %i.e. doesn't

The following computation should explain how this grammar is used:

aux('doesn''t'.like.it.[], Tail).
do('doesn''t'.like.it.[], Tl), terminal('not', Tl, Tail).
   Tl ← 'not'.L
dont('doesn''t'.like.it.[], L),
   terminal('not', 'not'.L, Tail).

```
terminal( 'doesn''t', 'doesn''t'.like.it.[], L ),
  terminal( 'not', 'not'.L, Tail ).
    L ← like.it.[]
terminal( 'not', 'not'.like.it.[], Tail ).
    Tail ← like.it.[]
success
```

Our last example is a small grammar that discards leading zeroes from an integer represented as a list of digits:

```
zeroes, [ D ] → [ 0 ], zeroes, [ D ], { digit( D ) }.
zeroes → [].
```

The reader may wish to trace the execution of the directives

```
:- zeroes( 0.3.[], Tail ).
:- zeroes( 0.0.[], Tail ).
```

3.4.3. Alternatives

Two or more grammar rules with the same lefthand side (including context and parameters of the non-terminal symbol) can be combined into a single rule with the common lefthand side and with the righthand side taking the form of **alternatives**—a sequence of original righthand sides separated by semicolons. For example:

```
list → [ '(', ')' ] ; [ '(' ], items, [ ')' ].
items → item ; item, [ ',' ], items.
item → atom ; list.
atom → letter ; letter, atom.
letter → [ L ], { isletter( L ) }.
```

Notice how—at last—we managed to come back rather closely to the original BNF grammar (3.1).

The translation of a rule with an alternative into an underlying clause is straightforward. One example should be sufficient:

```
items( K, N ) :- item( K, N ) ;
                 item( K, L ), terminal( ',', L, M ), items( M, N ).
```

The notation with alternatives is, strictly speaking, a "convenience" rather than a real extension, and—like alternatives in ordinary clauses (see Section 1.3.7)—it can sometimes adversely affect the grammar's readability.

3.4.4. Syntax of Grammar Rules: Summary

We shall now give a metamorphosis grammar that describes full syntax of grammar rules supported by Prolog-10. The principles of mapping rules onto underlying clauses have been discussed at length in the previous sections, so we choose not to overburden the grammar with parameters that would take care of the translation. However, we encourage the reader to try and augment the grammar along these lines. A hint: most of the non-terminal symbols should be given three parameters, two variables (to construct an input and output parameter) and a term (to hold the—partial—translation). For example:

> grammar_rule((Tr_of_left :- Tr_of_right), In_var, Out_var)
> → lefthand_side(Tr_of_left, In_var, Out_var), ['→'],
>   righthand_side(Tr_of_right, In_var, Out_var), ['.'].
> rule_items((Tr_of_item, Tr_of_items), Curr_in_var, Out_var)
> → rule_item(Tr_of_item, Curr_in_var, Mid_var), [','],
>   rule_items(Tr_of_items, Mid_var, Out_var).

In the actual translation we might eliminate the calls on the procedure *terminal*. Since *terminal(T, K, L)* means that K = T.L, we can substitute in advance T.L for K elsewhere in the clause. For example, in the clause

> list(K, N) :-
>   terminal('(', K, L), items(L, M), terminal(')', M, N).

we have K = '('.L and M = ')'.N, and after replacing K and M we obtain

> list('('.L, N) :- items(L, ')'.N).

This is, in fact, what is done in many implementations (see, e.g., Section 7.4.9). As we have executed both calls on *terminal* beforehand, every computation started by a call on *list* will be at least two steps shorter. Here are some other examples of such an improved translation of grammar rules:

> letter(Lett, Lett.L, L) :- isletter(Lett).
> p(Tl.T2.M, T1.T2.M) :- test(T1, T2).
> zeroes(0.L, D.N) :- zeroes(L, D.N), digit(D).

We shall now present the grammar *without* parameters (it is, really, equivalent to a BNF definition).

> grammar_rule → lefthand_side, ['→'],
>   righthand_side, ['.'].
> lefthand_side → nonterminal, context.
> context → terminals ; [].

righthand_side → alternatives.
alternatives → alternative ;
          alternative, [';'], alternatives.
alternative → [[]] ; rule_items.
rule_items → rule_item ; rule_item, [','], rule_items.
rule_item → nonterminal ; terminals ; condition ; [!] ;
          ['('] , alternatives , [')'].
nonterminal → name ;
          name, ['('], list_of_terms, [')'].
terminals → ['['], list_of_terms, [']'] ; string.
condition → ['{'], procedure_body, ['}'].
list_of_terms → term ; term, [','], list_of_terms.

Definitions of name, term, string and procedure_body are left as an
exercise for the reader.

It should be noted that the original appearance of grammar rules in the
Marseilles interpreter of Prolog I (Roussel 1975) was slightly different. In
particular, no alternatives were allowed, and terminal symbols and conditions could not be combined. Just to give the flavour of it, we shall rewrite
in Marseilles syntax some of the grammar rules for statements (Section
3.4.2).

```
:STATEMENTS( *STS ) == :STATEMENT( *ST )
   :OTHERST( *ST, *STS ).
:OTHERST( *ST1, SEQ( *ST1, *STS ) ) ==
   #; :STATEMENT( *ST2 ) :OTHERST( *ST2, *STS ).
:OTHERST( *ST, *ST ) #*DELIM ==
   #*DELIM –STSDELIM( *DELIM ).
:OTHERST( *DUMMY1, *DUMMY2 ) ==
   #*T :ERRONEOUS( *T ).
:OTHERST( *ST, *ST ) == .
   *THIS FOR THE LAST STATEMENT.
```

3.5. PROGRAMMING HINTS

3.5.1. Efficiency Considerations

Metamorphosis grammars correspond to Prolog programs which implement a very general parsing strategy: nondeterministic top-down parsing with backtracking (Aho and Ullman 1977; Gries 1971). The potential
cost of this strategy is exponential. This is the disadvantage of the gener-

ality and ease of programming with metamorphosis grammars. Well-known parsing algorithms for restricted classes of context-free grammars can be quite conveniently programmed in Prolog without metamorphosis grammars. See for example the operator precedence parser described in Section 7.4.3 and Appendix A.4. However, this requires explicit handling of the parsing stack, attributes etc., while metamorphosis grammars by themselves are as powerful as attribute grammars (Knuth 1968) or two-level grammars (van Wijngaarden 1976)—see the discussion in (Pereira and Warren 1980). Parameters and conditions/actions make it possible to construct an intuitively appealing, concise and readable metamorphosis grammar of any existing programming language (and of reasonable subsets of natural languages), capturing semantics as well as syntax—see e.g. (Moss 1979). At the same time, such a grammar can usually be used as a translator of this language, without additional effort on the part of the programmer, but there is often a certain price to be paid in efficiency.

One source of inefficiency is repetition. Consider two rules from the grammar for statements (Section 3.3):

relation(eq(E1, E2)) →
    expression(E1), ['='], expression(E2).
relation(lt(E1, E2)) →
    expression(E1), ['<'], expression(E2).

If a given relation is not an equality, we recognize this state of affairs only after parsing the first expression and failing to find an equals sign. We abandon the rule and choose the next but then we must once more parse the first expression (which may be quite large). The problem remains if we change the order of the rules.

To avoid this inefficiency, we may apply **factorization**—the technique already used in Section 3.4.2:

relation(R) → expression(E1), op_and_expr(E1, R).
op_and_expr(E1, eq(E1, E2)) → ['='], expression(E2).
op_and_expr(E1, lt(E1, E2)) → ['<'], expression(E2).

Another solution is to combine the original rules into a single rule by replacing the terminal symbols with a variable terminal, and adding a suitable condition:

relation(R) → expression(E1), [Op],
                { makestruct(Op, E1, E2, R) },
                expression(E2).
makestruct('=', E1, E2, eq(E1, E2)).
makestruct('<', E1, E2, lt(E1, E2)).

Notice the position of the condition: if we placed it at the end of the rule, we would run the risk of discovering an improper instance of Op only after parsing the whole input, say,

(A + b/2)*c   blah_blah   2*(n − (x + y)/4)

In its present position the condition fails as soon as it sees an invalid operator.

Both improvements of the original grammar eliminate possible repetitions. Both, though, seem to decrease the readability and elegance of the original solution, and we recommend that they be applied (if at all necessary) only in the late stages of program debugging.

3.5.2. Elimination of Left Recursion

We shall now discuss a problem which frequently arises with inexpert use of metamorphosis grammars. As an example, we shall consider the task of writing a workable grammar of simple arithmetic expressions (see Section 3.3). Here is the definition in BNF (for simplicity, we limit ourselves to two operators only):

< expression > ::= < add_expr > |
           < expression > + < add_expr > |
           < expression > − < add_expr >
< add_expr > ::= < constant >

We now give an obvious transcription of this definition into a metamorphosis grammar. Parameters are used to build the structure of a given expression—see (3.9).

expression(E) → add_expr(E).
expression(E1 + E2) →
    expression(E1), ['+'], add_expr(E2).
expression(E1 − E2) →
    expression(E1), ['−'], add_expr(E2).

The definition of *add_expr* will be left out (it can be simply an integer constant).

Unfortunately, this grammar—as a program—is not only inefficient but also incorrect. It goes into infinite (left) recursion whenever we give it an expression that contains a minus. Try to analyse the expression 2 − 3 + 5 (represented by 2.'−'.3.'+'.5.[]).

At first sight, it seems we can improve the situation by applying one of the techniques shown in the previous section. For example, the second technique gives the following rules:

expression(E) → add_expr(E).
expression(`E) → expression(E1), [Op],
                     { makesum(Op, E1, E2, E) },
                     add_expr(E2).
makesum('+', E1, E2, E1 + E2).
makesum('−', E1, E2, E1 − E2).

Now correct expressions will be parsed successfully, although an expression composed of n add-expressions will require $n - 1$ backtracks before reaching the solution. But the grammar will still fall into infinite recursion on any incorrect input (the reader may wish to check this on 2.+.[]). This means that it is of no practical value. As in all top-down parsing methods, we must eliminate left recursion to avoid trouble.

Suppose we reverse nonterminal symbols in the recursive rules in (3.10):

expression(E1 + E2) → add_expr(E1), ['+'], expression(E2).
expression(E1 − E2) → add_expr(E1), ['−'], expression(E2).

Now incorrect input causes the grammar to fail (without any error message, but this can be fixed). However, this grammar interprets operators as right-associative. The instantiation of its parameter for the expression $2 - 3 + 5$ will be $-(2, +(3, 5))$ rather than $+(-(2, 3), 5)$. Here is a possible solution to this new problem:

expression(E) → add_expr(E1), rest_of_expression(E1, E).
rest_of_expression(E1, E) →
     ['+'], add_expr(E2), rest_of_expression(E1 + E2, E).
rest_of_expression(E1, E) →
     ['−'], add_expr(E2), rest_of_expression(E1 − E2, E).
rest_of_expression(E1, E1) → [].

When we parse an expression, the parameter is initially uninstantiated. It is passed unchanged and instantiated after reaching the end of the expression. (In the terminology of attribute grammars this is a synthesized attribute.) The final structure is accumulated step by step. For example, during the parsing of the expression $2 - 3 + 4 - 5$, *rest_of_expression* will be activated four times, with $2, 2 - 3, (2 - 3) + 4$ and $((2 - 3) + 4) - 5$ as the first parameter. (This parameter is an inherited attribute.) Eventually the third rule will be chosen and E instantiated to $((2 - 3) + 4) - 5$.

We shall now present a grammar for expressions, complete with error handling, that fits the grammar for statements (see Sections 3.3 and 3.4.2). The definition of *erroneous* was given in Section 3.4.2.

```
expression( E ) → add_expr( E1 ), rest_of_expression( E1, E ).
rest_of_expression( E1, E ) →
        [ '+' ], add_expr( E2 ), rest_of_expression( E1 + E2, E ).
rest_of_expression( E1, E ) →
        [ '−' ], add_expr( E2 ), rest_of_expression( E1 − E2, E ).
rest_of_expression( E1, E1 ), [ Termin ] →
        [ Termin ], { expr_termin( Termin ) }.
rest_of_expression( _, _ ) → [ T ], erroneous( T ).
rest_of_expression( E1, E1 ) → [].
expr_termin( then ).          expr_termin( else ).
expr_termin( do ).            expr_termin( od ).
expr_termin( ';' ).           expr_termin( fi ).
add_expr( E ) → mult_expr( E1 ), rest_of_add_expr( E1, E ).
rest_of_add_expr( E1, E ) →
        [ '*' ], mult_expr( E2 ), rest_of_add_expr( E1*E2, E ).
rest_of_add_expr( E1, E ) →
        [ '/' ], mult_expr( E2 ), rest_of_add_expr( E1/E2, E ).
rest_of_add_expr( E1, E1 ), [ Termin ] →
        [ Termin ], { add_expr_termin( Termin ) }.
rest_of_add_expr( _, _ ) → [ T ], erroneous( T ).
rest_of_add_expr( E1, E1 ) → [].
add_expr_termin( Termin ) :- expr_termin( Termin ).
add_expr_termin( '+' ).
add_expr_termin( '−' ).
mult_expr( E ) → variable( E ).
mult_expr( E ) → constant( E ).
mult_expr( E ) → [ '(' ], expression( E ), [ ')' ].
```

To make the grammar really complete, we should also define variables and constants. We choose not to do it, because variables require symbol table handling—we shall discuss it in Section 4.2.2.

The techniques described above are only necessary if we want to perform analysis with a metamorphosis grammar. Even more: the transformed grammar is not good for synthesis, i.e. for constructing the sequence of terminal symbols given a (correct!) structure. Specifically, for synthesizing expressions, the only reasonable solution would be the original grammar (3.10).

4 SIMPLE PROGRAMMING TECHNIQUES

4.1. INTRODUCTION

Programming in Prolog differs from programming in classical (Pascal-style) languages primarily at the level of individual procedures. The larger the program, the more suitable the general recommendations of programming methodology. The advantages of systematic top-down design of programs, modularity[1], clean interfaces, etc., are certainly independent of the programming language used. Design and coding techniques specific to Prolog are due to its *logical* origin.

In Section 1.3.4 and Chapter 2 we discussed logical—static—interpretation of procedures. This interpretation makes it possible to design programs without paying attention—at least initially—to *how* the computation will proceed. One only needs to indicate *what* will be computed. Kowalski (1974, 1979a) coined an "equation",

Algorithm = Logic + Control

which helps clarify the distinctive feature of logic programming. It is maintained that logic programming relieves the programmer of the burden of specifying control information for her program. One would like to say: completely relieves, but unfortunately (at least in Prolog) this is not the case. Many useful built-in procedures, such as the cut, input/output and program modification procedures (assert, etc.; see Section 5.11), cannot be interpreted statically. As a result, a *practical* program may not usually be designed without paying regard to control information.

---

[1] At least on a conceptual level: most existing Prolog implementations do not support it explicitly.

In Section 4.3 we shall briefly consider the advantages and disadvantages of some side-effects in Prolog; we shall also present several simple tricks that help increase the efficiency of Prolog programs (especially their space requirements) in many existing implementations. Earlier, in Section 4.2, we shall give a few examples of Prolog implementation of commonly used data structures, in particular binary trees and linear lists. We shall show basic operations on those structures and a few typical applications. Section 4.4 contains small examples of program design.

4.2. EXAMPLES OF DATA STRUCTURES

We have chosen unbalanced binary search trees (BSTs) and one-way linear lists as an illustration of methods of implementing recursive data structures in Prolog. We assume you are familiar with basic definitions and algorithms; a detailed, though rather elementary presentation can be found, for example, in Wirth (1976) or Sedgewick (1983). Here, we shall refer only to common intuitions, and we shall concentrate on problems specific to Prolog.

We shall also briefly discuss representation of data structures by clauses—in particular, Prolog counterparts of arrays.

4.2.1. Simple Trees and Lists

Terms can usually be regarded as trees: the main functor labels the root, subtrees correspond to arguments. This is slightly imprecise, because multiple occurrences of variables represent more general structures—directed acyclic graphs (DAGs). However, the term f(A, A) which should be depicted as

can be thought of as

We must only remember that the two subtrees will remain identical, so instantiating variables in one will affect the other. Another difficulty is that it is possible to compute terms which are not even DAGs, and which should therefore be regarded as corresponding to infinite trees (see Section 1.2.3). All the same, an ordinary tree is a good intuition of the (general) term.

Terms are a convenient and concise representation of trees with irregular structure, where the information in the nodes determines both the shape of the tree and the repertory of applicable operations. The abstract syntax tree of Fig. 3.3, Section 3.3, is a typical example. However, programs that manipulate such irregular structures are usually problem-dependent, in that every principal functor (i.e. every type of node may require different computations.

There are other situations, typified by binary search trees, when we need a more uniform representation, because we use trees for contents rather than for structure. Suppose we represent the BST of Fig. 4.1 as the term

few(people(many(languages), speak))

Even if we disregard the ambiguity (is "languages" the left or right descendant of "many"?), main functors and their arguments must be isolated, that is, we must use the built-in procedure =.. ("univ"; see Section 5.10). To modify the tree, e.g. by adding a node, we must rebuild it completely, also using *univ*. This is not only inelegant, but inefficient as well (but see Section 4.2.6 for a discussion of such techniques).

We shall therefore represent empty binary trees by the atom

nil

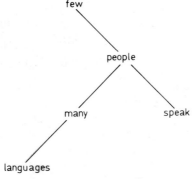

FIG. 4.1   A binary search tree.

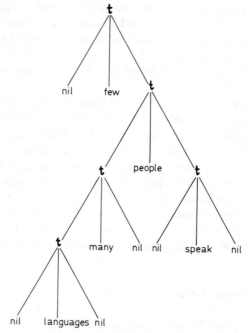

FIG. 4.2   A representation of the tree of Fig. 4.1.

and nonempty trees by three-argument terms

    t(Left_subtree, Node_info, Right_subtree)

For example, the BST of Fig. 4.1 will be represented by the term

    t(nil, few, t(t(t(nil, languages, nil), many, nil),
               people, t(nil, speak, nil)))

The term can be drawn as a tree (see Fig. 4.2). This method of representing binary trees can be readily adapted to trees of a different fixed degree, e.g. non-empty ternary trees can be represented by four-argument terms

    tt(Node_info, Left_subt, Middle_subt, Right_subt)

In Fig. 4.2 the contents of each node is only a key, but of course in practical applications nodes contain other information as well. The tree shown in Fig. 4.3 holds names and phone numbers of several persons—names are keys in lexicographic order. We use a nonassociative infix functor ':' to separate keys from other data.

An inorder traversal of a BST visits the nodes in increasing order, according to the ordering relation in the set of keys. For example, the

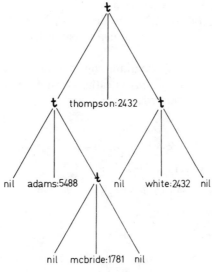

FIG. 4.3   Another BST.

following procedure can be used to write out name–phone pairs, sorted alphabetically by names:

```
write_sorted( nil ).
write_sorted( t( Left_subtree, Node_info, Right_subtree ) )    :-
        write_sorted( Left_subtree),
        write( Node_info),   nl,
        write_sorted( Right_subtree).
```

In this procedure, we need not test the actual ordering of nodes; this would not be the case if we wanted, say, to locate a node in a tree. Let the call

precedes(Node1, Node2)

succeed iff Node1 comes before Node2. For our name–number pairs the procedure can be defined simply as

precedes(Name1 :_, Name2 :_) :- Name1 @< Name2.

It is reasonable to expect that nodes are correctly built, e.g. that each key is a name, and other information a number. A good place to check this would be a procedure for inserting a node into a tree:

```
insert( Node, Tree, Newtree ) :-
    correct( Node ), !, ins( Node, Tree, Newtree ).
insert( Node, _ , _ ) :- signal_error( Node ).
```

However, such defensive programming is seldom necessary in practice.

The insertion procedure *ins* is rather straightforward. We must only take care to preserve the ordering relation:

```
% an empty tree will be replaced by a new leaf

ins( Node, nil, t( nil, Node, nil ) ).

ins( Node, t( Left, Root, Right), t( Newleft, Root, Right ) )   :-
        precedes( Node, Root ),   ins( Node, Left, Newleft ).

ins( Node, t( Left, Root, Right), t( Left, Root, Newright ) )   :-
        precedes( Root, Node ),   ins( Node, Right, Newright ).
```

The procedure fails when it tries to duplicate a key (both calls on *precedes* fail). If the keys need not be unique, we must relax one of the tests, e.g. by changing

precedes(Root, Node)

into

not precedes(Node, Root)

A BST can be built by successive insertions. We shall not discuss balanced trees. They present problems of their own, which can be solved by far in the same way as in classical programming languages (see e.g. Sedgewick 1983) but which can cause memory problems with some Prolog implementations. One example is an AVL-tree insertion program (van Emden 1981, Vasey 1982).

We need some thought to delete a node even from an unbalanced tree. If either of the subtrees of the deleted node is empty, the other subtree moves up and replaces the node. For example, deleting adams : _ from the tree in Fig. 4.3 gives the tree in Fig. 4.4. Suppose now that both subtrees are nonempty; we shall preserve the ordering if we replace the deleted node by that with the largest key in the left subtree (or else that with the smallest key in the right subtree). For example, deleting thompson : _ in Fig. 4.3 gives the tree in Fig. 4.5.

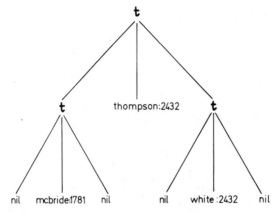

FIG. 4.4   The tree of Fig. 4.3 after deleting adams : _ .

The following procedures implement this algorithm. The second clause is for symmetry (and for efficiency) but it is not really necessary.

```
del( Node, t( nil, Node, Right ), Right ).

del( Node, t( Left, Node, nil ), Left).

del( Node, t( Left, Node, Right ), t( Newleft, Leftmax, Right ) )   :-
        remove_max( Left, Leftmax, Newleft ).

del( Node, t( Left, Root, Right ), t( Newleft, Root, Right ) )   :-
        precedes( Node, Root ),   del( Node, Left, Newleft ).

del( Node, t( Left, Root, Right ), t( Left, Root, Newright ) )   :-
        precedes( Root, Node ),   del( Node, Right, Newright ).


% find and remove the node with the largest key
remove_max( t( Left, Max, nil ), Max, Left ).

remove_max( t( Left, Root, Right ), Max, t( Left, Root, Newright ) )   :-
        remove_max( Right, Max, Newright ).
```

Normally we would call the procedure *del* with only the key given. We might encapsulate such calls:

```
delete( Key, Oldtree, Newtree ) :-
      del( Key : _, Oldtree, Newtree ).
```

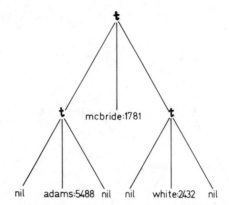

FIG. 4.5   The tree of Fig. 4.3 after deleting thompson : _.

The last basic operation on BSTs is the search itself:

```
search( Node, t( _, Node, _ ) ).

search( Node, t( Left, Root, _ ) )  :-

        precedes( Node, Root ),   search( Node, Left ).

search( Node, t( _, Root, Right ) )  :-

        precedes( Root, Node ),   search( Node, Right ).
```

Again, we can encapsulate typical calls—"find information associated with a given key":

find(Tree, Key, Data) :- search(Key : Data, Tree).

A slightly different method of representing binary trees consists in using

l(Node)

for leaves, instead of t(nil, Node, nil). However, with this representation we would have to distinguish empty trees from leaves of non-empty trees. For example, two more clauses would be necessary in the procedure for tree insertion.

As a very special case, we can consider trees of degree 1, that is, lists. Recall that a widespread convention (introduced in Chapter 1) is to denote empty lists by the atom

[]

and non-empty lists by infix terms

    Head.Tail

The period is used to build trees of degree 2, which are a convenient representation of lists. It plays the same role as **t** in our BST example. In Prolog-10 a special notation has been invented as yet another application of syntactic sugar. It is very commonly used, even though its advantages over dot notation are debatable. Instead of Head.Tail we shall write[2]

    [Head | Tail]

the list a.b.c.Tail will be written as

    [a, b, c | Tail]

and the list a.b.c.[] as

    [a, b, c]

To make sure you have mastered this notation, check that [c | [d]] is the same as [c, d].

    We shall remind you two list-manipulating procedures from Chapter 1. Membership:

    member(Item, [Item | Tail]).
    member(Item, [_ | Tail]) :- member(Item, Tail).

And list concatenation:

    append([], Second, Second).
    append([Head | First_tail], Second, [Head | Third_tail]) :-
        append(First_tail, Second, Third_tail).

    Here is another small example of operations on lists. Consider the following simple-minded sorting algorithm: given a list, put all its members in a BST and then apply the procedure *write_sorted,* defined above.

```
sort( List )  :-  buildtree( List, nil, Tree ), write_sorted( Tree ).

% 2nd and 3rd argument: the tree built so far, the final tree

buildtree( [], Finaltree, Finaltree ).

buildtree( [Item | Items], Currenttree, Finaltree )  :-
        insert( Item, Currenttree, Nexttree ),
        buildtree( Items, Nexttree, Finaltree ).
```

---

[2] Sometimes an equivalent notation is used: [Head,.. Tail], with ,.. written without blanks.

In Section 4.2.3 we shall define a more useful sorting procedure based on BSTs. It will construct the sorted permutation of a given list.

Just as in other programming languages, lists are used in Prolog primarily to represent sequences and sets. They can also be used in a standard way to represent trees of unspecified degree. For example, the tree of Fig. 4.6 might be represented by the list

[a, [b, [e]], [c], [d, [f], [g]]]

Lists are best utilized when items are processed sequentially from left to right, or when all processing takes place at the beginning of the list. In the latter case the list is used as a stack. The basic stack operations, *push* and *pop,* can be easily written in one procedure, e.g.

stack_op(Top, Rest_of_stack, [Top | Rest_of_stack]).

with the call

stack_op(Newtop, Stack, Newstack)

serving as *push,* and the call

stack_op(Top, Newstack, Stack)

to execute *pop.* However, in practice we would rather operate on the stack implicitly, by using appropriate terms in clause heads. One example is the procedure *reduce* (see Section 7.4.3) with old and new stacks as parameters. The clause

reduce([br(r, ’()’), t(X), br(1, ’()’), id(I) | S],
    [t(tr(I, X)) | S]).

describes an action that consists of four pops followed by one push.

Nonsequential access to a list requires, as might be expected, time proportional to the list's length. To build a list in linear time, we can

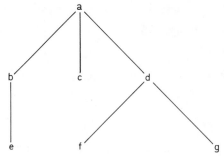

FIG. 4.6   A non-binary tree.

successively push incoming items, but the original sequence will be re-versed. Alternatively, we can use *append* to preserve the original order of items, but this would square the running time. Moreover, each call on *append* entails not only a traversal of the entire list, but also creation of its copy. Strictly speaking, a series of variables is produced and instantiated to successive tails. When executing the call

   append([It1, It2], [It3], X)

the following instantiations take place:

   X ← [It1 | Third_tail']
   Third_tail' ← [It2 | Third_tail"]
   Third_tail" ← [It3]

As a result, only the top-level structure is copied. The situation is roughly as in Fig. 4.7: the two lists share all items but the last.

We had a similar situation in the tree insertion procedure. Check that Fig. 4.8 properly illustrates the picture after inserting turner : 6481 into the tree of Fig. 4.3: we copy the top-level structure of the whole branch.

Copying structures upon modification is necessary because of the semantics of the operations: when we call *append(L1, L2, L3)* to concat-enate L1 and L2, we may wish to preserve an unmodified L1. If we want destructive modification operations, we must express this desire ex-plicitly.

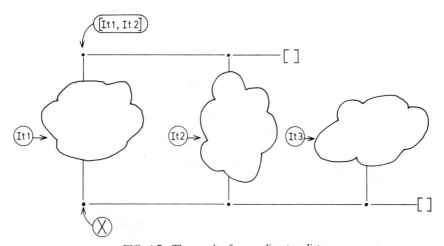

FIG. 4.7   The result of appending two lists.

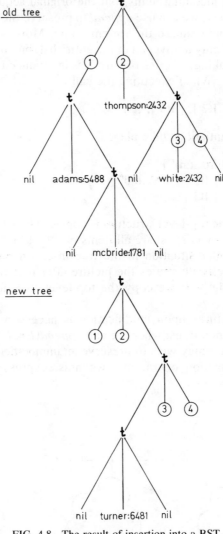

FIG. 4.8   The result of insertion into a BST.

4.2.2. Open Lists and Trees

If we want to build lists efficiently, we must avoid copying longer and longer initial segments of the final list. Recall how *append* extends the list piece by piece. After the call

append([It1, It2], [It3], X)

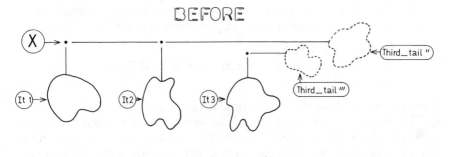

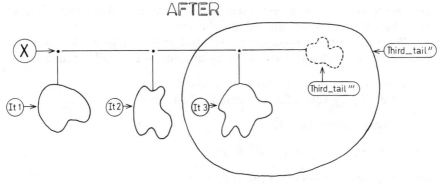

FIG. 4.9   Extending a list.

we get

X ← [It1 | Third_tail']
Third_tail' ← [It2 | Third_tail'']

and finally bind Third_tail''. The trick is to keep Third_tail'' ready for a subsequent instantiation:

Third_tail'' ← [It3 | Third_tail''']

The situation will be roughly as in Fig. 4.9. Figuratively speaking, we shall be able to resume *append* in the next step of computation. We only need to get hold of the variable Third_tail''', instantiate it:

Third_tail''' ← [It4 | Third_tail'''']

and so on. When we are through, we can instantiate, say,

Third_tail'''' ← []

and come up with the final instance of X,

[It1, It2, It3, It4]

We shall illustrate this with a procedure that reads in a sequence of letters (up to the first non-letter) and puts them in a list:

```
read_letters( [ L | Tail ] ) :-
    lastch( L ), letter( L ), !, rch, read_letters( Tail ).
read_letters( [] ).
```

(See Section 5.7.4 for the description of lastch and rch.)

The last tail variable can be left uninstantiated. Although the resulting structure will not be a proper list, it will be equally good as a representation of sequences. We shall call such structures **open lists**, and to avoid confusion we shall call proper lists, with [] at the end, **closed lists**. Empty open lists will be uninstantiated variables.

We must exercise some care if we deal with open lists. Consider the procedure that extends a given list by instantiating its tail variable:

```
extend( List, Ext ) :- var( List ), List = Ext.
extend( [ _ | Tail ], Ext ) :- extend( Tail, Ext ).
```

For example, after the call

```
extend( [ a, b | V ], [ c, d | W ] )
```

the first parameter becomes [a, b, c, d | W].

It is essential that the instantiation of the tail variable be delayed. Consider what would happen if we changed the first clause to (apparently equivalent)

```
extend( Ext, Ext ).
```

The result of the call

```
extend( [ X, Y, Z | End1 ], [ a, b | End2 ] )
```

(i.e. the first parameter's instantiation would be [a, b, Z | End1] instead of the expected [X, Y, Z, a, b | End2].

This version of *extend* can reasonably be used only in strictly deterministic fashion. Failure after a successful computation causes dummy elements to be inserted after the first list. For example, the calls

```
extend( [ a | E1 ], [ b | E2 ] ), fail
```

instantiate E1 as [b | E2], [_ , b | E2], [_, _, b | E2], etc. Therefore a more reasonable version would be that with a cut at the end of the first clause.

The reasoning that has led us to open lists can also be applied to trees. Uninstantiated variables represent empty **open trees**. Non-empty open trees will be represented as before. For example, the following term represents the tree of Fig. 4.1 (E1, ..., E6 are distinct variables):

t(E1, few, t(t(t(E2, languages, E3), many, E4),
people, t(E5, speak, E6)))

Again, we shall refer to trees discussed before as **closed trees**.

We need not copy anything to insert a node into an open tree. We can go down the appropriate branch, locate a suitable empty tree, i.e. a variable, and instantiate it to a new leaf:

```
ins( Node, Empty )    :-

        var( Empty ),   Empty = t( E1, Node, E2 ).
ins( Node, t( Left, Root, _ ) )    :-

        precedes( Node, Root ),   ins( Node, Left ).
ins( Node, t( _, Root, Right ) )    :-

        precedes( Root, Node ),   ins( Node, Right ).
```

If we rewrite the first clause as

ins(Node, t(E1, Node, E2)).

a subtle change in the procedure's behaviour will ensue. The procedure will insert nothing if this Node was already present in the tree. Surprisingly it will also be identical[3] to the procedure *search* from the previous section, and (as might be expected) will serve almost the same purpose. The overall effect of this insertion/search procedure can be described as follows. It looks for a given Node and succeeds after finding it. However, if there is no matching node in the tree, the procedure inserts Node and then "finds" it as well.

There are some strikingly elegant applications of this. A well-known example is maintenance of symbol tables for translators written in Prolog. If the translated language is not block structured, a symbol table usually cannot contain duplicate entries, and it normally only grows, so that keeping it in an open tree will require no copying at all.

The example we are going to present is, of necessity, rather involved. Before we proceed, you might find it helpful to return to Sections 3.3 and 3.4.1, where we described a simple Algol-like language and sketched a parser and a code generator.

We intend to produce object code for a single-address target machine.

---

[3] The only difference is strictly technical: in some Prolog implementations dummy variables cannot be used to pass information, so we must insert a leaf with fresh *named* variables.

For simplicity, we assume the code will not contain external references (we shall also not attempt any optimisations).

The code generator's output should be a list of "symbolic" instructions—terms described schematically as

Opcode(Address)

Each Address is an uninstantiated variable. There should be a unique Address for every addressable symbol of the source program (variable, constant, label), and for every label created by the code generator. By way of explanation, we give a possible translation of the assignment

x := x + y * y + 2

—most opcodes have obvious meaning.

```
[ load( A1 ),
  store( A2 ),
  load( A3 ),
  mult( A3 ),
  add( A4 ),
  add( A2 ),
  store( A1 ),
  stop( _ ),
  label( A1 ), data( _ ),    % x
  label( A2 ), data( _ ),    % temporary
  label( A3 ), data( _ ),    % y
  label( A4 ), data( 2 )     % constant 2
]
```

We want the same Prolog variable for all occurrences of a source variable; for example, A1 always stands for x.

To assemble this section of code, we should determine the base address and go down the list, counting bytes (or other units of storage). Each executable instruction would be assigned a final address. The pseudoinstruction *label* would be treated differently. We would instantiate Address as the current value of the location counter (without advancing the counter); this would instantiate *all* occurrences of Address (or of variables bound to it, if one wants such fine distinctions). Assuming each instruction takes four bytes and the fragment of code starts at location 1000, we would obtain

```
1000 : load( 1032 );
1004 : store( 1036 ),
1008 : load( 1040 ),
1012 : mult( 1040 ),
etc.
```

Conveniently enough, all we need to achieve this remarkable behaviour is the procedure *ins* (it should have rather been christened *table_lookup*). Whenever the translator encounters a symbol, say **x**, in the source program, it allocates a fresh variable V, to represent the symbol in subsequent processing. It also calls *ins* to locate or place the pair

p(x, V)

in the symbol table. On the first occurrence of **x** the pair will actually be inserted. A subsequent "insertion" of p(x, U) only binds V and U together, i.e. finds **x**'s "symbolic address".

For this scheme to work properly, each non-terminal symbol in the grammar that implements our code generator (see Section 3.4.1) must be furnished with one additional parameter to pass the symbol table[4]. The whole grammar should be called with an empty table:

generate_code(S, O) :-
    phrase(code(S, SymTab), O).

And here is a rule that might be used to generate code for assignments:

code(assign(Name, Expr), SymTab) →
    codeexpr(Expr, SymTab),
        % code for this arithmetic expression,
        % the value will be left in the accumulator
    [store(Addr)],
    { ins(p(Name, Addr), SymTab) }.

Symbol tables can also be implemented in open lists. For short tables lack of overhead due to key ordering tests can outweigh the loss due to worse performance. The simplest lookup procedure for open lists can be written as follows:

lookup(Entry, [Entry | Tail]).
lookup(Entry, [_ | Tail]) :- lookup(Entry, Tail).

This procedure, and two other versions (a bit more sophisticated) have been used in the Prolog part of ToyProlog implementation (see Section 7.4, Appendices A.3 and A.4), and in the program described in Section 8.2.

Open lists were first used in the bootstrapped Prolog interpreter from Marseilles (Battani and Méloni 1973, Roussel 1975). The technique shown in the code generator example was presented by Colmerauer (1975, 1978). Open trees were introduced by Warren (1977b, 1980b).

---

[4] For simplicity, we omitted the symbol table while developing the parser. We can save this particular program by doing symbol table management in the back-end, but of course the more proper way is to install symbols in the table in the front-end.

4.2.3. Difference Lists[5]

If the application does not require shortening a list, open lists can be constructed with no copying whatsoever. Successive instances of the originally empty list—a variable—are longer and longer open lists (assuming, of course, that we are careful to instantiate final variables appropriately). However, each time we add an item, the list must be traversed to find the final variable. To avoid this, we can keep this variable ready for instantiation:

　　　End = [NewItem | NewEnd]

and make NewEnd available for further processing.

The pair consisting of a list *and* its final variable can be considered another representation of the list—a little redundant for the sake of efficiency. It is reasonable to represent the term as a single term. We shall write it as

　　　OpenList -- ItsFinalVariable

with -- a nonassociative infix functor. For example:

　　　[a, b | X] -- X

To add an item at the end of a list we use the procedure

　　　additem(Item, List -- (Item | NewEnd), List -- NewEnd)

The call

　　　additem(4, [1, 2, 3 | X] -- X, NewList)

instantiates, as expected,

　　　NewList ← [1, 2, 3, 4 | NewEnd] -- NewEnd

because

　　　X ← [4 | NewEnd]

Consequently, the old list becomes

　　　[1, 2, 3, 4 | NewEnd] -- [4 | NewEnd]

To get a new list, we had to destroy the old one.

Fortunately, the destruction is apparent. The pair can still be regarded as a representation of the sequence 1, 2, 3. Notice that [4 |

---

[5] Difference lists (d-lists) were introduced by Clark and Tärnlund (1977).

NewEnd] is a tail of [1, 2, 3, 4 | NewEnd]. The sequence consists of those items we must pop off the first list to get its tail, i.e. of items by which the two lists differ—hence the name of this data structure: **difference list** (d-list for short).

Actually, a pair consisting of an open list and its tail is only a special case: a difference list is defined as a pair X -- Y such that X = Y or X = $[A_1, ..., A_n | Y]$ for some n ≥ 1. In general, no restrictions need be placed on the form of Y, although the most interesting applications of difference lists are those where Y is an open list.

Difference lists can be used to advantage whenever activity is expected at both ends of the sequence, e.g. when it is used as a queue. The procedure *additem* enqueues an item. To dequeue an item, we can use the obvious

remitem(Item, [Item | List] -- End, List -- End).

but the behaviour of this procedure is unsatisfactory for empty lists. The call

remitem(Item, E -- E, NewList)

instantiates NewList as List -- [Item | List], i.e. as a "negative difference list"[6]. A procedure which fails, given an empty list, may be written as follows:

removeitem(Item, List -- End, NewList -- End) :-
    not List = End, List = [Item | NewList].

Another nice feature of difference lists is the way they can be concatenated. Suppose we have two lists:

[a, b | X] --X   and   [c, d, e | Y] -- Y,

and we want to compute a list holding the sequence a, b, c, d, e. If we can assure that

X = [c, d, e | Y],

we shall have [a, b | X] = [a, b, c, d, e | Y], and

[a, b | X] -- Y

will be a solution. This is readily generalized as a procedure:

d_conc(List1 -- Tail1, Tail1 -- Tail2, List1 -- Tail2).

---

[6] This structure can be very useful in its own rights; see Shapiro (1983b), and Section 4.8).

Once again, it must be stressed that modification of such lists is destructive. For example, the second call below fails, because [c, d, e | Y] does not match [p | Z]:

d_conc([a, b | X] -- X, [c, d, e | Y] -- Y, ABCDE),
d_conc([a, b | X] -- X, [p | Z] -- Z, ABP).

We now return to the sorting algorithm based on BSTs (see Section 4.2.1). Instead of traversing the tree, built of a given list, and merely writing out the nodes, we would rather traverse it in order to construct the sorted permutation of the list:

tree_sort(List, SortedList) :-
    buildtree(List, nil, Tree),
    buildlist(Tree, SortedList).

The procedure buildlist "flattens" the tree (see Fig. 4.10 for an example). The general outline of the algorithm is rather obvious: we flatten the subtrees (recursively) and concatenate the resulting lists together with the root in between. Difference lists can be used to avoid numerous appends. Let the results of recursive calls be denoted by

LFlat -- LFlatE   and   RFlat -- RFlatE

The algorithm is programmed as follows:

flatten(nil, X -- X).
flatten(t(L, Root, R), Flat) :-
    flatten(L, LFlat -- LFlatE),
    flatten(R, RFlat -- RFlatE),
    d_conc(LFlat -- LFlatE, [Root | X] -- X, A),
    d_conc(A, RFlat -- RFlatE, Flat).

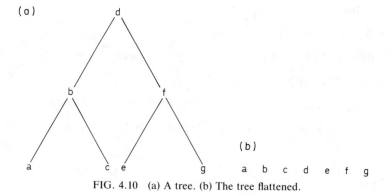

FIG. 4.10   (a) A tree. (b) The tree flattened.

This version is good for didactic purposes. Actually, we know that the following instantiations take place:

LFlatE ← [Root | X],   A ← LFlat -- X,
X ← RFlat,   Flat ← LFlat -- RFlatE

We can remove both calls on *d_conc* and end up with an equivalent form of the second clause:

flatten(t(L, Root, R), LFlat -- RFlatE) :-
    flatten(L, LFlat -- [Root | RFlat]),
    flatten(R, RFlat -- RFlatE).

We might similarly derive a "short cut" clause for leaves. We begin with

flatten(t(nil, Root, nil), LFlat -- RFlatE) :-
    flatten(nil, LFlat -- [Root | RFlat]),
    flatten(nil, RFlat -- RFlatE).

then make LFlat = [Root | RFlat] and RFlat = RFlatE, and remove the recursive calls. The special case becomes:

flatten(t(nil, Root, nil), [Root | RFlatE] -- RFlatE).

(as expected!).

After the call

flatten(Tree, List -- ListEnd)

we shall have List instantiated as

[$Node_1$, ..., $Node_n$ | ListEnd],

and all we shall need to get SortedList is close List by binding ListEnd to []. This is easily achieved by defining

buildlist(Tree, SortedList) :-
    flatten(Tree, SortedList -- []).

(or replacing the *buildlist* call in *tree_sort,* for that matter).

See Section 7.4.1 for a little more sophisticated application of difference lists.

4.2.4. Clausal Representation of Data Structures

A Prolog procedure built of unit clauses is a natural representation of sets and sequences. Under the static interpretation of programs, such a procedure models a relation, i.e. a set of tuples for which a certain relationship holds. For example:

name_phone(thompson, 2432).
name_phone(adams, 5488).
name_phone(white, 2432).
name_phone(mcbride, 1781).

In practice, unit clause procedures are sequences rather than sets, in that they are accessed sequentially. It is therefore possible to represent a list by a procedure, e.g.

list(b).
list(k).
list(q).
list(y).

The call

list(X)

tests membership for instantiated X, and serves as a generator for uninstantiated X. The whole list can be processed thus:

process_list :- list(X), process_item(X), fail.
process_list.

In general, clauses may be used to represent multidimensional matrices—we shall discuss this briefly in the next section.

The restriction to unit clauses is not essential. The clause

name_phone(X, 4396) :- office(X, room119).

will generate tuples one at a time, exactly as the other four clauses do. Similarly, we can add the clause

list(Item) :-
    digraph(Item), diphtong(Pronunciation, Item).

It is worth emphasizing that explicit and generated data are functionally indistinguishable. If five people sit in room 119, we can get up to nine name–phone pairs, without ever becoming aware of the "indirection" in one of the clauses.

Any structure expressible in terms of relations can be naturally cast in clauses. For example, a tree can be described as follows:

t(node1, node2, thompson : 2432, node3).
t(node2, nil, adams : 5488, node4).
t(node3, nil, white : 2432, nil).
t(node4, nil, mcbride : 1781, nil).
root(node1).

In particular, we can represent a list in this way:

    1(item1, b, item4).
    1(item2, y, nil).
    1(item3, q, item2).
    1(item4, k, item3).
    head(item1).

In general, every graph can be expressed as a unit-clause procedure. By way of explanation, here is a possible representation of the graph of Fig. 4.11 (see also Fig. 3.1):

    edge(e1, e2, o).
    edge(e1, e2, letter).
    edge(e1, e3, atom).
    edge(e2, e3, x).
    edge(e2, e3, letter).
    edge(e2, e3, atom).

And a representation of the graph of Fig. 4.15 (Section 4.4.3):

    arc(a, b).   arc(a, c).   arc(b, c).   arc(b, d).
    arc(b, e).   arc(c, d).   arc(c, e).   arc(d, e).

Clausal representation of trees, lists and the like is rather less convenient than representations described in previous sections. It cannot be passed as an actual parameter, so that its use can only be recommended when the bulk of data remains unchanged (see Section 8.1 for a non-trivial example). Since variables are local in clauses, clever techniques shown in Section 4.2.2 are hardly applied here. To build and modify data dynamically (e.g. add a node to a tree), we must apply "extralogical" built-in procedures *assert, retract,* etc., to the detriment of static interpretation of programs.

There are advantages, too. First of all, in Prolog implementations which support clause indexing, *direct* access to components can be possible. **Indexing** consists in finding matching clauses by hashing rather than by linear search, so that e.g. a node in a "tree" with **n** nodes can be located in constant time rather than in $\log_2 n$ steps (on the average).

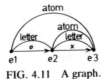

FIG. 4.11   A graph.

DEC-10 Prolog was the first to offer this possibility. If absent, it can be mimicked by means of the built-in procedure =.. (see the next section).

Clausal representation sometimes helps reduce the problem at hand to its bare essence. A case in point is an amazingly concise solution to a map colouring problem; we quote it after Pereira and Porto (1980b). A planar map is to be coloured with at most four colours so that contiguous regions are coloured differently. First we define the contiguity relation for colours:

```
next( red, blue ).        next( red, green ).       next( red, yellow ).

next( blue, red ).        next( blue, green ).      next( blue, yellow ).

next( green, red ).       next( green, blue ).      next( green, yellow ).

next( yellow, red ).      next( yellow, blue ).     next( yellow, green ).
```

The original map of Pereira and Porto (1980b) is shown in Fig. 4.12. A region is represented by its colour—this decision makes the solution beautifully terse. To find a colouring (if any) of the map, we must only call

```
:-    next( R1, R2 ),    next( R1, R3 ),    next( R1, R5 ),    next( R1, R6 ),

      next( R2, R3 ),    next( R2, R4 ),    next( R2, R5 ),    next( R2, R6 ),

      next( R3, R4 ),    next( R3, R6 ),    next( R5, R6 ),

      write( (R1, R2, R3, R4, R5, R6) ),    nl.
```

Structures represented by terms are usually traversed and manipulated by recursive procedures. Clauses are traversed by backtracking, either implicit (e.g. in the call above), or explicit (e.g. in the procedure

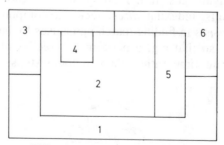

FIG. 4.12   A map to be coloured.

process_list). There is a fundamental discrepancy between these two modes, because backtracking *destroys* variable instantiations which are essential to recursive operations on data structures. Consider the task of computing a list of arcs exiting vertex b of the graph in Fig. 4.15. Arcs are available one at a time to a routine that "backtracks through" the procedure *arc*. If we want them to survive backtracking, we must "put aside", i.e. assert, those which contain b:

```
put_aside  :-  arc( X, Y ),  put_aside_if_b( X, Y ),  fail.


put_aside_if_b( X, Y )  :-  has( b, X, Y ),  assert( with_b( X, Y ) ).


has( X, X, _ )  :-  ! .
has( X, _, X ).


:-  put_aside.


% Now, a list can be created as follows:

collect_with_b( ThisList, FinalList )  :-
        retract( with_b( X, Y ) ),  !,
        collect_with_b( [ (X, Y) | ThisList], FinalList ).
collect_with_b( FinalList, FinalList ).


:-  collect_with_b( [], TheList),  write( TheList ),  nl.
```

Such operations are usually cast in terms of a general-purpose procedure that finds a set of all items for which a given condition holds. In our example, items would be (X, Y), and the condition

(arc(X, Y), has(b, X, Y))

The set is represented by a list, possibly with repetitions, so that it is called *bag* in the folklore. Here is our version of the procedure:

```
bagof(Item, Condition, _)  :-
        assert('BAG'('BAG')),        % a marker
        Condition,                   % generates an instance of Item
        assert('BAG'(Item)),         % saves it
        fail.                        % this clause eventually fails
bagof(_, _, Bag)  :-
        retract('BAG'(Item)), !,     % get the last Item saved
        collect(Item, [], Bag).


collect('BAG', FinalBag, FinalBag)  :-  !.    % this was the marker
collect(Item, ThisBag, FinalBag)  :-
        retract('BAG'(NextItem)), !,
        collect(NextItem, [Item ! ThisBag], FinalBag).
```

The marker enables us to use the procedure *bagof* within Condition.
An example of such nested computation is the following pair of calls
(Graph is to be a list of "bunches"—lists of arcs entering or leaving a
given vertex; the condition in the first call is an alternative, in the embedded one a conjunction):

```
:- bagof( X, ( arc(X, _); arc(_, X) ), Vertices ),
    bagof( Bunch,
                ( member(V, Vertices),
                    bagof( (Y, Z),
                                ( arc(Y, Z),  has(V, Y, Z) ),
                        Bunch
                    )
                ),
            Graph ).
```

Repetitions in a bag may be undesired. For example, the first call
above should rather find a *set* of all vertices—as it stands, Graph will
contain numerous duplicates. The procedure *setof* would call *bagof* and
then filter the resulting bag. In Prolog-10 and some other implementations

both *bagof* and *setof* are built-in procedures: *setof* even returns its output sorted. An implementation of *setof* in Prolog was presented by Pereira and Porto (1981).

4.2.5. Array Analogues in Prolog

There is no addressing mechanism in Prolog, no memory cells directly available to the programmer—for most applications this is simply unnecessary. Consequently, there are no arrays interpreted as contiguous, addressable areas. From a mathematical standpoint, arrays correspond to finite matrices, i.e. to mappings from finite sets of subscripts to sets of values. In theory, there are no restrictions on the form of subscripts, although integers are most commonly used.

In Prolog we can represent such mappings as procedures consisting of unit clauses, one clause for each sequence of subscripts and the corresponding value. This is but a special case of relation in the relational model of data (see Section 8.2).

Unit clauses are particularly convenient as a representation of sparse matrices, provided that clause indexing is supported by the Prolog implementation.

Another possibility is to represent a mapping as a list of n-tuples (subscripts, value), and to use list manipulation procedures. As a special case, a sequence subscripted by consecutive integers may be represented as a list of values. This approach may work for short lists, but in general it is prohibitively inefficient.

We shall now present an alternative way of storing integer-subscripted sequences, which is rather unlikely to outperform Prolog data bases (with indexing), but may be reasonable for sequences of moderate size. The method makes use of digital search trees (see e.g. Sedgewick 1983).

Branching in digital search trees is based on the values of successive digits of the key being looked for. Keys cannot be negative. The order of every node is equal to the base of the digital system, e.g. to 10 if keys are expressed in decimal. In Fig. 4.13 we show two trees, each containing 15 items numbered 0 through 14. A_i denotes the i-th item, the root is empty (i.e. contains a dummy value), and branches are labelled with digits. To find A_{13} in the binary tree, we take 1101, the binary code of 13, and go down selecting branches labelled with 1, 1, 0 and 1. To find A_{13} in the ternary tree, we use 111, the ternary code of 13.

Digital search trees are best implemented in Prolog by open trees. We shall demonstrate it in the case of ternary trees (other cases are basically

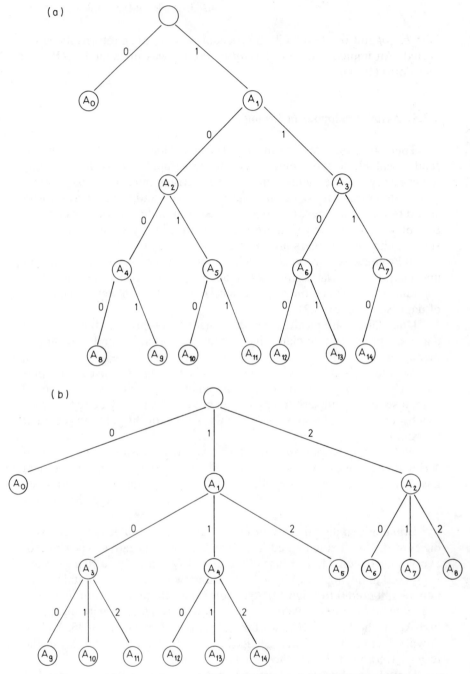

FIG. 4.13 Digital search trees: (a) Binary digital search tree. (b) Ternary digital search tree.

identical, although impractical if nodes have more than a few branches). A non-empty tree will be represented as

t3(Value, Left, Middle, Right)

and an empty tree as a variable. Explicit labels are unnecessary, as we may simply select Left or Middle, or Right upon encountering 0, 1 or 2, respectively.

A procedure that finds a value, given a ternary subscript and a tree, is quite straightforward. We assume that subscripts are represented as closed lists of digits:

```
find_3( [], t3( Value, _, _, _ ), Value ).

find_3( [0 | Sub], t3( _, Left, _, _ ), Value )    :-
         find_3( Sub, Left, Value ).

find_3( [1 | Sub], t3( _, _, Middle, _ ), Value )    :-
         find_3( Sub, Middle, Value ).

find_3( [2 | Sub], t3( _, _, _, Right ), Value )    :-
         find_3( Sub, Right, Value ).
```

The procedure fails if the first parameter is not a correct ternary subscript, or if the second parameter is not an open ternary tree. However, it does *not* fail when a nonexistent item is referred to. We shall discuss this phenomenon presently.

Now for a procedure that replaces an item. Two tree parameters are required, and the new tree is a copy of the old one, except for the replaced item. The amount of copying is similar to that illustrated in Fig. 4.8.

```
change_3( [], NewVal, t3( _, L, M, R ),
                t3( NewVal, L, M, R ) ).
change_3( [0 | Sub], NewVal, t3( OldVal, L, M, R ),
                t3( OldVal, NewL, M, R ) )    :-
         change_3( Sub, NewVal, L, NewL ).
change_3( [1 | Sub], NewVal, t3( OldVal, L, M, R ),
                t3( OldVal, L, NewM, R ) )    :-
         change_3( Sub, NewVal, M, NewM ).
```

```
change_3( [2 ! Sub], NewVal, t3( OldVal, L, M, R ),

                        t3( OldVal, L, M, NewR ) )  :-

      change_3( Sub, NewVal, R, NewR ).
```

Both procedures behave in the same way when the subscript is too large: they create a missing part of the tree, and then "find" or "change" the newly inserted item. For example, the call

find_3([2, 1, 0, 1], Tree, A64)

applied to the tree of Fig. 4.13b changes the node with item A7 into the tree of Fig. 4.14, or, in term notation, into

t3(A7, t3(Dummy21, Empty_i,
                      t3(A64, Empty_ii, Empty_iii, Empty_iv),
                      Empty_v),
          Empty_vi, Empty_vii)

The same effect will be achieved by the call

change_3([2, 1, 0, 1], A64, Tree, Tree)

The moral is that, first, no special insertion procedure is needed, and, second, the tree need not be full. It will contain only the inserted nodes together with the branches required to reach these nodes, but intermediate nodes may contain no meaningful information.

To make the story complete, here is a little procedure that converts nonnegative integers into lists of ternary digits. Note that there are two procedures here: conv_3/2 and (auxiliary) conv_3/3.

```
conv_3( 0, [0] ).

conv_3( N, TerN )  :-  integer( N ), 0 < N, conv_3( N, [], TerN ).


conv_3( 0, AllDigits, AllDigits )  :-  !.

conv_3( N, Z, AllDigits )  :-
        Digit is N mod 3, Nby3 is N / 3,
        conv_3( Nby3, [Digit ! Z], AllDigits ).
```

4.2.6. Access to the Structure of Terms

In Section 4.2.1 we dismissed the possibility of representing tree nodes with main functors: the term

few(nil, people(many(languages, nil), speak))

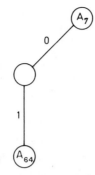

FIG. 4.14   Creation of the missing part of a tree.

would stand for the BST of Fig. 4.1. We shall now show an insertion routine for such trees. The built-in procedure =.. (*univ*) is used to circumvent the problem raised by the potential diversity of the functors.

```
insert( Node, Tree, NewTree )  :-
        Tree =.. [Root, Left, Right],
        insert( Node, Root, Left, Right, NewLeft, NewRight ),
        NewTree =.. [Root, NewLeft, NewRight].
insert( Node, nil, Node ).
insert( Node, Leaf, NewTree )  :-
        insert( Node, Leaf, nil, nil, Left, Right ),
        NewTree =.. [Leaf, Left, Right].


insert( Node, Root, L, R, NewL, R )  :-
        precedes( Node, Root ),  insert( Node, L, NewL ).
insert( Node, Root, L, R, L, NewR )  :-
        precedes( Root, Node ),  insert( Node, R, NewR ).
```

This application of *univ* is far from typical. As a more realistic example, consider the problem of translating an arithmetic expression into reverse Polish form, e.g.

y * sqrt(sqr(x) + f(1, y))

into

[y, x, sqr, 1, y, f, '+', sqrt, '*']

Here is a possible solution:

```
revpol( Expr, RevExpr )  :-
        Expr =.. [Fun | Args],  revargs( Args, [], RevArgs ),
        append( RevArgs, [Fun], RevExpr ).


revargs( [], RevAll, RevAll ).
revargs( [Arg | Args], RevTillNow, RevAll )  :-
        revpol( Arg, RevArg ),
        append( RevTillNow, RevArg, RevOneMore ),
        revargs( Args, RevOneMore, RevAll ).
```

We could use difference lists to decrease the cost of multiple append-ings, but the procedures would become even less readable (but try it—this would be an application of the "flatten" schema, although a little unwieldy because of the unknown number of arguments). However, a readable version would not only be much longer, but also less flexible:

```
revpol( A + B, RevExpr ) :-
    revpol( A, RevA ), revpol( B, RevB ),
    append( RevA, RevB, Aux ), append( Aux, [ '+' ], RevExpr ).
......
revpol( sin( A ), RevExpr ) :-
    revpol( A, RevA ),
    append( RevA, [ sin ], RevExpr ).
......
revpol( Atom, [ Atom ] ).
```

This is a closed schema: to be able to recognize a new function or operator, we must add a branch to this "case statement".

Perhaps one of the most important applications of *univ* (and related built-in procedures) is in bootstrapped implementations of Prolog. A basic interpreter (see Chapter 6 and Section 7.3) may support Prolog (with a very rudimentary syntax) furnished with built-in procedures analogous to *call* and *univ*. Various user interfaces can then be written in this simplified Prolog (see Section 7.4), provided we can convert texts to terms.

Assume we input the text

foo(fie(X), ok, X)

and produce its (intermediate) representation:

[[f, o, o], [[f, i, e], V], [[o, k]], V]

with uninstantiated V. (Try to write this reading program: a symbol table such as those described in Section 4.2.2 must be used to handle variable names properly.) Now we can glue the intermediate representation together:

```
glue( Inter, Inter )  :-  var( Inter ),  ! .
glue( [FunChars | InterArgs], Term )  :-
        not alldigits( FunChars ),
        glueargs( InterArgs, Args ),
        pname( Fun, FunChars ),  Term =.. [Fun | Args],
glue( [Digits], Number )  :-
        alldigits( Digits ),
        pnamei( Number, Digits ).


glueargs( [], [] ).
glueargs( [InterArg | InterArgs], [Arg | Args] )  :-
        glue( InterArg, Arg ),  glueargs( InterArgs, Args ).


alldigits( [Digit | Digits] )  :-
        digit( Digit ),  !,  alldigits( Digits ).
alldigits( [] ).
```

The procedure *glue* should be called with the second parameter uninstantiated.

In implementations that do not support indexing (see Section 4.2.4), *univ* helps avoid linear search of matching clauses. Consider, for example, a natural language application program which maintains a dictionary whose entries can look as follows:

    dict(program, noun(inanim) or verb(intrans)).
    dict(modular, adj).
    dict(an, article(indef)).

Next, assume that each word on input is filtered through this dictionary:

```
input_a_word( W, Features ) :-
    read_a_word( W ),
    ( dict( W, Features ), !; signal_unknown( W ) ).
```

Without indexing, dictionary lookup requires time proportional to the number of entries. Access to a procedure, i.e. to its first clause, usually requires approximately constant time (some form of hashing is used). We can have our dictionary in the form

```
program( noun( inanim ) or verb( intrans ) ).
modular( adj ).
an( article( indef ) ).
```

and define *dict* as

```
dict( W, Features ) :-
    Entry =.. [ W, Features ], Entry.
```

or—equivalently—as

```
dict( W, Features ) :-
    functor( Entry, W, 1 ), Entry, arg( 1, Entry, Features ).
```

A particularly simple dictionary is a table of keywords for a scanner of, say, Pascal:

```
const.       type.      array.      record.
function.    var.       begin.      do.
```

etc. To create the representation of a source program name, we can use this procedure:

```
key_or_id( Name, keyword( Name ) ) :- Name, !.
key_or_id( Name, ident( Name ) ).
```

As a final example, here is the crucial part of a definition of the procedure *phrase* which initiates processing based on a metamorphosis grammar:

```
phrase( InitialNonterminal, Terminals ) :-
    InitialNonterminal =.. [ Name | Parameters ],
    InitialCall =.. [ Name, Terminals, [] | Parameters ],
    InitialCall.
```

Note that input and output parameters are added at the beginning of the parameter list (rather than at the end, as suggested in Section 3.3).

4.3. SOME PROGRAMMING HINTS

We have collected here some down-to-earth suggestions which may help improve your coding technique in Prolog. Although style is largely a matter of taste, some of the things we have to say have long been present in the Prolog folklore, and we feel fairly confident they are worth presenting.

4.3.1. Using the Cut Procedure

Essentially, the cut commits the currently executing procedure to whatever it might have done since its activation. This is precisely what makes the cut a controversial feature: that it can only be interpreted dynamically. On the other hand, the variety of its uses and its power make it an important factor in the emergence of Prolog as a practical programming language.

In Chapters 1 and 2 we discuss the cut—in a very general manner—both as an extralogical mechanism and as a tool for improving efficiency. Here, we shall concentrate on its applications.

Despite Prolog's inherent nondeterminism, the usual computation is mostly deterministic: the majority of procedures are expected to produce a single, well-defined response to any particular set of input data. Most procedures are strictly deterministic: at most one clause of a procedure applies, regardless of the actual data.

With the procedural interpretation of Prolog in mind, clauses are commonly written as

head :- tests, actions.

A clause is executed for its *actions* which can be performed if and only if *head* matches the call and all *tests* succeed. This conforms to the fundamental notion of guarded commands (Dijkstra 1975). Some Prolog dialects, e.g. IC-Prolog (Clark *et al.* 1982), even provide special syntax for "guards".

If, during a deterministic computation, *tests* have succeeded, a cut executed immediately after *tests* commits our choice of the clause. The cut saves us further—unnecessary—attempts to execute the procedure in the case of a failure later on. As an example of this fairly typical situation, consider the following:

```
% Retrieve ( fetch ) the grammatical description of a word,
% fail if there is no such word in the dictionary.
```

```
% The word may be given as a string:
find( String, Description ) :-
    isletterstring( String ),      % yes, a string
    pname( Word, String ), fetch( Word, Description ).
% or as a word, i.e. nullary functor:
find( Word, Description ) :-
    isword( Word ),      % yes, a word
    fetch( Word, Description ).
% Reject bad data:
find( Bad, _ ) :-
    not isletterstring( Bad ),
    not isword( Bad ),      % yes, bad data
    signal( Bad ), fail.
```

In this procedure, cuts may be safely placed after tests. Notice, however, that a cut inserted *earlier* changes the procedure's behaviour, and a cut after *fetch* does not work if a word is absent from the dictionary. (It would also have ruinous effects if *fetch* were a nondeterministic generator of synonyms.)

When we adhere to the "guarded command" style of programming, the built-in procedure *not* is frequently used to invert tests (but see the beginning of the next section for a brief discussion of *not*'s peculiarities!). However, we would not like to perform expensive tests twice, as in this example:

```
addunique( Item, List ) :-
    presentinalonglist( Item, List ), signal_dupl( Item ).
addunique( Item, List ) :-
    not presentinalonglist( Item, List ), additem( Item, List ).
```

We can replace the inverted test with a cut after the original test:

```
addunique( Item, List ) :-
    presentinalonglist( Item, List ), !,
    signal_dupl( Item ).
addunique( Item, List ) :-      % not present...( Item, List )
    additem( Item, List ).
```

This procedure can be interpreted as

>**if** present...(Item, List) **then** signal_dupl(Item)
>   **else** additem(Item, List)

This is, perhaps, the most frequent application of the cut. It must be remembered, though, that this use of the cut is extralogical: a clause with a test removed means something else, and it cannot be understood in separation from the rest of the procedure. Still, the procedure as a whole is usually sufficiently readable, if we view it as a (possibly nested)

if … **then** … **else if** … **then** etc.

Sometimes cuts inside a procedure are undesirable. One example is a procedure that holds data, e.g.

```
father( jack, tom ).
father( bill, john ).
etc.
```

(with empty *tests* and *actions*). With a cut in each clause this would not only look ugly, the procedure would be of no use as a generator! Instead, we should commit the *call* on *father,* as in this procedure:

```
is_father( Person ) :- father( Person, _ ), !.
```

The cut serves as a firewall against unwanted backtracking.

Another example. Consider this group of grammar rules:

```
command( Cmd ) → stop( Cmd ).
command( Cmd ) → dump( Cmd ).
command( Cmd ) → load( Cmd ).
command( Cmd ) → create( Cmd ).
etc.
```

A "switch" such as *command* is best committed by the cut after a call, e.g.

```
phrase( command( Cmd ), Tokens ), !
```

This technique, however, has a disadvantage. The "committing" cut affects not only the call but also the calling procedure. If the call being committed happens to be the last *test* in a clause, then the cut plays two roles at once. Otherwise we should make it invisible to the surrounding clause. To achieve this, we can use this general-purpose "call-and-commit" procedure:

```
once( Call ) :- Call, !.
```

Other arguments against "cutting high" are implementation-dependent. First of all, in many implementations memory requirements are smaller when there are fewer fail-points, so it may be desirable to perform cuts as soon as possible. Some implementations also optimise storage utilisation of tail-recursive procedures (see Section 6.4). A procedure may become tail-recursive dynamically, after having its remaining clauses cut off. For example:

```
% Recognize a sequence of letters/digits.
ld( [ Ch | Chs ] ) → [ Ch ], { letter( Ch ) }, !, ld( Chs ).
ld( [ Ch | Chs ] ) → [ Ch ], { digit( Ch ) }, !, ld( Chs ).
ld( [] ) → [].
```

(Here, the cuts may protect us against deep recursion, effectively changing it into iteration.)

Sometimes the use of cuts should be recommended for clarity. We shall present two versions of the procedure that translates the term $(A_1, ..., A_n)$ into the list $[A_1, ..., A_n]$ and the term A (other than a comma-term) into [A]. First the version with "full guards":

```
c_list( AA, [ AA ] ) :- var( AA ).
c_list( AA, [ A | As ] ) :-
        not var( AA ), AA = ( A, AATail ), c_list( AATail, As ).
c_list( AA, [ AA ] ) :-
        not var( AA ), not AA = ( _ , _ ).
```

And the version with cuts (here the order of clauses is crucial):

```
c_list( AA, [ AA ] ) :- var( AA ), !.
c_list( ( A, AATail ), [ A | As ] ) :-
        !, c_list( AATail, As ).
c_list( AA, [ AA ] ).
```

In nondeterminisitic procedures cuts should be used cautiously, if we do not want to inadvertently lose some solutions. In particular, procedures that compute multiple answers (such as *append*) should not contain cuts. A cut after a call on a generator makes it yield only its first satisfactory answer, as in this small example:

```
int( 0 ).
int( NextN ) :- int( N ), NextN is N + 1.
:- int( X ), satisfactory( X ), !.
```

Cuts after tests in a procedure written according to the "guarded command" style implement Dijkstra's don't-care nondeterminism of **if** statements: any—exactly one—of the branches with true guards is chosen (in Prolog, the first one).

Special care must be exercised when adding cuts to procedures intended to be used in more than one way (such as grammar rules intended both for analysis and synthesis).

4.3.2. Failure as a Programming Tool

The procedure *not*, used to invert tests, owes its power and conciseness to the *combined* effect of three extralogical mechanisms in Prolog: variable calls, the cut, and forced failure. Recall the definition:

    not X :- X, !, fail.
    not _ .

Observe that the second clause performs no instantiations, and any instantiations in X must have been undone on failure. If *not* succeeds, its parameter will remain intact. Therefore, *not* will not return anything. For example, the call

    not student(X)

with uninstantiated X will not find a nonstudent (as might have been expected). Instead, it will fail if there is at least one student, e.g.

    student(jim).   student(jill).

Otherwise it will succeed with X still a variable. If we insist on finding nonstudents, we can look for them among NewYorkers:

    newyorker(tim).   newyorker(jim).
    newyorker(jill).   newyorker(amy).

Now the command

    :- newyorker(X), not student(X),
        write(X), nl, fail.

will print:

    tim
    amy

It must be emphasized that *not* called with a term containing variables does not implement negation properly (see Clark 1978). If the call *not student(X)* succeeds, then we shall actually prove that

$$\neg \, \exists x \; student(\, x \,)$$

which is equivalent to

$$\forall x \, \neg \, student(\, x \,)$$

On the other hand, suppose *not* means $\neg$. The command

    :- not student(X).

would then be interpreted (see Chapter 2) as

∀x ¬¬ student(x)

i.e. as ∀x student(x). Its negation—to be proved by **reductio ad absurdum**—is

∃x ¬ student(x)

This discrepancy was commented upon, for example, by Clark and McCabe (1980a, 1980b) and Dahl (1980). In IC-Prolog (Clark *et al.* 1982b) the problem was solved by treating *not* calls with variables as erroneous. This is to say, negation in their system is only applicable to ground predicates.

Except for *not*, forced failure is used primarily for efficiency. Many Prolog implementations have no garbage collection, but upon backtracking almost all of them very efficiently recover some storage holding control information and term instances (see Chapter 6). We can take advantage of this in a few rather unobvious but effective tricks. One of them is "double *not*".

On the face of it, the trick is pointless: the call

not not C

succeeds if and only if C does. We shall trace the execution of this call to show its hidden effect. Assume first that C succeeds; here are successive snapshots:

```
not not C
not C, !, fail
C, !, fail, !, fail
!, fail, !, fail
        % the cut will commit the internal not
fail, !, fail
        % RECOVER the storage used by C,
        % and backtrack in the external not
SUCCESS
```

Now, let C fail:

```
not not C
not C, !, fail
C, !, fail, !, fail
        % backtrack in the internal not,
        % succeed via the second clause
```

```
!, fail
```
    % the cut commits the external *not*
```
fail
FAILURE
```

Since "double *not*" does not instantiate anything, it can only be used in two situations. Either we want to perform a complicated "yes/no" test (with all interesting variables already instantiated), or we are only interested in some side-effects of C but we want to recover storage after its execution. For readability, we usually define two procedures:

```
check( Cond ) :- not not Cond.
side_effects( Goals ) :- not not Goals.
```

One example should suffice:

```
prettyprint( Term ) :- side_effects( doprettyprinting( Term ) ).
```

Suppose now that we need instantiations produced when executing a call, and that space still matters. To preserve the results (i.e. the appropriate terms) over backtracking, we must "put them aside". Only stored clauses are immune to failure. The following general-purpose procedure[7] executes a call, and at the same time "garbage collects" the storage used by the call:

```
with_gc( Call ) :-
    once( Call ), assert( 'ASIDE'( Call ) ), fail.
with_gc( Call ) :-
    retract( 'ASIDE'( Call ) ), !.   % commit retract
```

This method makes sense when *assert* requires less storage than Call, or when the implementation has no general garbage collector but reclaims storage left by retracted clauses.

with_gc can be employed in loop optimisation, which is an important application of forced failure. Essentially, recursion is the most natural Prolog counterpart of Pascal-like iteration. Consider a program that takes large chunks of an even larger text, extracts some data from them, and puts these data into an open tree. The storage for a step is worth recovering. Let *step* assert **basta.** after having encountered the final chunk. The loop can be written as follows:

```
buildtree( _ ) :- retract( basta ), !.  % remove the signal
buildtree( Tree ) :-
    with_gc( step( Tree ) ), buildtree( Tree ).
```

(Find a similar solution for closed trees.)

---

[7] This technique was advocated by R. A. Kowalski at the Logic Programming Workshop in Debrecen, Hungary, 1980.

Suppose now that steps of a loop have no common terms (which would have to be passed down the loop). This means that a step is executed only for its side-effects. For example, consider the problem of reading in a Prolog program up to the clause *end.*. Let the procedure *clause_in* perform one step: read a clause and assert it (unless it is *end.* or incorrect). The following procedure repeatedly calls on *clause_in*, and recovers storage after each step:

```
getprog :- clause_in( Clause ), Clause = end, !.
getprog :- getprog.
```

This loop can be made even more concise if we use a "failure screen". This is a procedure that always succeeds nondeterministically, i.e. leaves room for yet another success:

```
repeat.
repeat :- repeat.
```

(it is standard in some Prolog implementation). The loop can be expressed as

```
getprog :- repeat, clause_in( C ), C = end, !.
```

After C = end succeeds, the cut will remove the pending choice in *repeat*, and so terminate the loop.

For this technique to work, the core of the loop must be deterministic, as otherwise a failure of C = *end* would evoke another attempt to execute an already executed step. Usually it suffices to enclose the call for a step in once(_):

```
getprog :- repeat, once( clause_in( C ) ), C = end, !.
```

A special form of forced failure is caused by *tagfail*[8]. This built-in procedure is described in Section 5.12, together with other associated procedures. They are all primarily used for error handling, as they allow bypassing of large fragments of a computation. Here we shall present an application of *tag* and *tagfail* for exiting loops.

An extremely simplified interactive executor of Prolog commands can be programmed as follows:

```
ear :- tag( loop ).
ear.
loop :- repeat, read( C ), once( C ), fail.
```

---

[8] It is only available in Toy (see Section 5.12), but something similar is present or can be programmed in several other implementations of Prolog.

The execution of

   tagfail(loop)

terminates the loop: *tag(loop)* fails, and the second clause of *ear* promptly succeeds. With a step defined as

   step :- read(C), once(C).

and *loop* redefined as

   loop :- repeat, tag(step), fail.

we can also exit one step by calling

   tagfail(step)

4.3.3. Clauses as Global Data

   The program modification procedures—*assert, retract* and the like—are first of all used to maintain Prolog data bases (see Section 8.2). They can also be used in automodifying procedures, those which assert or retract their own clauses; this is an extremely dubious programming trick, and it is not recommended, especially since such programs tend to be rather subtly implementation-dependent.

   Modification procedures are also used to store so-called global data. In Prolog implementations that do not support modularisation, the data kept in program clauses (notably unit clauses) are accessible to all procedures, i.e. global. Such data are significant in Prolog because they are not affected by backtracking—see *with_gc* in the previous section. Also, they are sometimes more convenient to handle than information passed around via parameters. One example is a "switch"—a parameterless unit clause whose presence or absence provides a simple yes/no test. For instance, we can supply terse or wordy error messages:

   message(Code) :- terse, short_mes(Code), nl, !.
   message(Code) :- long_mes(Code), nl, !.
   short_mes(sym(S)) :- display('?sym '), display(S).
   ......
   long_mes(sym(S)) :-
       display('Unexpected symbol on input: '),
       display(S), nl,
       display(' The remainder of the command will be ignored.').

A switch can be easily turned on:

   turnon(Switch) :- Switch, !.   % already on
   turnon(Switch) :- assert(Switch).

and off:

> turnoff(Switch) :- retract(Switch), !.
>   % fails if Switch was off
> turnoff(_).   % already off

We can also revert the state of a switch (on → off, off → on):

> flip(Switch) :- retract(Switch), !.
> flip(Switch) :- assert(Switch).

Switches are really cumbersome to program without clausal data. It is not difficult to rewrite *message:*

> message(Code, terse) :- short_mes(Code), nl, !.
> message(Code, wordy) :- long_mes(Code), nl, !.

but the Terseness parameter ought to be carried everywhere throughout the program; and dynamic reversal of a switch can be somewhat messy.

Our final example demonstrates how assertions can be used to memorize results of expensive computations for future use. Let the procedure *integrate* perform symbolic integration of a given formula (and fail if it cannot be done). If we are going to use this procedure frequently, we may wish to avoid recomputing integrals. To this end, we should store every integral, once computed, and always try to find a ready answer before launching actual integration. Here is a possible solution:

> integral(Expr, IExpr) :- stored_integral(Expr, IExpr), !.
> integral(Expr, IExpr) :-
>   integrate(Expr, IExpr),
>   assert(stored_integral(Expr, IExpr)).

In fact, we have thus furnished our program with a primitive learning capacity.

4.4. EXAMPLES OF PROGRAM DESIGN

In this section we look at several tiny programming problems and their solutions which result from more or less formal analysis. This is not a real exercise in derivation of programs from formal specifications (see Hogger 1979; Gregory 1980; Burstall and Darlington 1977). This is, at best, an illustration of such derivation, not very rigorous and with formulae kept as simple as possible.

These particular problems present no difficulty to experienced programmers, who can readily solve them without resorting to sophisticated techniques. Simple as they are, they help demonstrate how logic formulae, which lend justification to a program designed in a traditional way, can also be viewed as the same program ("modulo" some clean transformations). Implications of this observation for logic programming are far-reaching and largely uninvestigated; see Shapiro (1983a) for fascinating examples of Prolog programs which are but a by-product of theoretical considerations.

Some of the procedures discussed below can be bi-directional, but we intentionally neglect such possibilities. As an exercise, try to discover some of their less obvious applications.

Formulae will be written according to the conventions of Prolog-10: variable names are capitalized, functor names begin with small letters.

4.4.1. List Reversal

Let $rev(X)$ denote the reversal of list X, let X *with* A denote the result of attaching A at the end of list X (e.g., [p, q] with r = [p, q, r]). Let X = Y mean: X matches Y.

Assuming that X *with* A has already been defined, a possible definition of rev is:

(4.1)   rev([]) = []
(4.2)   rev([A | Tail]) = rev(Tail) with A

Now, recall that in Prolog we can comfortably express relations such as "the reversal of X is Y" (which implicitly defines Y as rev(X)) without resorting to the notion of equality. To re-express (4.2) accordingly, we begin with the introduction of a new variable to denote rev(Tail):

(4.3)   T = rev(Tail) $\Rightarrow$ rev([A | Tail]) = T with A

This formula is equivalent to (4.2). Another new variable will denote T with A:

(4.4)   T = rev(Tail) $\Rightarrow$ (TA = T with A $\Rightarrow$
                    rev([A | Tail]) = TA)

which is equivalent to

(4.5)   (T = rev(Tail) $\wedge$ TA = T with A) $\Rightarrow$
                    rev([A | Tail]) = TA

We shall rewrite this implication, and the formula (4.1), using *reverse*(X, Y) instead of $rev(X) = Y$, and *attach*(X, Y, Z) instead of $Z = X$ *with* Y:

(4.6)   reverse(Tail, T) $\wedge$ attach(T, A, TA) $\Rightarrow$
                                    reverse([A | Tail], TA)

(4.7)   reverse([], [])

These two formulae are exactly the logical interpretation of the following procedure:

    reverse([A | Tail], TA) :-
        reverse(Tail, T), attach(T, A, TA).
    reverse([], []).

The procedure *attach* can be derived in a similar way:

(4.8)   [] with A = [A]

(4.9)   [B | Tail] with A = [B | (Tail with A)]

From (4.9) we can obtain

(4.10)   TA = Tail with A $\Rightarrow$ [B | Tail] with A = [B | TA]

and this (together with (4.8)) is rewritten as

(4.11)   attach(Tail, A, TA) $\Rightarrow$ attach([B | Tail], A, [B | TA])

(4.12)   attach ([], A, [A])

These derivations are by no means unique. Here is another reasoning that starts with (4.2). We first introduce TA to denote rev([A | Tail]), and get

(4.13)   TA = rev([A | Tail]) $\Rightarrow$ TA = rev(Tail) with A

which is equivalent to (4.2). Now we introduce T:

(4.14)   (TA = rev([A | Tail]) $\wedge$ T = rev(Tail)) $\Rightarrow$
                TA = T with A

This is easily translated into Prolog:

    attach(T, A, TA) :-
        reverse([A | Tail], TA), reverse(Tail, T).

In short: we managed to define *attach* by *reverse,* but the definition is only useful if we can define *reverse* independently of *attach*.

Another method of reversing a list stems from its interpretation as a stack (see Section 4.2.1). If we move the items of one stack onto another, they will come up in reversed order. Let Stack1 and Stack2 denote the stacks before this reversal. The final content of the second stack will be

    rev(Stack1) ++ Stack2

with X + + Y denoting the result of appending Y to X. The following two equalities define this structure recursively:

(4.15)   rev([]) + + Stack2 = Stack2

(4.16)   rev([A | Tail]) + + Stack2 = (rev(Tail) + + [A]) + + Stack2

Now, + + is associative, and [A] + + Stack2 = [A | Stack2], so that we can transform (4.16) into

(4.17)   rev([A | Tail]) + + Stack2 = rev(Tail) + + [A | Stack2]

Next, we introduce a new variable Final:

(4.18)   Final = rev(Tail) + + [A | Stack2] $\Rightarrow$
          Final = rev([A | Tail]) + + Stack2

Let *reverse2(X, Y, Z)* denote the formula $Z = rev(X) + + Y$. From (4.15) and (4.18) we get

(4.19)   reverse2([], Stack2, Stack2)

(4.20)   reverse2(Tail, [A | Stack2], Final) $\Rightarrow$
          reverse2([A | Tail], Stack2, Final)

(or, accordingly, the same in Prolog). For Y = [], reverse2(X, Y, Z) reads Z = rev(X), so to get the reversal of L we must call

    reverse2(L, [], LReversed)

—indeed, Stack2 must be initially empty.

Notice that in going from (4.17) to (4.18) another direction of the implication could have been chosen. This choice would lead to the Prolog clause

    reverse2a(Tail, [A | Stack2], Final) :-
        reverse2a([A | Tail], Stack2, Final).

which defined the shorter list in terms of the longer. Even though it is logically correct, operationally it is unrealistic: neither this nor (4.19) would match the initial call with non-empty L.

We shall conclude this section with an even less formal derivation of difference-list reversal. Let the list to be reversed be L -- Z, where L = $[A_1, ..., A_n | Z]$. We can write

    rev(L -- Z) = [A_n | X] -- Y

with X -- Y = rev($[A_1, ..., A_{n-1} | W]$ -- W). Since W is an arbitrary term, we can assume W = $[A_n | Z]$, so that

    X -- Y = rev(L -- [A_n | Z])

We now express the longer list by the shorter (see *reverse2a* above!):

$$\text{rev}(L -- [A_n \mid Z]) = X -- Y \Rightarrow$$
$$\text{rev}(L -- Z) = [A_n \mid X] -- Y$$

and rewrite it in Prolog, with reverse_d(X, Y) instead of rev(X) = Y:

reverse_d(L -- Z, [An | X] -- Y) :-
    reverse_d(L -- [An | Z], X -- Y).

The base clause,

reverse_d(Z -- Z, Y -- Y).

must come (i.e. be tried) first, because otherwise each call with a variable second parameter will fall into infinite recursion (you may wish to check this more thoroughly). This is where the peculiarities of Prolog come into play, and obscure the so-far clean derivation. It is even worse: we have missed one weakness of almost all Prolog implementations: the absence of so-called occur check during unification (see Section 1.2.3). Therefore, the base clause matches calls with a non-empty list as the first parameter, if only the list ends with a variable. For example, the call

reverse_d([a, b | Z] -- Z, Rev)

instantiates $Z \leftarrow$ [a, b | Z] and Rev $\leftarrow$ Y -- Y, contrary to our expectations. One possible remedy is to instantiate the final variable as [] before going on, but to this end both clauses of *reverse_d* must be duplicated. The complete procedure follows.

```
reverse_d( [] -- [], Y -- Y ).

reverse_d( L -- [], [An : X] -- Y )  :-

        reverse_d( L -- [An], X -- Y ).

reverse_d( Z -- Z, Y -- Y ).

reverse_d( L -- Z, [An : X] -- Y )  :-

        reverse_d( L -- [An : Z], X -- Y ).
```

Check that even this improved version loops for "negative" lists such as [b] -- [a, b]. As you see, difference lists are useful but can be rather tricky.

4.4.2. Sorting

We shall derive three procedures to sort a closed list of integers in ascending order. The first two implement insertion sort and a very simple transposition sort, a variation of "bubble sort". Both have running time proportional to the square of list length (but both seem passable because few Prolog applications require fast sorting procedures). The third procedure is the simplest quicksort, which takes less time but uses more space (the same justification applies).

Let X *into* Y denote the list that results from inserting the integer X into the ordered list Y. For example,

5 into [4, 7, 10] = [4, 5, 7, 10].

A possible definition of insertion consists of three formulae:

(4.21)   A into [] = [A]
(4.22)   A > B $\Rightarrow$ A into [B | Tail] = [B | (A into Tail)]
(4.23)   A=< B $\Rightarrow$ A into [B | Tail] = [A, B | Tail]

The formula (4.22) can be rewritten as

(4.24)   A > B $\wedge$ AT = A into Tail $\Rightarrow$ A into [B | Tail] = [B | AT]

and then we can use insert(X, Y, Z) instead of X *into* $Y = Z$ to get the following procedure:

```
insert( A, [], [ A ] ).
insert( A, [ B | Tail ], [ B | AT ] ) :- A > B, insert( A, Tail, AT ).
insert( A, [ B | Tail ], [ A, B | Tail ] ) :- A =< B.
```

Now, let *sorted*(X) denote the sorted permutation of the list X. We can define *sorted* in the following way:

(4.25)   sorted([]) = []
(4.26)   sorted([A | Tail]) = A into sorted(Tail)

The latter formula can be replaced by

(4.27)   ST = sorted(Tail) $\wedge$ AST = A into ST $\Rightarrow$
          sorted([A | Tail]) = AST

To express it in Prolog, we shall rewrite sorted(X) = Y as ins_sort(X, Y), and get these two clauses:

```
ins_sort( [], [] ).
ins_sort( [ A | Tail ], AST ) :-
    ins_sort( Tail, ST ), insert( A, ST, AST ).
```

The order of calls in the second clause is not accidental: the tests in *insert* require fully instantiated parameters, so the procedure would not work if *insert* came first!

Transposition sorting results from the observation that a sequence is unordered iff it contains an unordered pair of contiguous items (e.g. A, B such that A > B, if we consider the ascending order). Each step of a sorting algorithm should increase the "orderedness" of the sequence, e.g. by swapping A and B.

The following formula characterizes this sorting method:

(4.28) $L = X ++ [A, B | Y] \wedge A > B \wedge LT = X ++ [B, A | Y]$
          $\Rightarrow sorted(L) = sorted(LT)$

where $X ++ Y$ denotes Y appended to X. We should describe explicitly the "less ordered" sequence by the "more ordered", e.g. thus:

(4.29) $L = X ++ [A, B | Y] \wedge A > B \wedge LT = X ++ [B, A | Y]$
          $\wedge SL = sorted(LT) \Rightarrow SL = sorted(L)$

Using trans_sort(X, Y) for $sorted(X) = Y$, and append(X, Y, Z) for $X ++ Y = Z$, we can rewrite (4.29) into Prolog:

```
trans_sort( L, SL ) :-
    append( X, [ A, B | Y ], L ), A > B,
    append( X, [ B, A | Y ] LT ), trans_sort( LT, SL ).
```

Suppose now that for no X, A, B, Y we have $L = X ++ [A, B | Y] \wedge A > B$, i.e. that L is either ordered or too short (and also ordered!). More formally:

(4.30) $\neg (L = X ++ [A, B | Y] \wedge A > B) \Rightarrow L = sorted(L)$

When we rewrite this in Prolog, we shall drop the premise and place the resulting clause *after* the recursive one. The first two calls in that clause can be regarded as tests: does L contain a two-item subsequence, and is this subsequence unordered? The clause fails if this is not the case, and the premise of (4.30) becomes trivially true. We are left with the clause

```
trans_sort( L, L ).
```

which is exactly the required base clause: we proceed from "less ordered" sequences, so that eventually we must get an ordered permutation.

The arrangement of calls in the first clause is crucial. To begin with, we repeatedly isolate any two contiguous items (this fails if the list is too short), and we look at their ordering. The first improperly ordered pair terminates this process, and we recursively sort the "improved" sequence. The procedure is attributed to van Emden (Coelho *et al.* 1980).

The last sorting algorithm we are going to program in Prolog is the well-known quicksort (Hoare 1962). For a given sequence L and its element A, let small(L, A) denote the subsequence consisting of all items smaller than A, and large(L, A) those larger than A. Items equal to A will fall, say, into small(L, A). The following formulae describe two possible situations:

(4.31)   sorted([A | L]) = sorted(small(L, A)) ++ A ++
                    sorted(large(L, A))

(4.32)   sorted([]) = []

The usual transformations of (4.31) give, for example,

(4.33)   small(L, A) = LAs $\land$ large(L, A) = LAl $\land$
          sorted(LAs) = SLAs $\land$ sorted(LAl) = SLAl $\Rightarrow$
          sorted([A | L]) = SLAs ++ [A] ++ SLAl

When implementing quicksort, a standard practice is to compute small(L, A) and large(L, A) simultaneously, i.e. to introduce

    partition(L, A, LAs, LAl)

instead of the first two equalities in (4.33). Here is the Prolog code for *partition* (it can be derived in a straightforward way):

```
partition( [ X | Tail ], A, [ X | Small ], Large ) :-
    X =< A, partition( Tail, A, Small, Large ).
partition( [ X | Tail ], A, Small, [ X | Large ] ) :-
    X > A, partition( Tail, A, Small, Large ).
partition( [], _, [], [] ).
```

The formula (4.33) should be transformed in the usual way:

(4.34)   partition(L, A, LAs, LAl) $\land$
          sorted(LAs) = SLAs $\land$ sorted(LAl) = SLAl $\land$
          SLAs ++ [A | SLAl] = Sorted $\Rightarrow$
          sorted([A | L]) = Sorted

This is directly expressible in Prolog, with quick_sort(X, Y) denoting the equality sorted(X) = Y:

```
quick_sort( [ A | L ], Sorted ) :-
    partition( L, A, LAs, LAl ),
    quick_sort( LAs, SLAs ), quick_sort( LAl, SLAl ),
    append( SLAs, [ A | SLA1 ], Sorted ).
quick_sort( [], [] ).
```

In the worst case, the cost of appending sorted fragments is proportional to n^2 for a list of length n. We can avoid appending altogether exactly as we did in *reverse2* in the previous section. We take the empty stack, sort large(L, A) and push sorted(large(L, A)) onto the stack. Next, we stack A, and finally sorted(small(L, A)).

The formulae corresponding to (4.31), (4.32)—and similar to (4.15), (4.16)—are as follows:

(4.35)   sorted([A | L]) ++ Stack2 =
              sorted(small(L, A)) ++ [A] ++
                  sorted(large(L, A)) ++ Stack2

(4.36)   sorted([]) ++ Stack2 = Stack2

We can now repeat the same reasoning and replace (4.35) with

(4.37)   partition(L, A, LAs, LAl) $\wedge$
              sorted(LAs) ++ [A] ++ sorted(LAl) + Stack2 = Sorted
                  $\Rightarrow$ sorted([A | L]) ++ Stack2 = Sorted

The lefthand side equality in (4.37) must be rewritten as

(4.38)   sorted(LAl) ++ Stack2 = LargeStacked $\wedge$
              sorted(LAs) ++ [A] ++ LargeStacked = Sorted

We introduce q_sort(X, Y, Z) for the equality sorted(X) ++ Y = Z, and get the following procedure:

```
q_sort( [ A | L ], Stack2, Sorted ) :-
    partition( L, A, LAs, LAl ),
    q_sort( LAl, Stack2, LargeStacked ),
    q_sort( LAs, [ A | LargeStacked ], Sorted ).
q_sort( []. Stack2, Stack2 ).
```

And wrap it in

```
quick_sort_2( List, Sorted ) :- q_sort( List, [], Sorted ).
```

This version of quicksort is also attributed to van Emden (Coelho *et al.* 1980).

Notice that the recursive calls on *q_sort* can be interchanged. A partly uninstantiated stack will be appended to sorted(small(L, A)); the other call will then fully instantiate the stack. Actually, the pairs Sorted, [A | LargeStacked] and LargeStacked, Stack2 can be interpreted as difference lists. Try to derive more formally a version of quicksort with difference lists.

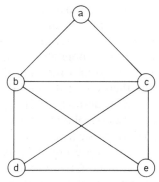

FIG. 4.15   A graph.

4.4.3. Euler Paths[9]

We shall try to solve in Prolog the problem of finding Euler paths in an undirected graph. For the sake of completeness, here are the basic definitions. An **undirected graph** is the pair (v, $\mathscr{E}$), with V a finite set of **vertices** and $\mathscr{E}$ a set of edges. A vertex is labelled with a unique name. An **edge** is an unordered pair of different vertices, usually interpreted as a connection between them. A graph is often modelled by a drawing with a point for each vertex and a line (connecting the two vertices) for each edge. Figure 4.15 shows a graph which consists of five vertices and eight edges. A **path** from vertex X to vertex Y is a sequence of edges such that contiguous edges share a vertex, X belongs to the first edge, Y to the last. For example,

(a, b), (b, c), (c, d), (d, e)

is a path from **a** to **e** in the graph of Fig. 4.15. The same path can be unambiguously represented as a sequence of vertices:

a b c d e

An **Euler path** is a path passing through all vertices, in which every edge occurs exactly once. An **Euler graph** is a graph that contains an Euler path. For our graph,

d b a c b e c d e

---

[9] The problem (described as "drawing a picture") was solved in Prolog by Szeredi (1977).

is an example of Euler path. If we remove the edge **bc**, the resulting graph will not be an Euler graph (you may wish to check this).

We shall develop a very simple program, depending only on the most intuitive properties, which looks somewhat blindly for Euler paths. A more efficient algorithm arises from a theorem that characterizes Euler graphs. We shall quote the theorem at the end of this section.

At first, we must choose a method of representing graphs. We can assume that the graph contains no isolated vertices (vertices which do not belong to any edge); otherwise, it is certainly not an Euler graph. A graph without isolated vertices can be represented by its set of edges alone. An edge is an unordered pair, i.e. a set of two vertices. Since we have no sets in Prolog (as in most programming languages), we shall represent edges with ordered pairs:

$$V1 \leftrightarrow V2$$

($\leftrightarrow$ is a non-associative infix functor), and we shall try to make the program account for the cummutativity of pairs.

Euler graphs have the following two properties:

1. A graph with one edge is an Euler graph.
2. Suppose we take out an edge, and what remains is a Euler graph with an Euler path starting with one of this edge's vertices; then the whole graph is an Euler graph (and we happened to have removed a terminal edge of an Euler path).

Let paths be represented with lists of vertex names, and let *path(E,P)* mean "E is the set of edges of an Euler graph, and P is an Euler path in this graph". The first property above can be rewritten as two formulae:

(4.39)   path({ V1 $\leftrightarrow$ V2 }, [V1, V2])
(4.40)   path({ V2 $\leftrightarrow$ V1 }, [V1, V2])

In other words, both arrangements of vertices are equally satisfactory.

Here is how the second property can be formalized (\ denotes set subtraction):

(4.41)   path(E \ { V1 $\leftrightarrow$ V2 }, [V2 | RestofPath]) $\Rightarrow$
                path(E, [V1, V2 | RestofPath])
(4.42)   path(E \ { V2 $\leftrightarrow$ V1 }, [V2 | RestofPath]) $\Rightarrow$
                path(E, [V1, V2 | RestofPath])

Before we rewrite (4.39–4.42) into Prolog, we must finally decide how to represent sets. We can use any structure capable of holding uniform data; to keep things simple we shall use lists. (Another possibility would be to represent each edge as a separate clause, but then we would have no easy way of passing a set of edges as a parameter to a path-finding procedure.)

The formulae (4.41) and (4.42) must be transformed to get rid of the complicated expression inside *path*; for example, (4.41) becomes

(4.43) $E1 = E \setminus \{ V1 \leftrightarrow V2 \} \wedge$ path(E1, [V2 | RestofPath]) $\Rightarrow$
          path(E, [V1, V2 | RestofPath])

With the set $\{V1 \leftrightarrow V2\}$ represented as the list [V1 <−> V2], and with *takeout(X, Y, Z)* denoting the equality $X \setminus \{Y\} = Z$, we can write down the procedure *path*:

    path([V1 <−> V2], [V1, V2]).
    path([V2 <−> V1], [V1, V2]).
    path(E, [V1, V2 | RestofPath]) :-
        takeout(E, V1 <−> V2, E1), path(E1, [V2 | RestofPath]).
    path(E, [V1, V2 | RestofPath]) :-
        takeout(E, V2 <−> V1, E1), path(E1, [V2 | RestofPath]).

Notice that details of set representation are transparent to the recursive clauses.

A list version of *takeout* can be defined in a straightforward manner, so we shall skip a detailed derivation:

    takeout([V1 <−> V2 | E1], V1 <−> V2, E1).
    takeout([Edge | Edges], TheEdge, [Edge | Remainder]) :-
        takeout(Edges, TheEdge, Remainder).

This program is crying out for optimisation: in the worst cases we can traverse the list E *twice* before locating the edge to be taken out. One solution, actually presented in Szeredi (1977), is to make *takeout*, rather than *path*, sensitive to the order of vertices. This can be easily achieved by adding another base clause to *takeout*:

    takeout([V2 <−> V1 | E1], V1 <−> V2, E1).

and deleting any of the two recursive clauses of *path*.

The procedure *path* can be used non-deterministically, to produce all Euler paths in a given graph, or with a cut, to check whether the graph is an Euler graph (and find an instance of Euler path). It can also be used the other way round: given a path it computes a list that represents the Euler graph with this path (or all such lists, but this would be overzealous).

We shall need a few more definitions to formulate Euler's fundamental theorem on Euler graphs. A graph is **connected** if for each two vertices V1, V2 there is a path from V1 to V2. For example, the graph of Fig. 4.15 is connected. The **degree** of a vertex is the number of edges which contain the vertex. For example, **b** in our graph is a vertex of degree 4, and **e** of degree 3.

The theorem states that a graph is an Euler graph if and only if it is connected and contains either no vertices of an odd degree, or exactly two such vertices. In the latter case, the two odd-degree vertices are terminal vertices of each Euler path. In the former case, each Euler path is a cycle, i.e. a path that returns to the starting point. In our example, **d** and **e** are the only vertices of odd degree.

If the graph is known to be an Euler graph, an Euler path can be found in time proportional to the number of edges. Once removed, the edge can be attached to the path for good. You may find it amusing to modify the above program in this direction.

5 SUMMARY OF SYNTAX AND BUILT-IN PROCEDURES

This chapter describes Prolog as defined by Toy, the implementation presented in Chapter 7. The supported dialect is very similar to Prolog-10 (Pereira *et al.* 1978, Bowen 1981, Clocksin and Mellish 1981); some, but not all, differences are noted. Other "standard" versions will be similar: use the appropriate reference manuals.

The user communicates with Toy through an interactive interface (see Sections 1.2.2 and 7.4.2).

5.1. PROLOG SYNTAX

A program can be regarded (roughly) as a sequence of clauses. Definitions and grammar rules in the sequence are grouped in procedures. There are quite a few principles that govern "consulting"/"reconsulting", and dynamically asserting/retracting clauses (with the *redefinition* switch on or off). Therefore a formal definition of procedures would be unnecessarily involved: it should account for the fact that procedures change in time.

The notation used is extended BNF. Non-terminal symbols will be boldfaced, and some of them subscripted (this is the first extension). A BNF rule takes the general form

lhsnonterm ::= **rhs**$_1$ | ...... | **rhs**$_n$

(**lhsnonterm** is either **rhs**$_1$ or ... or **rhs**$_n$).

Each **rhs** is a sequence of non-terminals and terminals. The second extension: zero or more occurrences of a sequence **s** are denoted as {**s**}. To avoid confusion, terminal symbols | {} will be boldface. Throughout the description, we assume standard operator declarations are in force.

Many special forms, such as integer expressions to be evaluated by *is*,

=:=, etc., or lists of single characters, will not be described. See Section 5.2 and on for applications of these forms in built-in procedures.

Some comments in plain English will be interspersed in the BNF description. See also the notes at the end of this section.

clause ::= **definition** | **grammarrule** | **directive**
definition ::= **nonunitclause** | **unitclause**
nonunitclause ::= **head** :- **body**
unitclause ::= **head**
                COMMENT the main functor of **head** is not a binary :-
head ::= **nonvarint**
body ::= **bodyalt** { ; **bodyalt** }
bodyalt ::= **call** { , **call** }
call ::= **nonvarint** | **variable** | (**body**)
nonvarint ::= **term**
                COMMENT not a variable or an integer (a formal definition would be straightforward but cumbersome)
grammarrule ::= **lhside** → **rhside**
                COMMENT the arrow is written as -->
lhside ::= **nonterminal context** | **nonterminal**
nonterminal ::= **nonvarint**
context ::= **terminals**
rhside ::= **alternatives**
alternatives ::= **alternative** { ; **alternative** }
alternative ::= **ruleitem** { , **ruleitem** }
ruleitem ::= **nonterminal** | **terminals** | **condition** | ! | (**alternatives**)
terminals ::= **list** | **string**
                COMMENT only closed lists are allowed
condition ::= **curlyterm**
directive ::= **command** | **query**
command ::= :- **body**
query ::= **body**
                COMMENT **body**'s main functor is not a unary :-
term ::= term_{1200}
term_N ::= $\text{op}_{fx,N} \text{term}_{N-1}$ | $\text{op}_{fy,N} \text{term}_N$ | $\text{term}_{N-1} \text{op}_{xf,N}$ | $\text{term}_N \text{op}_{yf,N}$ | $\text{term}_{N-1} \text{op}_{xfx,N} \text{term}_{N-1}$ | $\text{term}_{N-1} \text{op}_{xfy,N} \text{term}_N$ | $\text{term}_N \text{op}_{yfx,N} \text{term}_{N-1}$ | term_{N-1}

COMMENT $1 =< N =< 1200$; $\mathbf{op}_{\text{Type},N}$ is an operator of type Type and priority N; $\mathbf{term}_N$ can be called "term with priority N"

$\mathbf{term}_0$ ::= **variable** | **integer** | **string** |
  list | **noop** |
  noop(term{ **, term** }) |
  (**term**) | **curlyterm**

curlyterm ::= { **term** }

noop ::= **functor**

$\mathbf{op}_{T,N}$ ::= **functor**

  COMMENT T is one of fx, fy, xf, yf, xfx, xfy, yfx, N is in the range 1..1200; see also note 1

list ::= [] | [$\mathbf{term}_{999}$ { , $\mathbf{term}_{999}$ }] |
  [$\mathbf{term}_{999}$ { , $\mathbf{term}_{999}$ } | **term**]

  COMMENT terms with priority 999 can be safely conjoined by commas which are infix functors with priority 1000

functor ::= **word** | **qname** |
  symbol | **solochar**

word ::= **wordstart** { **alphanum** }

wordstart ::= **smalletter**

alphanum ::= **smalletter** | **bigletter** |
  digit | _

qname ::= '{ **qitem** }'

qitem ::= '' | **nonquote**

  COMMENT **nonquote** is any character other than '

symbol ::= **symch** { **symch** }

variable ::= **varstart** { **alphanum** }

varstart ::= **bigletter** | _

integer ::= − **digit** { **digit** } | **digit** { **digit** }

string ::= "{ **sitem** }"

  COMMENT in Toy a string is equivalent to a list of character names; in Prolog-10, to a list of their ASCII codes

sitem ::= "" | **nondquote**

  COMMENT **nondquote** is any character other than "

smalletter ::= a | b | c | d | e | f | g | h | i |
  j | k | l | m | n | o | p | q | r |
  s | t | u | v | w | x | y | z

bigletter ::= A | B | C | D | E | F | G | H | I |
  J | K | L | M | N | O | P | Q | R |
  S | T | U | V | W | X | Y | Z

digit ::= 0 | 1 | 2 | 3 | 4 | 5 | 6 | 7 | 8 | 9
symch ::= . | : | - | < | = | > | + | / |
         * | ? | & | $ | @ | # | ¬ | \
         COMMENT a lone dot followed by white space is not a symch
                but a fullstop
solochar ::= , | ; | !
token ::= **functor** | **variable** | **integer** |
         string | **bracketbar**
         COMMENT tokens are listed to explain note 6 below
bracketbar ::= (|) | [|] | { | } | |
comment ::= % { **nonlineend** } **lineend**
         COMMENT **lineend** is an end-of-line (linefeed)
                character; **nonlineend** is any other
                character. Toy converts line-ends to
                single linefeeds
whitespace ::= { **layoutchar** }
         COMMENT **layoutchar** is blank or tab or **lineend**
                or any nonprintable character (in
                ASCII these are characters with codes
                =< 31)
fullstop ::= . **layoutchar**

Notes:

1. Mixed functors have not been described, but their inclusion is straight-forward:

   $$\textbf{term}_N ::= \textbf{op}_{[\text{ xfy,fx }],N}\ \textbf{term}_{N-1}$$

   and 11 other combinations. In Toy, a mixed functor can only have one binary and one unary type, both with the same priority.
2. There are numerous ambiguous combinations of contiguous operators. This grammar does not account for them. See Section 7.4.3 (and Appendix A.4) for a rather detailed description in Prolog.
3. Not all functors can be declared as operators. Quoted names are always taken as "normal" functors.
4. In the definition of **body**, commas and semicolons need not have been actually singled out, because they are regular infix functors. The definition

   body ::= **nonvarint**

   would not, however, emphasize the most common structure of **body**.

5. The syntax of directives conforms to the convention adopted in Toy. See Section 7.4.2 for details.
6. Comments and whitespace can be freely inserted before and after a token, and cannot be inserted in the middle of a token. Remember that a comment extends till end-of-line.
7. Whitespace must be inserted between an unsigned integer and a minus which is to be treated as a functor. A minus immediately preceding a sequence of digits is taken as a part of the integer.
8. If curly brackets are not available, the usual practice is to use "decorated brackets": %(and %). This requires some care in the treatment of comments.
9. A term on input must be terminated with a full stop not embedded in a quoted name, string or comment.

5.2. BUILT-IN PROCEDURES: GENERAL INFORMATION

For the purposes of this chapter, built-in procedures fall into two groups. System procedures are implemented in the interpreter described in Section 7.3. Predefined procedures are written in Prolog; they belong to the user interface described in Section 7.4. Together, these two groups cover the basic set of Prolog-10 procedures. Differences and extensions are noted where appropriate but this is a description of Toy and it is not intended as a replacement for the Prolog-10 manual. The procedures are roughly classified according to their purpose.

A system procedure call may fail, succeed or raise an error. Failure or success is equivalent to a failure or success of a normal procedure call. The only difference is that success is usually accompanied by a side-effect, such as writing a character, setting a switch, etc. A failing system procedure does not usually cause any side-effects (input procedures are a notable exception).

An error is raised when a system procedure detects an incorrect parameter (or parameters). If the description of a procedure mentions the form of expected parameters, parameters of unlisted forms will cause an error to be raised. There is no guarantee that the error will be raised before any actions are performed, though this is usually so.

Raising an error consists in invoking procedure *error*/1, with its single parameter instantiated to the offending system procedure call. In general, *error* behaves as if its call were present in the program instead of the erroneous system procedure call. An explicit call to *error* is also possible. *error* is a Prolog procedure: the standard library contains a simple version which outputs a message and fails. The user can augment this procedure to his liking, possibly providing different clauses as "error handlers" for different system procedures. Redefinition of *error* requires removing it from the standard library (see Section 7.4.5)—in the present version it is protected together with the whole library. Some predefined procedures invoke *error*, and so can the user's programs.

   error is not in Prolog-10.

   The following are conventions observed throughout this chapter. (Additional conventions or explanations appear under some group headings.)

   Whenever we say that a procedure "tries to unify" we mean that it fails or succeeds depending on the outcome. Success means that unification is performed.

   When we say that a procedure "tests" something, we mean that it fails or succeeds according to the result.

   Acceptable parameters are indicated by conventional names listed below:

TERM—any term will do
INTEGER—an integer
VAR—a variable
NONVARINT—a non-variable, non-integer term
CALL—same as NONVARINT
ATOM—a NONVARINT without arguments
NAME—same as ATOM
CHAR—a NAME consisting of a single character
FILENAME—a NAME conforming to the implementation-dependent
    conventions for specifying files
CALLIST—a list (possibly empty) of CALLs
CHARLIST—a list (possibly empty) of CHARs
DIGITLIST—a CHARLIST built of digit characters

In descriptions, PAR1, PAR2 etc. stand for actual parameters in the built-in procedure call.

   Note that '123' is a name, and 123 an integer. 9 is the integer nine, and '9' is the digit (character). The output procedures do not always distinguish between the two (*writeq* does).

   Toy introduces a number of predefined operators. Some of them are used as infix or prefix procedure names. Table 5.1 is the list of predefined operators:

TABLE 5.1

Predefined Operators

Name	Type	Priority
:-	xfx	1200
:-	fx	1200
-->	xfx	1200
;	xfy	1100
,	xfy	1000
not	fy	900
=	xfx	700
is	xfx	700
=:=	xfx	700
=\=	xfx	700
<	xfx	700
=<	xfx	700
>	xfx	700
>=	xfx	700
@<	xfx	700
@=<	xfx	700
@>	xfx	700
@>=	xfx	700
==	xfx	700
\==	xfx	700
=..	xfx	700
+	yfx	500
+	fx	500
−	yfx	500
−	fx	500
*	yfx	400
/	yfx	400
mod	xfx	300

5.3. CONVENIENCE

true

    always succeeds.

fail

    always fails.

not CALL

    the "not" procedure (but see Section 4.3.2!): succeeds only when the parameter fails. Defined in Prolog:

      not C :- C, !, fail.
      not _ .

CALL , CALL

the "and" procedure: succeeds only when both arguments succeed. Defined in Prolog:

A, B :- A, B.

See also the description of the cut.

CALL ; CALL

the "or" procedure: succeeds only if either of the parameters succeeds. Defined in Prolog:

A; _ :- A.
_; B :- B.

See also the description of the cut.

check(CALL)

succeeds only when the parameter succeeds, but instantiates no variables—only side-effects of CALL remain. Defined in Prolog:

check(Call) :- not not Call.

Not in Prolog-10.

side_effects(CALL)

exactly equivalent to check(Call), but used when the parameter is to be executed for its side-effects rather than to test something. Not in Prolog-10.

once(CALL)

executes CALL deterministically. Defined in Prolog:

once(Call) :- Call, !.

Not in Prolog-10.

5.4. ARITHMETIC

In the descriptions, div stands for integer division, and mod for taking the remainder of integer division.

The following are correct invocation patterns for *sum*/3 (not in Prolog-10).

sum(INTEGER, INTEGER, INTEGER)

succeeds only if PAR1 + PAR2 = PAR3

sum(INTEGER, INTEGER, VAR)

succeeds after unifying PAR3 with the value of PAR1 + PAR2

sum(INTEGER, VAR, INTEGER)

succeeds after unifying PAR2 with the value of PAR3 − PAR1

sum(VAR, INTEGER, INTEGER)
  succeeds after unifying PAR1 with the value of PAR3 − PAR2

The following are correct invocation patterns for *prod*/4 (not in Prolog-10).
prod(INTEGER, INTEGER, INTEGER, INTEGER)
  succeeds only if PAR1 ∗ PAR2 + PAR3 = PAR4
prod(INTEGER, INTEGER, INTEGER, VAR)
  succeeds after unifying PAR4 with the value of PAR1 ∗ PAR2 + PAR3
prod(INTEGER, INTEGER, VAR, INTEGER)
  succeeds after unifying PAR3 with the value of PAR4 − PAR1 ∗ PAR2
prod(INTEGER, VAR, VAR, INTEGER)
  succeeds after unifying PAR2 with the value of PAR4 div PAR1 and PAR3 with the value of PAR4 mod PAR1
prod(VAR, INTEGER, VAR, INTEGER)
  like the previous one, but with PAR1 and PAR2 exchanged
prod(INTEGER, VAR, INTEGER, INTEGER)
  fails if (PAR4 − PAR3) mod PAR1 is not zero; otherwise succeeds after unifying PAR2 with the value of (PAR4 − PAR3) div PAR1
prod(VAR, INTEGER, INTEGER, INTEGER)
  like the previous one, but with PAR1 and PAR2 exchanged

TERM is TERM
  the procedure *is* assumes PAR2 is an integer expression, i.e. a term composed of integers by means of standard arithmetic functors: + (binary and unary), − (binary and unary), ∗, /, mod. The procedure fails if PAR2 is not an integer expression. Otherwise it evaluates the expression and tries to unify the value with PAR1. According to Prolog-10 conventions, *is* can also evaluate a list

  [INTEGER]

  as this INTEGER; e.g. 55 *is* [55] succeeds. (This is needed in Prolog-10 mainly for evaluating single character strings to ASCII codes.) Defined in Prolog.

5.5. COMPARING INTEGERS AND NAMES

less(INTEGER, INTEGER)
  succeeds only if PAR1 < PAR2. Not in Prolog-10.

TERM =:= TERM

PAR1 and PAR2 are treated as integer expressions and evaluated. The procedure succeeds only if both parameters are proper integer expressions (see *is/2*) and their values are equal. Defined in Prolog.

TERM =\= TERM

as above, but tests whether the values are nonequal

TERM < TERM

as above, but tests whether the value of PAR1 is less than that of PAR2

TERM =< TERM

as above, but tests whether the value of PAR1 is not greater than that of PAR2

TERM > TERM

as above, but tests whether the value of PAR1 is greater than that of PAR2

TERM >= TERM

as above, but tests whether the value of PAR1 is not less than that of PAR2

NAME @< NAME

succeeds only when PAR1 precedes PAR2 in the lexicographic order (as defined by the underlying ASCII collating sequence).

NAME @=< NAME

like @<, but tests whether PAR2 does not precede PAR1. Defined in Prolog.

NAME @> NAME

like @<, but tests whether PAR2 precedes PAR1. Defined in Prolog.

NAME @>= NAME

like @<, but tests whether PAR1 does not precede PAR2. Defined in Prolog.

5.6. TESTING TERM EQUALITY

TERM = TERM

tries to unify PAR1 and PAR2. Defined in Prolog:

X = X.

eqvar(VAR, VAR)

succeeds only when the parameters are two occurrences of the same nondummy variable. Not in Prolog-10.

TERM == TERM
>succeeds only when the parameters are two occurrences of the same term. For example, if A, B are uninstantiated,

>p(A) == p(B)

>fails, even though

>p(A) = p(B)

>succeeds. Defined in Prolog.

TERM \== TERM
>succeeds only when the parameters are not two occurrences of the same term. Defined in Prolog.

5.7. INPUT/OUTPUT

5.7.1. Switching Streams

This set of procedures can be used to dynamically change the files read or written by the input/output procedures. The user's terminal is treated like any other file: its name is *user* (both for input and output); the terminal is read from and written on by default.

Ideally, one should be able to open a file with *tell* or *see*, stop using it with another *tell* or *see*, start using it from the current position after a second *tell* or *see*, and close it with *told* or *seen*. There should be no limits on the interleaving introduced by using a file in the middle of using a file in the middle etc.

The procedures are described as if this situation were real. In practice, things are very implementation-dependent. The version of Toy presented in Chapter 7 and Appendix A.1 has only two input and two output streams: one for the terminal and one for a disk file in each direction. Also, Toy has no code for dealing with incorrect file names, nonexistent files and the like. All this is too dependent on the environment in which it is implemented.

see(FILENAME)
>the specified file becomes the current input file; the terminal's name is *user*

seeing(TERM)
>tries to unify the parameter with the name of the current input file

seen
>closes the current input file; *user* becomes current. Has no effect if the current file is *user*

tell(FILENAME)
>the specified file becomes the current output file; the terminal's name is *user*

telling(TERM)
>tries to unify the parameter with the name of the current output file

told
>closes the current output file; *user* becomes current. Has no effect if the current file is *user*

5.7.2. Listing Control

The Toy-Prolog interpreter contains a listing switch. If the switch is on, each line read in from the current input is listed on the user's terminal: this is useful when one wants to see what is being read from a disk file.

echo
>succeeds after turning the listing switch on; has no effect if the switch is already on. Not in Prolog-10.

noecho
>succeeds after turning the listing switch off; has no effect if the switch is already off. Not in Prolog-10.

5.7.3. Terms

display(TERM)
>writes the term onto the current output. The term is written in standard notation (prefix with parentheses) and identifiers are not quoted even if they normally should be. Variables are written as _n, where n is an address. There is no guarantee that a variable will be printed as the same address in different invocations of *display*. In Prolog-10, *display* is a little different: it always writes on the user's terminal.

write(TERM)
>writes the term onto the current output. The term is written according to operator declarations currently in force. No identifiers are quoted. Variables are written as X1, X2 etc. Each invocation of *write* begins numbering from 1, so that e.g. the calls

    write(X), write(f (Y, X))

will produce

    X1f(X1, X2)

Defined in Prolog. CAUTION: in Toy, *write* uses *numbervars* (see Section 5.15) which binds variables in the term to 'V'(N) for N = 1, 2, etc. Hence, *write* cannot output any term 'V'(INTEGER) properly.

writeq(TERM)

same as *write*, but quotes identifiers that are not proper words or symbols, and also those identifiers that coincide with operator names; e.g. a 3-parameter **is** would be quoted. However, a quote within a quoted name will not be doubled (this is a bug, actually). Otherwise, a term written by *writeq* can be read back by *read*.

read(TERM)

reads from the current input a term, terminated with a full stop. Succeeds only when PAR1 unifies with this term. Operator declarations currently in force are taken into account. Recall that a quoted name cannot be an operator. If the text on input is not a correct term, *read* print the message

+ + + Bad term on input. Text skipped:

skips and reprints the input until the first (still unprocessed) full stop, and tries to unify PAR1 with 'e r r'. (If the erroneous line does not contain a full stop, you should input one before Prolog resumes.) See the next section for behaviour on file end detecting. Defined in Prolog in terms of single-character input (see the next section).

op(INTEGER, TERM, ATOM)

declares an operator with PAR3—the name, PAR1—the priority (1 =< PAR1 =< 1200, and PAR2—the type. PAR1 is usually less than 1000, to avoid conflicts with clause-constructing operators (see the table in Section 5.2); operators with lower priority take precedence over those with a higher priority. PAR2 must be a proper word or symbol. Admissible types of operators are fx, fy (unary, prefix); xf, yf (unary, postfix); xfx, xfy, yfx (binary, infix). The types fx, xf, xfx are non-associative; fy, yf, associative; xfy, right-associative; yfx, left-associative. Any other PAR2 causes an error.

If an operator declaration with this name but another priority is already in force, the procedure replaces the old declaration with the new one. If a declaration with the same name and priority exists, three possibilities arise:

—both operators are binary or both unary; the old definition is replaced;
—the old operator is unary (binary), the new—binary (unary); a mixed functor is created;

—the old operator is mixed, the new—binary (unary); the binary (unary) type in the mixed functor declaration is replaced with PAR2.

Defined in Prolog.

delop(ATOM)

the operator declaration with the name given by PAR1 is deleted. The name should be quoted to prevent it from being treated as an (erroneous) operator with missing arguments. Defined in Prolog. Not in Prolog-10.

5.7.4. Single Characters

The Toy interpreter contains a single-character input buffer called the **current character**. Initially, it contains a blank and is then refilled by each reading operation. In the presented version, each line end is treated as if it were a linefeed character (ordinal number 10, see the procedure *iseoln*). Behaviour upon detection of end-of-file depends on the current input. If the input is *user* (i.e. the terminal), Prolog is terminated; otherwise an automatic *seen* is performed and the reading operation is restarted.

The operations presented here (except *nl*) differ from those in Prolog-10. In Toy, the arguments of input/output operations are characters, and the internal buffer can be used to rescan the current input character. In Prolog-10 there is no such buffer and the arguments of the operations are *integers*, i.e. character codes. These operations could be defined as follows:

```
get0( Ord ) :- rch, lastch( Ch ), ordchr( Ord, Ch ).
get( Ord ) :-  rch, skipbl, lastch( Ch ),
               ordchr( Ord, Ch ).
skip( X ) :-   repeat, get0( X ), !.
put( Ord ) :-  ordchr( Ord, Ch ), wch( Ch ).
```

This would not assure complete compatibility, however. Erroneous calls would be handled a little differently and so would line ends. See also the description of strings.

rch

succeeds after filling **current character** with the next character from current input (but see the introductory remarks for effects of line end or end-of-file)

skipbl

succeeds after ensuring that **current character** is a printing character

with ordinal number greater than 32. Does nothing if it already is such
a character; otherwise repeatedly invokes *rch*.

lastch(TERM)

tries to unify its parameter with **current character**

wch(CHAR)

writes the character on current output (the linefeed character is interpreted as line terminator)

nl

terminates the current output line. Defined in Prolog:

:- ordchr(10, Ch), assert((nl :- wch(Ch))).

rdch(TERM)

gets the next character from current input (by invoking **rch**). Makes a
copy of **current character**, treating a non-printing character (including
line end) as a blank; tries to unify the copy with its parameter. Defined in Prolog.

rdchsk(TERM)

same as above, but preceded by a call on **skipbl**

5.7.5. Others

These procedures are not really concerned with input/output, but the
only effect of *status* is to write something, and *ordchr* is most useful when
reading or writing non-printing characters. They all are not in Prolog-10.

ordchr(INTEGER, CHAR)

succeeds only when PAR1 is the ordinal number of PAR2

ordchr(VAR, CHAR)

succeeds after unifying the variable with the ordinal number of the
character

ordchr(INTEGER, VAR)

succeeds after unifying the variable with the character whose ordinal
number is the value of PAR1 mod 128

iseoln(TERM)

tries to unify PAR1 with the end-of-line character. Defined in Prolog:

:- ordchr(10, Ch), assert(iseoln(Ch)).

status

writes memory utilisation information on the current output

See also *consult*/1, *reconsult*/1, *listing*/0 and *listing*/1 in Section 5.11.

5.8. TESTING CHARACTERS

Each of these procedures fails or succeeds depending on whether its parameter is a character belonging to a particular class. They are designed to help the user interface (see Section 7.4) in reading Prolog terms, but some of them are of general utility. The procedures *iseoln*/1 and *ordchr*/2 (see Section 5.7.5) are also used to test characters.

smalletter(TERM)

    tests whether the parameter is a lower case letter

bigletter(TERM)

    tests whether the parameter is an upper case letter

letter(TERM)

    tests whether the parameter is an upper or lower case letter

digit(TERM)

    tests whether the parameter is a decimal digit

alphanum(TERM)

    tests whether the parameter is a letter, a digit or an underscore character

bracket(TERM)

    tests whether the parameter is one of the following characters:

$$( ) [ ] \{ \}$$

solochar(TERM)

    tests whether the parameter is one of the following characters:

$$! , ;$$

symch(TERM)

    tests whether the parameter is one of the following characters:

$$+ - * / = @ \# \$ \& : . ? < > \neg \backslash$$

5.9. TESTING TYPES

These procedures fail or succeed depending on the form of their arguments.

var(TERM)

    tests whether the parameter is an uninstantiated variable

integer(TERM)

    tests whether the parameter is an integer

nonvarint(TERM)

   tests whether the parameter is a NONVARINT (neither a variable nor an integer); not in Prolog-10

atom(TERM)

   tests whether the parameter is an atom (a NONVARINT without arguments)

5.10. ACCESSING THE STRUCTURE OF TERMS

The procedures *pname* and *pnamei* are not in Prolog-10. They replace *name*/2, which is similar, but which uses lists of integers (ASCII codes) in place of our lists of characters (see Section 5.7.4).

pname(NAME, TERM)

   builds a list of characters forming the name and tries to unify it with PAR2

pname(VAR, CHARLIST)

   succeeds after unifying the variable with a NAME formed of the characters on the list. (Note that pname(X, [1, 2, 3]) binds X to the name '123', and not to the integer 123).

pnamei(INTEGER, TERM)

   builds a list of decimal digit characters (constituting the written form of the integer) and tries to unify it with the term; the integer must not be negative.

pnamei(VAR, DIGITLIST)

   succeeds after unifying the variable with an integer whose written form is given by the digit characters on the list. Even when the parameters are formally correct, an error may be raised if the specified integer is too large.

functor(VAR, INTEGER, 0)

   PAR3 is the integer zero; succeeds after unifying the variable with PAR2 (this version is allowed for completeness, see below for sensible uses of *functor*)

functor(VAR, NAME, INTEGER)

   succeeds after unifying the variable with a term whose main functor has the name and arity defined by PAR2 and PAR3, and whose arguments are different variables; PAR3 must not be negative

functor(INTEGER, TERM, TERM)

   tries to unify PAR2 with PAR1 and PAR3 with the integer zero

functor(NONVARINT, TERM, TERM)
>   tries to unify PAR2 and PAR3 with the name and arity of the main
>   functor in PAR1

arg(INTEGER, NONVARINT, TERM)
>   fails if the integer is smaller than 1 or greater than the arity of the
>   main functor in PAR2. Otherwise tries to unify PAR3 with that argu-
>   ment of PAR2 whose number is given by PAR1.

The following are correct invocation patterns for the procedure =..
(pronounced "univ"), which is defined in Prolog.

VAR =.. [INTEGER]
>   succeeds after unifying the variable with the integer
VAR =.. [NAME | TERM]
>   if the term is not a closed list, an error in the procedure *length*/2 is
>   raised (=.. uses *length*). Otherwise a term with NAME as its name
>   and TERM as its argument list is created and unified with VAR.
INTEGER =.. TERM
>   tries to unify the term with [PAR1]
NONVARINT =.. TERM
>   constructs a list, with PAR1's main functor as the head and the list of
>   PAR1's arguments as the tail. Tries to unify the list with PAR2.

5.11. ACCESSING PROCEDURES

The Toy-Prolog interpreter supports *assert*/3, *retract*/3 and *clause*/5.
These are low-level, but quite powerful procedures (see the editor in
Appendix A.5). Parameters representing clause bodies have the form of
lists of calls (an empty body is [ ]).

The Prolog library uses these low-level routines to define Prolog-10
procedures *assert*/1, *asserta*/1, *assertz*/1, *retract*/1 and *clause*/2. Unlike
most other built-in procedures, *retract*/1 and *clause*/2 are non-determinis-
tic. Parameters representing clause bodies have the form of terms used in
the external representation, i.e. sequences built with commas (an empty
body is *true*).

An attempt to apply any of these procedures to system routines defined by the interpreter is treated as an erroneous call. So is an attempt to
modify protected procedures. (There is a diagnostic printout which cannot be suppressed by redefining *error*/1.)

Caution: Remember the standard operator declarations listed in Section 5.2. To be safe, always enclose a clause-representing term in paren-

theses. For example,

assert((a :- b, c))

is okay, but

assert(a :- b, c)

is a call on *assert*/2. In some versions of Prolog, even

assert(a :- b)

is incorrect.

assert(NONVARINT, CALLIST, INTEGER)
> PAR1 is treated as a clause's head, PAR2 as its body. The clause is asserted immediately after the n-th clause of this procedure (where n is PAR3 if a clause with this number exists, and the last clause's position if PAR3 is too large; if the procedure is empty or PAR3 < 1, the clause is asserted as first). Not in Prolog-10.

retract(NAME, INTEGER, INTEGER)
> PAR2 must not be negative. PAR1 and PAR2 define the name and arity of a predicate symbol. If the associated procedure does not contain a clause whose number is given by PAR3 (the first clause has number 1), *retract* fails. If the clause does exist, it is logically removed from the procedure and *retract* succeeds. A removed clause does not disappear from storage and its active instances can still run to completion. Not in Prolog-10.

clause(NAME, INTEGER, INTEGER, TERM, TERM)
> PAR2 must not be negative. PAR1 and PAR2 are treated as the name and arity of a predicate symbol. If the associated procedure has no clause whose number is given by PAR3 (in particular, if it is a system routine) then *clause* fails. Otherwise it tries to unify PAR4 with the head of the clause and PAR5 with its body. Not in Prolog-10.

asserta(NONVARINT)
> treats the parameter as a clause (non-unit if its main functor is :-/2, unit otherwise). An error is raised if the first argument of a :- is not a NONVARINT. Asserts the clause at the beginning of its procedure, creating the procedure if it does not exist. Defined in Prolog.

assertz(NONVARINT)
> same as above, but the assertion is at the end of the procedure.

assert(NONVARINT)
> equivalent to *asserta*(PAR1).

retract(NONVARINT)
> the parameter is treated as a clause (non-unit if its main functor is :-/2 and unit otherwise). An error is raised if the first argument of :- is not

a NONVARINT. The first matching clause is retracted, and a fail point created (see Section 5.12). On failure, the next matching clause will be retracted. Note: if PAR1 has the form *nonvarint:-var* then it matches only clauses with a single variable call in their bodies. Defined in Prolog.

clause(NONVARINT, TERM)

locates the first procedure whose head matches PAR1 and whose body matches PAR2; the body of a unit clause is the term *true*. After successful unification, establishes a fail point and succeeds; the next matching clause is sought on failure. Defined in Prolog. Not in Prolog-10.

redefine

this procedure is needed to implement *reconsult* and should not be used directly. It modifies the effects of *assert*: if the procedure to which a clause is added is different from that affected by the last assertion, an automatic *abolish* is invoked before the *assert*. The next invocation of *redefine* restores the original situation.

protect

succeeds after ensuring that all procedures already defined, except those whose heads are single characters with no arguments (this restriction is imposed by a minor technical difficulty), are protected. An attempt to modify a protected procedure (by means of *assert*, *retract*, *abolish*, *consult*, *reconsult*) is treated as an erroneous invocation of the system procedure in question. (The user interface in Toy protects all its procedures.) Not in Prolog-10.

abolish(NAME, INTEGER)

PAR2 must not be negative. PAR1 and PAR2 are treated as the name and arity of a predicate symbol. All the clauses of this procedure are logically removed (retracted) and *abolish* succeeds.

predefined(NAME, INTEGER)

PAR2 must not be negative. PAR1 and PAR2 are treated as the name and arity of a predicate symbol. If the procedure associated with this symbol is a system procedure, *predefined* succeeds; otherwise it fails. Not in Prolog-10.

consult(FILENAME)

sees the named file and enters program definition mode: successive terms are read-in and stored via *assertz* (see the convention for *asserta*'s parameters) and asserted (but see *protect*). There are two exceptions: the term *end* causes the file to be closed and definition mode to be exited; terms with the unary :- as a main functor are treated as commands, and immediately executed. Defined in Prolog.

reconsult(FILENAME)

as above, but *redefine* is called at the beginning and at the end of processing. Contiguous sequences of clauses with the same predicate symbol in their heads are treated as complete definitions of procedures and supersede previous definitions.

listing(NONVARINT)

PAR1 must be an ATOM, or a term of the form ATOM/INTEGER or a list of such terms (possibly multi-level). Each atom is treated as a procedure's name, each integer as a procedure's arity. All relevant procedures are listed on the current output. Defined in Prolog.

listing

as above, but for all defined procedures (including procedures defined in the monitor and library, but excluding built-in system procedures).

5.12. CONTROL

Whenever a procedure call activates a clause which is not the last clause in its procedure, we say that a fail point is associated with the call. A fail point is something to backtrack to: it saves information necessary for reestablishing the state of the computation and proceeding with the next clause.

The immediate descendants of a call **C** are the calls in the procedure which **C** activated. The immediate ancestor of a call **C** is the call which activated the procedure containing **C**. An ancestor is the immediate ancestor or an ancestor of the immediate ancestor. A descendant is defined similarly.

!

the cut procedure; succeeds after finding the nearest ancestor which is not a *call*/1, *tag*/2, ,/2 or ;/2 and removing all existing fail points associated with this ancestor and all its descendants.

repeat

an endless "generator of successes" (see Section 4.3.2). Defined in Prolog:

    repeat.
    repeat :- repeat.

call(CALL)

behaves exactly as if its parameter were in its place, with the exception that an incorrect parameter (an integer or uninstantiated variable) is detected at run time rather than at clause-definition time. In top-level syntax, one can use a variable instead of a predicate—this is converted to an invocation of *call*.

halt(ATOM)

>   stops the interpreter after writing the atom. Not in Prolog-10.

stop

>   stops the interpreter. Not in Prolog-10.

The following procedures are not in Prolog-10. They are useful for error handling, but are "dirty", and should be used sparingly.

tag(CALL)

>   this is a form of *call*/1 which can be referred to by *tagfail*/1, *tagexit*/2, *tagcut*/2 and *ancestor*/2. The parameter of *tag* is called a "tagged ancestor" of its descendants; it is never removed from the stack as a result of tail recursion optimisation (see Sections 6.4 and 7.1).
>   NOTE: a tag is recognized only when explicitly written in its clause. In particular call(tag(C)) is equivalent to call(call(C)).

ancestor(TERM)

>   searches for the nearest tagged ancestor unifiable with the parameter; fails if no such ancestor is found, otherwise unifies and succeeds.

tagcut(TERM)

>   searches for the nearest tagged ancestor unifiable with the parameter. Fails if no such ancestor is found; otherwise unifies, removes all existing fail points associated with the ancestor and its decendants and succeeds.

tagfail(TERM)

>   equivalent to

>   tagcut(PAR1), fail

>   i.e. if the appropriate tagged ancestor is found, the ancestor fails immediately; otherwise *tagcut* fails.

tagexit(TERM)

>   searches for the nearest tagged ancestor unifiable with the parameter; fails if no such ancestor is found, otherwise unifies and passes control to the ancestor, which succeeds immediately.

5.13. DEBUGGING

The built-in debugging facilities of Toy are very primitive. There is only a wall-paper trace which displays all calls with a plus or a minus to indicate success or failure respectively (e.g. if a call fails to match two clauses and activates the third, it is shown twice with a minus and once with a plus).

A more useful—selective—tracer is listed in Appendix A.5.

There is also a switch which may cause the interpreter to output warning messages upon encountering calls on non-existent procedures. It is good practice to turn it on when debugging a program.

All these procedures are not in Prolog-10, which has a more sophisticated set of debugging aids.

debug
> succeeds after turning tracing on (no effect if already on)

nodebug
> succeeds after turning tracing off (no effect if already off)

nonexistent
> succeeds after turning on warning about calls on nonexistent procedures (no effect if already on)

nononexistent
> succeeds after turning off warning about calls on nonexistent procedures (no effect if already off)

5.14. GRAMMAR PROCESSING

phrase(CALL, TERM)
> treats CALL as a nonterminal symbol of a grammar rule, schematically

> nt(PAR1, ..., PARn),

> and initiates grammar processing—with this initial symbol—by calling

> nt(TERM, [], PAR1, ..., PARn)

> Defined in Prolog (see Section 4.2.6).

5.15. MISCELLANEOUS

length(NONVARINT, TERM)
> PAR1 must be a closed list. Computes the length of this list and tries to unify the resulting integer with PAR2. Defined in Prolog.

isclosedlist(TERM)
> succeeds only when the term is a closed list. Defined in Prolog. Not in Prolog-10.

numbervars(TERM)

instantiates TERM's variables as 'V'(1), 'V'(2), etc. Variables bound
together instantiated as the same 'V'(i). As a result, the term becomes ground. Defined in Prolog.

member(TERM, TERM)

establishes the relationship: PAR1 is a member of the list PAR2.
Defined in Prolog:

member(X, [X | Y]).
member(X, [_ | Y]) :- member(X, Y).

bagof(TERM, CALL, TERM)

tries to unify PAR3 with the list of PAR1's instantiations after all
possible computations of PAR2 (see Section 4.2.4 for details). Pro-
log-10 has a more sophisticated version of this procedure. Defined in
Prolog.

6 PRINCIPLES OF PROLOG IMPLEMENTATION

6.1. INTRODUCTION

This chapter is but a bird's-eye view on implementation techniques specific to Prolog. We assume you know how conventional block structure languages are implemented: a competent programmer could hardly escape learning these things. The discussion is kept at a level free of representation details. Chapter 7 provides a rather detailed and complete case study of one of the many ways in which the basic principles can be applied in practice.

Two topics are missing: compilation and garbage collection. To compile Prolog programs is to apply the general principles in such a way that a program is executed particularly efficiently. This is done partly by taking advantage of the underlying machine (e.g. by using machine code instead of a more compact representation of programs, trading speed for memory) and partly by performing special case analysis to detect operations which can be simplified (e.g. unification with a variable which is known to be uninstantiated). We decided that compilation is beyond the scope of this book (which already discusses implementation issues more thoroughly than the usual introduction to a programming language). The problem and techniques of garbage collection are well known, and are best studied independently of a particular programming language (though you will find that in Prolog one has to do with one of the harder variants of the problem).

6.2. REPRESENTATION OF TERMS

If we disregard the possibility of forming cyclic structures (see Section 1.2.3), we can see that all terms are directed acyclic graphs (DAGs). They are not necessarily trees, because different branches can converge to a common component: in linear notation we express this phenomenon by repetition, as in t(p(X), q(p(X), Y)).

In a Prolog program, several identical occurrences of a term within a single clause denote the same object. Properly speaking, this is not an object but a descriptor, or template. At execution time, it corresponds to different objects in different instances of the clause. In this and the next chapter we shall reserve the unadorned word "term" for **term instances**. Terms written in a program will be referred to as **term descriptions**. A description can have several occurrences; similarly, an instance can have several parents in a DAG.

There are many possible representations of a DAG. For our present purposes they are all equivalent, provided that it is possible to distinguish nodes corresponding to Prolog variables. On a more abstract level, however, two very different methods are used to implement term instances. Accordingly, all existing implementations of Prolog can be classified as either Structure Sharing or Non–Structure Sharing (NSS).

In principle, to form a new term instance in a Non–Structure Sharing system, one must create a new DAG. We are talking about creating new instances that correspond to term descriptions (present in the program text, or in clauses asserted after having been constructed by a program); creation of new terms as a result of unification is different. Variables are bound by being associated with pointers directed at their instantiations. These pointers are invisible, i.e. automatically dereferenced, whenever the DAG is traversed. Figure 6.1 illustrates—in a representation-independent manner—two terms, before and after unification.

A Structure Sharing system takes advantage of the fact that different instances of the same term differ only in their variable bindings. Whereas two instances of

t(p(X), q(p(X), Y))

can be

t(p(c), q(p(c), d))   and
    t(p(r(a)), q(p(r(a)), r(a)))

respectively, their general structure remains the same. The main functor must be a **t** of two arguments; **t**'s first argument must also be the first

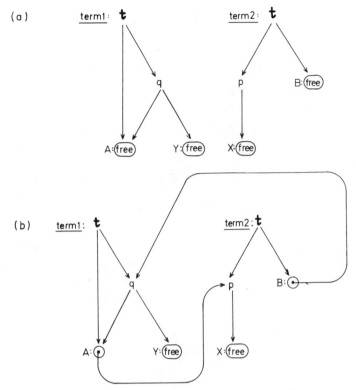

FIG. 6.1 The Non–Structure Sharing representation of terms: (a) t(A, q(A, Y)) and t(p(X), B) before unification. (b) t(A, q(A, Y)) and t(p(X), B) instantiated to t(p(X), q(p(X), Y)) after unification.

argument of the two-argument **q** which is **t**'s second argument; and so on. Consequently, all instances of the term may share this structural information, if only care is taken to let them have different variables. This is easily achieved by associating each instance with a different **variable frame**: a chunk of storage holding variable instances. The internal representation of a term description—we shall call it **prototype**—is a DAG in which each variable node is represented by information about the offset of the variable's location in a variable frame. All terms—including variable bindings—are now represented not by single pointers, but by two-pointer **term handles**[1]

< prototype, variable frame >

[1] Another terminology, introduced by Warren (1977a), is to call prototypes **skeletons**, and handles **molecules**. We do not like the mixed metaphor.

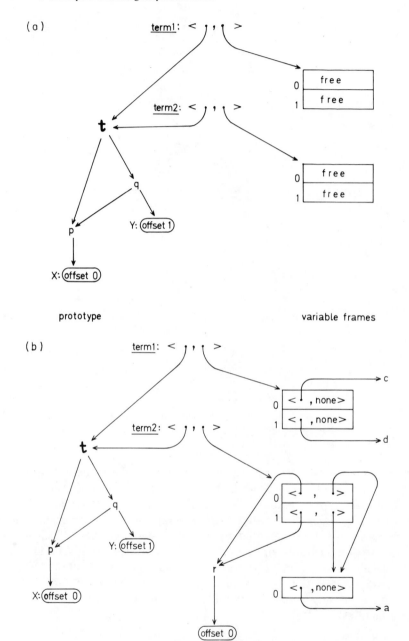

FIG. 6.2   The Structure Sharing representation of terms: (a) Two instances of t(p(X), q(p(X), Y)), both sharing the same prototype. (b) term1 instantiated to t(p(c), q(p(c), d)) and term2 instantiated to t(p(r(a)), q(p(r(a)), r(a))).

Figure 6.2 illustrates the principle of Structure Sharing. Figure 6.3 corresponds to Fig. 6.1. If we find general DAGs less convenient than trees, Structure Sharing makes it easy to employ trees by providing implicit links to variables from all occurrence sites. This is shown in Fig. 6.4.

Inside a clause, different occurrences of the same variable description can appear within different term descriptions. There is the problem of

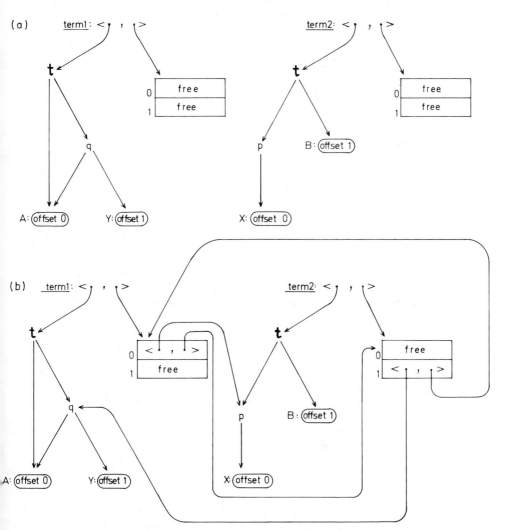

FIG. 6.3 The Structure Sharing representation of terms: (a) t(A, q(A, Y)) and t(p(X), B) before unification. (b) t(A, q(A, Y)) and t(p(X), B) instantiated to t(p(X), q(p(X), Y)) after unification.

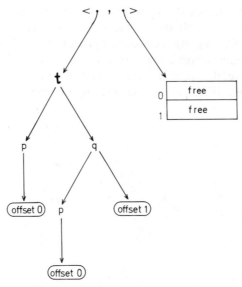

FIG. 6.4   Structure Sharing: the DAG t(p(X), q(p(X), Y)) represented by a tree.

ensuring that the same variable becomes a part of all the corresponding terms associated with a clause instance. With Structure Sharing, this is done by allocating a single frame for all the variables appearing in a clause, at the moment of its activation. All occurrences of a variable within this clause's prototypes are encoded as the same *offset* in the common variable frame (this is just an application of the technique demonstrated in Fig. 6.4).

In practice, most NSS implementations use a very similar approach to solve the problem (despite its name, it is a hybrid method). Term instances are also encoded as prototypes, with variables represented by offsets into a clause's variable frame. One difference is that variable frame locations hold only single pointers rather than term handles. The other—more important—difference is that terms formed in this way are only "virtual" instances. This is to say that they may be used only as data selectors, directing unification to instantiate variables in the variable frame. Whenever one of these terms is to *become* a variable's instantiation, a "real" instance (a new DAG) must be built. If this new instance contains a variable, its variable node becomes a copy of the appropriate location in the variable frame, while the location is made to hold a pointer to the node. This ensures that all future references to the variable will end up in the node.

The process is shown in Fig. 6.5. Note that here, too, prototypes can

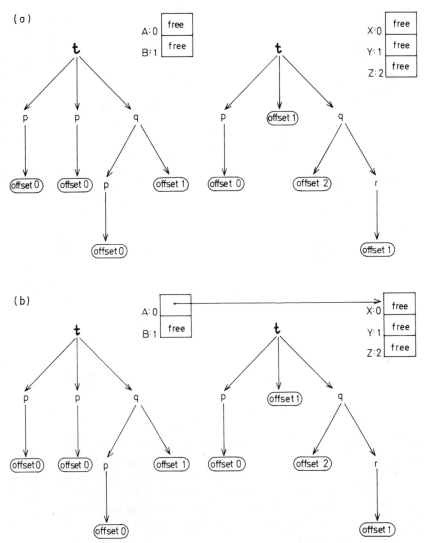

FIG. 6.5 "Virtual" and "real" instances in Non–Structure Sharing: (a) proc(t(p(A), p(A), q(p(A),B))) is called with proc(t(p(X), Y, q(Z, r(Y))))—both terms are "virtual" before unification. (b) The first occurrence of p(A) acts as a selector—A is bound to X. (c) The second occurrence of p(A) acts as a constructor—Y is bound to its copy (a "real" instance). (d) q(p(A), B) and q(Z, r(Y)) both act as selectors, but p(A) and r(Y) are constructors—both terms are now t(p(X), p(X), q(p(X), r(p(X)))), represented by a mixture of "real" and "virtual" instances. (*continued*)

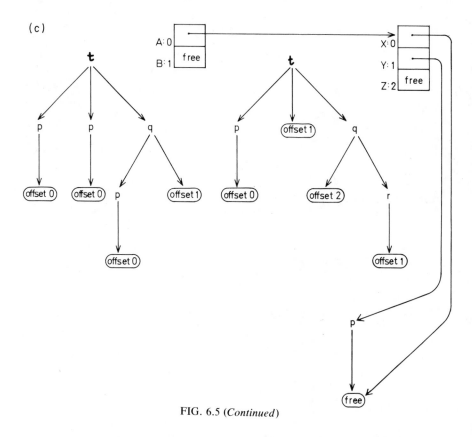

FIG. 6.5 (*Continued*)

be trees, and more general DAGs are implemented by variable bindings. In general, the process of term creation can give rise to several copies of a single term instance (p(A) in the example), but these are indistinguishable.

The process of copying an uninstantiated variable might seem a little roundabout: why don't all copies simply contain pointers to the variable frame location? Indeed, why are there any copies at all: is not Structure Sharing always better?

Recall from chapter 1 (see Fig. 1.6) that a term's lifetime may have to exceed that of the encompassing clause instance. Yet it is obvious that we would like to regard a variable frame—which is created when a clause is activated—as a part of the clause's activation record. If we are careful to represent variable–to–variable bindings so that younger variables point at older ones rather than the other way round, *and* if term copies contain no pointers into variable frames, then there is no risk of leaving dangling

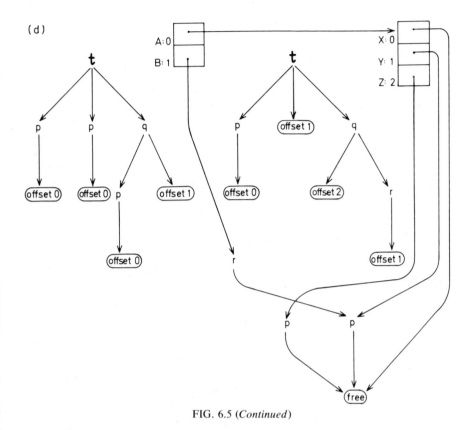

FIG. 6.5 (*Continued*)

pointers as activation records are deallocated upon procedure completion (according to the normal stack regime)[2].

The situation is quite similar to that encountered in Pascal, say: an object which is to live longer than the procedure which has created it is allocated in the heap, i.e. a memory area distinct from the activation stack. The NSS heap is called a **copy stack**. It is a true stack, because term copies can obviously be discarded when the program backtracks past their point of creation. They can become inaccessible much earlier, too, and a garbage collector could be very useful, but it is not essential to Prolog as it is to Lisp. One must remember, however, that without garbage collection the copy stack's size is roughly proportional to the amount of time spent in forward execution (without backtracking), and

[2] But this is not always possible (see the next section).

that one may need to alleviate that by introducing artificial failures in a few well-chosen places (see Section 4.3.2).

In the simplest form of Structure Sharing, a variable frame is an integral part of the representation of a number of term instances, and cannot—in principle—be deallocated so long as any of these terms is accessible. It must be allocated on a variable stack, which closely resembles the copy stack of NSS (except that a garbage collector, if required, is harder to implement). The activation stack is smaller, as it only holds control information.

The most important advantage of NSS is that retention past the moment of procedure termination concerns only those terms which become variable instantiations. With simple Structure Sharing, on the other hand, all terms are retained. As it turns out, terms are often used as selectors rather than constructors, and clauses frequently propel a computation along without creating many long-lived objects. The copy stack is therefore usually smaller than the variable stack, and the effects of memory requirements being a function of time are much less pronounced with NSS.

Starting with DECProlog-10, many Structure Sharing implementations take advantage of the difference between terms which must live longer than their clauses and those which need not. As a clause is read in, it is analysed to detect variables which cannot, under any circumstances, be used to form instantiations of variables outside the clause. These are classified as **local** variables, whereas the others are called **global**. The variable names are all local to the clause, of course—the terminology is to convey that global variables are long-lived, while local variables may be allocated (and deallocated) with the clause's activation frame. The activation stack is accordingly referred to as the **local stack**, and the **global stack** holds global variables.

A simple, though not necessarily the most subtle, classification criterion is whether a variable appears inside a term (i.e. is not only a procedure's parameter). For example, in

a(X, f(Y)) :- b(X, g(Z)).

we find that X is local. The rule about directing variable–to–variable references towards the bottom of the stack suffices to ensure that its deallocation will not leave dangling pointers. The variable Y is obviously global, as the clause can "export" it after having been activated by

a(Something, Variable).

The status of Z is uncertain. It can be bound to a variable in **b**, but we are really interested only in those outside variables which outlive **a**. If the body of **a** were

b(g(Z))

then Z could conceivably be classified as local (according to our experience, though, allowing such cases could complicate the implementation). But as the clause stands, we need to analyse **b** (assuming it will not subsequently be modified!) to check whether g(Z) can be made an instantiation of a variable to which X is bound. For example, with **b** defined as

b(V, V)

the call

a(P, Q)

would instantiate P ← g(Z) and Q ← f(Y)—both Y and Z would be "exported." Variables that do not appear in terms can only be used to carry information around the clause; it is safest to assume that all others will be used to form structures.

This assumption does not yet allow Structure Sharing to be really competitive with NSS. To achieve this, we must declare our intentions by providing so-called **mode declarations**. In Prolog-10 one writes

:- mode member(?, +).

to inform Prolog that the second parameter of *member* will never be a variable, though its first parameter might be one. This means that the procedure

member(E, [E | L]).
member(E, [X | L]) :- member(E, L).

will not be invoked as a generator of lists, so compound terms will only be used as selectors and all the variables—even those global by the general criterion—can be classified as local[3].

Providing mode declarations may seem a nuisance, but they are good documentation (and are *not* compulsory). The declarations are static and must necessarily be less informative than the dynamic special-case analysis of NSS. In common cases, however, the difference is not detectable and this form of Structure Sharing is, in fact, as good as NSS with regard to memory utilisation. This does not mean that the two behave identically. Programs can be written which make any one method almost arbitrarily worse than the other (how would you go about devising such a program?).

[3] A compiler can also use this information to generate faster code.

Structure Sharing tends to be faster, but it is more complicated. There is the problem of analysing clauses, utilising mode declarations and manipulating term handles instead of single pointers. Moreover, system routines such as *clause* are harder to write because a clause can contain references to local variables and its instance is not therefore a correct term. If you want to write a simple memory-efficient interpreter, use Non–Structure Sharing.

6.3. CONTROL

One of the keys to the success of a Prolog implementation is the efficiency of backtracking. Whenever a fail point is established (see Section 1.3.2), the computation's state must be saved, so that it can be restored upon failure. Both the saving and the restoration of a state are frequent events, which must take place as rapidly as possible.

The state of a computation can be reduced to the contents of the control stack and the heap[4]. Obviously, Prolog's special requirements rule out checkpointing (i.e. dumping memory contents) as a means of saving the state. Logging (i.e. recording changes made to the state) is a more hopeful technique, as differences between successive states of interest are usually minute in comparison to the amount of information contained in a state. The technique is particularly suitable—and universally used—for dealing with the evolution of variable instantiations. Only uninstantiated variables can be modified, so the old value need not be remembered and it is enough to record a modified variable's address.

While logging is also a viable method of handling activation record traffic on the control stack, it would not be able to take advantage of the disciplined manner in which procedure instances are created and destroyed. A better method, well known since the appearance of (Bobrow and Wegbreit 1973), can roughly be described as using the log itself to define a new state.

As a fail point is established, a **fail point record** is pushed onto a special stack. (We are interested in a conceptual description. In practice, this stack is often implemented by a chain of pointers threaded through activation records.) The fail point record stores information about current sizes of memory areas and a pointer to the list of untried clauses likely to match the current call. In other words, it contains information essential to Prolog's ability to recommence computations from this fail point. To

---

[4] The generic terms are meant to emphasize that this discussion is valid for Structure Sharing and NSS alike.

make this information *sufficient*, stack and heap areas below the levels indicated by a fail point record are treated as **frozen**, i.e. under special protection.

Binding a frozen variable is allowed, but must be logged by pushing its address onto a fourth stack, called the **trail** (its size is also remembered in a fail point record). The control stack, however, is frozen quite literally. Whenever a terminating procedure would cause control to be returned to an activation record (AR) within the frozen area, a *copy* of the AR is created just above the protected part of the stack. The copy defines the current procedure's environment: an ancestor link provides access to the frozen AR of the procedure's caller. To avoid copying that part of an AR which contains variables[5], the variables of a clause are associated with the AR of its caller rather than with its own AR. An AR's copy will be used to perform a new call: the original describes the previous call, so its variables are irrelevant. All this is illustrated in Fig. 6.6.

With these precautions, backtracking consists in undoing bindings made after creating the most recent fail point record FR (a simple matter of resetting locations referenced in the top-most fragment of the trail), popping all stacks to the levels indicated by FR, grabbing the untried clause list and popping FR itself. This is rapid enough; the unescapable penalty is that of maintaining (several copies of) frozen substacks which would normally disappear with the shortening of call chains. One of the reasons why judicious use of the cut is so important (see Section 4.3.1) is that it allows Prolog to reclaim stack storage. To invoke the cut is to pop a number of fail point records, thereby unfreezing areas of memory.

6.4. TAIL RECURSION OPTIMISATION

Many programming tasks are inherently iterative. For example, to test whether an item is present in a list, we must look at successive elements until either the list is exhausted or the item is found. But in Prolog we can only define *member* as a recursive procedure. Recursion is more expensive than iteration in that it requires not only time but also stack storage which grows linearly with the number of turns. Storage is often a scarce resource, and it would be very unsatisfactory if each decision to traverse a list had to be accompanied by speculations about the potential length of the list. In Prolog, using recursion instead of iteration is all the more serious because the stack may have to be frozen.

---

[5] Local variables of Structure Sharing, "virtual" variable instances of NSS.

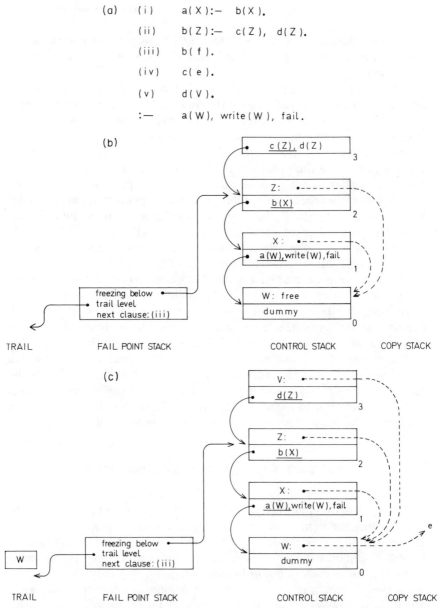

FIG. 6.6 Control stack management: (a) The example program. (b) Clause (iv) is invoked. (Solid lines in control stack are the ancestor links, dotted lines are variable bindings. Active calls are underscored, remaining calls in each clause are also shown. The model is NSS.) (c) One step later, d is ready to return. (d) After returning from d and b. (Frame 3 is a copy of 1, executing the next call. The variable Z was destroyed when the stack was popped—it was just above the freezing level.) (e) After failure, before invocation of clause (iii). (f) Clause (iii) and (i) terminated, directive in control.

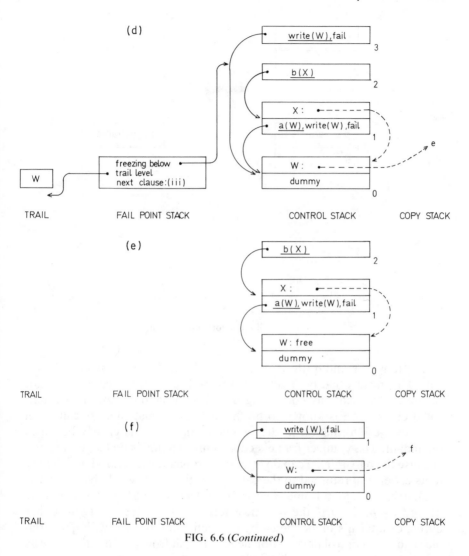

FIG. 6.6 (*Continued*)

Tail recursion optimisation (TRO) is the technique of replacing some forms of recursion with iteration. Despite its name, it is also useful in situations where there is no direct recursion, or even no recursion at all—just a long chain of procedure calls.

The general idea is illustrated in Fig. 6.7. Assume that **q** is the last call in **p** and that **p** is deterministic, i.e. there are no fail points between the

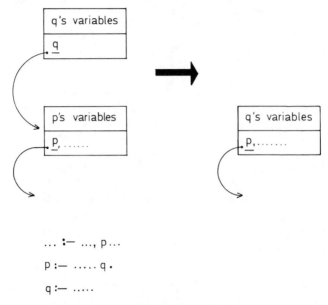

FIG. 6.7   Tail recursion optimisation.

invocations of **p** and **q** (they were not established or were removed by a cut). This means that both activation records are not frozen, and are not separated by locations containing useful information. Now, if the activated clause of **q** is known to be the last clause matching its call, then some of the information in the two activation records clearly becomes redundant. The younger frame's control information is no longer needed, because the only thing **p** can do after **q**'s termination is return immediately to its caller: if **q** returned to the caller of **p**, the effect would be the same. Similarly, the older frame's variables (local or "virtual") will not be needed by **p**. TRO is the technical term for replacing the two—either during or after **q**'s invocation—by one activation record, with **q**'s variables and with control information needed to exit from **p**. If **q** is the same as **p** (or contains a tail recursive call on **p**, or the like), many calls may be executed without increasing the size of the control stack. (The heap may grow, though, if the computation constructs some long-lived objects.)

Several methods of implementing TRO are described in the literature, and we shall not discuss them here. An important feature of some is that they allow **delayed** TRO, i.e. merging of our two activation records after **q** performs a cut, even though its initial invocation is not deterministic. In Section 7.3.4 you will find one such method, which we favour for its simplicity.

6.5. BIBLIOGRAPHIC NOTES

The idea of structure sharing comes from Boyer and Moore (1972). It was used in the original Marseilles interpreter (Battani and Méloni 1973, Roussel 1975), which, actually, was preceded by an earlier, experimental version (Colmerauer *et al.* 1972). That interpreter did not have anything like fail point records. Though variables were allocated on a separate stack, control frames were also—as a rule—popped only on backtracking. Classification of variables into local and global was introduced with the DECProlog compiler. Warren (1977a) is the original reference, see also Warren *et al.* (1977) and Warren (1980b). A preliminary report on the first NSS implementation is Bruynooghe (1976).

The idea of tail recursion optimisation is well known. Bruynooghe was the first to use TRO in Prolog, while Warren used a different method as an afterthought; see Warren (1980a).

A good detailed explanation of the implementation principles is Bruynooghe (1982b). It stresses both the similarity of structure sharing to conventional handling of procedure instances and the similarity of Prolog's control structures to a proof tree. Van Emden (1982) contains a disciplined derivation of the control algorithm, starting from search-tree traversal.

Most implementations merge fail point records and control frames into a single type of record. To our knowledge, they were first separated in Donz (1979), an early approach to global optimisation, where they were talked of as the and-nodes and or-nodes of a search tree. We like the separation because it brings to light the fact that backtracking is implemented almost exactly as proposed—in a more general setting—in Bobrow and Wegbreit (1973), the classic paper on implementation of unconventional control structures.

A comparison of NSS and structure sharing can be found in Mellish (1982), with some comments in Bruynooghe (1982b).

Mellish (1981) is an early approach to automatic production of mode declarations by means of global flow analysis. Other papers concerned with global analysis, though not for the sake of efficiency, are Bruynooghe (1982a) and Mycroft and O'Keefe (1983).

At the time of this writing we know of two new compilers being developed. The references are Bowen *et al.* (1983) and Ballieu (1983).

See also Section 2.5 for references on Prolog implementations with coroutining and parallelism.

As a point of interest, we shall mention two papers describing implementations of Prolog done by embedding it in another programming language: Lisp (Komorowski 1982) or POP-11 (Mellish and Hardy 1983).

7 TOY: AN EXERCISE IN IMPLEMENTATION

7.1. INTRODUCTION

This chapter is a case study of Toy—a simple but fairly complete implementation of Prolog. Only the most important (or least obvious) information is presented here, and it should be read *together with the listings* in the appendices.

While designing Toy, we attempted to strike a compromise between several conflicting goals. We wanted to write:

—A clean, readable interpreter which you could find useful for "getting a feel" of what is involved in implementing a "life-size" Prolog system;
—A usable interpreter, which we could use to test all the programming examples in this book (our extant implementations were quite incompatible with Prolog-10) and which you might use to experiment with Prolog if you have a lot of time but no access to a machine running one of the commercially available Prolog systems;
—A large fragment of the implementation in Prolog itself, to provide a sizable example of using the language for solving well-known but not completely trivial programming tasks at a relatively low level;
—An interpreter which, though useful, would have little commercial value.

We decided to use Pascal, because it is easy to read, well known and generally available. The program is not written to be very efficient: concern for readability and conciseness almost always prevailed. It is not particularly short and elegant either, as we wanted it to support a

185

fairly complete version of Prolog modelled after the Prolog-10 dialect. There are two principal reasons why we call it *Toy*:

—The user interface is written in Prolog, and this makes it rather slow;
—There is no garbage collector, and moreover, partitioning storage into several disjoint fixed-length areas makes it easier to encounter a memory overflow condition.

If you decide to use Toy, you will quickly find that the time taken to read and write terms requires some patience. We had to rewrite *read*, *write* and *op* in Pascal for our purposes, and it is but a moderately difficult task. A rather straightforward implementation resulted in another 1000 lines of code, but a lot of it is dedicated to handling mixed functors (see Section 7.4.3).

We used Toy on two minicomputers: a PDP 11/40 look-alike running RSX11M, and a Polish computer called Mera 400. The PDP has an address space of 64KB; we used it to bring the system up, but it was a tight squeeze. You might do better with a P-code system rather than with a native-code compiler of Pascal, such as the one we had to use. The Mera had a 128KB address space and a fairly good native-code compiler (but with no attempt at global optimisation): we could easily load and execute both the whole Prolog interface and programs such as WARPLAN or Toy-Sequel (see Chapter 8). We tested all our programs and had quite a bit of memory to spare, running in a 104KB space.

The moral is that you should have no trouble running Toy on a 16-bit micro. If you feel like punching it in and playing with it, do so, but remember it is copyrighted. No version of this implementation may be used or distributed for gain, all listings must contain our copyright notice, and the heading produced by *status* (see Section 5.7.5) must contain the texts "Toy-Prolog" and "IIUW Warszawa". Otherwise you are welcome to modify it, give it to friends, etc. If you have any comment to make, we shall be happy to hear from you.

7.2. GENERAL INFORMATION

Toy is a Non–Structure Sharing interpreter (see Chapter 6). The program written in Pascal supports a limited syntax, which we shall call Toy-Prolog, and only a subset of the usual system (built-in) procedures. The full user interface and library is implemented in Prolog (see Section 7.4)—this approach was taken in the original Marseilles implementation, and in a number of implementations since. A short program called the "bootstrapper" (see Section 7.4.1), written in Toy-Prolog, is used to translate into Toy-Prolog other parts of the user interface, which are written in a slightly restricted form of the usual syntax. Next, various interface programs can be loaded during initialization (see Section 7.3.6).

A Prolog program called the "monitor" supports an interactive programming regime (see Section 7.4.2). Full Prolog-10 syntax can be used (see sections 7.4.3–7.4.5). A program called the "translator" can be used to convert Prolog-10 programs into Toy-Prolog (see Section 7.4.6). The translator shares most of the monitor's routines. It can be used for large (interactively debugged) programs which are to be loaded quickly, without repeated syntactic analysis by the rather slow parser in the monitor. See Appendix A.5 for a few examples of such programs.

We shall finish this section with an example of Toy-Prolog syntax. There is no point in providing a precise description of this language, as it is very simple and the recursive-descent parser (a fragment called the READER in the listing of Appendix A.1) is so straightforward that it can easily be used to resolve all doubts. Our example is

p([a, [b, c], d | X], Y) :- q(Y, X), r(s(Y), _).
:- p(Z, (t :- u, v)).

To make it directly acceptable to the READER, we write

p(a.(b.c.[]).d.:0, :1) : q(:1, :0) . r(s(:1), _) . []
: p(:0, ':-'(t, ','(u, v))) . []#

See Appendix A.3 for further examples. The syntax is not nice, but is very close to the internal representation of clauses.

7.3. THE TOY-PROLOG INTERPRETER

7.3.1. The Principal Storage Areas

Toy uses several disjoint areas of memory for its data structures (see Fig. 7.1). They are listed below.

—CT (character table), used to store strings: print names of Prolog functors and predicate symbols;
—AT (atom table), used to store atoms. In this chapter "atom" does *not* denote a functor with no arguments. It is the generic name of a record containing useful information about a symbol (a functor or predicate symbol in our case);

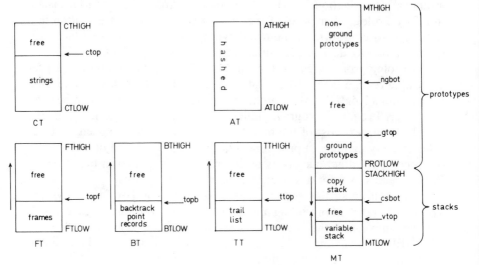

FIG. 7.1   The main data areas.

—MT (main table), used to store term instances and prototypes. There are two subareas here:

—Prototype storage, which is further divided into disjoint storage areas for ground (variable-free) prototypes and for those that contain variables. The classification is important because a ground prototype can be used to represent all its instances, and need not be copied onto the copy stack;

—Stack storage, which is further divided into disjoint areas for the copy stack and the variable stack (the variable stack holds variables from activation records: Pascal's type mechanism made it more convenient to keep control information from activation records in a separate table FT);

—FT (frame table), used as the activation record stack (but variables are stacked in MT);

—BT (backtrack table), used as the fail-point stack (here called backtrack-point stack—we just needed a different letter to label the table);

—TT (trail table), used as the trail stack;

—Pascal's heap, used to store procedure descriptors;

—Pascal's stack, used for recursion in unification and term-copying operations.

In what follows, we shall use the word **pointer**, or **address**, to denote both Pascal pointers and indices into the tables.

7.3.2. The Dictionary: Atoms and Procedure Descriptions

The character and atom tables form the **dictionary**: a data structure used primarily as an aid in translating between the external and internal forms of Prolog terms and clauses. It also supports access to procedures, making it easier to implement variable calls and clause manipulation.

An atom is a record containing information about a functor and/or a predicate symbol. The difference between a term and a procedure depends only on context and is not always recognized. Predicate symbols are denoted by functors when clauses are treated as terms (e.g. in *assert*); conversely, a functor may be used to invoke a procedure (as in *call*).

The attributes of an atom are

—Its print name (a pointer to a string in CT);
—Its arity;
—The procedure of this name and arity (a pointer to a procedure descriptor, or **nil**).

Atoms are accessed through direct pointers or through a hashing procedure. Direct pointers are present in the representation of terms (including clauses; see the next section). The pointers are used for

—Printing a functor,
—Determining arity,
—Finding a procedure.

In particular, the representation of a call contains a pointer to an atom as the only handle on its procedure. Addition and deletion of clauses in the procedure does not therefore require modification of its calls.

Hashing is used to locate appropriate atoms during conversion from external representation. Such conversion takes place when terms are read in or when they are created by *functor* and *pname*. For simplicity, linear rehash is used in the current version: you might wish to improve it.

Print names are represented in CT by contiguous sequences of characters terminated with EOS characters (zero bytes). As a name is created by pname or the READER, its characters are pushed on top of the string area in CT (procedure *buildname*). On termination of the string, *wrapname* is invoked to locate an atom with the same printname. If such an atom is found, the string is obliterated; otherwise a new atom is created and returned. Since this atom's arity is unknown, the arity field is set to the special value of *noarity* (procedure *findname*).

Atoms are located by the READER in a two-phase process. First, *buildname* and *wrapname* are used to find the first atom with this name; then a single scan through the (virtual) hash chain finds an atom with correct arity, or detects its absence and creates it (procedure *findatom*). Conversion between atoms of different priorities, needed to implement *functor*, requires invocation of the hash algorithm to locate the beginning of the appropriate hash chain (procedure *samename*).

Procedure descriptors are allocated in the Pascal heap. Descriptors are formed of lists of records, each of them with:

—a pointer to the next element in the list;
—the number of variables in an activation record;
—either the number of a system procedure, or pointers to the prototypes of a clause's head and body.

A system procedure descriptor is formed of a single such record. The descriptor of a Prolog procedure is a list of records, one for each clause. The head predicate's atom always points at the first element of this list.

A clause body is represented by the prototype of a Prolog list containing its calls. Figure 7.2a illustrates the layout (recall that the binary dot is the Prolog list constructor).

7.3.3. Prototypes and Term Instances

The main table, MT, holds a variety of objects which are distinguished partly by their addresses and partly by their contents. Addresses are used to distinguish between prototypes and term instances (fields denoting variables contain variable offsets in prototypes, and variable bindings in term instances). Prototypes of ground terms, which contain no variables, are also used as instances: this helps keep down the size of the copy stack.

Instances of non-ground terms are kept in the stack area. It is divided into the copy stack and the variable stack. The variable stack holds activation-record variables and is separated from the copy stack because it can shrink on procedure return and not only upon backtracking (see Chapter 6).

Object contents are used to distinguish between integers, variables, and "normal" terms with functors.

—Integers are two-word objects. The second word holds the integer and the first—a special marker INT, which prevents the interpreter from treating integers as pointers.

—Variables hold values less or equal to VARLIM (both INT and pointers to MT or AT objects have values greater than VARLIM). VARLIM is kept only inside the dummy variable (_) prototype, whose address is DUMVARX—this prototype is treated as ground. The value FREEVAR (equal to VARLIM − 1) fills free variable instances. Values below FREEVAR are negative: in prototypes their absolute values denote offsets in variable frames, and in instances their absolute values

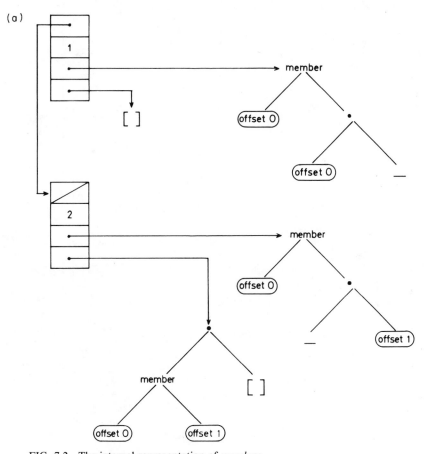

FIG. 7.2 The internal representation of *member*:

member(:0, :0._) : []

member(:0, _.:1) : member(:0, :1) . []

(a) The abstract form. (b) The data structures (variable offsets adjusted by offoff; []/0, ./2, ./0, member/2 denote addresses). (*continued*)

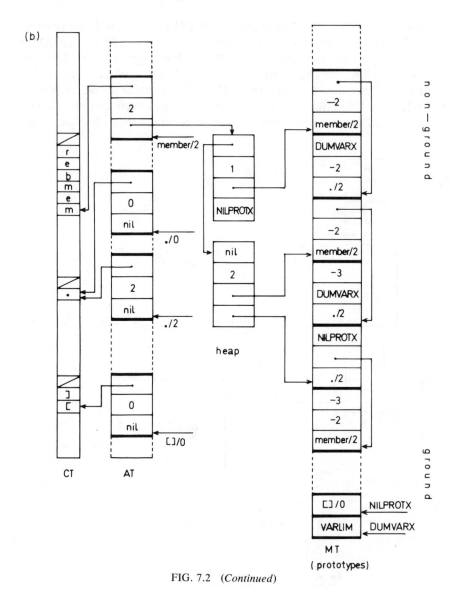

FIG. 7.2   (*Continued*)

are pointers to variable bindings. (Actually, the situation is slightly different: INT = 1, VARLIM = 0 and FREEVAR = −1. All negative entries denote non-dummy variables. MT's lower index is 2, but variable frame offsets start from 0 and are therefore adjusted by the constant OFFOFF = 2; −2 stands for offset 0, −3 for offset 1, etc.)

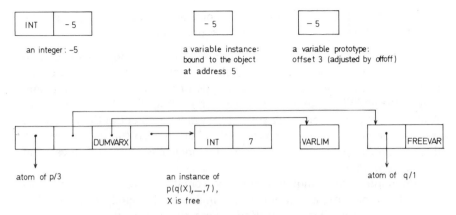

FIG. 7.3   Internal representation of terms.

—"Normal" terms are contiguous sequences of words. The first word holds a pointer to the main functor's atom (its arity field defines the length of the sequence). Other words represent arguments. For variable arguments see above; other arguments are represented by pointers to appropriate objects (see procedures *getarity* and *getarg* in the listing).

Figure 7.3 illustrates these conventions. Figure 7.2b shows the complete internal representation of a procedure.

As explained in Chapter 6, term instances are pushed onto the copy stack only when absolutely necessary (when they become variable bindings) and are otherwise represented as in Structure Sharing. It is therefore convenient to represent all instances by a pair of pointers. If the first pointer addresses a prototype, the second (which we shall call the prototype's **environment**) is a pointer to an area in the variable stack. If the first pointer addresses a term instance, the second is disregarded. Note that— unlike in Structure Sharing implementations—the environment need never change as term arguments are accessed: variable bindings are never nonground prototypes and require no environment.

The normal mechanisms of object recognition and creation are circumvented in two major cases (see procedure *loadsyskernel*).

—To avoid creation in the copy stack of too many integer objects representing intermediate results, a range of the most frequently used integers ($-1..10$ in this version) is maintained in the form of unique ground prototypes.

—To avoid the overhead of locating character atoms, checking whether functors represent characters, and duplicating character prototypes or instances, ground prototypes of ASCII characters are kept in a contiguous area of MT. Accessing a character prototype requires only the addition of its ordinal number to this area's address.

Certain other objects also have representations at addresses known to the interpreter. Apart from "popular" integers, characters and the dummy variable, there is also a prototype of the atom [] (see the beginning of the global variable declarations for a listing of all these addresses). Addresses of atoms requiring special treatment are kept in the table STD (see the definition of type *stdatomid*). There is also the prototype of a dummy clause, whose body consists of a single call to *error*/1, located at address *errcallseq*.

Procedures for handling term representations are quite straightforward. Only prototype creation might not be immediately obvious. The method is quite similar to that used for creating entries in the dictionary. A prototype is allocated by invoking *initprot* with information about the main functor. Arguments are then filled in by *newparg* and *newpvararg*, and the process is terminated by *wrapprot*. This procedure checks if all the arguments are ground—when this is the case, the prototype is moved to the ground prototype area. Note that the process is inherently recursive, as argument prototypes may be created before their parent term's prototype is wrapped up. This is why *initprot* must be used: piecemeal allocation would not preserve contiguity.

A short comment about *terminst*, the procedure usually used to create terms on the copy stack. Non-variable arguments are represented not by direct pointers, but by negative values, as if they were all formed by instantiating pre-existing variables. This is necessary because the procedure *argument* (which follows chains of variable bindings to locate the final instantiation) expects variable arguments directly inside the representation of their parent terms. A recursive call on *terminst* can return a variable and treating the variable as a normal argument—by inserting a positive pointer to it—would break the chain of references. (Such things are not easily seen, and the erroneous situations are rather infrequent: this bug was the hardest to locate!)

7.3.4. Control

In Toy, clause bodies are represented as prototypes of lists. The list elements are prototypes of calls, and none of them is an integer or a variable. While not directly related to the external form of clauses in Prolog-10, this representation is very regular and easy to handle.

The method of representing control state is almost exactly like that described in Chapter 6. The principal difference is that the variable part of

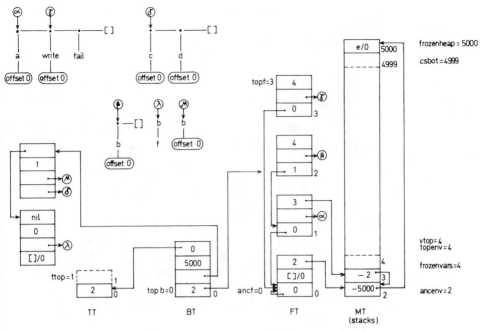

FIG. 7.4   A more detailed form of Fig. 6.6d.

an activation record is kept on a separate stack. Figure 7.4 is a detailed version of Fig. 6.6d. We shall comment only on the variables used as "control registers".

The crucial variables are:

—*topf*, a pointer to the current control frame (i.e. activation record), which is always on top of the stack in FT;

—*topb*, a pointer to the current backtrack point (i.e. fail point) record, which is always on top of the stack in BT;

—*csbot*, a pointer to the first free location below the copy stack in MT (this stack grows downwards);

—*vtop*, a pointer to the first free location above the variable stack in MT;

—*ttop*, a pointer to the first free location above the trail stack in TT.

Five auxiliary variables contain copies of information available elsewhere. They are used for efficiency:

—*ancf* is a pointer to the current control frame's parent frame;

—*topenv* is a pointer to the current variable frame (associated with *topf*);

—*ancenv* is a pointer to the variable frame associated with *ancf*;

—*frozenheap* is a pointer to the first free location below the frozen part of the copy stack;

—*frozenvars* is a pointer to the first free location above the frozen part of the variable stack.

Execution of a Prolog program is driven by the procedure *resolve*. Each turn of its loop is an attempt to match a call against a clause head, or to execute a system procedure. At the beginning of this step the situation is as shown in Fig. 7.4: a control frame for the current call is on top of the stack, but the clause is not yet invoked and the associated variable frame is empty. If the call was an erroneous system procedure call, the error handler is activated (see below).

If the step is unsuccessful (the head did not match the call, or the system procedure failed), the interpreter backtracks. Otherwise it enters the procedure or—if it was a system procedure or a unit clause—exits it. Entering a procedure consists in setting up the control state so that the next call to be executed will be the first call in the freshly activated clause. Exiting is the process of finding the next pending call: either the one immediately following the successful current call, or (if this was the last in its clause) a call following the nearest ancestor which is not the last call in its clause.

To stop the execution, the flag *stop* must be set. This is done either by the system procedure *halt*, or by *backtrack* when there are no fail points left (i.e. when the directive failed) or by *exitt* when it cannot find a pending call (i.e. when the directive succeeded).

Two auxiliary variables play the role of a program counter:

—*ccall* contains a pointer to the prototype of the current call (it is the prototype of the first element in the list indicated by the current control frame's calls field, unless that element is an invocation of *call* or *tag*: *ccall* is then the outermost argument which is neither of these);

—*cproc* contains a pointer to the descriptor of the procedure invoked by *ccall* (for Prolog procedures, this is the first clause's descriptor when in forward execution, and a pointer recovered from a backtrack point record's *resume* field when immediately after a failure).

Notice that a fail point's *resume* field points at the predecessor of the clause which is to be retried. This is so to make *retract* correct.

The algorithm used for tail recursion optimisation (procedure *trooverlay*) merits some explanation. We employ the naive method suggested by Fig. 6.7. After unification is over, procedure *candotro* checks whether the current call is an untagged tail call and whether the ancestor frame is not frozen. If so, neither the call nor the variable frame associated with the ancestor frame will ever be needed again. The current variable frame is shifted to replace the ancestor variable frame, and the control stack is popped so that the ancestor control frame becomes topmost (the most recently activated clause is still accessible through *cproc*). The algorithm is made a little complicated by the fact that the shifted variables may be instantiated to one another or to the destroyed (overlaid) variables. Both cases are illustrated in Fig. 7.5.

The cut procedure simply removes as many backtrack point records as necessary (possibly none) to ensure that the call invoking the procedure containing the cut—and all subsequent calls—will not be retried. (There are exceptions to this rule: notice that ,/2, ;/2 and *call*/1 are transparent to the cut.) After popping off backtrack points, the interpreter must purge the topmost section of the trail to remove references to variables which are no longer frozen. This is necessary, because such variables can be popped off or shifted during TRO. Notice that the method of TRO applied

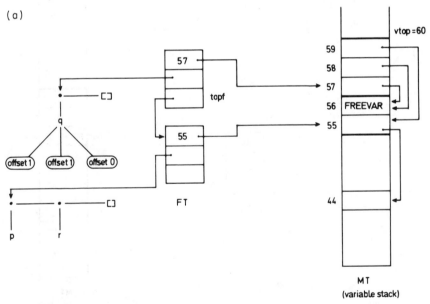

FIG. 7.5 Tail recursion optimisation: merging two frames. (a) The initial situation. Both frames are not frozen, the call is tail recursive. The variables at 57 and 58 are instantiated to the same free variable, the variable at 59 is instantiated to the variable at 44. (b) Adjustment pass. (i) The first variable (at 57) points at an overlaid free variable (at 56). The direction of the pointer is reversed. (ii) The second variable (at 58) is dereferenced to that at 57 through that at 56. The reference is remapped: the second variable points at 55—the *future* location of the variable now at 57. (iii) The third variable (at 59) is dereferenced to that at 44 through that at 55. (c) Shifting pass overlays the parent's variable frame with the current variable frame; the parent's control frame becomes current. (*continued*)

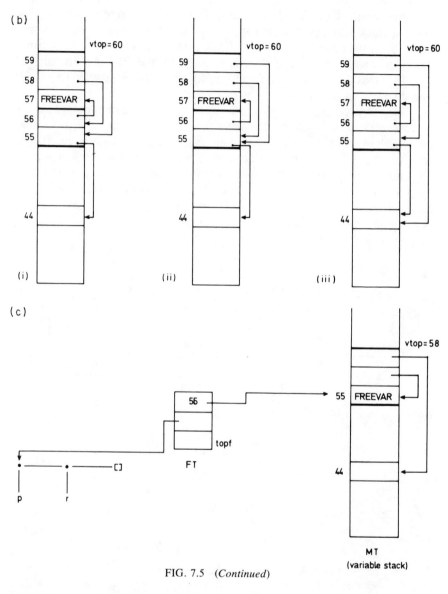

FIG. 7.5 (*Continued*)

here makes it fairly easy to perform **delayed** frame merging after things are made deterministic by the cut. We shall not enter into the details of this and of *tagcut*: this is a simple exercise.

The last thing worth mentioning is the handling of erroneous calls to system procedures. This involves pushing a dummy variable frame, with a single variable instantiated to the erroneous call. The current control frame (in which the call was invoked) is associated with this variable frame and becomes the ancestor of *error*/1. As a result, the parameter of *error*/1 is the right instance of the erroneous call. The process is illustrated in Fig. 7.6.

The program maintains several important invariants, such as "there are no outside references to non-frozen variable frames except from variables higher in the variable stack". We decided to let you have the fun of discovering them for yourself (after all, these are the real trade secrets).

7.3.5. System Procedures

We shall not give a detailed description of the system routines. There are too many of them, and the listing is more or less self-explanatory. The general principles are as follows:

—All system procedures are invoked through procedure *sysroutcall*;
—*sysroutcall* sets up pointers to their parameters in table SPAR (the values of integer parameters are also passed through table SPARV);
—System procedures that can fail or succeed indicate the result by setting a Boolean parameter (*success*) passed by *sysroutcall*;
—Whenever a system procedure detects an error, it sets the global flag *syserror*, which forces the interpreter to invoke *error*/1 (see the end of the previous section).

There are no tricks, except in the procedure concerned with creating new clauses. It is important that several occurrences of a variable be represented by occurrences of the same offset when a term is translated into a prototype. To achieve this, addresses of variables appearing in an asserted clause are stacked in the free area above the topmost variable frame. With each variable occurrence, this temporary variable dictionary is searched linearly and, possibly, augmented. The position of a variable in this dictionary is treated as its offset.

To add a new system procedure, one must:

—Write its code;
—Insert its identifier in type *sysroutid* (its place there defines its position);
—Insert its call in procedure *sysroutcall* (in the same position);
—Insert its name and arity in the kernel file (in the same position)—see the next section.

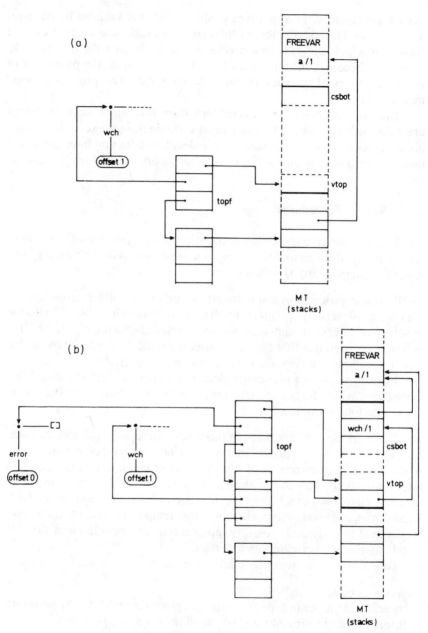

FIG. 7.6 Handling erroneous calls to system routines. (a) *wch* detects an incorrect argument: a(V). (b) a call to *error*/1 is set up.

7.3.6. Initialisation

Initialisation is done in three phases. First, most of the variables are set by procedure *initvars*. Then two portions of data are read from the so-called "kernel file". One portion defines the names and arities of standard atoms whose addresses must be known to the interpreter. They are created and their addresses are stored in table STD. The other portion defines the names and arities of system procedures: as the atoms are created, they are associated with system procedure descriptors. The number and order of all these atoms is known to the interpreter. Arities are important, but printnames are arbitrary and *can be changed at will*.

The last phase of initialisation consists in creating a number of standard objects. Their addresses are known to the interpreter but they cannot be created before the addresses of standard atoms are fixed. The objects are:

—The prototype of [ ];
—The prototypes of characters;
—The prototypes of the integers −1, 0, ..., 10;
—The dummy clause body used to invoke *error* (it is the prototype of [error(X)]);
—The prototype of *user*, needed by the stream switching procedures (see Section 5.7.1).

After initialisation, the interpreter begins normal execution, reading the current file. This is normally the kernel file, containing some useful library procedures. One can also append the bootstrapper or the translated monitor (see below).

7.4. INTERPRETATION OF PROLOG-10 IN TOY-PROLOG

7.4.1. Intermediate Language

Even a modest program in Toy-Prolog can be unmanageable. To write the monitor, we use a subset of full Prolog, without operators and grammar rule notation. Commas and the symbol :- are treated as separators. List notation is allowed, with one restriction: an X in [...... | X] must be a variable. This subset is translated into Toy-Prolog by a "bootstrapper" written in Toy-Prolog. Debugging and testing the monitor required frequent retranslations of its small pieces, but the gain in readability is worth this extra effort. Of course, once the monitor works, the bootstrapper is no longer needed.

The bootstrapper is listed in Appendix A.3. Comments starting with %% associate mnemonics with variable numbers. The main procedure is *translate* (lines 2–13), with two parameters—the names of the source and output files. The unit processed with each turn of the failure-driven loop is a single clause or a comment. The loop stops upon encountering a @ in place of the first non-blank character of a unit. The translation of a clause is a string which is built "on the fly" on a difference list of characters; the list is represented by the two parameters christened *termrepr* and *rest_of_termrepr*. Here is how the clause in lines 54–55 would look after rewriting it into full Prolog and combining those parameters:

```
ctailaux( Fterm_firstch, Termrepr -- Rest_of_termrepr,
                Sym_tab ) :-
    fterm( Fterm_firstch, Fterms_firstch,
          Termrepr -- [' ', '.' | Middletermrepr ], Sym_tab ),
    fterms( Fterms_firstch, Middletermrepr -- Rest_of_termrepr,
                Sym_tab ).
```

Fterms_firstch is the first non-blank following a functor-term; in a correct clause, it can only be a dot, or a comma (see lines 58–66).

Comments embedded in a clause are copied at once (lines 50–53). Moreover, the string contains end-of-line and blank characters which improve the appearance of the translation.

Error in a clause causes a message to be printed and the input up to the nearest dot to be reprinted and skipped (see lines 15–21). The program assumes the data are correct, and protests upon encountering the first unexpected character.

Output for each clause with variables is followed by a comment that associates variable numbers with source names taken from a symbol table for this clause (lines 219–226). The table is an open list of names. Their positions are used as variable numbers in the translation. Up to 99 variables can occur in a clause. The number–name pairs are written six in a line (line 224).

There are some other minor points worth noticing. For example, the output string gets closed eventually due to the [] in the initial call on *clause* (line 11); translations of lists within lists are parethesized, see the fifth parameter of *term* (lines 131, 136, 137); identifiers are enclosed in quotes by *fterm* (lines 69–70); etc. etc. However, the rest of the program should be self-explanatory. A hint: it can be viewed as a metamorphosis grammar used for synthesis, driven by input data, with the two components of a difference list serving as an input and output parameter (see Section 3.1).

7.4.2. Overview of the Monitor

The core of the monitor is an implementation of the built-in procedure *read* that is used in user programs (see Section 7.4.3). The user communicaes with Prolog via an interactive "driver" which operates in a loop terminated by executing the procedure *stop*. In each cycle the driver prompts the user with

?-

and then reads and executes a directive. The symbol table (returned by the two-parameter *read*; see the end of the next section) pairs source names of variables with variables proper. After successful execution, the symbol table is used to display final instances of these variables, and the driver awaits a printable character. If it is a semicolon, execution resumes with forced failure, else processing of this directive terminates.

A directive can be prefixed with :- (we call such a directive a *command*, and that without the prefix a *query*). It will then be executed deterministically, and variable instances will not be printed. However, neither a non-unit clause nor a grammar rule make sense when read directly by the driver: a two-parameter procedure :- or --> (presumably undefined) would be called. User procedures can be defined by calling the built-in procedure *consult* or *reconsult*; both are implemented in the driver. In "consult mode", term L --> R is treated as a grammar rule and translated by the procedure *transl_rule* (see Section 7.4.4). A one-parameter term :-C is treated as a command and executed. Other terms are treated as program clauses.

The monitor is listed in Appendix A.4.

7.4.3. Reader

The syntax of Prolog-10 is only deceptively simple, so the reader is rather involved. One wonders whether a simpler syntax would necessarily be less user friendly.

The main component of the reader is a parser which produces internal representations of terms on input (Appendix A.4, lines 90–332). Translation of an internal representation into a term proper is quite straightforward (look at the listing of the procedure *maketerm*, lines 334–357, after reaching the end of this section).

The parser is a classic operator precedence parser; those parsers belong to the "shift–reduce" class—they are bottom-up and deterministic (Gries 1971, Aho and Ullman 1977).

Recall that, roughly, an operator precedence grammar has no production with two consecutive non-terminals, and all its productions are such that a shift–reduce parser can determine the handle by comparing neighbouring terminals in a sentential form. This is possible when each pair of terminals is in at most one of the three relations denoted by $<$, $=$, $>$. The relations are defined as follows (p, q are terminals, U, V, W non-terminals):

—$p = q$ if there exists a production of the form

$$U \to \cdots pq \cdots$$
$$\text{or}\quad U \to \cdots p\ V\ q \cdots$$

—$p < q$ if there exists a production of the form

$$U \to \cdots p\ V \cdots$$
where $q \cdots$ or $W\ q\cdots$ can be derived from V

—$p > q$ if there exists a production of the form

$$U \to \cdots V\ q \cdots$$
where $\cdots p$ or $\cdots p\ W$ can be derived from V

A parser shifts (i.e. scans a sentential form from left to right) until it detects a pair of terminals related by $>$. It then scans backwards until the nearest pair of terminals related by $<$. The $<$ and $>$ are assumed to be brackets delimiting the handle in a canonic parse: the handle is reduced and the process continues.

Note that $<$, $=$ and $>$ have nothing to do with the common number-ordering relations. However, if terminals are operators as in arithmetic expressions, these relations reflect operator priority: the grammar is structured so that higher priority operators (with operands) are reduced first. The situation is similar in the case of Prolog "operators" (even though in Prolog-10 weaker operators are given the higher priority). We shall say—very informally—that f is weaker than g if $f < g$ or $g > f$. But note that, for example, $+ < ($, $(=)$, and $+ >)$.

We shall now return to our program. We assume that the input is delimited by two additional operators. The rightmost delimiter is weaker than any operator to its left; the leftmost is weaker than any operator to its right (except the other delimiter). Notice that an empty input is erroneous.

The parser maintains a stack of symbols. Initially the stack contains

only the leftmost delimiter. The first true terminal becomes the current
input terminal. In each step, the current input terminal is compared to the
topmost terminal on the stack. Three situations are possible:

1. The input is erroneous—the parser stops "with error";
2. The topmost terminal is stronger—there must be a production with the
   righthand side consisting of a number of topmost symbols on the stack;
   we reduce the stack by replacing all these symbols with a corresponding lefthand side;
3. The topmost terminal is not stronger, i.e. no righthand side has been
   completed—we shift the current input terminal onto the stack and
   make the next terminal current.

The operator grammar of Prolog-10 terms assumes seven classes of
terminals and one class of nonterminals, t (for terms). Parameters of
symbols are used to build the internal representation of a given term.

Terminal symbols are read by a scanner (see Appendix A.4, lines
361–480). The procedure *absorbtoken* (lines 379–409) reads and constructs a "raw" token:

—id(NameString)	from words, symbols, and solo-characters;
—qid(NameString)	from quoted names;
—var(NameString)	from variables;
—num(NumberString)	from integers;
—str(String)	from strings;
—br(LeftRight, Type)	from brackets (LeftRight is l or r, Type is '()', [], or '{}');
—bar	from |;
—dot	from a full stop.

Next, the procedure *maketoken* (lines 457–480) constructs a terminal
symbol:

—vns(Variable)	from var(NameString);
—vns(Number)	from num(NumberString);
—vns(String)	from str(String);
—ff(Name, Types, Priority)	from id(NameString) (when this functor is an operator);
—id(Name)	from id(NameString) (when this functor is not an operator) and from qid(Name-String) (i.e. a quoted name never de-notes an operator);
—br(LR, T)	from br(LR, T);

| —bar | from bar; |
| —dot | from dot. |

The terminal symbol *dot* is used as the rightmost delimiter of the input. The leftmost delimiter (and the seventh terminal) is *bottom*. It is never returned by the scanner: the parser's main procedure, *gettr*, pushes it onto the initially empty stack. Both delimiters never appear in productions.

The Types argument of *ff* is a list of functor types: [Binary], or [Unary], or [Binary, Unary] (see the definition of the built-in procedure *op* lines 656–718)).

A symbol table in an open list is used to relate a variable's name to a Prolog variable.

The grammar underlying the parser is given in the listing (lines 99–107). The definition of internal representation can be read off the *reduce* procedure (lines 158–179). Incidentally, the procedure can be paraphrased as a metamorphosis grammar. For example, the fifth and sixth clause would be rewritten as

t(tr(Type, X)) → [br(1, Type)], t(X),
               [br(r, Type)].
t(bar(X, Y)) → [br(1, [])], t(X), [bar],
               t(Y), [br(r, [])].

Notice, however, that top-down analysis based on such a grammar would not be deterministic.

There are five types of internal representations:

—arg0(X)	for X a variable, name, string, or nullary functor;
—tr1(Name, X)	for a prefix or postfix term (X is the representation of the argument);
—tr2(Name, X, Y)	for an infix term (X, Y are the representations of the arguments; in particular, the comma is an infix functor, so "comma-lists" of terms are represented with tr2—for example, the representation of

        a, b, c

is

    tr2(',', arg0(a),
          tr2(',', arg0(b), arg0(c)));

| —bar(X, Y) | for a list with front X and tail Y; X is often the representation of a comma-list; |

—tr(Name, X)   for all other valid situations:

tr('()', X) is equivalent to X;

tr([ ], X) represents a list (of definite length), X usually represents a comma-term

tr('{}', X) represents the term {(Cond)} where Cond is the term represented by X (this is used in grammar rules);

tr(Name, X) with Name other than a bracket type (and X—usually the representation of a comma-term) represents a normal term; for example, the term

foo(''p'', 5)

is represented by

tr(foo, tr2(',', arg0([p]), arg0(5)))

The parser's entry point is the procedure *gettr* (lines 125–127), and the main loop is implemented as the procedure *parse* (lines 129–138). The loop terminates successfully when the original input (*bottom* and *dot* included) reduces to the sequence

bottom   t(InternalRepresentation)   dot

The parser fails in two situations:

—when the procedure *establish_precedence* fails, i.e. when the topmost terminal on the stack and the current input terminal do not compare;

—when the procedure *reduce* fails, i.e. the top segment of the stack does not match any production.

The procedure *topterminal* (lines 140–143) returns Top, the topmost stack terminal, and its position: 1 means Top is the top item, 2 means it is covered by a t(_).

The precedence relations are summarized in Table 7.1. We treat all operators jointly with respect to other terminals. Empty slots signify erroneous combinations of contiguous terminals.

A functor–functor relationship is the only potentially conflicting one: to establish the precedence relation for a given Top and Input, we must consider their priorities and types (sometimes even some broader context should be considered but this might require changes in the otherwise deterministic algorithm). If the priorities differ, the functor with lower priority is taken as stronger, according to the conventions of Prolog-10. (Notice, however, that when Top is stronger, Input cannot be a

TABLE 7.1

Precedence Relations for the Operator Grammar of Terms

Top \ Input	vns	id	(	)	[	|	]	{	}	ff	bottom	dot
vns				>		>	>		>	>^{b}		>
id			=	>		>	>		>	>^{b}		>
(	<	<	<	=	<			<		<		>
)				>		>	>		>	>^{b}		>
[	<	<	<		<	=	=	<		<		>
|	<	<	<		<		=	<		<		>
]				>		>	>		>	>^{b}		>
{	<	<	<		<			<	=	<		>
}				>		>	>		>	>^{b}		>
ff	<^{a}	<^{a}	<^{a}		<^{a}			<^{a}		<^{a} >^{b}		>
bottom	<	<	<	<	<	<	<	<	<	<	<	>
dot												

^{a} Top can be any prefix or infix functor, i.e. Types = [xf] and Types = [yf] are excluded.

^{b} Input can be any infix or postfix functor, i.e. Types = [fx] and Types = [fy] are excluded.

prefix functor, and when Input is stronger, Top cannot be postfix.) If Top and Input have equal priorities, their types must be examined (see below).

Mixed[1] functors require special treatment. In most contexts, their inherent ambiguity is apparent: only one of a functor's types can be properly attributed to it. For example, let Input be &, an [xfy, fy] functor, and Top a left parenthesis not covered by a non-terminal:

...... (& ......

Surely, & can only be a prefix variation of this mixed functor—an infix variation is excluded. Likewise, if Top is $, an [xfx, xf] functor, covered

---

[1] Recall that our version of Prolog allows a mixed functor to have only one binary and one unary type, both with the same priority.

by a non-terminal, and Input a right bracket:

...... $ Term] ......

then $ certainly cannot be a postfix functor. In such situations, we can "disambiguate" the mixed functor by removing the incompatible type from its representation. For example, we replace ff('&', [xfy, fy], Priority) with ff('&', [fy], Priority).

The relation in Table 7.1 is implemented by the procedure *establish_precedence* (lines 195–204), which takes the two terminals and the position of Top. It fails given an incorrect combination, otherwise it succeeds with the fourth parameter instantiated as *gt* (Top is stronger) or *lseq* (Top is not stronger). When both terminals are mixed functors, the procedure tries to disambiguate their types. The last two parameters are instantiated as the new top and new input terminal, to be used in the next step (usually they remain unchanged).

The real job is done by the procedure *p* which returns *gt* or *lseq*, or—when functors are involved—gt(NewTop, NewInput) or lseq(NewTop, NewInput). It fails given an erroneous pair of terminals.

Table 7.1 has 80-odd nonempty entries, but it can be easily simplified. First of all, we can treat *bottom* and *dot* separately; see the last two clauses of *p* (lines 240–241). Next, we consider slots with "="—the first four clauses (lines 206–209) take care of this, and the remainder of *p* can operate with the six slots cleared. Now we are left with a 10 × 10 table with three different rows and three columns. Table 7.2 depicts the situation after combining identical rows and columns.

TABLE 7.2

Simplified Precedence Relations

Input / Top	vns id ([{	)] } |	ff
vns id)] }		>^{a}	>^{b}
([{ |	<^{a}		<
ff	<^{c}	>	<^{c} >^{b}

^{a} Top and Input cannot be separated by a non-terminal.

^{b} Input cannot be a prefix functor.

^{c} Top cannot be a postfix functor.

The next six clauses of *p* (lines 211–222) take care of the six nonconflicting slots in Table 7.2. The procedure *restrict* (lines 265–271) is used to test and possibly disambiguate the type of a functor. The procedure performs set subtraction for sets given as lists; it will fail if the difference is an empty set.

Now we must try to resolve a conflict in the remaining slot. A closer look at the grammar allows a refinement of this slot (see Table 7.3). The 12th and 13th clauses of *p* (lines 229–238) are responsible for situations when the priorities differ. Again, we also attempt a disambiguation of types.

The 11th clause (lines 225–227) applies to functors with equal priorities. Table 7.4 shows the precedence relation in this case. We allow all combinations that can be disambiguated without analysing broader context to the left or to the right of the two functors. For example, an xfy functor f is weaker than an xfx functor g because the term

A f B g C

cannot be interpreted as

(A f B) g C

—g's left argument would have, incorrectly, the same priority as g.

The relation of Table 7.4 is implemented by the procedure *ff_p* (lines 319–332), which returns *lseq*, *gt* or *err*. Conflict resolution is performed by the procedure *res_confl* (lines 273–291), which also returns *lseq*, *gt* or *err* (*err* is later rejected by *do_rels* called in *p*). It also returns disambiguated—sometimes unchanged—functors.

If only one of the terminals is a mixed functor, we choose a nonconflicting interpretation by comparing slots in Table 7.4. This is done by

TABLE 7.3

A Refinement for Two Operators

Top \ Input	prefix	infix	postfix
prefix	<	< >	< >
infix	<	< >	< >
postfix		>	>

TABLE 7.4

Precedence Relations for Operators with Equal Priorities

Top's type \ Input's type	xfy	xfx	xf	yfx	yf	fy	fx
yfx				$>^a$	$>^a$		
xfx				$>^a$	$>^a$		
fx				$>^a$	$>^a$		
xfy	$<^a$	$<^a$	$<^a$			$<^b$	$<^b$
fy	$<^a$	$<^a$	$<^a$			$<^b$	$<^b$
yf				$>^b$	$>^b$		
xf				$>^b$	$>^b$		

[a] Top and Input must be separated by a non-terminal.
[b] Top and Input must not be separated by a non-terminal.

the procedure *match_rels* (lines 297–300). For two mixed functors we extract a subtable of relations for each possible pair of interpretations; see Table 7.5 (and lines 286–289). The situation is clear if all four slots are the same. Otherwise there are only four patterns which can be correct: when one of the rows or one of the columns contains two *err* slots. Details—in the procedure *res_mixed* (lines 302–317).

The procedure read(Term, SymbolTable) performs the two phases of the reader—see lines 65–69. It returns the symbol table with variables from this term. The table is used by the interactive driver (see Section

TABLE 7.5

The Subtable Template for Two Mixed Functors: the Binary and Unary Types Are Compared with Each Other

	TInpBin	TInpUn
TTopBin	RelBB	RelBU
TTopUn	RelUB	RelBB

7.4.2). If data are incorrect, the parser will stop on the first bad symbol and *read*/2 will skip characters up to the nearest full stop after this symbol (which may also be a full stop). The built-in procedure *read*/1 simply encapsulates *read*/2.

7.4.4. Grammar Preprocessor

The grammar rule preprocessor (lines 482–583 in Appendix A.4) operates according to the principles presented in Chapter 3. The list of lefthand side terminals (usually empty) is connected to the output variable of the lefthand side non-terminal. Calls on the procedure *terminal* (Section 3.1) are "pre-executed" for efficiency. By way of explanation, here are two examples. The rule

a → [p], b, [q, r], c.

is translated into

a([p | X], Z) :- b(X, [q, r | Y]), c(Y, Z).

The rule

a → b, [q, r], c, [s].

is translated into

a(X, Z) :- b(X, [q, r | Y]), c(Y, [s | Z]).

(The translation of a list of terminals is *true*, absorbed by the next item's translation; see *combine*, lines 540–542).

Conditions/actions (other than a single cut) are passed to the preprocessor as '{}'(C); see the procedure *maketerm* in the reader, lines 345–346). The functor '{}' is stripped off by the procedure *transl_item*, line 550.

Righthand sides separated by semicolons are preceded by a non-terminal defined as

'   dummy' → [].

This is necessary when alternatives start with different terminals. For example, the rules

a → [p], b.   and   a → [q], c.

would be translated with

a([p | Y], Z)   and   a([q | Y], Z)

as a lefthand side. Consequently the rule

a → [p], b; [q], c.

must be translated as

a(X, Z) ;- ' dummy' (X, [p | Y]), b(Y, Z) ;
     ' dummy' (X, [q | V]), c(V, Z).

For simplicity, this has been applied to all rules with alternatives.

7.4.5. Library

The library (Appendix A.4, lines 585–1002) contains definitions of about 20 built-in procedures (note that several simple procedures are also defined in the kernel file, appendix A.2). Their definitions in Chapter 5 can be treated as design documentation. Their implementation is largely straightforward. We shall comment on a few not quite obvious passages.

The procedures clause(Head, Body) and retract(Clause) are "backtrackable", i.e. can be used in failure-driven loops that generate or remove all matching clauses. Here is a description of the generator (the other procedure is programmed similarly). We are going to visit all clauses of a procedure and suspend execution each time we get to a matching one. This is achieved by setting up a recursive loop with its step distributed between two clauses (see the procedure *remcls*/7, lines 814–822). The first clause does the matching. Upon mismatch, we immediately proceed with the second clause, i.e. conclude the step. If the matching succeeds, the generator succeeds, too, but with a pending alternative. A failure later on resumes the second half of the step.

The procedures *write* and *writeq* both encapsulate the procedure out-term(Term, With_or_without_quotes) which first uses *numbervars* (lines 623–632) to bind all variables in Term, and next calls

outt(Term_after_numbervars, Context, With_or_without_quotes).

Context specifies the essential features of a functor whose argument is Term. If it is not an operator, or there is no external functor, then Context is fd(_, _). Otherwise, Context is fd(ff(Priority, Associativity), Dir). Term may be to the left (Dir = l) or to the right (Dir = r) of the functor. Associativity may be a(l) or a(r) for left- and right-associative functors, and na(l), na(r), or na(_) for non-associative functors. Context is tested by the procedure *outff*/5 (lines 933–935) to decide whether Term should be parenthesized to avoid ambiguity in the case of equal priorities. Actually, the test—performed by *agree* (lines 939–943)—is rather crude (see the previous section!): sometimes we overparenthesize. The parameter of *na* has only been added for homogeneity, but it could be used in a more subtle detection of non-ambiguous cases.

7.4.6. Translator

The translator of Prolog-10 into Toy-Prolog (Appendix A.4, lines 1004–1088) is invoked by the call

translate(SourceFileName, OutputFileName).

Commands are translated and also executed (deterministically), so that, for example, a declaration of an infix functor affects subsequent parts of the input program. The translator terminates (and succeeds) after reading in the unary clause

   end.

The program is quite easy to understand. Only the procedure *lookup* may require an explanation. The table pairs variables of the clause with consecutive integers, starting from 0. A variable is a key, so we must use the built-in procedure *eqvar* to locate variables already present in the table. The third parameter of the procedure *lookup* indicates the last number encountered (initially, -1), so that only a new variable requires one addition. A more simple-minded solution would be to keep only variables in the table, and count them during lookup. This would require at least $(n - 1) * n/2$ additions for a clause with n variables. (In Toy, integers are implemented in a particularly simple way, so this might fill the copy stack with many dead integers. Another possibility is to apply the procedure *numbervars*—inside *put*—to Head and Body jointly.

The translator outputs bare translations. It would be helpful to have source comments transferred to the translation, and to get source variable names paired with numbers (see Section 7.4.1). Try this exercise for yourself.

8 TWO CASE STUDIES

8.1. PLANNING

We shall consider planning with respect to a finite, usually small, set of **objects** to which simple **actions** from a finite, and also small, set are applicable. Objects constitute a closed "**world**". The **state** of the "world" is, by definition, the set of all **relationships** that hold between its objects; we also call these relationships **facts** about objects. As a result of an action, some relationships cease or begin to hold; we say that an action **deletes** or **adds** facts. A fact established by an action is also called a **goal achieved** by this action. Every action transforms one state into another. **Planning** consists in finding a sequence of actions that lead from a given **initial state** to a given **final state**.

As an example, we shall describe one of the so-called cube worlds. There are three cubes, *a, b, c,* and *floor*. All we can do with them is stack cubes on cubes or on the floor. There are two types of facts concerning a cube U and an object W: U is sitting on W, and U is clear (this means that nothing is sitting on U). The set of possible states is determined by naming all meaningless (i.e. impossible or forbidden) combinations of facts:

—A cube X sitting on a *clear* cube Y;
—A cube sitting on two different objects;
—Two different cubes sitting on the same cube;
—An object sitting on itself.

There is one kind of action: move a single clear block, either from another block onto the floor, or from an object onto another clear block (the object must differ from both blocks). As a result of moving X from Y onto Z, X is sitting on Z instead of Y, Y is clear (unless it is the floor), Z is not clear (unless it is the floor).

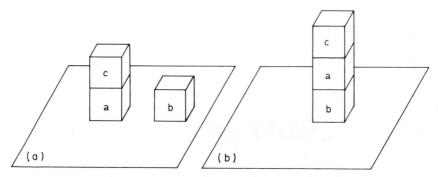

FIG. 8.1   (a) An initial state of the cubes world. (b) A final state of the cubes world.

Even in this microscopic world, planning may require some sophistication. It is reasonable to postulate that a desirable fact, once added, will never be deleted (otherwise we risk an infinite loop). However, let the initial state be that of Fig. 8.1a, described by a conjunction of five facts:

a on floor, b on floor, c on a, clear(b), clear(c).

Let the final state be that of Fig. 8.1b, described by a conjunction of two goals: c on a, a on b. The first goal is trivially achieved. To put a on b, though, we must remove c from a, i.e. destroy an already achieved goal. The simple strategy of achieving goals one by one (and freezing all relevant facts) would not work in this case.

In a more crowded "world", a state might comprise so many facts that its direct representation (as a list, say) would be impractical. Moreover, even a small change might require copying large data structures. Clausal representation is free from this disadvantage but it is unwieldy when a change must be undone, and of course planning is a trial–and–error process. What we need is a method of incrementally describing incremental changes, and making them easily undoable.

A state and an action determine the next state, if we assume that the action does not affect facts not mentioned explicitly in the description of the action's effects as added or deleted. Given an initial state and a plan, i.e. a sequence of actions, we can check whether a fact holds in the resulting final state. To undo an action, we remove it from the plan (in practice, this may be slightly more complicated).

For any particular planning problem, the initial state can be considered fixed. The final state should be given implicitly, as a conjunction of facts to be established by a plan we are going to find. This approach was taken by D. H. D. Warren in his remarkable planning program, WAR-PLAN.

In WARPLAN, world description is separated from the planning procedure (see Listing 8.1, pp. 221–223, lines 1–26, for the description of our cube world). Objects are given implicitly, in descriptions of actions and facts. Actions are defined by three procedures. The two-parameter procedure

    can(Action, Precondition)

serves as a catalogue—one clause per action; Precondition is a conjunction of facts that must hold for Action to be applicable. A conjunction is either a fact, or a pair of conjunctions constructed by the infix functor &, e.g. c on a & a on b.

Two other procedures,

    add(Fact, Action)
    del(Fact, Action)

give facts added and deleted by available actions (and, conversely, actions which can add or delete a fact). Impossible combinations of facts are listed in the procedure

    imposs(Conjunction)

In these four procedures, we can use variables instead of world objects to express general laws, e.g. "a clear cube U is sitting on a cube V":

    U on V & notequal(V, floor) & clear(U)

For efficiency, facts that hold in the initial state, and are unaffected by any action, are listed in the procedure

    always(Fact)

Other facts that hold in the initial state are supplied by the procedure

    given(InitialStateName, Fact)

The initial state is denoted by its name, e.g. *start*. A state derived from it by actions A1, ..., An is denoted by the term

    InitialStateName : A1 : ··· : An,

e.g.

    start : move(c,a, floor) : move(a, floor, b) : move(c, floor, a)

The planning program (Listing 8.2, pp. 224–226) operates independently of specific world descriptions. It assumes the presence of an appropriate data base whose coherence is the responsibility of the user.

The program begins with a conjunction of facts (i.e. the description of a desired final state) and the empty plan. In each step, the conjunction shrinks and/or the plan grows; successive intermediate states approximate the final state. Roughly speaking, the plan is constructed backwards: we look for preconditions of actions that achieve the final state, then for preconditions of actions that achieve those preconditions, etc. Unless a fact holds in an intermediate state, the program chooses an action that adds this fact, inserts the action into the current partial plan, removes the fact from the current conjunction and adds to it the action's preconditions.

A partial plan usually contains variables. For example, to achieve a on b, we use the action move(a, V, b), whose precondition includes the fact a on V (for an unknown V). Such variables require some care: the fact U on c may, in general, differ from a on V, even though the two terms are unifiable. We can either use the built-in procedure == to compare facts, or temporarily instantiate their variables (by the built-in procedure *numbervars*) prior to the comparison.

In addition to the current conjunction and plan, the program maintains a conjunction of desirable facts already planned for. No newly inserted action can destroy any of these *preserved* facts.

The program is amazingly concise. In Warren's original paper it was accompanied by many pages of detailed considerations. Hence, the absence of proper comments in the program text. Below we shall present, in our own words, some indispensable technical explanations.

The main planning routine, *plan*, is called only if the final state description is not inconsistent (lines 10–13), i.e. if it does not imply one of the impossible combinations of facts. *plan* has three input parameters—facts to be achieved, facts already achieved (initially *true*; see line 13) and the current plan—and one output parameter, the final plan. The procedure *solve* is called for each fact of the initial goal list (see lines 30–32). It has five parameters: a fact to be established, preserved facts, the current plan, preserved facts after *solve* has succeeded and the new plan.

Every clause of *solve* accounts for a different status of the fact (lines 35–39). It may be always true; it may be true by virtue of general laws external to "worlds" (e.g. equality or inequality of objects will be checked by this clause); it may hold in the state described by the current plan (to preserve it, we add it to the facts planned for; see lines 83–84); otherwise (the last clause) we choose an action and call *achieve*.

The procedure *achieve* (lines 41–49) tries to apply a given action, i.e. to insert it into the current plan (as the last action, or as the last but one, etc.). The action U is applicable if it deletes none of the preserved facts, and if its precondition is consistent with these facts and if a plan for achieving this precondition can be constructed. Notice that possible additions to P (preserved facts) made by the recursive call on *plan* are invisible to *achieve*: they are only needed "locally" during the construction of the intermediate plan T1. The additional call on *preserves* (line 45) is necessary because of variables in the plan. For example, the action move(b, a, W) need not delete the fact clear(c), so *preserves* lets it through; however, *plan* may instantiate W as c, and this ought to cause a failure.

If, for any of these reasons, the action U cannot be added at the end of the plan, *achieve* will try to undo the last action V and insert U earlier into the plan. This is only possible if V does not delete the fact to be added by U. The procedure *retrace* (lines 65–73) removes from the set of preserved facts all facts that may be established by V but are different from V's preconditions. Specifically, it removes the facts added by V (lines 68–69) and the facts that constitute the precondition of V (lines 70–71)—the latter facts will be re-inserted by *append* (see lines 66, 86–87)[1].

A few comments on the remaining procedures. A fact holds after executing a given plan (lines 52–55), if it is *given* or added by one of the actions, and preserved by all subsequent actions (if any). Two conjunctions, C and P, are inconsistent (lines 76–78, 93–97) if C&P contains all facts of an impossible combination S, except those which—like *not-equal*—are tested "metaphysically" (see line 95). For disjoint C, S this cannot be the case—hence the call on *intersect* which is relatively cheap. Two object descriptions X and Y, with variables instantiated by *number-vars* in *mkground* (line 101), may refer to the same object if X = Y or X = 'V'(_) or Y = 'V'(_)—see line 99. The procedure *elem* (lines 89–91) extracts single facts from a nested conjunction; it can be used both to test membership, and to generate facts.

Now that you have acquainted yourself with the planning program, try it on a richer world. Here is the world of a robot that walks around several rooms, moves some boxes, etc. (see Listing 8.1, lines 33–101). Figure 8.2 depicts an initial state of this world. There are six points, five rooms, four doors, three boxes, a light switch, and the robot. Nine types of facts are considered: at(Object, Point), on(Object, Box), nextto(Object1, Object2), pushable(Object), inroom(Object, Room), locinroom(Point, Room), connects(Door, Room1, Room2), status(Lightswitch, OnOff), onfloor—the latter characterizes the robot. Only the robot performs actions—there are seven of them (see lines 64–77).

---

[1] The special treatment of V's preconditions is necessary for actions which add facts listed among their own preconditions. If *retrace* simply deleted V's effects, such preconditions could be lost from the list of facts which must be preserved by U, and those parts of the plan which achieve "locally desirable" goals could inadvertently be destroyed in the insertion process.

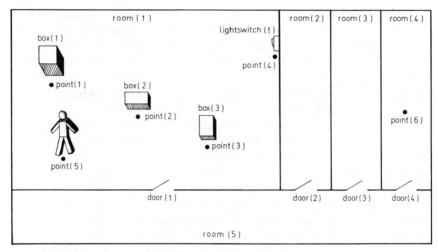

FIG. 8.2   "STRIPS" world.

The procedure *del* merits a comment. It is supposed to delete more than it should—we count on *add* to straighten the situation out. For example, the action turnon(S) removes whatever status of S may be recorded (line 54); "a moment later" it adds the appropriate fact (line 39). The clauses in lines 49–50 say that a moved object X is no longer "next to" anything. However, this does not apply to the robot manipulating a box (lines 46–48)—*del* fails, i.e. the fact is *not* deleted.

For sample results, see Listing 8.3, p. 227.

Although WARPLAN is a feat of ingenuity, there is much more to planning than it does account for. For one thing, the plans it generates need not be optimal, i.e. contain the least possible number of actions. For example, action U in *achieve* (lines 47–49) is executed when it preserves V's precondition P; if we checked that U establishes P, we might delete actions which had been planned to establish it. A much more profound problem: in general, it is likely that conditional or iterative plans will be required, rather than sequential (the robot explores the world).

Even with these (and other) limitations, and despite exponential time complexity, WARPLAN is an excellent tool for experiments with rigorous world descriptions. One example is the world of a robot that assembles cars. Warren has also demonstrated how his program can be used to compile arithmetic expressions into machine code (the code is treated as a plan for placing some values in some registers).

```
1   % % % % % %   WARPLAN -- cube worlds
2
3   :- op( 50, xfx, on ).
4
5   add( U on W, move( U, V, W ) ) :-
6   add( clear( V ), move( U, V, W ) ).
7
8   del( U on Z, move( U, V, W ) ) :-
9   del( clear( W ), move( U, V, W ) ).
10
11  can( move( U, V, floor ),
12      U on V & notequal( U, floor ) & clear( U ) ).
13  can( move( U, V, W ),
14      clear( W ) & U on V & notequal( U, W ) & clear( U ) ).
15
16  imposs( X on Y & clear( Y ) ).
17  imposs( X on Y & X on Z & notequal( Y, Z ) ).
18  imposs( X on Z & Y on Z & notequal( Z, floor ) & notequal( X, Y ) ).
19  imposs( X on X ).
20
21  % The three blocks problem.
22  given( start, a on floor ).
23  given( start, b on floor ).
24  given( start, c on a ).
25  given( start, clear( b ) ).
26  given( start, clear( c ) ).
27
28  :- plans( c on a & a on b, start ).
29  :- plans( a on b & b on c, start ).
30  :- delop( 'on' ), redefine.
31  % -----------------------------------------
32
33  % % % % % %   WARPLAN -- the STRIPS problem
34
35  add( at( robot, F ), goto1( F, R ) ).
36  add( nextto( robot, X ), goto2( X, R ) ).
37  add( nextto( X, Y ), pushto( X, Y, R ) ).
38  add( nextto( Y, X ), pushto( X, Y, R ) ).
```

LISTING 8.1 WARPLAN—Examples of worlds. (*continued*)

```prolog
39   add( status( S, on ) ), turnon( S ) ) ).
40   add( on( robot, B ) ), climbon( B ) ) ).
41   add( onfloor, climboff( B ) ) ).
42   add( inroom( robot, R2 ), gothrough( D, R1, R2 ) ) ).
43
44   del( at( X, Z ), U ) :-          moved( X, U ) ).
45   del( nextto( Z, robot ), U ) :- !, del( nextto( robot, Z ), U ) ).
46   del( nextto( robot, X ), pushto( X, Y, R ) ) :- !, fail.
47   del( nextto( robot, B ), climbon( B ) ) :- !, fail.
48   del( nextto( robot, B ), climboff( B ) ) :- !, fail.
49   del( nextto( X, Z ), U ) :-      moved( X, U ) ).
50   del( nextto( Z, X ), U ) :-      moved( X, U ) ),
51   del( on( X, Z ), U ) :-          moved( ,X, U ) ).
52   del( onfloor, climbon( B ) ) ).
53   del( inroom( robot, Z ), gothrough( D, R1, R2 ) ) ).
54   del( status( S, Z ), turnon( S ) ) )
55
56   moved( robot, goto1( F, R ) ) ).
57   moved( robot, goto2( X, R ) ) ).
58   moved( robot, pushto( X, Y, R ) ) ).
59   moved( X, pushto( X, Y, R ) ) ).
60   moved( robot, climbon( B ) ) ).
61   moved( robot, climboff( B ) ) ).
62   moved( robot, gothrough( D, R1, R2 ) ) ).
63
64   can( goto1( F, R ),
65   locinroom( F, R ) & inroom( robot, R ) & onfloor ) ).
66   can( goto2( X, R ),
67   inroom( X, R ) & inroom( robot, R ) & onfloor ) ).
68   can( turnon( lightswitch(S) ),
69   on( robot, box(1) ) & nextto( box(1), lightswitch(S) ) ) ).
70   can( pushto( X, Y, R ),
71   pushable( X ) & inroom( Y, R ) & inroom( robot, R ) &
72   nextto( robot, X ) & onfloor ) ).
73   can( gothrough( D, R1, R2 ),
74   connects( D, R1, R2 ) & inroom( robot, R1 ) &
75   nextto( robot, D ) & onfloor ) ).
76   can( climboff( box(B) ), on( robot, box(B) ) ) ).
```

```
77   can( climbon( box(B) ) , nextto( robot, box(B) ) ) & onfloor ) .
78
79   always( inroom( D, R1 ) )             :-  always( connects( D, R1, R2 ) ) .
80   always( connects( D, R2, R1 ) )       :-  connects1( D, R1, R2 ) ) .
81   always( connects( D, R1, R2 ) )       :-  connects1( D, R1, R2 ) ) .
82   always( pushable( box(N) ) ) .
83   always( locinroom( point(N), room(1) ) )      :-  range( N, 1, 5 ) ) .
84   always( locinroom( point(6), room(4) ) ) .
85   always( inroom( lightswitch(1), room(1) ) ) .
86   always( at( lightswitch(1), point(4) ) ) .
87
88   connects1( door(N), room(N), room(5) )        :-  range( N, 1, 4 ) ) .
89
90   range( M, M, _ ) .
91   range( M, L, N ) :-
92       L < N,  L1 is L + 1,  range( M, L1, N ) .
93
94   imposs( at( X, Y ) & at( X, Z ) & notequal( Y, Z ) ) .
95
96   given( strips1, at( box(N), point(N) ) )      :-  range( N, 1, 3 ) .
97   given( strips1, at( robot, point(5) ) ) .
98   given( strips1, inroom( box(N), room(1) ) )   :-  range( N, 1, 3 ) .
99   given( strips1, onfloor ) .
100  given( strips1, status( lightswitch(1), off ) ) .
101  given( strips1, inroom( robot, room(1) ) ) .
102
103  % A few tests.
104  :- plans( at( robot, point(5) ), strips1 ) .
105  :- plans( at( robot, point(1) ) & at( robot, point(2) ), strips1) .
106  :- plans( at( robot, point(4) ), strips1) .
107  :- plans( status( lightswitch(1), on ), strips1) .
108  :- plans( at( robot, point(6) ), strips1) .
109  :- plans( nextto( box(1), box(2) ) & nextto( box(3), box(2) ), strips1) .
```

LISTING 8.1 *(Continued)*

WARPLAN - A System for Generating Plans

```
1   % % % % %
2   % % % % %
3   % % % % %
4
5   % % % The general planner.
6   %
7   :- op( 200, xfy, & ), op( 100, xfx, : ).
8
9   % Generate and output a plan.
10  plans( C, _ ) :-
11      inconsistent( C, true ), !, write( "Impossible." ), nl.
12  plans( C, T ) :-
13      plan( C, true, T, T1 ), output( T1 ), !.
14  plans( _, _ ) :-
15      write( "Can''t do this." ), nl.
16
17  output( Xs::X ) :-
18      numbervars( Xs::X, 1, _ ), output1( Xs ), output2( X, "." ), nl.
19  output( _ ) :- write( "Nothing need be done." ), nl.
20
21  output1( Xs::X ) :- !, output1( Xs ), output2( X, " :" ).
22  output1( X ) :- output2( X, " :" ).
23
24  output2( Item, Funct ) :- write( Item ), write( Funct ), nl.
25
26  % Main planning routine.
27  % Definitions of 'always', 'imposs', 'given', 'can', 'add', 'del' --
28  % see specific world descriptions.
29
30  plan( X&C, P, T, T2 ) :-
31      !, solve( X, P, T, P1, T1 ), plan( C, P1, T1, T2 ).
32  plan( X, P, T, T1 ) :- solve( X, P, T, _, T1 ).
33
34  % Ways of solving a goal.
35  solve( X, P, T, P, T ) :- always( X ).
36  solve( X, P, P, P, T ) :- X.
```

```
37  solve( X, F, T, F1, T )  :-  holds( X, T ),   and( X, F, F1 ).
38  solve( X, F, T, X&F, T1 )  :-
39      add( X, U ) ,  achieve( X, U, F, T, T1 ).
40
41  % Methods of achieving a goal
42  % by extension:
43  achieve( _, U, F, T, T1:U )  :-
44      preserves( U, F ),  can( U, C ),  not inconsistent( C, F ),
45      plan( C, F, T, T1 ),  preserves( U, F ).
46  % by insertion:
47  achieve( X, U, F, T1:V, T1:V )  :-
48      preserved( X, U ),  retrace( F, V, F1 ),
49      achieve( X, F1, T, T1 ),  preserved( X, U ).
50
51  % Check if a fact holds in a given state.
52  holds( X, _:=V )  :-  add( X, V ).
53  holds( X, T:V )  :-
54      !,  preserved( X, V ),  holds( X, T ),  preserved( X, V ).
55  holds( X, T )  :-  given( T, X ).
56
57  % Prove that an action preserves a fact.
58  preserves( U, X&C )  :-  preserved( X, U ),  preserves( U, C ).
59  preserves( _, true ).
60
61  preserved( X, V )  :-  check( pres( X, V ) ).
62  pres( X, V )  :-  mkground( X&V ),  not del( X, V ).
63
64  % Retracing a goal already achieved.
65  retrace( F, V, F2 )  :-
66      can( V, C ),  retrace( F, V, C, F1 ),  append( C, F1, F2 ).
67
68  retrace( X&F, V, C, F1 )  :-
69      add( Y, V ),  X == Y,  !,  retrace( F, V, C, F1 ).
70  retrace( X&F, V, C, F1 )  :-
71      elem( Y, C ),  X == Y,  !,  retrace( F, V, C, F1 ).
```

LISTING 8.2   WARPLAN—The general planner. (*continued*)

```prolog
72  retrace( X&P, V, C, X&P1 ) :-    retrace( P, V, C, P1 ).
73  retrace( true, _, _, true ).
74
75  % Inconsistency with a goal already achieved.
76  inconsistent( C, P ) :-
77      mkground( C&P ), imposs( S ),
78      check( intersect( C, S ) ), implied( S, C&P ), !.
79
80  % % % Utilities.
81  % -------------
82
83  and( X, P, P ) :-    elem( Y, P ),    X == Y,    !.
84  and( X, P, X&P ).
85
86  append( X&C, P, X&P1 )    :-    !,    append( C, P, P1 ).
87  append( X, P, X&P ).
88
89  elem( X, Y&_ )   :-    elem( X, Y ).
90  elem( X, _&C )   :-    !,    elem( X, C ).
91  elem( X, X ).
92
93  implied( S1&S2, C )   :-    !,    implied( S1, C ),    implied( S2, C ).
94  implied( X, C )   :-    elem( X, C ).
95  implied( X, _ )   :-    X.
96
97  intersect( S1, S2 )   :-    elem( X, S1 ),    elem( X, S2 ).
98
99  notequal( X, Y )   :-    not X==Y,    not X='V'(_),    not Y='V'('') .
100
101 mkground( X )   :-    numbervars(X, 0, _ ).
```

LISTING 8.2 (*Continued*)

```
1
2     c on a  &  a on b
3
4     start :
5     move( c, a, floor ) :
6     move( a, floor, b ) :
7     move( c, floor, a ).
8
9     a on b  &  b on c
10
11    start :
12    move( c, a, floor ) :
13    move( b, floor, c ) :
14    move( a, floor, b ).
15
16    at( robot, point(5) )
17
18    Nothing need be done.
19
20    at( robot, point(1) )  &  at( robot, point(2) )
21
22    Impossible.
23
24    at( robot, point(4) )
25
26    strips1 :
27    goto1( point( 4 ), room( 1 ) ).
28
29    status( lightswitch(1), on )
30
31    strips1 :
32    goto2( box( 1 ), room( 1 ) ) :
33    pushto( box( 1 ), lightswitch( 1 ), room( 1 ) ) :
34    climbon( box( 1 ) ) :
35    turnon( lightswitch( 1 ) ).
36
37    at( robot, point(6) )
38
39    strips1 :
40    goto2( door( 1 ), room( 1 ) ) :
41    gothrough( door( 1 ), room( 1 ), room( 5 ) ) :
42    goto2( door( 4 ), room( 5 ) ) :
43    gothrough( door( 4 ), room( 5 ), room( 4 ) ) :
44    goto1( point( 6 ), room( 4 ) ).
45
46    nextto( box(1), box(2) )  &  nextto( box(3), box(2) )
47
48    strips1 :
49    goto2( box( 1 ), room( 1 ) ) :
50    pushto( box( 1 ), box( 2 ), room( 1 ) ) :
51    goto2( box( 3 ), room( 1 ) ) :
52    pushto( box( 3 ), box( 2 ), room( 1 ) ).
```

LISTING 8.3   WARPLAN—Sample results.

BIBLIOGRAPHIC NOTES

WARPLAN is described in Warren (1974). Our presentation has been greatly influenced by this excellent paper. The program we publish here is a slightly cleaned-up version of the text given in Coelho *et al.* (1980), where all the mentioned examples of worlds can also be found. The robot's world was introduced by Fikes and Nilsson (1971) as a test case for their system STRIPS; Warren (1974) used it to compare the performance of the two systems. An extension of WARPLAN, intended for generating conditional plans, was described in Warren (1976).

8.2. PROLOG AND RELATIONAL DATA BASES

In this section, we shall be primarily concerned with data bases in the limited sense: a **data base** is a purposefully structured collection of stored data, often pertaining to an organisation (e.g. a bank, factory, university, warehouse). In a **relational** data base all data are conceptually grouped into relations, which are usually depicted as rectangular tables as in Fig. 8.3. A column in the table is called an **attribute** and referred to by a name, e.g. *dno*. All values of an attribute belong to a common **domain**, e.g. each salary belongs to integers. A relation is a set of **tuples** (table rows) which

EMP

empno	name	dno	salary	mgrno
13	Miller	0	1 500	19
21	Jones	1	1 000	13
35	Brown	1	1 000	21
38	White	1	800	35
43	Smith	2	1 200	13
61	Thomas	1	850	21
89	Morgan	1	1 050	35
42	Miller	1	850	35

DEPT

dno	name	mgrno
1	PublicRelations	21
2	Security	43

FIG. 8.3   Contents of a relational data base.

consist of attribute values, e.g.

< 38, White, 1, 800, 35 >.

Tuples belong to the set described by a **relation schema** which specifies names, domains and order of attributes, e.g.

EMP < integer empno, string name, integer dno,
                     integer salary, integer mgrno >
DEPT < integer dno, string name, integer mgrno >

Two tuples may share the value of an attribute, and thus implicitly fall into one group; for example, Brown and Thomas are both subordinates of a manager whose number is 21.

A relation can be changed by inserting, deleting or updating some of its tuples. These operations are referred to as **data manipulation**.

A query to the data base is answered by enumerating tuples of the resulting relation (or by computing an **aggregate function**, such as "average" or "total", over these tuples). Most queries are expressible in terms of the following primitive operations on relations.

—**Selection** chooses tuples for which a given condition holds; for example, we can select from EMP those employees of department 1 who earn over 900 (there are three such tuples).
—**Projection** neglects some attributes and (possibly) reorders the remaining ones; for example, we can project EMP over *name*, *empno*, and *salary*, to get

< Miller, 13, 1500 >

and seven other triples.
—**Join** of two relations A, B forms a new relation. It consists of those concatenations of tuples from A with tuples from B, for which a given condition holds. For example, the join of EMP and DEPT, such that department numbers coincide, consists of the tuple

< 21, Jones, 1, 1000, 13, 1, PublicRelations, 21 >

and six other 8-tuples.
—Unconditional join is a **product**; for EMP and DEPT the product consists of sixteen 8-tuples.
—Finally, set operations, namely **union**, **intersection** and **difference**, can be applied to two relations whose corresponding attributes belong to the same domain, i.e. whose schemata differ only in names.

Much of this conceptual framework is naturally translated into Prolog. A relation is modelled as a procedure made of unit clauses which correspond to tuples, for example:

> 'EMP'(13, 'Miller', 0, 1500, 19).
> 'EMP'(21, 'Jones', 1, 1000, 13).
> etc.

(we use quotes to prevent capitalized names from being treated as variables). To change a relation, we use the built-in procedures *assert* and *retract*.

Primitive operations on relations are expressed in terms of procedure calls. For example, the procedure

> s(Empno, Name, Dno, Salary, Mgrno) :-
>   'EMP'(Empno, Name, Dno, Salary, Mgrno),
>   Dno = 1, Salary > 900.

can be used to generate all tuples for employees of department 1 who earn over 900 (i.e. to implement selection):

> :- s(E, N, D, S, M), write((E, N, D, S, M)), nl, fail.

Better still, we can substitute 1 for Dno and remove the test:

> s(E, N, 1, S, M) :- 'EMP'(E, N, 1, S, M), S > 900.

The procedure **p** can be used to implement projection:

> p(Name, Empno, Salary) :-
>   'EMP'(Empno, Name, _, Salary, _).

The composition of these two operations can be expressed in Prolog quite succintly:

> s_then_p(Name, Empno, Salary) :-
>   'EMP'(Empno, Name, 1, Salary, _), Salary > 900.

Or we can put this directly into a query:

> :- 'EMP'(E, N, 1, S, _), S > 900,
>   write((N, E, S)), nl, fail.

Finally, here is the join of EMP and DEPT over coinciding department numbers:

> j(Empno, NameE, DnoE, Salary, MgrnoE, DnoE, NameD,
> MgrnoD) :-
>   'EMP'(Empno, NameE, DnoE, Salary, MgrnoE),
>   'DEPT'(DnoE, NameD, MgrnoD).

All these operations are neatly explained in terms of static interpretation of procedures (try for yourself!). Set operations are even more straightforward. Let $a(X_1, \ldots, X_n)$ and $b(X_1, \ldots, X_n)$ denote generators of tuples, such as 'DEPT'(D, N, M) or p(N, E, S). We have

aUNIONb($X_1, \ldots, X_n$) :-
    a($X_1, \ldots, X_n$) ; b($X_1, \ldots, X_n$).
aINTERSECTIONb($X_1, \ldots, X_n$) :-
    a($X_1, \ldots, X_n$) , b($X_1, \ldots, X_n$).
aDIFFERENCEb($X_1, \ldots, X_n$) :-
    a($X_1, \ldots, X_n$) , not b($X_1, \ldots, X_n$).

Queries which involve only primitive operations can be answered without actually creating the resulting relation. Its tuples can be generated by a failure-driven loop and displayed immediately. To compute an aggregate function, however, we need the whole attribute (column) at once. We can construct it by means of the procedure *bagof* (see Section 4.2.4); for example:

:- bagof(Salary, 'EMP'(_, _, _, Salary, _), Salaries),
    max_of(Salaries, MaxSal), write(MaxSal), nl.

Sometimes we can also use *bagof* for efficiency. For example, we look for employees of department 1 who earn no more than a 1000 and who are FTU members since at least 1980:

:- 'EMP'(E, N, 1, S, _), S =< 1000,
    'FTU'(E, _, _, DateJoined), DateJoined =< 1980,
    write((E, N)), nl, fail.

With those implementations of Prolog which do not support clause indexing, the entire relation FTU would be scanned many times. Instead, we can precompute the necessary set:

:- bagof(Empno, ('FTU'(Empno, _, _, DateJoined),
              DateJoined =< 1980), FTUMembers),
    'EMP'(E, N, 1, S, _), S =< 1000,
    member(E, FTUMembers), write((E, N)), nl, fail.

There are queries which cannot be expressed as a composition of selections, projections, joins and aggregate functions. A classical example: find every employee who earns more than at least one of her/his superiors. The relation "is a superior of" is inherently transitive, but we can only express the relations "is an immediate manager of", "is an immediate manager of an immediate manager of" etc. In Prolog, however, the problem is easily solved. For example, we can define a procedure to generate managers' salaries:

```
mgr_sal( Mgrno, Salary ) :- 'EMP'( Mgrno, _, _, Salary, _ ).
mgr_sal( Mgrno, Salary ) :-
    'EMP'( Mgrno, _, _, _, MgrMgrno ),
    mgr_sal( MgrMgrno, Salary ).
```

(try to rewrite it so as to avoid repeated pass through EMP). From the standpoint of the caller, this generator is indistinguishable from those made of unit clauses. The query can be written as follows:

```
:- 'EMP'( Empno, _, _, Salary, Mgrno ),
    once( ( mgr_sal( Mgrno, MgrSal ), MgrSal < Salary ) ),
    write( Empno ), nl, fail.
```

A relation which is computed rather than stored (e.g. s, p, s_then_p, j above) is called a **view** in the relational data base terminology. A view results from primitive operations on stored relations—also indirectly, via other views—and it changes as those relations change (and conversely, a change in a view might influence those relations—but this poses quite nontrivial problems). The relation *mgr_sal,* however, can only be obtained by embedding primitive operations in a host programming language, furnished with recursion or iteration. An important advantage of Prolog is its ability to express tuples, views, and special programs in the same language. In particular, it offers a possibility of enforcing **integrity constraints**—application-specific conditions of the coherence of data. Constraints should be tested prior to any change to a relation. For example, we can use this procedure to insert only correct tuples:

```
insert( Tuple ) :-
    correct_insert( Tuple ), !, assertz( Tuple ).
insert( Tuple ) :- signal_violation( Tuple ).
correct_insert( 'EMP'( E, _, D, _, M ) ) :-
    !, E =\= M, 'DEPT'( D, _, _ ).    % there is such a dept
correct_insert( _ ).                  % others are OK
```

On the whole, Prolog is a powerful tool for data base applications. Admittedly, there is more to data base systems than our presentation suggests. For one thing, the size of a real data base may far exceed the capacity of any existing Prolog implementation. The model described in Chapter 6 ought to be augmented: clauses would be stored on disk and handled by standard or specialized access methods. Second, every practical data base implementation should address problems such as concurrent execution of users' commands, recovery after hardware failures, etc., etc. There are no ready solutions in Prolog but presumably they can be programmed into it.

Surprisingly, Prolog is, in a sense, too strong, too unrestricted. For example, to ensure the conformance of a tuple with the relation schema, some form of type checking is required, presumably as explicit tests. Unrestrained use of assert/retract may also ruin the integrity of a data base in other ways. Consequently, Prolog should rather be considered a tool for implementing more restricted user interfaces: queries and commands in a user language are analysed (types checked, integrity ensured, etc.), and only then translated into Prolog.

A particularly attractive option would be to query the data base in a natural language. Several encouraging small experiments have been carried out. At the moment, though, this is much more a research problem in its own right than a generally available programming technique.

Relational data languages, notably Sequel and Query-by-Example, provide syntactic sugar for relation schema definitions, data manipulation and queries (involving Boolean expressions and compositions of primitive relational operations). In contrast with natural language interfaces, a Prolog implementation of a relational data language is a programming task of moderate complexity.

We shall now present Toy-Sequel, a relational data language patterned after Sequel and implemented in Prolog (see Listing 8.4). With the exception of aggregate functions, expressions in tuple specifications and some exotic features, it supports all that is essential in Sequel. Extensions are relatively easy to introduce (we left them out to make the program shorter). To give the flavour of the language, here is an annotated conversation with our program, initiated by the call

```
:- toysequel.
```

To begin with, we specify a few relation schemas:

```
create EMP < string name, integer salary, integer dno >.
create DEPT < integer dno, string manager >.
create BoardMembers < string name, string position,
                      integer seniority >.
```

Now we insert some tuples:

```
into EMP insert < "Brown", 1000, 1 >, < "White", 800, 1 >,
                < "Miller", 850, 1 >, < "Barry", 900, 2 >,
                < "Thomas", 850, 1 >, < "Morgan", 1050, 1 >.
into DEPT insert < 1, "Jones" >, < 2, "Smith" >.
```

We can ask what relations the data base contains; Toy-Sequel displays their names (its responses are italicized):

relations.
BoardMembers
DEPT
EMP

What is the schema of EMP?

relation EMP.
string name
integer salary
integer dno

A select expression determines a set of tuples. They may be displayed. For example, who in departments other than 2 earns at least 1000?

select from EMP tuples < name, salary >
    where dno < > 2 and salary > = 1000.
Brown 1000
Morgan 1050

Or they may be inserted elsewhere:

into EMP insert
    select from DEPT tuples < manager, 1000, dno >.

In the absence of "where ...", the condition is taken as true.
    Both managers have the salary 1000. We can given Smith a raise:

update EMP so that salary = 1200 where name = "Smith".

Fire Barry:

from EMP delete tuples where name = "Barry".

If several relations are involved, e.g. in a join, attribute names may be ambiguous. To disambiguate, qualify them with relation names. For example:

select from EMP, DEPT tuples < name, EMP_dno, manager >
    where EMP_dno = DEPT_dno.

(Actually, EMP_dno may be replaced with dno: an unqualified attribute name is qualified with the leftmost appropriate relation name.)
    A relation may be accessed in several places at once. For example, to compare salaries of different employees we need the product of EMP by EMP. We must give one of the occurrences an alias name and so allow

unambiguous references to attribute values. The following query joins the relations EMP, DEPT and EMP alias Mgr, to find employees who earn more than their (immediate) manager:

> select from EMP, DEPT, Mgr = EMP tuples < EMP_name >
> where EMP_dno = DEPT_dno
> and DEPT_manager = Mgr_name
> and Mgr_salary < EMP_salary.
> *Morgan*

Again, the qualification with EMP is superfluous, as well as the qualification of *manager*.

A similar condition can be used to give a raise of half the difference in salaries to those who earn over 100 less than their manager:

> update EMP using DEPT, Mgr = EMP
> so that salary = EMP_salary + (Mgr_salary − EMP_salary)/2
>
> where EMP_dno = DEPT_dno
> and manager = Mgr_name
> and Mgr_salary > EMP_salary + 100.

Two miscellaneous queries. Find employees whose names do not begin with M:

> select from EMP tuples < name >
> where name < "M" or name > = "N".

(five of them). And find EMP tuples with a nonexistent department number—this is a kind of (manual...) integrity checking:

> select from EMP tuples < name, salary, dno > where
> not < dno > in select from DEPT tuples < dno >.

in denotes set membership. The name *dno* in the nested select expression pertains to DEPT.

Time to finish. The relation BoardMembers will not be necessary, after all:

> cancel BoardMembers.

Store the data base in a file:

> dump to AAA.

(next time we shall begin with

> load from AAA.

and resume at this point). Finally, return control to Prolog:

stop.

We shall not go into details of the Toy-Sequel interpreter. The rationale for its design was given above; the program is (almost) self-documenting. The following remarks account for a few central technical decisions.

The main procedure, *toysequel* (lines 4–7 in the listing), repeatedly reads and executes commands. The procedure *getcommand* (lines 9–11) returns a Prolog goal, which is the translation of a command, and a flag. The flag remains uninstantiated if the command is correct, otherwise it is instantiated as *error*. The procedure *docommand* (lines 13–14) executes a correct command's translation, and does nothing in the case of errors.

A command is processed in three phases. The text, terminated with a dot, is read in (lines 32–43) and then passed through a scanner, implemented as a metamorphosis grammar (lines 45–84). It classifies tokens as names, strings, integers and single non-alphanumeric characters. A list of tokens goes to the command compiler—a metamorphosis grammar which is the core of the interpreter. The grammar consists of 11 parts, one for each Toy-Sequel command (see lines 113–123).

All commands, except *load* and *stop*, manipulate the relation catalogue. The catalogue is implemented as a three-parameter procedure 'r e l', with a unit clause for each relation schema. A schema stores the name of a relation, a generator of this relation's tuples and a "frame" of symbol table entries linking attribute names and types to variables in the generator (see lines 131–141). For example, the command

create EMP< string name, integer salary, integer dno >.

adds the clause

'r e l'('EMP', ' EMP'(Name, Salary, Dno),
    [attr(name, string, Name), attr(salary, integer, Salary),
    attr(dno, integer, Dno)]).

Blanks are added to relation names in generators to make conflicts with other procedures less plausible.

The command processors for *select*, *insert*, *delete* and *update* maintain a symbol table—a stack of frames taken from the catalogue. For example, attribute names in the command

select from EMP, Mgr = EMP, DEPT
    tuples < name, Mgr_dno, manager >
    where dno = DEPT_dno and manager = Mgr_name
               and salary > Mgr_salary.

will be looked for in the following symbol table (see lines 208–223, and 96–102):

```
[ 'EMP' : [ attr( name,  string, NameEMP ),
            attr( salary, integer, SalaryEMP ),
            attr( dno, integer, DnoEMP ) ],
  'Mgr' : [ attr( name,  string, NameMgr ),
            attr( salary, integer, SalaryMgr ),
            attr( dno, integer, DnoMgr ) ],
  'DEPT' : [ attr( dno, integer, DnoDEPT ),
             attr( manager, string, ManagerDEPT ) ] ]
```

(Nested select expressions would push their own frames onto this stack— see line 277.)

The product of these three relations will be generated by the following calls retrieved from the catalogue:

```
' EMP'( NameEMP, SalaryEMP, DnoEMP ),
' EMP'( NameMgr, SalaryMgr, DnoMgr ),
' DEPT'( DnoDEPT, ManagerDEPT )
```

The condition will be translated into a Prolog goal (see lines 236–237, 239–362). The goal will be executed immediately after the generators (lines 166–168). Attribute names in the condition will be translated into variables from the symbol table. Thus,

salary > Mgr_salary

will become

SalaryEMP > SalaryMgr

The "equalities"

DnoEMP = DnoDEPT, ManagerDEPT = NameMgr

will be processed at compile time, by binding variables together (line 318), so that actually only six different variables will occur in the generators.

The tuple pattern (lines 225–234) will also contain variables from the symbol table:

[NameEMP, DnoMgr, ManagerDEPT]

One such tuple will be displayed in every step of the failure-driven loop (lines 166–168).

A construction that would certainly benefit from a more detailed explanation is *update*. We shall comment on the example shown in the listing (lines 396–411):

> update EMP using DEPT, Mgr = EMP
> so that salary = salary + (Mgr_salary − salary) / 5
> where salary < Mgr_salary − 1000 and Mgr_name = manager
> and DEPT_dno = dno and not< Mgr_name > in
> select from BoardMembers tuples < name >.

First, two copies of the stack frame are created, and two call patterns (OldTup and NewTup):

> ' EMP'(Name, Salary, Dno)
> ' EMP'(NewName, NewSalary, NewDno)

Now, *makemodlist* creates a raw modification list:

> [modif(attr(name, string, Name), NewName, ModName),
>   modif(attr(salary, integer, Salary), NewSalary, ModSalary),
>   modif(attr(dno, integer, Dno), NewDno, ModDno)]

A symbol table is constructed, first a frame for EMP (note that *old* attribute values will be retrieved and used), next for DEPT and EMP (with the alias name Mgr). During the construction of Modifications (lines 420–421, 410), the raw list is changed by *findmname* (lines 454–465, 434): ModSalary is instantiated as true (line 462) to note that the salary will be modified. Finally, *closemodlist* (lines 447–452, 422) binds together variables that stand for unmodified attributes, i.e. Name with NewName and Dno with NewDno. Also, equalities in lines 398–399 cause two other pairs of variables to be bound together (see line 318).

A comment on error treatment. Incorrect data do not terminate processing. Instead, the procedure *ancestor* instantiates the variable Errflag (lines 5, 484, 488)—this prevents the command from being executed (lines 13–14), but the analysis continues. The grammar rules *synerrc* (lines 486–498) display the troublesome token and the others to its right, and then succeed leaving the token list intact.

In actual use, Toy-Sequel would probably be found too simple. However, many extensions are quite straightforward. As an exercise, try to augment Toy-Sequel with defined views, e.g.

> view EMP1 < name, salary > as
> select from EMP tuples < name, salary > where dno = 1.

Another extension: "wild card" tuple specifications, e.g.

> select from EMP tuples *.
>   (i.e. tuples < name, salary, dno >)

select from EMP, DEPT tuples < EMP_*, manager >
   where EMP_dno = DEPT_dno.
(i.e. tuples < name, salary, EMP_dno, manager >).

And aggregate functions, e.g.

select from EMP average of < salary >.

An example of less straightforward modifications is query optimisation. Consider the command:

select from EMP, DEPT tuples < name, salary >
   where dno = DEPT_dno and manager = ''Jones''.

The answer will be generated by the calls

' EMP'(Name, Salary, Dno), ' DEPT'(Dno, ''Jones'')

which access every EMP tuple, even though only one department is involved. The same set of tuples would be generated by the calls

' DEPT'(Dno, ''Jones''), ' EMP'(Name, Salary, Dno)

but now other departments' tuples would never be retrieved. This optimisation could speed things up considerably for Prolog implementations with clause indexing.

BIBLIOGRAPHIC NOTES

The bibliography on data bases is enormous. We shall only name a few positions relevant to our presentation which (of necessity) has only touched on basic facts. Two widely accepted introductory textbooks on data bases in general are Ullman (1982) and Date (1982). The relational model of data was introduced by Codd (1970) and further elaborated by many, including Codd himself (1979). The most popular relational data languages are probably Quel, used in the data base system INGRES (Stonebraker *et al.* 1976), Sequel, created for the system R (Astrahan 1976; Chamberlin *et al.* 1976) and Query-by-Example (Zloof 1977).

In the proceedings of conferences on logic in data bases (Gallaire and Minker 1978, Gallaire *et al.* 1981) there are, in particular, papers on the role of logic programming in data base theory and applications. The advantages of Prolog (and logic programming at large) for data bases have been advocated by quite a few authors, e.g. Kowalski (1978), Gallaire (1983) and Lloyd (1982). A practical demonstration of Prolog's power is Chat80 (Warren and Pereira 1982; Warren 1981), a system with natural language interface. Queries in English are translated into Prolog calls; they are similar to those produced by Toy-Sequel, but Chat80 performs some query optimisation. Several other data base applications with natural language interface are described in Dahl (1977), Coelho (1982), and Filgueiras and Pereira (1983).

Another example of data base application of Prolog is an implementation of Query-by-Example (Neves and Williams 1983; Neves *et al.* 1983). Chomicki and Grudziński (1983) describe a system, based on extendible hashing, that manipulates tuples stored on disk. The system has been designed to support data-base-oriented implementations of Prolog.

The Toy-Sequel interpreter was rewritten as a sized-down version of SPOQUEL, a program which we had written with Włodek Grudziński in early 1982. It helped us through a difficult winter.

```
1    % -- -- --  Toy-Sequel interpreter  -- -- -- --
2    % (c) COPYRIGHT 1983  -- Feliks Kluzniak, Stanislaw Szpakowicz
3    %              Institute of Informatics, Warsaw University
4    toysequel  :-- write( '-- Toy-Sequel, IIUW Warszawa 1983 --' ), nl,
5                   repeat, tag( setcommand( Cmd, Errflag ) ),
6                          tag( docommand( Cmd, Errflag ) ),
7                          Cmd = sequelstop, !.
8
9    setcommand( Cmd, Errflag ) :--
10                   readcmd( CmdString ),
11                   scan( CmdString, TList ), compile( TList, Cmd ).
12
13   docommand( Cmd, Errflag ) :-- var( Errflag ), !, Cmd.
14   docommand( _, _ ).
15
16   scan( CmdString, TList ) :--
17                   phrase( tokens( TList ), CmdString ), tracescan( TList ).
18
19   compile( TList, Cmd ) :--
20                   phrase( command( Cmd ), TList ), !, tracecompile( Cmd ).
21   compile( _, error ) :-- synerr( badcommand ).
22
23   tracescan( Cmd ) :-- tracescan, !, write( '--scanned' ( Cmd ) ), nl.
24   tracescan( _ ).
25
26   tracecompile( Cmd ) :-- tracecompile, !, write( '--compiled' ( Cmd ) ), nl.
27   tracecompile( _ ).
28
29   tracescan.              tracecompile.
30
31   % -- -- -- reader and scanner -- -- --
32   % Reader stops on the first dot outside strings.
33   readcmd( String )  :-- rdchsk( Ch ), readcmd( Ch, String ).
34
35   readcmd( '.', [] ) :-- !, rch.
36   readcmd( '"', ['"' | Rest] ) :--
37                   !, rdch( Ch ), readstr( Ch, Rest, RestAfter ),
38                   rdch( Nextch ), readcmd( Nextch, RestAfter ).
39   readcmd( Ch, [Ch | Rest] ) :-- rdch( Nextch ), readcmd( Nextch, Rest ).
```

LISTING 8.4 Toy-Sequel interpreter. (*continued*)

```prolog
40
41  readstr( '''', [''' | Rest], Rest ) :- !.
42  readstr( Ch, [Ch | Rest], RestAfter ) :-
43      rdch( Nextch ), readstr( Nextch, Rest, RestAfter ).
44
45  % This scanner recognizes names, strings, integers, and single
46  % characters. Strings are returned as lists of characters.
47  % The tokens are: n(Name), s(String), i(Integer), ASingleCharacter.
48  tokens( [T | Ts] ) --> token( T ), !, sp, tokens( Ts ).
49  tokens( [] ) --> [].
50
51  token( n( Name ) ) -->
52      letter( L ), namechars( NN ), { pname( Name, [L | NN] ) }.
53  token( s( String ) ) --> [''''], stringchars( String ).
54  token( i( Integer ) ) --> sign( S ), digit( D ), digits( DD ),
55      sign( S ), digit( D ), digits( DD ),
56      { pnamei( I, [D | DD] ), signed( S, I, Integer ) }.
57  token( Ch ) --> [Ch].
58
59  letter( Ch ) --> [Ch], { letter( Ch ) }.
60
61  namechars( [Ch | Chs] ) --> letter( Ch ), !, namechars( Chs ).
62  namechars( [Ch | Chs] ) --> digit( Ch ), !, namechars( Chs ).
63  namechars( [] ) --> [].
64
65  % '''' in a string stands for a single '''
66  % (readcmd treats '''''''' as two adjacent strings).
67  stringchars( ['''' | Chs] ) --> [''''], [''''], !, stringchars( Chs ).
68  stringchars( [] ) --> [''''], !.
69  stringchars( [Ch | Chs] ) --> [Ch], stringchars( Chs ).
70
71  digit( Ch ) --> [Ch], { digit( Ch ) }.
72
73  digits( [D | DD] ) --> digit( D ), !, digits( DD ).
74  digits( [] ) --> [].
75
76  sign( '-' ) --> [ '-' ].
77  sign( '+' ) --> [ '+' ].
78  sign( '+' ) --> [].
```

242

```
79   signed( "+", I, I ).
80   signed( "-", I, Integer ) :-- Integer is - I.
81
82
83   sp --> [" "], sp.                 % optional spaces
84   sp --> [].
85
86   % These are used for attributes.
87   aname( Qual-Name ) --> En( Qual ), " ", n( Name )], '.
88   aname( Variable-Name ) --> En( Name )].      % ie fits all qualifiers
89
90   constant( Int, integer ) --> Ci( Int )], '.
91   constant( Str, string ) --> Cs( Str )].
92
93   % -- -- -- symbol table operations -- -- -- -- --
94   :-- op(100, xfx, '''').
95
96   % Given a relation name and an alias (cf select expression, procedure
97   % relname), use the relation's schema to push a new set of items onto
98   % symbol table stack and to return the generator. The format
99   % of a schema is described with create (procedure newrel).
100  newrelname( RelNm, Alias, Generator, OldST, [Alias :: RelST : OldST] ) :--
101      'r e l'( RelNm, Generator, RelST ), '.
102  newrelname( RelNm, _, fail, OldST, OldST )  :--  symerr( norelname(RelNm) ).
103
104  % Given a qualified name, return its associated variable and type.
105  findattr( Q-Nm, Var, Type, EQ = RelST : RelST ) :--
106      member( attr( Nm, Type, Var ), RelST ), '.
107  findattr( QNm, Var, Type, [_ : ST] ) :-- ; findattr( QNm, Var, Type, ST ) :-
108  findattr( QNm, _, _, [] ) :-- symerr( noattribute( QNm ) ).
109
110  % -- -- -- command compiler -- -- -- -- --
111  % See the various commands for examples of use.
112  % Command interpretation routines listed alongside command grammar processors.
113  command( Cmd ) --> create( Cmd ).
114  command( Cmd ) --> cancel( Cmd ).
115  command( Cmd ) --> select( Cmd ).
116  command( Cmd ) --> relations( Cmd ).
117  command( Cmd ) --> relation( Cmd ).
```

LISTING 8.4 (*Continued*)

```
118  command( Cmd )  --)  insert( Cmd ) .
119  command( Cmd )  --)  delete( Cmd ) .
120  command( Cmd )  --)  update( Cmd ) .
121  command( Cmd )  --)  stop( Cmd ) .
122  command( Cmd )  --)  dump( Cmd ) .
123  command( Cmd )  --)  load( Cmd ) .
124  % -- create a new relation --
125  % Eg: create EMP ( string name, integer salary, integer dno ) .
126  % Eg: create DEPT(integer dno,string manager).
127  % Eg: create BoardMembers(string name, string position, integer seniority).
128  % Note that lower and upper case letters are different. Keywords must be
129  % in lower case, otherwise use any convention you like.
130  create( newrel( RelName, [V : Vs], [attr(Nm, Type, V) : As] ) )  --->
131      [n( create ), n( RelName )],
132      ['('], typnam( Type, Nm ), typnams( Vs, As ), [')'].
133
134  typnams( [V : Vs], [attr( Nm, Type, V ) : As] )  --->
135      [','], typnam( Type, Nm ), typnams( Vs, As ).
136  typnams( [], [] )  --> [].
137
138  typnam( string, Nm )  --> [n( string ), n( Nm )].
139  typnam( integer, Nm )  --> [n( integer ), n( Nm )].
140  typnam( notype, Nm )  --> synerr( typeexpected ).
141
142  % A schema stores a pattern for invoking the relation's tuples (the generator),
143  % and a list of symbol table entries linking attribute names and types with
144  % variables in the generator.
145  newrel( RelName, Vars, RelST )  :-
146      not 're l'( RelName, _, _ ),
147      mksen( RelName, Vars, Generator ),
148      assert( 're l'( RelName, Generator, RelST ) ).
149  newrel( RelName, _, _ )  :-  namerr( duprelname( RelName ) ) .
150
151  % Add a blank for (rudimentary) security.
152  mksen( RelName, Vars, Generator )  :-
153      pname( RelName , Chars ), pname( RelNm, [' ' : Chars] ),
154      Generator =.. [RelNm : Vars].
155
156
```

```
157  % -- cancel a relation -- --
158  % Eg:  cancel EMP.
159  cancel( cancel( RelName ) ) ---> [n( cancel ), n( RelName ) ].
160
161  cancel( RelName )  :-  retract( "r e l"( RelName, Generator, ... ) ), !,
162                         retract( Generator ), fail.
163  cancel( RelName )  :-  namerr( unknown( RelName ) ).
164
165  % -- queries --
166  % List the set generated by a select expression.
167  select( ( Generators, Filter, writetuple( Tup ), fail ) ) --->
168       selectexp( set( Generators, Filter, Tup, ... ), [] ).
169
170  writetuple( [] )  :- !, nl.
171  writetuple( [Val | Vals] )  :-
172       write( Val ), write( ' ' ), writetuple( Vals ).
173
174  % List all relations. Eg:  relations.
175  relations( ( "r e l"( RelNm, ... ), write( RelNm ), nl, fail ) ) --->
176       [n( relations )].
177
178  % List the attributes of a relation. Eg:  relation EMP.
179  relation( relation( Name ) )  ---> [n( relation ), n( Name )].
180
181  relation( RelNm )  :-  "r e l"( RelNm, ... , Attrs ), !, listattrs( Attrs ),
182  relation( RelNm )  :-  write( RelNm ), write(' is not a relation'), nl.
183
184  listattrs( [] )  :- !.
185  listattrs( [attr( Name, Type, ... ) ! Attrs ] ) :-
186       write( Type ), write( ' ' ), write( Name ), nl,
187       listattrs( Attrs ).
188
189  % -- select expression -- --
190  % Eg:  select from EMP, Mgr=EMP, DEPT tuples ( name, dno )
191  %      where salary > Mgr.salary*85/100
192  %      and Mgr_name = manager and DEPT_dno = EMP_dno
193  %      and ( manager ) in (<"Smith">, <"Jones">, <"Brown">) .
194  % (ie set names and department numbers of those subordinates of Smith,
195  % Jones or Brown who earn more than 85% of their manager's salary )
```

LISTING 8.4 (*Continued*)

```
196  % Generators pick up tuples from named relations, Filters pass only tuples
197  % fitting the where-clause, Tuple is instantiated to the passed tuples (one by
198  % one), Types is the tuple's pattern with types instead of attributes (used for
199  % type checking).
200  % The example compiles to :
201  %
202  % set( ( ' EMP', Name, Salary, Dno ), ' EMP', ( MgrName, MgrSalary, MgrDno ),
203  %                                    , ' DEPT', ( Dno, MgrName )          ),
204  %    ( Salary > MgrSalary*85/100, true, true,
205  %    ( member( MgrName, ("Smith", "Jones", "Brown") ), true ) ),
206  %    [ Name, Dno ], [ string, integer ]  )
207  %
208  selectexp( set( Generators, Filter, Tuple, Types ), InitST ) --->
209      [n( select ), n( from )], relnames( Generators, InitST, ST ),
210      [n( tuples )], tuplepattern( Tuple, Types, ST ),
211      whereclause( Filter, ST ).
212
213  % One or more relation names, possibly "aliased" - Symbol table fragments are
214  % stacked in reverse order, so attribute search order will be that of
215  % the from-list (using-list for update) relations.
216  relnames( ( Gen, Gens ), OldST, NewST ) --->
217      relname( Name, Alias ), [','], relnames( Gens, OldST, TempST ),
218      { newrelname( Name, Alias, Gen, TempST, NewST ) }.
219  relnames( Gen, OldST, NewST ) --->
220      relname( Name, Alias ), { newrelname( Name, Alias, Gen, OldST, NewST ) }.
221
222  relname( Name, Alias ) ---> [n( Alias ), '=', n( Name ) ], !.
223  relname( Name, Name ) ---> [n( Name )].
224
225  % tuplepattern is also invoked by inexp.
226  tuplepattern( [A : As], [T : Ts], ST ) --->
227      [''], attrpatt( A, T, ST ), attrpatts( As, Ts, ST ), ['''].
228
229  attrpatts( [A : As], [T : Ts], ST ) --->
230      [','], !, attrpatt( A, T, ST ), attrpatts( As, Ts, ST ).
231  attrpatts( [], [] ) ---> [].
232
233  attrpatt( Attribute, Type ) ---> constant( Attribute, Type ), !.
234  attrpatt( A, T, ST ) ---> aname( QN ), { findattr( QN, A, T, ST ) }.
```

246

```
235  whereclause( Filter, ST )  --->  En( where )], '; ', boolexp( Filter, ST ) ).
236  whereclause( true, _ )  --->  [].
237
238  %  -- Boolean expressions -- --
239  % Eg:  salary > Mgr_salary * 85/100
240  %      or <name> in select from BoardMembers tuples <name>
241  % Note that embedded select expressions do not modify the symbol table,
242  % whose extensions are visible only in the nested constructs.
243  boolexp( E, ST )  --->  bterm( T, ST ), rboolexp( T, E, ST ).
244
245
246  rboolexp( L, (L ; R), ST )  --->  En( or )], '; ', boolexp( R, ST ).
247  rboolexp( E, E, _ )  --->  [].
248
249  bterm( T, ST )  --->  bfactor( F, ST ), rbterm( F, T, ST ).
250
251  rbterm( L, (L , R), ST )  --->  En( and )], '; ', bterm( R, ST ).
252  rbterm( T, T, _ )  --->  [].
253
254  bfactor( not F, ST )  --->  E"("], En( "not" )], '; ', bfactor( F, ST ) ).
255  bfactor( E, ST )  --->  E"("], '; ', boolexp( E, ST )], E")"].
256  bfactor( E, ST )  --->  inexp( E, ST )], '; '.
257  bfactor( E, ST )  --->  relexp( E, ST ).
258
259  %  -- set membership -- --
260  % Eg:  < dno, name > in < 1, "Jones" >, < 2, "Smith" >
261  % Eg:  < name > in (select from BoardMembers tuples <name>)
262  inexp( ( Generator, Filter ), ST )  --->
263         tuplepattern( Patt, Type, ST ), En( in )],
264         setexp( set( Generator, Filter, Tuple, Types ), ST ) ),
265         matchpatterns( Patt, Type, Tuple, Types ).
266
267  % matchpatterns is a rule, so that synerrc can show context.
268  matchpatterns( Patt, Types, Patt, Types )  --->  !.
269  matchpatterns( F1, T1, F2, T2 )  --->
270         synerrc( badinexppattern( T1, F1, T2, F2 ) ).
271
272  %  -- set expressions -- --
273  % A sequence of tuples or a select expression, possibly in parentheses.
```

LISTING 8.4 (*Continued*)

247

```
% The generator for a sequence of tuples is a call on member with second
% parameter instantiated to a list of these tuples.
setexp( Set, ST ) ---> ['v'], !, setexp( Set, ST ), ['v'].
setexp( Set, ST ) ---> selectexp( Set, ST ), !.
setexp( set( member( Patt, [Tup : Tups], true, Patt, Types ), ST ) --->
    tuple( Tup, Types ), tuples( Tups, Types ),
    ( mkpattern( Types, Patt ),
setexp( set( fail, fail, [], [] ), _ ) ---> synerr( badsetexpression ) .

tuples( [Tup], Types ) ---> ['v'], !, tuple( Tup, TupTypes ),
    ( checktype( Types, TupTypes ), tuples( TupTypes ) .
tuples( [], _ ) ---> [].

tuple( [A : As], [T : Ts] ) --->
    ['v'], constant( A, T ), constants( As, Ts ), ['v'], !.
tuple( [], [] ) ---> ['v'], synerr( badtuple ), { fail }.

constants( [A : As], [T : Ts] ) --->
    ['v'], !, constant( A, T ), constants( As, Ts ).
constants( [], _ ) ---> [].

checktype( Type, Type ) :- !.
checktype( T1, T2 ) :- synerr( inconsistent( T1, T2 ) ).

% Patt in set(_, _, Patt, _) is a list of n fresh variables
% (n is the length of tuples in this set).
mkpattern( [], [] ) :- !.
mkpattern( [_ : Types], [V : Vs] ) :- mkpattern( Types, Vs ).

% --- relational expressions ---
relexp( E, ST ) --->
    simplexp( LeftE, LeftType, ST ), relop( Op ), !,
    simplexp( RightE, RightType, ST ),
    { consrel( LeftE, LeftType, Op, RightE, RightType, E ) }.

relop( '=<' ) ---> ['=','<'].       relop( '==' ) ---> ['=','='].
relop( '=\=' ) ---> ['=','\','='].  relop( '<' ) ---> ['<'].
relop( '>=' ) ---> ['>','='].       relop( '>' ) ---> ['>'].
```

```
313   consrel( L, Type, Op, R, Type, E ) :- consrel( L, Op, R, Type, E ), !.
314   consrel( L, LType, Op, R, RType, fail ) :-
315      E =.. [Op, L, R], synerr( typeconflict( LType, RType, E ) ).
316
317   % The first clause does compile-time equality.
318   consrel( Arg, '==', Arg, _, true ).
319   consrel( L, '==', R, string, fail ).
320   consrel( L, '=\=', R, string, fail ).
321   consrel( L, Op, R, integer, E ) :- E =.. [Op, L, R].
322   consrel( L, '<', R, string, lstr( L, R ) ).
323   consrel( L, '=<', R, string, ( lstr( L, R ) ; L == R ) ).
324   consrel( L, '>', R, string, lstr( R, L ) ).
325   consrel( L, '>=', R, string, ( lstr( R, L ) ; R == L ) ).
326
327   % Compare strings lexicographically.
328   lstr( [], [_|_] ) :- !.
329   lstr( [Ch1 | _], [Ch2 | _] ) :- Ch1 @< Ch2, !.
330   lstr( [Ch1 : Chs1], [Ch1 : Chs2] ) :- lstr( Chs1, Chs2 ).
331
332   % -- simple expressions --
333   simplexp( E, string, ST ) --> stringexp( E, ST ), !.
334   simplexp( E, integer, ST ) --> arithexp( E, ST ).
335
336   stringexp( Str, _ ) --> Ls( Str ), !.
337   % Type checking is delayed to avoid error messages -- might be integer.
338   stringexp( Var, ST ) -->
339      qname( QN ), { findattr( QN, Var, Type, ST ), Type = string }.
340
341   arithexp( E, ST ) --> aterm( T, ST ), rarithexp( T, E, ST ).
342
343   rarithexp( L, E, ST ) -->
344      ['+'], !, aterm( T, ST ), rarithexp( L+T, E, ST ).
345   rarithexp( L, E, ST ) -->
346      ['-'], !, aterm( T, ST ), rarithexp( L-T, E, ST ).
347   rarithexp( E, E, _ ) --> [].
348
349   aterm( T, ST ) --> afactor( F, ST ), raterm( F, T, ST ).
350
351   raterm( L, T, ST ) -->
```

LISTING 8.4 (*Continued*)

```
3352   raterm( ["*"], !, afactor( F, ST ), raterm( L*F, T, ST ) .
3353   raterm( L, T, ST ), -->
3354   raterm( ["/"], !, afactor( F, ST ), raterm( L/F, T, ST ) .
3355   raterm( T, T, _ ) --> [].
3356
3357   afactor( E, ST )  --> ["("], !, arithexp( E, ST ), [")"].
3358   afactor( Int, _ ) --> [i:Int)], [], !.
3359   afactor( Var, ST ) -->
3360      aname( QN ), { findattr( QN, Var, Type, ST ), Type == integer }, !.
3361   afactor( 0, _ ) --> aname( QN ), !, synerrc( notinteger( QN ) ) .
3362   afactor( 0, _ ) --> synerrc( nointegerfactor ) .
3363
3364   % -- -- insert -- --
3365   % Eg: into EMP insert ("Jones",1000,1), ("Smith",1200,2).
3366   % Eg: into EMP insert select from DEPT tuples (manager 1050, dno).
3367   insert( Generators, Filter, assertz( NewTuple ) , fail ) --->
3368      [n(into), n( RelName )],
3369      {"r e l"( RelName, _, RelST ) }, !, [n( insert )],
3370      setexp( set( Generators, Filter, Tuple, Types ), [] ),
3371      { checktypes( Types, RelST ),
3372        mksen( RelName, Tuple, NewTuple ) }.
3373   insert( fail ) ---> [n(into), n( RelNm )],
3374                       synerrc( norelname( RelNm ) ) .
3375
3376   checktypes( [], [] ) --> !.
3377   checktypes( [T:Ts], [attr( _, T, _ ):As] ) --> !, checktypes( Ts, As ) .
3378   checktypes( Types, Attributes ) --> synerrc( badsettype( Types, Attributes ) ) .
3379
3380   % -- delete -- --
3381   % Eg: from EMP delete all tuples.
3382   % Eg: from EMP delete tuples where salary < 1000 and
3383   %           (dno) in select from DEPT tuples (dno)
3384   % (ie fire all subordinates of Smith who earn less than a 1000 )
3385   %           where manager == "Smith" .
3386   delete( ( RelGen, RelFilter, retract( RelGen ), fail ) ) --->
3387      [n( from ), n( RelNm )],
3388      { newrelname( RelNm, RelNm, RelGen, [], ST ) },
3389      [n( delete )], delfilter( RelFilter, ST ) .
3390
```

250

```
391  delfilter( true, _ ) --> [n( all ), n( tuples )].
392  delfilter( RelFilter, ST ) -->
393       [n( tuples ), n( where )], boolexp( RelFilter, ST ).
394  X -- -- update -- --
395  X Eg: update EMP using DEPT, Mgr=EMP
396  X     so that salary = salary + (Mgr_salary - salary)/5
397  X     where salary < Mgr_salary - 1000 and Mgr_name = manager
398  X     and DEPT_dno = dno
399  X     and not <Mgr_name> in
400                 select from BoardMembers tuples <name>.
401  X (ie to all employees who earn over a 1000 less than their manager
402  X give a raise equal to 20% of the difference provided the manager
403  X does not sit on the board)
404  X This is compiled to :
405  X  , EMP, ( Name, Salary, Dno ),                                       % OldTup
406  X (, DEPT, (Dno,Manager), , EMP, (Manager,MgrSalary,MgrDno)),          % UseGens
407  X (Salary < MgrSalary - 1000, true, true,
408  X    not (, BoardMembers, (Manager,_,_), true) ),                      % Filter
409  X NewSalary is Salary + (MgrSalary - Salary)/5,                        % Modifications
410  X retract(, EMP, (Name,Salary,Dno), assert(, EMP, (Name,NewSalary,Dno), fail
411
412  update( ( OldTup, UseGens, Filter, Modifications,
413          retract( OldTup ), assert( NewTup ), fail ) ) -->
414       [n( update ), n( RelNm )],
415       ( , r e l ,( RelNm, OldTup, OldST ),
416       ,r e l ,( RelNm, NewTup, NewST ), !,
417       makemodlist( OldST, NewST, MList ) ),
418       usingclause( UseGens, UseST ), ( ST = [RelNm = OldST ! UseST ],
419       [n( so ), n( that )],
420       modifier( Modification, MList, ST ),
421       modifiers( Modification, Modifications, MList, ST ),
422       ( closemodlist( MList ) ), whereclause( Filter, ST ).
423  update( fail ) --> [n( update )], synerrc( noupdatedrelation ).
424
425  usingclause( Gens, ST ) --> [n( using )], relnames( Gens, [], ST ).
426  usingclause( true, ST ) --> [].
427
428  modifiers( M, (M, Ms), MList, ST ) -->
```

LISTING 8.4 *(Continued)*

251

```
429        [L",'], !, modifier( MM, MList, ST ),
430        modifiers( M, Ms, MList, ST ).
431    modifiers( M, M, _ ) --> [].
432
433    modifier( AttrVar is Expr, MList, ST ) --->
434        En( Nm )], ( findmname( Nm, AttrVar, Type, MList ) ),
435        [L"="], simplexp( Expr, EType, ST ),
436        ( mtype( Type, EType, Nm ) ).
437
438    % A "modlist" lists updated relation's attributes together with new variables
439    % forming new tuple's attributes and Mod variables which are used to flag
440    % an attribute's modification when it is detected on the left hand side of
441    % an equality in "so that"-list.
442    makemodlist( [Old : Olds], [attr( _, _, NewV) : NewVs],
443                 [modif( Old, NewV, Mod ) : Mods] ) :-
444        !, makemodlist( Olds, NewVs, Mods ).
445    makemodlist( [], [], [] ).
446
447    % Bind old and new variables in "modlist" entries with clear flag.
448    closemodlist( [Mod : Mods] ) :- closemod( Mod ), !, closemodlist( Mods ).
449    closemodlist( [] ).
450
451    closemod( modif( attr( _, _, OldV ), OldV, Mod ) ), !,    var( Mod ).
452    closemod( _ ).
453
454    % Flag an updated attribute in "modlist".
455    findmname( Nm, NewV, T, MList ) :-
456        member( modif( attr( Nm, T, _ ), NewV, Mod ), MList ), !,
457        mmod( Mod, Nm ).
458    findmname( Nm, _, _ ) :- synerr( notinupdatedrel( Nm ) ).
459
460    % If no errors the first clause of mmod fails, the second binds.
461    mmod( Mod, Nm ) :- not var( Mod ), !, synerr( updatedtwice( Nm ) ).
462    mmod( true, _ ).
463
464    mtype( Type, Type, _ ) :- !.
465    mtype( T1, T2, Nm ) :- synerr( typeconflict( T1, Nm, T2 ) ).
466
```

```
467    % -- -- control commands -- -- --
468    stop( sequelstop )        -->  En( stop ) ( ).
469
470    sequelstop.               % do nothing (cf the main procedure)
471
472    load( consult( FileName ) )  -->  En( load ), n( from ), n( FileName ) ].
473
474    dump( dump( FileName ) )    -->  En( dump ), n( to ), n( FileName ) ].
475
476    dump( FileName )  :-  tell( FileName ),
477              'r e l'( Nm, Gen, ST ), wclause( 'r e l'( Nm, Gen, ST ) ),
478              Gen, wclause( Gen ), fail.
479    dump( _ )  :-  write( 'end.' ), nl, told .
480
481    wclause( Cl )  :-  writeq( Cl ), write( '.' ), nl.
482
483    % -- -- -- error handling ("bare bones" version) -- -- -- : --
484    synerr( Info )  :-  synmes( Info ), ancestor( setcommand( _, error ) ) .
485
486    synmes( Info )   -->  { synmes( Info ), write( 'Context: ' ) },
487                      context. % will fail eventually!
488    synerrc( _ )     -->  { nl, ancestor( setcommand( _, error ) ) }.
489
490    synmes( Info )  :-  nl, write( '-- Syntactic error: '), write( Info ), nl.
491
492    context   -->  [Token], { wtoken( Token ) }, context.
493    context   -->  [ ].
494
495    wtoken( T )  :-  wt( T, Name ).
496    wt( n( Name ), Name ) .
497    wt( i( Integer ), Integer ) .
498    wt( s( String ), String ) .
499    wt( Char, Char ) .
500
501    namerr( Info )  :-  nl, write( '*** Error: ' ), nl,
502              write( Info ), nl, tagfail( docommand( _, _, _ ) ) ).
```

LISTING 8.4 (*Continued*)

253

9 PROLOG DIALECTS[1]

9.1. PROLOG I

The idea of logic programming emerged in Marseilles in the first half of 1972 while Robert Kowalski was visiting the artificial intelligence team founded by Alain Colmerauer at the University of Marseilles. Colmerauer with his team prepared the design specification of the programming language Prolog (Colmerauer *et al.* 1972). The language resembled a theorem prover rather closely, but it already possessed the essential properties of contemporary Prolog, and even some features reintroduced quite recently, e.g. delaying calls till appropriate instantiation of their arguments. Almost at the same time Kowalski advocated predicate calculus as a formalism for expressing algorithms without commitment to a specific strategy of their execution; the short note (1972) was later expanded to a larger paper (1974). Hence the two pioneers of logic programming took from the outset different approaches to the problem of changing the idea into reality. Although developed in close interaction, these different attitudes still manifest themselves in logic programming research.

The language described in Colmerauer *et al.* (1972) was implemented in Algol W on IBM 360/67 by Philippe Roussel and used at once in several applications (Colmerauer *et al.* 1973, Pasero 1973, Kanoui 1973, Joubert 1974; Bergman and Kanoui 1973, 1975, Battani and Méloni 1975, Guizol 1975). It was quickly replaced by an improved version, coded partly in Fortran by Battani and Méloni (1973) and partly in Prolog by Colmerauer and Roussel. This was the first version of Prolog used outside Marseilles. Although not christened so by its authors, it deserves the name of Prolog I, especially as its commonly used name "Marseille Prolog" has become ambiguous.

---

[1] This chapter was contributed by Janusz S. Bień, Institute of Informatics, Warsaw University, Warsaw, Poland.

The original reference to Prolog I is Roussel (1975); some historical information can be found in Battani and Méloni (1973) and Kluźniak (1984). The syntax of the language is illustrated below by the sample clauses:

+APPEND(NIL, *X, *X).
+APPEND(*X.*Y, *Z, *X.*V) −APPEND(*Y, *Z, *V).

This should be preceded by the declaration of the infix dot:

−AJOP(".", 1, "X'(X'X)")!

And a sample directive (SORT means *write*):

−APPEND(A.B.NIL, C.NIL, *X) −SORT(*X) −LIGNE!

Positive literals (see Chapter 2) are preceded with +, negative with −; the notation allows representation of non-Horn clauses. This was a natural requirement, because the early versions of Prolog were intended to implement a general theorem-proving method known as linear resolution with selection function (Kowalski and Kuehner 1971). Program clauses were distinguished from directives by a different terminator. The syntax survived its original motivation and is still used in some versions of the language (Kluźniak and Szpakowicz 1983).

9.2. PROLOG II

After Prolog I was released, Colmerauer's team experimented with various mutations of the language; some of them have been described in Guizol and Méloni (1976), Colmerauer *et al.* (1979) and Kanoui and Van Caneghem (1980). Finally it was announced that the goal of creating "the ultimate Prolog" was achieved (Colmerauer *et al.* 1981). The new language was called Prolog II by its authors (Colmerauer 1982, Van Caneghem 1982, Kanoui 1982).

The most important innovation of Prolog II is the treatment of cyclic data structures (see Section 1.2.3). They are simply valid representations of infinite trees, which can be manipulated in a similar way to other terms (Colmerauer 1979, 1982). However, the same infinite tree can be represented by different data structures; to let them be matched correctly it appeared necessary to treat functors in the same way as arguments (Filgueiras 1982). As a result, a functor can be a variable or a compound term. In Prolog II, the standard form of terms is considered just a shorthand notation for a more general form called tuple. For example, ff(x) stands for <ff, x>, while <x, y> and <<ff(x)>, y> are also legal terms (single-letter names denote variables, ff is a constant). Instead of unifying two tuples, Prolog II constructs a system of equations. For example, matching <x> with <ff(x)> corresponds to solving in x the equation

$$x = ff(\, x \,).$$

The solution of this equation is the infinite tree ff(ff(ff(...))), which is represented by an appropriate cyclic data structure.

The behavior of Prolog programs is described as incremental solving of the system of equations introduced by program clauses, which can also be seen as rewriting rules. The execution of a call is viewed as the operation of erasing it by applying the rules and solving the appropriate equations. This viewpoint manifests itself in the syntax of clauses by an arrow leading from the head to the (possibly empty) body, e.g.

```
append( nil, x, x ) → ;
append( x.y, z, x.v ) → append( y, z, v ) ;
```

This approach makes it possible to describe the principles of Prolog II in a compact and self-contained way, relieved from the references to theorem-proving techniques and relying only on the most fundamental and intuitive notions of logic (Colmerauer 1983).

Prolog II offers a simple yet powerful coroutining mechanism (see Chapter 2). A call may require its parameter to be instantiated. Given a variable, it waits for it to become bound. This is achieved by the built-in procedure *geler* ("freeze"), whose first argument is a "trigger" (usually a variable to be bound) and the second a call (to be delayed). If the "trigger" is already bound, *geler* simply executes the call.

Another coroutining primitive is *dif*, which succeeds if its parameters are not "perfectly" equal (see the built-in procedure = =, Section 5.5.6). If during the execution of *dif* ("down the terms' structure") a variable is encountered, *dif* waits until it becomes bound and only then resumes the comparison.

The coroutining mechanism will be illustrated by two examples adapted from Colmerauer *et al.* (1983). The first example is a procedure that takes two trees represented as deeply nested dotted list structures. It succeeds when both structures can be flattened to the same linear list. A built-in procedure *ident* is used to check whether the argument is a constant.

```
sameleaves( a, b ) → leaves( a, u ) leaves( b, u ) list( u );

leaves( a, u ) → geler( u, leaves1( a, u ) );
```

```
leaves1( a, a.nil ) → ident( a );
leaves1( a.l, a.u ) → ident( a ) leaves( l, u );
leaves1( ( a.b ).l, u ) → leaves1( a.b.l, u );

list( nil ) →;
list( a.u ) → list( u );
```

The second example is a procedure that generates a list of digits 1, 2, 3 such that all three elements are different.

```
perm( x.y.z.nil ) → alldifferent( x.y.z.nil )
                    alldigits( x.y.z.nil );

alldigits( nil ) →;
alldigits( x.l ) → digit( x ) alldigits( l );
digit( 1 ) →; digit( 2 ) →; digit( 3 ) →;

alldifferent( nil ) →;
alldifferent( x.l ) → outside( x, l ) alldifferent( l );

outside( x, nil );
outside( x, y.l ) → dif( x, y ) outside( x, l );
```

Prolog II supports a kind of modularisation implemented by so-called "worlds", each with a unique name. Worlds are organised into a tree structure. The root is the world "origine", which has two subworlds "ordinaire" and "?????". Subworlds of "ordinaire" (which is the default) can be created by the user who can walk up and down the tree, and also create and discard worlds. "?????" contains the Prolog II supervisor and cannot be used as the current world. Every procedure name is associated with the world in which it was first mentioned ("declared"). It is accessible in this world and its descendants but not in its siblings. Moreover, a name N and the same name N declared in a superworld later on refer to different procedures.

   Clauses are available for all manipulations (including initial definition) only in the world where the procedure name has been declared and in its direct subworlds. For example, standard procedure names are introduced in "origine"—with clauses defined in "?????"—and used in "ordinaire". So, the user cannot change a standard procedure definition. Clause indexing is provided, or rather tuple indexing. The leftmost name in the tuple is used as a key.

   The purpose of Toy's *tag, tagexit* etc. (see Section 5.12) is served in Prolog II by a pair of built-in procedures *bloc, fin-bloc*. In the call *bloc(l, t)*, *t* is the call to be executed in the block. When, during the execution of *t*, a call of the form *fin-bloc(ll)* is encountered, the most recent call on *bloc(l, t)* with *l* unifiable with *ll* is sought. If none is found, an error condition is raised, else this call on bloc succeeds deterministically. This feature is used for error handling and for exiting loops.

We have presented here only some of the Prolog II features, and the interested reader is referred to Colmerauer *et al.* (1983). It is interesting that the pilot implementation of Prolog II which is described here was done on an Apple II microcomputer using software paging on floppy disks.

9.3. MICRO-PROLOG AND MPROLOG

micro-Prolog is the dialect used by Kowalski's team at Imperial College of Science and Technology in London. micro-Prolog was developed and implemented by McCabe (1981); his main goal was to install Prolog on a cheap 8-bit microcomputer. micro-Prolog uses lists to represent terms, calls and clauses, e.g.

((Append() x x))
((Append (x | X) Y (x | Z)) (Append X Y Z))

The list notation has several advantages: predicates and functors need not have a fixed number of arguments (i.e. the whole argument list can be bound to a single variable); their names can be arbitrary list structures (for technical reasons this is not allowed for predicates). micro-Prolog also supports a simple form of modularity: modules are created dynamically and the accessibility of names is determined by export/import lists.

A typical user is not expected to interact directly with micro-Prolog, because a special front-end called Simple is provided to conceal the low-level language features. Here is the *append* example in the Simple syntax:

Append(( ) x x)
Append((x | X) Y (x | Z)) if Append(X Y Z)

Simple was used as a computer language for children; other interesting applications are expert systems. The language is subject to various experiments and extensions, such as an explanation facility or an original form of input/output operations called query–the–user (Sergot 1982); Simple and other extensions are all written in micro-Prolog. Both micro-Prolog and some of its applications are extensively documented in Ennals (1983) and Clark and McCabe (1984).

MPROLOG was developed at the Institute for Co-ordination of Computer Techniques, in Budapest (Bendl *et al.* 1980, SzKI 1982), using the programming language CDL2 (Koster 1974). MPROLOG is an upward-compatible extension of Prolog-10, intended for creating production software for mainframe computers. The crucial extension consists in introducing a form of modularity, based on the ideas of Szeredi (1982) and similar in spirit to that found in many other languages. The modules are syntactic units and contain explicit export/import lists determining the visibility (i.e. the accessibility) of names; a visible name can serve as a functor or as a predicate name. When a program is entered, only the main module is loaded and executed; other modules must be loaded explicitly by calling appropriate built-in procedures.

MPROLOG is a large system which includes several components. The pretranslator produces an internal form of a program module; the consolidator links the modules into a program; the interpreter executes it. The program development support system (PDSS) provides a dedicated editor and debugging aids. A compiler and an optimizer are under development. The language offers a multitude of built-in procedures (probably more than any other Prolog system) and interfaces to user-supplied procedures written in CDL2 and Fortran.

APPENDICES

APPENDIX A.1

Toy-Prolog Interpreter

```
1    program Toy ;
2
3    (* (C) COPYRIGHT 1983  --   Feliks Kluzniak, Stanislaw Szpakowicz
4                                 Institute of Informatics, Warsaw University   *)
5
6    label 1, 2;  (* error halt & almost-fatal error recovery only *)
7
8
9    const
10
11       maxint   =  32767;
12       eos      =      0 ;   (* end-of-string character ord *)
13       eol      =     10;    (* end-of-line character ord *)
14       maxchar  =    127;    (* maximum character ord *)
15
16       (* table limits *)
17       ctlow   =  0;  cthigh  =   4000;   (* character table *)
18       atsize  = 1009;                    (* atom table size: a prime *)
19       atlow   =  2;  athigh  =   1010;   (* athigh=atlow-1+atsize****** *)
20       ttlow   =  0;  tthigh  =    800;   (* trail table *)
21       btlow   =  0;  bthigh  =    300;   (* backtrack point table *)
22       btbelow = -1;                      (* = btlow - 1, for initialisation *)
23       ftlow   =  0;  fthigh  =    800;   (* frame table *)
24       ftbelow = -1;                      (* = ftlow - 1, for initialisation *)
25       mtlow   =  2;  mthigh  =  16000;   (* main table *)
26                                          (* mt , see also var declarations *)
27       (* at *)
28       noarity = -1;                   (* used when an atom is only a name handle *)
29       emptyatom =      = cthigh;      (*name value marking unused atom entries
30                                         can't be a name - no room for eos *)
31       (* mt , see also var declarations *)
```

262

```
32   stacksize = 5000;    (* size of var & copy stack area *)
33   int       = 1;       (*marker for integer objects, = varlim+1******)
34   varlim    = 0;       (* fields holding (= varlim are vars,
35                            only dumvarx holds varlim     *)
36   freevar   = -1;      (* filler for free vars in stack area *)
37   offoff    = 2;       (* variable prot with offset k is
38                            represented as -(k + offoff)  *)
39   minstdint = -1;      (* integers in this range are given *)
40   maxstdint = 10;      (*  standard prototypes to save memory *)
41
42   (* various *)
43   maxvarnumb = mthish;   (* max number of different vars
44                               in a clause - 1 *)
45   maxargnumb = mthish;   (* max number of args in a term *)
46   maxsyspars = 5;        (* max number of parameters in a
47                               system routine *)
48   car = 1;             (* dot's argument number ( sequence head ) *)
49   cdr = 2;             (* ------------- '' ------------- tail *)
50
51   (* character class encodings, see array cc & initvars *)
52   (*note that (= csmalletter is letter and (= cunderscore is alphameric*)
53   cbigletter = 'a';  csmalletter = 'b';  cdigit = 'c';
54   cunderscore = 'd';  cbracket = 'e';  csolochar = 'f';
55   csymch = 'g';  cother = 'h';
56
57   (* i / o *)
58   maxlinesize = 80;
59
60
61 type
62   (* index ranges *)
63   ctx = ctlow .. cthigh;   (* character table index *)
64   atx = atlow .. athigh;   (* atom table index *)
65   ttx = ttlow .. tthigh;   (* trail table index *)
```

(continued)

```
66      btx       =   btlow .. bthigh;        (* backtrack point table index *)
67      ftx       =   ftlow .. fthigh;        (* frame table index *)
68      mtx       =   mtlow .. mthigh;        (* main table index *)
69
70      stackx    =   mtx; (* i.e.mtlow .. stackhigh; stack area index in mt.*)
71      protx     =   mtx; (* i.e.protlow .. mthigh; prototype area index in mt*)
72
73      (* sundry ranges *)
74      varnumb   =   0 .. maxvarnumb;         (* number of vars / var offset *)
75      argnumb   =   noarity .. maxargnumb;   (* number of arguments *)
76      nsysparam =   0 .. maxsyspars;  (* number of system routine params *)
77      classofchar   =   cbigletter..cother;
78
79      (* standard atoms ( indexing table std ) :=
80                            ';'/2, ','/2, 'call'/1, 'tag'/1,
81                       'L]'/0, '.'/2, 'error'/1, 'user'/0  *)
82      stdatomid  =  ( atmsemcol, atmcomma, atmcall, atmtag,
83                       atmnil, atmdot, atmerror, atmuser   );
84
85
86      (* system routine identifiers *)
87      sysroutid  =  ( idfail, idtag, idcall,
88                       idslash,
89                       idtascut, idtasfail, idtasexit, idancestor,
90                       idhalt, idstatus,
91                       iddisplay, idrch, idlastch, idskipbl, idwch,
92                       idecho, idnoecho, idsee, idseeing, idseen,
93                       idtell, idtelling, idtold,
94                       idordchr, idsum, idprod, idinf, idnameinf,
95                       idsmalletter, idbisletter, idletter, iddisit,
96                       idalphanum, idbracket, idsolochar, idsymch,
97                       ideqvar, idvar, idatom, idinteger, idnonvarint,
98                       idfunctor, idarg, idpname, idpnamei,
99                       idproc, idproclimit, idprocinit,
```

```
100        idclause, idretract, idabolish,
101        idassert, idredefine, idpredefined, idprotect,
102        idnonexistent, idnonexistent,
103        iddebug, idnodebug,           );
104        idtrue                    );
105
106  (* error codes *)
107  errid  = ( ctovflw, atovflw, ttovflw, btovflw,
108             ftovflw, stackovflw, protovflw,
109             syntax, loadfile, sysinit, usereof,
110             longfilename, unifyerr     );
111
112
113
114  (* objects *)
115
116  procptr  = @ proc;
117
118  proc  .:=  record          (* a procedure descriptor *)
119             next  :  procptr;      (* what to do after failure *)
120             nvars :  varnumb;      (* size of variable frame *)
121             case systemroutine : boolean of
122               true :  ( sysid : sysroutid );
123               false : ( head, body : protx )
124             end;
125
126  atom  =    record  (* unique functor/predicate representation *)
127             name  :  ctx;          (* printname string,
128                                    = emptyatom if not used *)
129             arity :  argnumb;
130             proc  :  procptr       (* associated proc or nil *)
131             end;
132
133  backpt  =  record          (* backtrack-point (fail-point) *)
```

(continued)

265

```
134         frozenframe  :  ftx;          (* where to resume *)
135         resume       :  procptr;      (* what to resume *)
136         copylev      :  stackx;       (* copy stack level *)
137         traillev     :  ttx           (* trail stack level*)
138       end;
139
140 frame =  record              (* environment frame *)
141         anc    :  ftx;               (*to caller frame (but TRO)*)
142         calls  :  mtx;               (* call is 1st in this seq. *)
143         vars   :  stackx             (* variables of this frame *)
144       end;
145
146 var
147                 :  mtx;
148 (* mt address constants ( alas, no compile-time expressions ) *)
149 stackhigh,      (* mtlow-1+stacksize; top of var.& copy stack area *)
150 protlow,        (* stackhish+1, bottom of prototype area *)
151 dumvarx,        (* protlow, the unique dummy variable prototype *)
152 nilprotx,       (* dumvarx+1, a prototype of '[]'/0 *)
153 minchprotx,     (* nilprotx+1, low end of unique char prot area *)
154 maxchprotx,     (* minchprotx+maxchar, high end of char prot area *)
155 stdintprotx     (* maxchprotx+1, low end of std int prot area *)
156                 :  mtx;
157
158 (*** variables ***)
159
160 ci, co, mc (*,si,so*) :  text;   (*input,output,sysfile,seefile,tellfile*)
161 seeing, telling  :  boolean;     (* terminal/file i/o flags *)
162 seeobj, tellobj  :  mtx;         (* terms with current file names *)
163 sysloading  :  boolean;          (* on when loading system file *)
164 colinesize, solinesize :  0 .. maxlinesize;
165 echo  :  boolean;                (* input echo switch *)
166
167 ct  =  array [ ctx ] of char;    (* character string table *)
```

```
168  ctop ,        : ctx;                         (* first free *)
169  builtname     : ctx;                         (* first char of constructed name *)
170
171  at       : array [ atx ] of atom;            (* atom table = hashed *)
172  freeatoms : integer;                         (* >= 1, 1 kept as sentinel *)
173
174  tt       : array [ ttx ] of stackx;          (* trail table *)
175  ttop     : ttx;                              (* first free *)
176
177  bt       : array [ btx ] of backpt;          (* backtrack-point table *)
178  topb     : btbelow .. bthigh;    (* last used = current backpt *)
179
180  ft       : array [ ftx ] of frame;           (* environment frame table *)
181  topf     : ftbelow .. fthigh;    (* last used = current frame *)
182
183  mt       : array [ mtx ] of integer;         (* main memory table *)
184  vtop ,                                       (* first free above variable stack *)
185  csbot ,                                      (* first free below term copy stack *)
186  stop ,                           (* first free above ground prot area *)
187  nsbot    : mtx;                  (* first free below non-ground prot area *)
188  sprotected, nsprotected : protx; (* clauses with heads below or above
189                                             these can't be redefined     *)
190
191  (* storage utilisation = low level markers for status only *)
192  tminfree , bminfree , fminfree ,
193  stackminfree              : integer ;
194
195  (* control state registers ( see also topf and topb ) *)
196  ancf     : ftx;                  (* = ft [ topf ]. anc *)
197  topenv , : ftx;                  (* = ft [ topf ]. vars, current clause's
198                                             variable environment    *)
199  ancenv : stackx;                 (* = ft [ ancf ]. vars, current call's
200                                             variable environment    *)
201  ccall    : mtx;                  (* the current call *)
```

(continued)

```
202    cproc        : procptr;     (* the current proc *)
203
204    frozenvars ,               (* = ft [ bt [ topb ]. frozenframe ]. vars *)
205    frozenheap   : stackx;     (* = bt [ topb ]. copylev *)
206
207    debug        : boolean;    (* wallpaper trace switch *)
208
209    (* standard system routine interface *)
210    syserror : boolean;        (* turned on for bad system routine calls *)
211    spar : array [ 1 .. maxsyspars ] of mtx;     (*parameters (in ancenv)*)
212    sparv : array [ 1 .. maxsyspars ] of integer; (*values of int spars*)
213
214    (* standard atom pointers ( constants ) *)
215    std : array [ stdatomid ] of atx;
216
217    (* pointers to standard objects in prototype area ( constants) *)
218    errorcallseq  : protx;     (* '.'('error'(':0'),'[]') *)
219    userprot      : protx;     (* prototype of 'user'/0 *)
220
221    (* assert etc. *)
222    lastasserted    : atx;     (*head atom of most recently asserted clause*)
223    redefining      : boolean; (* redefinition switch cf. redefine *)
224    vardictbot      : stackx;  (* first location of temporary
225                                  variable dictionary above
226                                  topmost variable frame - used
227                                  only by storeclause & helpers *)
228    procindx        : integer; (* used by genproc & helpers *)
229    shownonexistent : boolean; (* show calls to empty procs ? *)
230
231    (* reader & high i/o *)
232    cch     : char;    (* current input character *)
233    nclvars : varnumb; (* number of vars in currently read clause *)
234    whaterr : errid;   (* syntax or loadfile according to context *)
235
```

```
236   (* character class mapping (chars in the external form of a Prolog
237        program, but bisletter through cdisits used also by "internal"
238        form reader). the classes are encoded as characters, as this
239        is the only way to obtain a packed table with some Pascal
240        implementations.                                             *)
241   cc    :   array [ char ] of classofchar;
242
243   (* main program variables *)
244   terminate  :  boolean;              (* flag set by system routine halt *)
245   goalstmnt  :  protx;                (* current initial goal statement *)
246   nsoalvars  :  varnumb;              (* and the number of its variables *)
247
248
249
250   (*-------- e r r o r s --------*)
251
252   procedure putline;
253   forward; (*-------*)
254
255   procedure halt;
256   (* this might be implementation-dependent *)
257   begin  writeln ( co ); writeln (co, ' *******toyprolos aborted*******');
258        goto 1
259   end;
260
261   procedure status;
262   const field = 8;
263   type tablename = array [ 1..9 ] of char;
264   procedure line ( caption : tablename; size, free, unused : integer );
265        begin writeln ( co, '',
266                     caption, size : field, free : field, unused : field )
267        end;
268   begin  writeln ( co );
269        writeln ( co, ' Toy Prolos    version 1 (MERA)   -  IIUW Warszawa 1983' ) ;
```

(continued)

269

```
270      writeln ( co, ' table   size   free   unused' );
271      line ( 'character', cthigh, cthigh - ctop; cthigh - ctop );
272      line ( 'atom     ', atsize, freeatoms, freeatoms );
273      line ( 'prototype', mthish - protlow, nsbot - stop, nsbot - stop );
274      line ( 'trail    ', tthish, tthish - ttop, tminfree );
275      line ( 'backpt   ', bthish, bthish - topb, bminfree );
276      line ( 'frame    ', fthish, fthish - topf, fminfree );
277      line ( 'var/copy ', stackhigh - mtlow, csbot - vtop, stackminfree );
278      write( co, ' ' );   colinesize:= 0
279   end;
280
281   procedure error ( id : errid );
282   begin writeln ( co );
283      write ( co, '++++++error : ' );
284      case id of
285         ctovflw       :  write ( co, 'character' );
286         atovflw       :  write ( co, 'atom' );
287         ttovflw       :  write ( co, 'trail' );
288         btovflw       :  write ( co, 'backtrack-point' );
289         ftovflw       :  write ( co, 'frame' );
290         stackovflw    :  write ( co, 'variable/copy' );
291         protovflw     :  write ( co, 'prototype' );
292         syntax        :  write ( co, 'bad system program syntax' );
293         loadfile      :  write ( co, 'bad system kernel file' );
294         sysinit       :  write ( co, 'interpreter initialisation error' );
295         usereof       :  write ( co, 'user eof ' );
296         longsfilename :  write ( co, 'file name too long' );
297         unifyerr      :  write ( co, 'error in unify, interpreter bad' )
298      end;
299      if id <= protovflw then begin
300         write ( co, ' table overflow' );
301         putline; status
302      end;
303      putline;
```

```
304            if id in [ ctovflw, protovflw, loadfile, sysinit, usereof ] then halt
305            else goto 2
306    end;
307
308    (* procedure check ( n : integer;  b : boolean );
309    (* (* debugging help : abort if b false *)
310    (* begin  if not b then begin
311    (*                      writeln ( co );
312    (*                      writeln (co, ' +--+--+--+ check failure ', n );
313    (*                      halt
314    (*                end
315    (* end;
316    (**)
317
318
319
320    (*-------  l o w   i n p u t / o u t p u t  -------*)
321
322            (* file opening/closing is implementation-dependent.
323               see also procedure loadsyskernel ( initialisation ). *)
324
325
326    procedure closefile ( forinput : boolean );
327    (* close mc,si or so, switching to user terminal.
328       forinput signals whether the current input or the current output file
329       is to be closed. no effect if the file is not open.             *)
330    begin  if forinput then begin
331              if seeing then begin
332                           (* close ( si ); *)      seeing:= false
333              end
334              else
335              if sysloading then begin
336                           (* close ( mc ); *)      sysloading:= false
337              end
```

(continued)

```
338            end
339         else    if telling then begin
340                    (* close ( so ) ; *)    telling:= false
341
342                end
343    end (*closefile*);

344    procedure openfile ( name : ctx; forinput : boolean );
345    (* open the file (si or so according to 2nd parameter)
346       whose name is given by a string in character table.
347       a file is opened rewound. if a previous file is open, it is closed.  *)
348    const  ln = 35; (* for RSX-11 *)
349    var  nm : array [ 1..ln ] of char;   k : 1..ln;
350    begin(*
351       while ( k <> ln ) and ( ct [ name ] ( <> chr ( eos ) ) ) do begin
352          nm [ k ] := ct [ name ];   name:= name + 1;   k:= k + 1
353
354       end;
355       if ct [ name ] ( <> chr ( eos ) then error ( longfilename );
356       for k:= k to ln do nm [ k ] := ' ';
357       closefile ( forinput );  *)            (* only 1 file per stream *)
358       if forinput then begin
359                   (* reset ( si, nm, 'pli' ) ; *)   seeing:= true
360          end
361       else begin
362                   (* rewrite ( so, nm, 'plo' ); *)    telling:= true;
363                   write( so, ' ' );    solinesize:= 0
364
365       end
366    end (*openfile*);

367    procedure putline;
368    (* start a new output line *)
369    begin  if telling then begin
370                   writeln ( so );    solinesize:= 0
371           end
           else begin
```

```
372          writeln ( co ); write( co, ' ' ); colinesize:= 0
373       end
374    end;
375
376    procedure setline;
377    (* start a new input line *)
378    var keep : boolean;
379    begin if sysloading then readln ( mc )
380       else
381          if seeing then readln ( si )
382          else readln ( ci );
383       if echo then begin
384          keep:= telling; telling:= false;
385          putline; telling:= keep
386       end
387    end;
388
389    procedure putch ( c : char );
390    (* put a character onto the current output file *)
391    (* characters are counted to avoid line overflow *)
392    begin if telling then begin
393          if solinesize >= maxlinesize then putline;
394          write( so, c ); solinesize:= solinesize +1
395       end
396       else begin
397          if colinesize >= maxlinesize then putline;
398          write( co, c ); colinesize:= colinesize + 1
399       end
400    end;
401
402    procedure getch ( var c : char );
403    (* get a character from the current input file *)
404    var keep : boolean;
405    begin if sysloading then read ( mc, c )
```

273

(continued)

```
406            else
407              if seeing then read ( si, c )
408              else read ( ci, c );
409          if echo then begin
410                keep:= telling;  telling:= false;
411                putch ( c );  telling:= keep
412              end
413        end;
414
415  procedure putint ( i : integer );
416  (* output an integer without blanks *)
417  var divisor : integer;
418  begin  if i < 0 then begin
419                putch ( '-' );  i:= - i
420              end;
421          divisor:= 10000;                    (***16 bit version***)
422          while ( i div divisor = 0 ) and ( divisor <> 1 ) do
423                                          divisor:= divisor div 10;
424          repeat  putch ( chr ( i div divisor + ord ( '0' ) ) );
425                i:= i mod divisor;  divisor:= divisor div 10
426          until divisor = 0
427  end;
428
429  function endofline : boolean;
430  (* eoln on the current input file ? *)
431  begin  if sysloading then endofline:= eoln ( mc )
432          else
433          if seeing then endofline:= eoln ( si )
434          else endofline:= eoln ( ci )
435  end;
436
437  function endoffile : boolean;
438  (* eof on the current input file ? *)
439  begin  if sysloading then endoffile:= eof ( mc )
```

```
440        else
441        if seeing then endoffile:= eof ( si )
442        else endoffile:= eof ( ci )
443    end;
444
445
446
447
448
449    (*---------- d i c t i o n a r y ----------*)
450
451        (* string representation is known to initprot, sterm & nameexplode *)
452
453
454    function compstrings ( s1, s2 : ctx; equality : boolean ) : boolean;
455    (* equality --> s1 = s2 ?  # not equality --> s1 < s2 ? *)
456    begin  while ( ct[s1] = ct[s2]) and ( ct[s2] <> chr(eos) ) do begin
457                   s1:= s1 + 1;  s2:= s2 + 1
458    end;
459        if equality then compstrings:= ct[s1] = ct[s2]   (* both are eos ? *)
460        else compstrings:= ct[s1] < ct[s2]        (* note that eos = 0 *)
461    end;
462
463    function charlast ( string : ctx ) : ctx;
464    (* locate the last character (except eos) of this string *)
465    begin  while ct [ string ]<> chr ( eos ) do string:= string + 1;
466           charlast:= string - 1   (*correct because lowest string not empty*)
467    end;
468
469    procedure newatom ( where : atx; printname : ctx; narity : argnumb ) ;
470    (* create a new atom ( at least one empty atom needed as sentinel ) *)
471    begin  if freeatoms = 1 then error ( atovflw ) ;
472           with at [ where ] do begin
473                   name:= printname;   arity:= narity;   proc:= nil
```

(continued)

275

```
474          end;
475          freeatoms:= freeatoms - 1
476      end;
477
478  function findname ( firstch, lastch : ctx ) : atx;
479  (* find the first occurence of an atom with name in ct firstch
480     through lastch. create one ( with noarity ) if none .        *)
481  var  a : atx;
482  begin  (* a simple hash on first and last char *)
483      (* ***linear rehash used : don't forget findatom when improving*** *)
484      a:= ( ord(ct[firstch])*256 + ord(ct[lastch]) ) mod atsize + atlow;
485      (* rehash loop stopped by empty sentinel ( freeatoms >= 1 ) *)
486      while ( at[ a ]. name <> emptyatom ) and
487                      not compstring= ( at[ a ]. name, firstch, true ) do
488          if a <> athish then a:= a + 1
489          else a:= atlow;
490      if at[ a ]. name = emptyatom then newatom ( a, firstch, noarity );
491      findname:= a
492  end;
493
494  function findatom ( nameatom : atx; narity : argnumb ) : atx;
495  (* given the first atom with name, find or create one with name and arity *)
496  var  a : atx;  thename : ctx;
497  begin  if at[ nameatom ]. arity = noarity then begin (*just a name handle:*)
498              at[ nameatom ].arity:= narity;         (* so use it !       *)
499              findatom:= nameatom
500          end
501      else begin    (* linear rehash (there is an empty atom sentinel) *)
502          thename:= at[ nameatom ]. name;   a:= nameatom;
503          while ( at[ a ]. name <> emptyatom ) and
504                  ( (at[a].name<>thename) or (at[a].arity<>narity) ) do
505              if a <> athish then a:= a + 1
506              else a:= atlow;
507          if at[ a ]. name = emptyatom then newatom(a, thename, narity);(*5*)
```

```
508                findatom:= a
509       end
510    end;
511  procedure buildname ( c : char );
512  (* add a character to the currently-constructed name *)
513  begin  if ctop = cthigh then error ( ctovflw );
514         ct[ ctop ]:= c;   ctop:= ctop + 1
516  end;
518  function wrapname  : atx;
519  (* the constructed name is complete =  return the first atom with this name *)
520  var  nm : atx;
521  begin  buildname ( chr ( eos ) );          (* terminate the string *)
522         nm:= findname ( builtname, ctop - 2 );
523         if at [ nm ]. name <> builtname then   (* copy already exists    *)
524                ctop:= builtname            (* so destroy the new one *)
525         else builtname:= ctop;             (* prepare for next name *)
526         wrapname:= nm
527  end;
529  function samename ( atom : atx; narity : argnumb ) : atx;
530  (* return the first atom ( in the appropriate hash chain ) with
531     the same name as atom but with. arity ( which may be different )    *)
532  begin  with at [ atom ] do
533         samename:= findatom ( findname ( name , charlast ( name ) ), narity )
534  end;
536  procedure putname ( c : ctx );
537  (* output the print name starting at c *)
538  begin  while ct[ c ]<> chr ( eos ) do begin
539                putch ( ct[ c ]);   c:= c + 1
540         end
541  end;
```

(continued)

```
542
543
544
545
546    (*-------------- t e r m   r e p r e s e n t a t i o n --------------*)
547
548         (* pt stands for a prototype or a term instance *)
549         (* note: chars have unique prots, cf newprot & charprot,
550              so have integers in the most frequently used range *)
551
552
553    procedure protspace ( size : integer ) ;
554    (* enough space in prototype area ? *)
555    begin  if nsbot - stop < size then error ( protovflw )
556    end;
557
558
559    (* function isnonsroundprot ( pt : mtx ) : boolean;
560    (* (* is it a non-ground prototype ( a prot with variables ) ? *)
561    (* (* expanded in varadr and terminst *)
562    (* begin   isnonsroundprot:= pt > nsbot
563    (* end;
564    (**)
565
566    function isvar ( pt : mtx ) : boolean;
567    (* a variable ? *)
568    begin  isvar:= mt [ pt ] <= varlim
569    end;
570
571    function isndvar ( pt : mtx ) : boolean;
572    (* a non-dummy variable ? *)
573    (** expanded in unify, terminst & argument *)
574    begin  isndvar:= mt [ pt ] < varlim
575    end;
```

```
576  (* function isframevar ( t : mtx ) : boolean;
577  (* (* a variable environment stack var ? *)
578  (* (** expanded in bind2vars & terminst *)
579  (* begin  isframevar:= t < vtop
580  (* end;
581
582  (**)
583
584  function isint ( pt : mtx ) : boolean;
585  (* an integer ? *)
586  (** expanded in unify *)
587  begin  isint:= mt [ pt ] = int
588  end;
589
590  function intval ( pt : mtx ) : integer;
591  (* an integer : return its value *)
592  (** expanded in unify *)
593  begin intval:= mt [ pt + 1 ]
594  end;
595
596  function isnormal ( pt : mtx ) : boolean;
597  (* not a variable or integer ?  note that int = varlim + 1 *)
598  (** expanded in unify *)
599  begin  isnormal:= mt [ pt ] > int
600  end;
601
602  function isargless ( pt : mtx ) : boolean;
603  (* a non-variable, non-integer prot/term without arguments ? *)
604  begin  if mt [ pt ] <= int then isargless:= false
605         else isargless :=  at [ mt [ pt ] ] . arity  =  0
606  end;
607
608  function ischar ( pt : mtx; var c : char ) : boolean;
609  (* is it a character term ? if so, what is the character ? *)
```

```
610   var  val : integer;
611   begin  val:= pt - minchprotx;
612      if ( val < 0 ) or ( val > maxchar ) then ischar:= false
613      else begin
614                 c:= chr ( val );    ischar:= true
615          end
616   end;
617
618   function charprot ( c : char ) : protx;
619   (* return this character's prototype *)
620   begin  charprot:= minchprotx + ord ( c )
621   end;
622
623   function setarity ( pt : mtx ) : argnumb;
624   (* return the narity of pt's functor *)
625   (** expanded in unify and terminst *)
626   begin  setarity:= mt [ pt ] ] . arity
627   end;
628
629   function setargs ( pt : mtx;  n :, argnum ) : mtx;
630   (* return pt's n'th argument (for prots only prot arg returned) *)
631   (** expanded in argument *)
632   begin  (* check(1, isnormal( pt ) and ( n)= 0 ) and ( n <= setarity( pt ))) *)
633      if mt [ pt + n ] <= varlim then setargs:= pt + n
634      else setargs:= mt [ pt + n ]
635   end;
636
637   function isstdint ( val : integer; var prot : protx ) : boolean;
638   (* if val is a standard integer, return its unique prototype *)
639   begin  if ( val < minstdint ) or ( val > maxstdint ) then isstdint:= false
640      else begin
641              prot:= stdintprotx + ( val - minstdint ) * 2;
642              isstdint:= true
643          end
```

```
644       end;
645       procedure mkint ( val : integer );
646       (* build an integer prototype on top of ground area *)
647       begin   protspace ( 2 );
648
649            mt [ stop ] := int;   mt [ stop + 1 ] := val;   stop := stop + 2
650       end;
651
652       function newintprot ( val : integer ) : protx;
653       (* return an integer prototype (ground) *)
654       var   p : protx;
655       begin   if isstdint ( val, p ) then newintprot := p
656            else begin
657                 newintprot := stop;   mkint ( val )
658            end
659       end;
660
661       function initprot ( atom : atx ) : protx;
662       (* create a prototype whose functor is described by atom.
663            note that it will need argument filling and wrapping.
664            guards uniqueness of character prototypes.            *)
665       var   size : integer;   achar : boolean;
666       begin   with at [ atom ] do begin
667                 size := 1 + arity;                  (* 1 for the functor *)
668                 if size <> 1 then achar := false
669                 else achar := ct [ name + 1 ] = chr ( eos ) ;
670                 if achar then initprot := charprot ( ct [ name ] )
671            end;
672            if not achar then begin
673                 protspace ( size );   ngbot := ngbot - size;
674                 mt [ ngbot + 1 ] := atom;            (* functor filled *)
675                 initprot := ngbot + 1
676            end
677       end;
```

281

(continued)

```
678    procedure newpvarg ( p : protx; n : argnumb; v : varnumb ) ;
679    (* insert this variable offset as the n'th argument of a constructed prot *)
680    begin  mt [ p + n ] := - ( v + offoff )
681    end;
682
683
684    procedure newpars ( p : protx; n : argnumb; arg : integer ) ;
685    (*insert the n'th (non-var or dummy var) argument into constructed prototype*)
686    begin  (* check (2, arg >= protlow ) ; *)
687           mt [ p + n ] := arg
688    end;
689
690    function wrapprot ( p : protx ) : protx;
691    (* p is a recently constructed prototype. return its final address
692    after attempting to move it to the ground prot area. the manner of
693    construction ensures that p can't be ground if it is not directly above
694    nsbot ( or already in the ground area - applies to chars & std ints ) .         *)
695    var  arity, k : argnumb;  ground : boolean;
696    begin  if p <> nsbot + 1 then wrapprot:= p
697           else begin                        (* see if all args are ground *)
698                  arity:= setarity ( p ) ;  k:= 0;  ground:= true;
699                  while ( k <> arity ) and ground do begin
700                         ground := setargs ( p, k ) ;  <  stop
701                         k:= k + 1;
702                  end;
703                  if not ground then wrapprot:= p
704                  else begin
705                         wrapprot:= stop;
706                         for k:= 0 to arity do begin        (*0 for the functor*)
707                                nsbot:= nsbot + 1;
708                                mt [ stop ] := mt [ nsbot ];
709                                stop:= stop + 1
710                         end
711                  end (**ground*)
```

(* shift to ground area *)

end (*ground?*)

282

```
712  end (*wrapprot*) ;
713
714
715
716
717
718  (*--------- t e r m   i n s t a n c e s ---------*)
719
720       (* pt stands for a copy stack term instance or
721          for a prototype in variable environment env *)
722
723
724  procedure stackspace ( size : integer ) ;
725  var  left : integer;
726  begin  left:= csbot - ( vtop + size ) ;
727       if left < 0 then error ( stackovflw ) ;
728       if left < stackminfree then stackminfree:= left
729  end;
730
731  procedure pushvars ( n : varnumb ) ;
732  (* push n free variables onto the variable environment stack *)
733  begin if n <> 0 then begin        (* test just for efficiency *)
734            stackspace ( n ) ;
735            for n:= n downto 1 do begin
736                 mt [ vtop ]:= freevar;   vtop:= vtop + 1
737            end
738       end
739  end;
740
741  function heapint ( i : integer ) : mtx;
742  (* create an integer object on the copy stack or return std int prot *)
743  var  p : protx;
744  begin  if isstdint ( i , p ) then heapint:= p
745         else begin
```

(continued)

283

```
746                   stackspace ( 2 ) ;
747                   mt [ csbot ] := i;      mt [ csbot - 1 ] := int;
748                   heapint:= csbot - 1;    csbot:= csbot - 2
749          end
750   end;
751   function heapdot ( head, tail : mtx ) : stackx;
752   (* create an instance of .(head, tail) *)
753   begin  stackspace ( 3 ) ;
754          mt [ csbot ] := tail;     mt [ csbot - 1 ] := head;
755          mt [ csbot - 2 ] := std [atmdot];     heapdot:= csbot - 2;
756          csbot:= csbot - 3
757
758   end;
759   function sterm ( atom : atx ) : stackx;
760   (* create a most general term instance for this atom, i.e. a term with
761      different variables for arguments; but guard char uniqueness.             *)
762   var   thisarity : argnum;  thisname : ctx;
763   begin  with at [ atom ] do begin
764                   thisarity:= arity;   thisname:= name
765          end;
766          if ( thisarity = 0 ) and ( ct [ thisname + 1 ] = chr( eos ) ) then
767                   sterm:= charprot ( ct [ thisname ] )
768          else begin
769                   stackspace ( 1 + thisarity ) ;    (* 1 for the functor *)
770                   for thisarity:= thisarity downto 1 do begin
771                           mt [ csbot ] := freevar;   csbot:= csbot - 1
772                   end;
773                   mt [ csbot ] := atom;   sterm:= csbot;   csbot:= csbot - 1
774          end
775   end;
776
777   procedure bind ( v : stackx; t : mtx ) ;
778   (* bind variable instance v to term t, pushing a trail if necessary *)
779
```

```
780 begin    (* check (3, isndvar ( v ) and ( mt [ v ] = freevar ) ); *)
781       mt [ v ] := - t;
782       if ( v > frozenheap ) or ( v < frozenvars ) then begin
783          if ttop = tthigh then error ( ttovflw );
784          tt [ ttop ] := v;  ttop := ttop + 1;
785          if tminfree > tthigh - ttop then tminfree := tthigh - ttop
786       end
787 end;
788
789 procedure undo ( tlev : ttx );
790 (* bring trail level down to tlev and undo the bindings referenced by    *)
791     popped trail entries.
792 begin   while ttop > tlev do begin
793              ttop := ttop - 1;   mt [ tt [ ttop ] ] := freevar
794          end
795 end;
796
797 procedure bind2vars ( v1, v2 : stackx );
798 (* v1 and v2 are free variable instances. if they are of the same kind,
799    bind the younger to the older. otherwise bind the frame variable to
800    the copy stack ( heap ) variable.
801 ** v < vtop is expanded isframevar                                       *)
802 begin   (* check (4, isndvar ( v1 ) and isndvar ( v2 ) ); *)
803     if v1 = v2 then          (* no action - must remain free *)
804     else
805     if v1 < vtop then                              (*v1 frame*)
806        if v2 < vtop then                           (*v2 frame*)
807           if v1 < v2 then bind ( v2, v1 )          (*v1 older*)
808           else bind ( v1, v2 )                     (*v2 older*)
809        else bind ( v1, v2)                         (*v1 frame, v2 heap*)
810     else
811     if v2 < vtop then bind ( v2, v1 )              (*v2 frame, v1 heap*)
812     else
813     if v1 < v2 then bind ( v1, v2 )                (*v2 older*)
```

285

(continued)

```
814          else bind ( v2, v1 )                              (*v1 older*)
815    end;
816
817    function varadr ( v : mtx; env : stackx ) : stackx;
818    (* v is a variable prototype or instance. if a prototype,
819       find its instance in variable environment env. **isnonsroundprot expanded *)
820    begin   (* check (5; isndvar ( v ) ); *)
821          if not ( v ) nsbot ) then varadr:= v
822          else varadr:= env + ( - mt [ v ] - offoff )
823
824    end;
825    function argument ( pt : mtx; env : stackx; n : argnumb ) : mtx;
826    (* pt is a term instance or a prototype in variable environment env,
827       and is neither a variable nor an integer. return its dereferenced
828       n'th argument. instead of a variable prototype return
829       a frame variable cell index. ** setars expanded here.            *)
830    var  field; arg : mtx;
831    begin   field:= pt + n;
832          if mt [field] > varlim then arg:= mt [field]           (* non-var *)
833          (* mt [ field ] :: varlim impossible; as only dumvarx holds varlim *)
834          else begin     (* non-dummy var; dereference binding if any *)
835                   arg:= varadr ( field; env ) );
836                   (*note that nonvars or free vars will stop the loop *)
837                   while mt [ arg ] < freevar do arg:= - mt [ arg ]
838          end;
839          argument:= arg
840    end;
841    function terminst ( pt : mtx; env : stackx ) : mtx;
842    (* if pt is a term instance ( a ground prototype or a copy-stack object ),
843       return its address. if it is a non-ground prototype use env as
844       the proper variable environment and return the address of a new copy
845       in the copy stack. free frame variables are bound to their copies.    *)
846    (* ***isnonsroundprot; setarity and isndvar expanded *)
847
```

286

```
848  var    arity, k : argnumb;   copy : stackx;   arg : mtx;
849  begin   if not ( pt > ngbot ) then terminst:= pt     (* not isnonsroundprot *)
850          else    (* the following branch for stand-alone frame variables *)
851          if mt[ pt ] < varlim then begin  (*isndvar: build a new heap variable*)
852              stackspace ( 1 );
853              mt [ csbot ] := freevar;   copy:= csbot;   csbot:= csbot - 1;
854              bind ( varadr ( pt, env ), copy ) ;   terminst:= copy
855          end
856          else begin
857              arity:= at [ mt [ pt [ ].arity;
858              stackspace ( 1 + arity ) ;   (* 1 for the functor *)
859              csbot:= csbot - ( 1 + arity ) ;    copy:= csbot + 1;
860              mt [ copy ] := mt [ pt ];          (* functor *)
861              for k:= 1 to arity do begin       (* arguments *)
862                  arg:= argument ( pt, env, k ) ;
863                  if arg < vtop then begin (*framevar,evidently free*)
864                      bind ( arg, copy + k ) ;
865                      mt [ copy + k ] := freevar
866                  end
867                  else mt [ copy + k ] := - terminst ( arg, env )
868                      (*ie.args always linked as if through vars,
869                      because terminst can return a variable.   *)
870              end;
871              terminst:= copy
872          end
873  end;

875  function unify ( c : mtx;   cenv : stackx;   h : mtx;   henv : stackx )
876                                                  : boolean;
877  (* c and h are terms ( possibly prototypes in variable environments cenv and
878     henv ), but neither is a non-dummy variable prototype ( cf. argument ). -
879     try to unify, but don't undo on failure.                            *)
880  var   success : boolean;   arity, n : argnumb;   mth, mtc : integer;
881  begin   (* check(6, not ( isndvar( c ) and isnonsroundprot( c ) ) and
```

(continued)

287

```
882    success:= true;      not ( isndvar( h ) and isnonsgroundprot( h ) ) ); *)
883    mth:= mt [ h ]; mtc:= mt [ c ];      (* let's be optimistic for a change *)
884    (* first branch if same prots and environment or same terms and      (* more wieldy & efficient *)
885       environment doesn't matter (i.e. not non-ground prots),
886       i.e. an attempt to unify a term with itself : no action required *)
887
888    if ( h = c ) and ( ( henv = cenv ) or ( h <= ngbot ) ) then
889    else
890    if ( mth > int ) and ( mtc > int ) then                    (*both are "normal" *)
891            if mth <> mtc then success:= false                 (*different functors*)
892            else begin                                         (*try the arguments *)
893                    n:= 0; arity:= at [ mth ]. arity;
894                    while ( n <> arity ) and success do begin
895                            n:= n + 1;
896                            success:= unify( argument( c, cenv, n ), cenv,
897                                             argument( h, henv, n ), henv)
898                    end
899            end
900    else                                                       (* at least one int or var *)
901    if ( h = dumvarx ) or ( c = dumvarx ) then                 (*no action*)
902    else
903    if mth = freevar then
904            if mtc = freevar then bind2vars ( h, c )           (*isndvar(h)*)
905            else bind ( h, terminst( c, cenv ) )               (*isndvar(c)*)
906    else
907            if mtc = freevar then bind ( c, terminst ( h, henv ) )   (*isndvar(c)*)
908    else
909    if mth = int then
910            if mtc <> int then success:= false                 (* not isint( c ) *)
911            else success:= mt [ h + 1 ] = mt [ c + 1 ]         (*intvals*)
912    else
913    if mtc = int then success:= false                          (*isint(h)*)
914    else error ( unifyerr );
915    unify:= success
```

288

```
916    end;
917    procedure display ( pt : mtx; env : stackx ) ;
918    (* output pt in standard form *)
919    var   arity, k : argnumb;
920    begin  if isvar ( pt ) then begin
921           putch ( '_' ) ;
922           if pt <> dumvarx then putint ( varadr ( pt, env ) )
923           end
924    else
925           if isint ( pt ) then putint ( intval ( pt ) )
926    else begin
927           putname ( at[ mt[ pt ] ].name ) ;   arity:= getarity ( pt ) ;
928           if arity <> 0 then begin
929                  putch ( '(' ) ;  putch ( ' ' ) ;
930                  for k:= 1 to arity do begin
931                         display ( argument ( pt, env, k ), env ) ;
932                         if k <> arity then putch ( ',' ) ;
933                         putch ( ' ' )
934                         end;
935                  putch ( ')' )
936                  end (*arity<>0*)
937           end
938    end (*display*) ;
939
940    function iscallsequence ( pt : mtx; env : stackx ) : boolean;
941    (* is this term a dotted list without integer or variable elements ? *)
942    var   is : ( no, dontknow, yes ) ;
943    begin  is:= dontknow;
944           repeat if not ( isnormal ( pt ) ) then is:= no
945           else
946                  if mt[ pt ] = std [atmnil] then is:= yes
947           else
948                  if mt[ pt ] <> std [atmdot] then is:= no
```

(continued)

289

```
950                         else begin
951                            if not isnormal( argument(pt, env, car)) then is:= no;
952                            pt:= argument ( pt, env, cdr )        (* tail *)
953                     end
954               until is <> dontknow;
955               iscallsequence:= is = yes
956       end;




961   (*---------------     c o n t r o l     ------------*)
962
963       (* note that call sequence prototypes have non-variable elements.
964          thus mt [ seq + car ] and mt [ seq + cdr ] access the first
965          call in a sequence and the sequence tail respectively.          *)
966
967
969   procedure sysroutcall ( id : sysroutid;   var success, stop : boolean );
970   forward; (*----------------------------------------------------------*)
971
972
973   function isnonunitclause ( proc : procptr ) : boolean;
974   (* is proc a clause, and does it have any calls ? *)
975   begin  if proc = nil then isnonunitclause:= false
976          else with proc @ do
977             if systemroutine then isnonunitclause:= false
978             else isnonunitclause:= mt [ body ] <> std [atmnil]
979   end;
980
981   procedure pushbackpt ( proc : procptr );
982   (* push a backtrack point freezing the current frame for resumption of proc *)
983   begin  if topb = bthigh then error ( btovflw );
```

```
984     topb:= topb + 1;
985     if bminfree > bthish - topb then bminfree:= bthish - topb;
986     with bt [ topb ] do begin
987        frozenframe:= topf;    resume:= proc;
988        copylev:= csbot;    traillev:= ttop
989     end;
990     frozenvars:= topenv;    frozenheap:= csbot
991  end;
992
993  procedure popbackpt;
994  (* topb <> btlow. return to the previous backtrack point *)
995  begin (* check (7, topb <> btlow ) ; *)
996     topb:= topb - 1;
997     with bt [ topb ] do begin
998        frozenheap:= copylev;    frozenvars:= ft [ frozenframe ]. vars
999     end
1000 end;
1001
1002 procedure pushframe ( ancestor : ftx; callsequence : protx );
1003 (* create a new (current) environment frame with no variables (as yet) *)
1004 begin if topf = fthish then error ( ftovflw );
1005    topf:= topf + 1;
1006    if fminfree > fthish - topf then fminfree:= fthish - topf;
1007    with ft [ topf ] do begin
1008       anc:= ancestor;    calls:= callsequence;    vars:= vtop
1009    end;
1010    topenv:= vtop;    ancf:= ancestor;    ancenv:= ft [ ancf ]. vars,
1011 end;
1012
1013 procedure backtrack ( var stop : boolean );
1014 (* set stop if no backtrack points left; otherwise restore the state frozen
1015    by the current backpt and set cproc to the clause to be attempted next *)
1016 begin if topb = btlow then stop:= true
1017    else begin
```

(continued)

```
1018              csbot:= frozenheap;  vtop:= frozenvars;
1019              with bt [ topb ] do begin
1020                undo ( trailev );
1021                (* if frozenframe = topf, we are only backtracking
1022                from a non-matching clause head :: the control
1023                resisters need not change.                    *)
1024                if frozenframe <> topf then begin
1025                    topf:= frozenframe;  topenv:= ft [topf].vars;
1026                    ancf:= ft [topf].anc; ancenv:= ft [ancf].vars;
1027                    (* set ccall, skipping call & tas ::
1028                     no error possible, we've been here *)
1029                    ccall:= mt [ ft [ topf ]. calls + car ];
1030                    while ( mt [ ccall ] = std [atmcall] ) or
1031                      ( mt [ ccall ] = std [atmtag] ) do
1032                        ccall:= arsument( ccall, ancenv, 1 )
1033                end;
1034                cproc:= resume @. next;
1035                if cproc = nil then popbackpt
1036              else
1037                if cproc @. next = nil then popbackpt
1038              else resume:= cproc
1039          end (*with*)
1040        end
1041    end (*backtrack*);
1042
1043    procedure exitt ( var stop : boolean );
1044    (* starting from the most recently activated procedure ( system routine or
1045      unit clause ) exit until a pending call is found. set stop if none.   *)
1046    var f, anc : ftx; nextcseq : protx;  found : boolean;
1047    begin   found:= false; f:= topf; stop:= false;
1048        repeat   (* tentative exit until nonterminated frame or stack bottom *)
1049            nextcseq:= mt [ ft [ f ]. calls + cdr ];
1050            if mt [ nextcseq ] = std [atmdot] then found:= true
1051            else begin                            (* no more calls *)
```

292

```
1052        end
1053        f := ft [ f ]. anc;   stop := f = ftlow
1054    until found or stop;
1055    if found then begin        (* finalise exit and set next proc *)
1056        ancf := ft [ f ]. anc;   ancenv := ft [ ancf ]. vars;
1057        if f > bt [ topb ]. frozenframe then topf := f
1058        else begin              (* frozen : must activate a copy *)
1059            topf := bt [ topb ]. frozenframe + 1;
1060            with ft [ topf ] do begin
1061                anc := ancf;   vars := frozenvars
1062            end
1063        end;
1064        with ft [ topf ] do begin        (* advance in frame *)
1065            calls := nextcseq;   topenv := vars
1066        end;
1067        vtop := topenv    (* discard exited nonfrozen var env frames *)
1068    end
1069 end (*exitt*);

1070
1071 function candotro ( frame : ftx ) : boolean;
1072 (* can we apply tail recursion optimisation (tro) to this frame, i.e.
1073    destroy it after shifting its variables over those of its ancestor ?
1074    we can if its call is last in its clause ( and is not an outermost
1075    tag ) and the ancestor is not frozen.                    *)
1076 begin  with ft [ frame ] do
1077    if anc <= bt [ topb ]. frozenframe then candotro := false
1078    else candotro := ( mt [ mt [ calls + cdr ] [ ] = std [atmnil] ) and
1079                     ( mt [ mt [ calls + car [ ] = std [atmtag] )
1080 end;

1081
1082 procedure trooverlay ( var younsframe : ftx;   var younsenv : stackx;
1083                       var oldframe : ftx;   var oldenv : stackx ) ;
1084 (* apply tail recursion optimisation :  overlay old frame's variable
1085    environment (oldenv) with that of younsframe (younsenv), then
```

293

(continued)

```
1086      let youngsframe reference oldframe and oldframe's ancestor.
1087      youngsenv must be the youngest variable environment on the stack.
1088      both frames must not be frozen (vars not referenced from trail)     *)
1089  var  low, high : stackx;  shiftby, v : integer;
1090  begin  if oldenv <> youngsenv then begin  (*shift after reference adjustment*)
1091           high:= youngsenv;  shiftby:= youngsenv - oldenv;
1092           while high < vtop do begin       (*adj. refs to shifted/overlaid*)
1093             v:= - mt [ high ];             (*  value of shifted var *)
1094             if ( v >= oldenv ) and ( v < youngsenv ) then begin
1095               (*ref to overlaid. if overlaid free, reverse
1096                 pointers so that all vars bound to it will
1097                 be rebound to high; otherwise follow the
1098                 overlaid ref & repeat adjustment loop for
1099                 this high to deal with new mt[high].        *)
1100               if mt [ v ] = freevar then begin
1101                 mt [ high ] := freevar;
1102                 mt [ v ] := - high;
1103                 high:= high + 1
1104               end
1105             else mt [ high ] := mt [ v ]
1106             end (*to overlaid*)
1107           else begin  (*if ref. to shifted, adjust to new adr*)
1108             if ( v >= youngsenv ) and ( v < vtop ) then
1109               mt [ high ] := - ( v - shiftby );
1110             high:= high + 1
1111             end
1112           end (*adjustment loop*) ;
1113           low:= oldenv;
1114           for high:= youngsenv to vtop - 1 do begin    (* shift *)
1115             mt [ low ] := mt [ high ];  low:= low + 1
1116           end;
1117           vtop := low
1118         end (*tricks dealings*) ;
1119    youngsenv:= oldenv;  youngsframe:= oldframe;
```

```
1120        oldframe:= ft [ youngframe ]. anc;   oldenv:= ft [ oldframe ]. vars
1121    end (*trooverlay*);
1122
1123    procedure enter;
1124    (* build a frame for the first call in cproc. *)
1125    begin (* check (8, ( cproc <> nil ) and not cproc@.systemroutine ); *)
1126      if candotro ( topf ) then trooverlay ( topf, topenv, ancf, ancenv ) ;
1127      pushframe ( topf, cproc @. body )
1128    end;
1129
1130    procedure errsetup;
1131    (* invoked upon detection of an erroneous system routine call ( so topf is not
1132       frozen ). top frame is associated with a variable bound to the bad call,
1133       then a call to 'error'/1 is set up.                                  *)
1134    begin (* check (9, topf > bt [ topb ]. frozenframe ); *)
1135      topenv:= vtop;  ft [ topf ]. vars:= topenv;  pushvars ( 1 );
1136      bind ( topenv, terminst ( mt [ ft [topf].calls + car ], ancenv ) ) ;
1137      pushframe ( topf, errorcallseq );  ccall:= mt [ errorcallseq + car ]
1138    end;
1139
1140    procedure preparestep;
1141    (* load ccall, stripping off tos & call, then load cproc and
1142       push a backtrack-point if needed.                           *)
1143    begin  ccall:= mt [ ft [ topf ]. calls + car ];
1144      while ( mt [ ccall ] = std [atmcall] ) or
1145           ( mt [ ccall ] = std [atmtas] ) do begin
1146        ccall:= argument ( ccall, ancenv, 1 );
1147        if not isnormal ( ccall ) then errsetup       (*affects ccall*)
1148      end;
1149      cproc:= at [ mt [ ccall ]. proc;
1150      if cproc <> nil then
1151        if cproc @. next <> nil then pushbackpt ( cproc )
1152    end (*preparestep*);
1153
```

295

(continued)

```
1154   procedure onestep ( var success, stop : boolean ) ;
1155   (* perform a single resolution step.
1156   on entry success is false immediately after a backtrack, true otherwise. *)
1157        procedure showcall;
1158        (* show the call in wallpaper trace *)
1159        var keep : boolean;
1160        begin  keep:= telling;  telling:= false;
1161               display ( ccall, ancenv );  telling:= keep
1162        end;
1163        procedure showresult;
1164        (* show the call's result in wallpaper trace *)
1165        var keep : boolean;
1166        begin  keep:= telling;  telling:= false;
1167               if success then writeln ( co, "*+*" )
1168               else writeln ( co, "*--*" );
1169               putline;  telling:= keep
1170        end;
1171        procedure shownoproc;
1172        (* output a message for a call to a nonexistent procedure *)
1173        var keep : boolean;
1174        begin  keep:= telling;  telling:= false;
1175               putline;
1176               write(co, "---failing call to non existent procedure:") ;
1177               putline;  putname ( at[ mt[ ccall ] ].name ) ;
1178               putch ( "," ) ;
1179               putint( setarity ( ccall ) ) ;  putline;
1180               telling:= keep
1181        end;
1182   begin  if success then preparestep;           (* otherwise backtrack did *)
1183          if debug then showcall;
1184          if cproc = nil then begin                (*empty proc called*)
1185                  success:= false;
1186                  if shownonexistent then shownoproc
1187
```

296

```
1188          end
1189        else with cproc @ do begin
1190          pushvars ( nvars ) ;
1191          if systemroutine then sysroutcall ( sysid, success, stop )
1192          else success:= unify( ccall, ancenv, cproc @, head, topenv )
1193        end (*with*);
1194      if debug then showresult
1195   end (*onestep*);

1196
1197   procedure startresolution ( goalsequence : protx; ngoalvars : varnumb ) ;
1198   (* initialise stacks in preparation for this goal's execution. the lowermost
1199      frame is associated with goal's variables, the lowermost backtrack point
1200      freezes it and acts as a sentinel. both have some dummy entries.         *)
1201   begin ttop:= ttlow; vtop:= mtlow; csbot:= stackhigh;
1202         topf:= ftbelow; topb:= btbelow;
1203         pushframe ( ftlow, nilprotx ) ;          (* dummy call *)
1204         pushbackpt ( nil ) ;
1205         pushvars ( ngoalvars ) ;   pushframe ( topf, goalsequence )
1206   end;

1207
1208   procedure resolve ( goalsequence : protx; nvarsingoalseq : varnumb ) ;
1209   (* execute this ( initial ) goal sequence *)
1210   var success, stop : boolean;
1211   begin startresolution ( goalsequence, nvarsingoalseq ) ;
1212         stop:= false; success:= true; (* false only on failure *)
1213         repeat
1214           onestep ( success, stop ) ;
1215           if not stop then
1216             if syserror then begin
1217               syserror:= false;       success:= true;
1218               errsetup
1219             end
1220             else
1221               if not success then backtrack ( stop )
```

(continued)

```
1222                              else
1223                              if isnonunitclause ( cproc ) then enter
1224                              else exitt ( stop )
1225                   until stop
1226         end (*resolve*);
1227
1228
1229
1230
1231   (*----------- c o n t r o l   d i s r u p t i o n   e t c .  -----------*)
1232         (* note that only explicit, outermost tags are detected.
1233            eg. in "call( tag(...))" tag is ignored :
1234            tags are tricky enough as it is.
1235            cf. also candotro, backtrack and preparestep in control. *)
1236
1237
1238   procedure purgetrail ( low : ttx );
1239   (* remove unnecessary trail entries at and above low , either after
1240      a successful unifyordont call or after popping backtrack-points in
1241      a non-backtracking context ( unfreeze ). this is necessary, as
1242      unfrozen vars might be moved or destroyed -- it also saves trail space. *)
1243   var high : ttx;
1244   begin  for high:= low to ttop - 1 do
1245              if (tt [high] < frozenvars) or (tt [high] > frozenheap)
1246                                                                then begin
1247                            tt [ low ] :=  tt [ high ];   low:= low + 1
1248                  end;
1249         ttop:= low
1250   end;
1251
1252   function unifyordont ( c : mtx; cenv : stackx; h : mtx; henv : stackx )
1253                                                               : boolean;
1254   (* same as unify, but undo effects on failure.
1255      this is done by ensuring that all bindings are trailed. *)
```

```
1256  var    success : boolean;         fv, fh : stackx;      tlev : ttx;
1257  begin   fv:= frozenvars;          fh:= frozenheap;      tlev:= ttop;
1258          frozenvars:= vtop;        frozenheap:= csbot;
1259          success:= unify ( c, cenv, h, henv ) ;
1260          frozenvars:= fv;          frozenheap:= fh;
1262          if success then purgetrail ( tlev )
1263          else undo ( tlev ) ;
1264          unifyordont:= success
1265  end;
1266  procedure unfreeze ( frame : ftx ) ;
1267  (* remove as many backtrack points as necessary to unfreeze frame ( >ftlow) *)
1268  var    chansed : boolean;
1269  begin   chansed:= false;
1270          while frame <= bt [ topb ]. frozenframe do begin (*sentinel at btlow*)
1271                 chansed:= true;  popbackpt
1272          end;
1273          if chansed then purgetrail ( bt [ topb ]. traillev )
1274  end;
1275  procedure cutcleanup;
1276  (* destroy cut-off frames between cut or tagcut and its immediate ancestor. *)
1277  var    ancancf : ftx;   ancancenv : stackx;   owncalls : protx;
1279  begin   if topf <> ancf + 1 then begin
1280                 vtop:= ft [ ancf + 1 ] .vars;
1281                 ft [ ancf + 1 ] := ft [ topf ];    topf:= ancf + 1;
1282                 ft [ topf ] .vars := vtop
1283          end;
1284          if candotro ( ancf ) then begin          (* tro for ancf *)
1285                 ancancf:= ft [ ancf ]. ancf;
1286                 ancancenv:= ft [ ancancf ]. vars;
1287                 owncalls:= ft [ topf ]. calls;  (*save continuation*)
1288                 trooverlay( ancf, ancenv, ancancf, ancancenv ) ;
1289                 topf:= ancf + 1;     (* args were just chansed *)
```

(continued)

```
1290              with ft [ topf ] do begin          (*rebuild own frame*)
1291                      calls:= owncalls;    anc:= ancf;
1292                      vars:= vtop; topenv:= vtop
1293              end
1294        end (*tro*)
1295 end (*cutcleanup*);
1296
1297 procedure slash;
1298 (* perform the "cut" operation :: unfreeze the nearest ancestor which
1299    is not ";"(_,_) or ";"(_,_,_) (after stripping off "tag" and "call";)
1300    attempt a delayed tro for the immediate ancestor.                   *)
1301 var f,ancancf : ftx; ancancenv : stackx; found : boolean;
1302     call : mtx;
1303 begin   f := ancf;   found:= false;
1304         while ( f <> ftlow ) and not found do begin
1305             call:= mt [ ft [ f ]. calls + car ];
1306             ancancf:= ft [ f ]. anc;   ancancenv:= ft [ ancancf ]. vars;
1307             while (mt[call]= std[atmtag]) or (mt[call]= std[atmcall]) do
1308                         call:= argument ( call, ancancenv, 1 );
1309             if ( mt [ call ] <> std [ atmsemcol ] [ ] ) and
1310                ( mt [ call ] <> std [ atmcomma ] ) then found:= true
1311             else f:= ancancf
1312         end;
1313         if found then begin
1314             unfreeze ( f );          cutcleanup
1315         end (*found*)
1316 end (*slash*);
1317
1318 function gottagged ( var f : ftx;   pt : mtx;   env : stackx ) : boolean;
1319 (* among the ancestors of f search for the nearest tagged call unifiable
1320    with pt in env. if found, unify and return true with f pointing at
1321    the tagged frame; if not, return false with f undefined.            *)
1322 var   call : protx;   callenv : stackx;   found : boolean;
1323 begin   found:= false;
```

```
1324   while ( f <> ftlow ) and not found do
1325       with ft [ f ] do begin
1326           call:= mt [ calls + car ]; callenv:= ft [anc]. vars;
1327           if mt [ call ] = std.[atmtag] then found:=
1328               unifyordont( argument(call, callenv, 1),
1329                                       callenv, pt, env ) ;
1330           if not found then f:= anc
1331       end (*with*) ;
1332       gottagged:= found

1334 end;
1335 procedure ancestor ( var success : boolean ) ;
1336 (* try to unify sysrout arg with a tagged ancestor. *)
1337 var  frame : ftx;
1338 begin  frame:= ancf;    success:= gottagged ( frame, spar [ 1 ], ancenv )
1339 end;

1341 procedure tagcut ( var success : boolean ) ;
1342 (* if a tagged ancestor unifies with the sysrout parameter, unfreeze it *)
1343 var  frame : ftx;
1344 begin  frame:= ancf;
1345     if gottagged ( frame, spar [ 1 ], ancenv ) then begin
1346             unfreeze ( frame ) ;    cutcleanup
1347     end
1348     else success:= false
1349 end;


1352 procedure tagfail ( var success : boolean ) ;
1353 (* if a tagged ancestor unifies with the sysrout parameter, cause
1354     the ancestor to fail immediately, otherwise simply fail.   *)
1355 begin  tagcut ( success ) ;              (* if ancestor unfrozen, it will fail now *)
1356     success:= false
1357 end;
```

(continued)

```
1358  procedure tagexit ( var success : boolean );
1359  (* if a tagged ancestor unifies with the sysrout parameter, unify and
1360     immediately exit to the ancestor by resetting ancf and changing topf's
1361     call sequence to errorcallseq ( only because it has an empty tail, sorry ! ),
1362     and cproc to nil. otherwise fail.                                          *)
1363  var  frame : ftx;
1364  begin   frame:= ancf;
1365     if gottagged ( frame, spar [ 1 ], ancenv ) then
1366     begin
1367        with ft[ topf ] do begin
1368           calls:=errorcallseq;    cproc:= nil;
1369           anc:=frame;  ancf:= frame
1370        end
1371     end
1372     else success:=false
1373  end;
1374
1375
1376  (*--------  a r i t h m e t i c ,  c h a r s  --------*)
1377
1378  procedure bindpar ( v : nsysparam; t : mtx );
1379  (* v is the number of a variable sysrout parameter :  bind it to t.
1380     -------> used also outside arithmetic (------                   *)
1381  begin   if spar [ v ]<> dumvarx then bind ( varadr( spar [ v ], ancenv ), t )
1382  end;
1383
1384  procedure arithans ( answar : nsysparam; answer : integer );
1385  (* sysrout parameter answar is a variable :  bind it to answer *)
1386  begin   bindpar ( answar, heapint ( answer ) )
1387  end;
1388
1389  procedure arithpars ( k : nsysparam; var code : integer );
1390  (* k is the number of parameters in spar. for each integer parameter set
1391
```

```
1392         a bit in the rightmost k bits of code, only integers and variables    *)
1393         allowed: syserror is set for others.
1394 var i : nysparam;
1395 begin   code:= 0;
1396     for i:= 1 to k do begin
1397         code:= code * 2;                    (* shift left *)
1398         if isint ( spar [ i ] ) then code:= code + 1    (* set bit *)
1399         else
1400             if not isvar ( spar [ i ] ) then syserror:= true
1401         end
1402 end (*arithpars*);
1403
1404 procedure sum ( var success : boolean );
1405 (* a + b = x or a + x = c or x + b = c or a + b = c ? *)
1406 var  code : 0..7;
1407 begin  arithpars ( 3, code );
1408     if not syserror then
1409         case code of
1410             0, 1, 2, 4 :  syserror:= true;   (* not enough integers *)
1411 (*011*)     3 :  arithans ( 1, sparv [ 3 ] - sparv [ 2 ] );
1412 (*101*)     5 :  arithans ( 2, sparv [ 3 ] - sparv [ 1 ] );
1413 (*110*)     6 :  arithans ( 3, sparv [ 1 ] + sparv [ 2 ] );
1414 (*111*)     7 :  success:=  sparv [ 1 ] + sparv [ 2 ] = sparv [ 3 ]
1415             end
1416 end (*sum*);
1417
1418 procedure prod ( var success : boolean );
1419 (* a*b+c = x or a*x+c = d or ( a*x+c = d & y < a ) or
1420    ( x*b+y = d & y < a ) or  x*b+c = d or a*b+c = d ?    *)
1421 var  code : 0..15;
1422     procedure divmod ( x, by : nysparam );
1423     begin if sparv [ by ] = 0 then syserror:= true
1424         else begin
1425             arithans ( 3, sparv [ 4 ] mod sparv [ by ] );
```

(continued)

```
1426                                  arithans ( x, sparv [ 4 ] div sparv [ by ] )
1427           end
1428       end;
1429       procedure division ( x, by : nsysparam ) ;
1430       begin  if sparv [ by ] = 0 then syserror := true
1431           else begin
1432                   if (sparv[ 4 ] - sparv[ 3 ] ) mod sparv[ by ] <> 0
1433                                                then success := false
1434                   else arithans(x, (sparv[4] - sparv[3]) div sparv[by])
1435           end
1436       end;
1437  begin  (* prod *)
1438       arithpars ( 4, code ) ;
1439       if not syserror then
1440           case code of
1441           0,1,2,3,4,6,8,10,12 :  syserror := true;   (* ambiguous *)
1442  (*0101*)    5 :  divmod ( 1, 2 ) ;
1443  (*0111*)    7 :  division ( 1, 2 ) ;
1444  (*1001*)    9 :  divmod ( 2, 1 ) ;
1445  (*1011*)   11 :  division ( 2, 1 ) ;
1446  (*1101*)   13 :  arithans ( 3, sparv [ 4 ] - sparv [ 1 ] * sparv [ 2 ] ) ;
1447  (*1110*)   14 :  arithans ( 4, sparv [ 1 ] * sparv [ 2 ] + sparv [ 3 ] ) ;
1448  (*1111*)   15 :  success := sparv [ 1 ] * sparv [ 2 ] = sparv [ 4 ] - sparv [ 3 ]
1449           end
1450  end (*prod*);
1451
1452  procedure inf ( var success : boolean ) ;
1453  (* a < b ? *)
1454  var  code : 0..3;
1455  begin  arithpars ( 2, code.) ;
1456       if not syserror then
1457           if code <> 3 then syserror := true     (* 2 ints needed *)
1458  (*11*)      else success := sparv [ 1 ] > sparv [ 2 ]
1459  end;
```

304

```
1460  procedure nameinf ( var success : boolean );
1461  (* implement '@' : sysrout parameters are argless functors,
1462     check their lexicographic ordering.      *)
1463  begin if not isargless ( spar [ 1 ] ) or not ( isargless ( spar [ 2 ] ) )
1464                                              then syserror:= true
1465        else success:== compstrings( at [ mt [ spar [ 1 ] ]. name,
1466                                      at [ mt [ spar [ 2 ] ]. name, false )
1467  end;
1468
1469  procedure ordchr ( var success : boolean );
1470  (* chr ( a mod nch ) = x or x = ord ( b ) or a mod nch = ord ( b ) ?
1471     nch is the number of characters, i.e. maxchar + 1 ( 128 for ASCII )  *)
1472  var ch : char; isch : boolean;
1473  begin isch:== ischar ( spar [ 2 ], ch );       (* ch defined if isch *)
1474        if isint ( spar [ 1 ] ) then
1475                   if isvar ( spar [ 2 ] ) then
1476                           bindpar( 2, charprot( chr( sparv[1] mod (maxchar+1))))
1477                   else
1478                   if isch then success:== sparv[1] mod (maxchar+1) = ord ( ch )
1479                   else syserror:= true
1480        else
1481        if isch and isvar ( spar [1] ) then arithans ( 1, ord ( ch ) )
1482        else syserror:= true
1483  end (*ordchr*);
1484
1485  procedure chiclass ( class : classofchar; var success : boolean );
1486  (* if the sysrout parameter is not a character, fail.
1487     otherwise check if it is of this class.       *)
1488  var c : char;
1489  begin if ischar ( spar [ 1 ], c ) then success:== cc [ c ] = class
1490        else success:=false
1491  end;
1492
1493
```

(continued)

```
1494  procedure ch2class ( class : classofchar;   var success : boolean );
1495  (* like chclass1, but c ( class is also ok *)
1496  var  c : char;
1497  begin  if ischar ( spar [ 1 ], c ) then success:= cc [ c ] <= class
1498         else success:= false
1499  end;
1500
1501
1502
1503
1504
1505  (*————————  s t r u c t u r e   a c c e s s  ————————*)
1506
1507  function atomspar ( name, arity : nsysparam )  : atx;
1508  (* extract an atom description from a sysrout call specifying name & arity.
1509    ————> used also outside structure access (————                     *)
1510  begin  if not isargless( spar [name]) or not isint( spar [arity]) then begin
1511              syserror:= true;  atomspar:= atlow      (* a dummy value *)
1512          end
1513          else atomspar:= samename ( mt [spar [name][], sparv [arity] )
1514
1515  end;
1516
1517  procedure eqvar ( var success : boolean );
1518  (* are both sysrout parameters the same non-dummy variable ? *)
1519  begin  if not isndvar( spar[1]) or not isndvar( spar[2]) then success:= false
1520         else success := spar [ 1 ] = spar [ 2 ]
1521  end;
1522
1523  procedure functor ( var success : boolean );
1524  (* implement functor( term, func, narity ) *)
1525  var  atom : atx;
1526  begin  if isvar ( spar [ 1 ] ) then        (* construct most general term *)
1527         if isint ( spar [ 2 ] ) then
                if not isint ( spar [ 3 ] ) then syserror:= true
```

```
1528              else
1529                if sparv[ 3 ] <> 0 then syserror:= true
1530              else bindpar ( 1, spar [ 2 ] )
1531            else begin
1532              atom:= atomspar ( 2, 3 );
1533              if not syserror then bindpar ( 1, sterm ( atom ) )
1534            end
1535          else   (* match term's functor with arity and func *)
1536            if isint ( spar [ 1 ] ) then
1537              if unify ( spar [ 2 ], ancenv, spar [ 1 ], vtop ) then
1538                success:= unify( spar[3], ancenv, heapint( 0 ), vtop )
1539              else success:= false
1540                                (* try narity, then func *)
1541            if unify( spar[3], ancenv, heapint( setarity( spar[1] ) ), vtop ) then
1542              success:= unify( spar [ 2 ], ancenv,
1543                         sterm( samename( mt [ spar[[1] ,0 ) ), vtop )
1544            else success:= false
1545   end (*functor*);
1546
1547   procedure arg ( var success : boolean );
1548   (* implement arg ( number, term, argument ) *)
1549   begin if not isint( spar[1]) or not isnormal( spar [2]) then syserror:= true
1550        else
1551          if (sparv[1]<1) or (sparv[1] > setarity(spar[2])) then success:= false
1552          else success:= unify ( spar [ 3 ], ancenv,
1553                         argument (spar[2], ancenv, sparv[1]), ancenv )
1554   end (*arg*);
1555
1556   function intexplode ( n : integer ) : mtx;
1557   (* produce a list of n's digits ( in character form ) *)
1558   var list : mtx;
1559   begin  list:= nilprotx;
1560     repeat  list:= heapdot( charprot( chr( n mod 10 + ord('0'))), list );
1561        n:= n div 10
```

307

(continued)

```
1562            until n = 0;
1563       intexplode:= list
1564    end;
1565
1566    function nameexplode ( firstc : ctx )  : mtx;
1567    (* produce a list of this printname's characters *)
1568    var  list : mtx;  lastc : ctx;
1569    begin  list:= nilprotx;
1570       for lastc:= charlast ( firstc ) downto firstc do
1571          list:= heapdot ( charprot ( ct [ lastc ] ), list );
1572       nameexplode:= list
1573    end;
1574
1575    function trydigseq ( list : mtx; env : stackx; var num : integer )  : boolean;
1576    (* if list is a digit sequence ( in character form ), convert it to num;
1577    otherwise yield false. an empty list is not a digit sequence !    *)
1578    var  is : ( no, dontknow, yes );   dig : char;   d : integer;
1579         err, turn1 : boolean;
1580    begin  is:= dontknow;   err:= false;   num:= 0;   turn1:= true;
1581       repeat if not isnormal ( list ) then is:= no
1582          else
1583             if mt [ list ] = std [ atmnil ] then
1584                if turn1 then is:= no
1585                else is:= yes
1586             else
1587                if mt [ list ] <> std [ atmdot ] then is:= no
1588                else begin     (* ischar defines dig for all branches ! *)
1589                   if not ischar( argument( list, env, car ), dig ) then
1590                                                            is:= no
1591                   else
1592                      if ( dig < '0' ) or ( dig > '9' ) then is:= no
1593                      else
1594                         if num > maxint div 10 then err:= true
1595                         else begin
```

308

```
1596                               num:= num * 10;    d:= ord( dig ) - ord( '0' ) ;
1597                               if num <> 0 then
1598                                           if ( maxint div num = 1 ) and
1599                                              ( d > maxint mod num ) then
1600                                                           err:= true;
1601                               if not err then num:= num + d
1602                       end;
1603                       list:= argument ( list, env, cdr );        (*tail*)
1604                       turn1:= false
1605               end
1606       until ( is <> dontknow ) or err;
1607       trydisseq := is = yes
1608
1609   end;

1610   function trycharseq ( list : mtx;  env : stackx;  var atom : atx )  : boolean;
1611   (* if list is a character sequence, construct a name and return
1612       its atom ( null arity ). otherwise yield false.
1613       an empty list is a character sequence !                     *)
1614   var  is : ( no, dontknow, yes );  c : char;
1615   begin  is:= dontknow;
1616       repeat  if not isnormal ( list ) then is:= no
1617               else
1618               if mt [ list ] = std [ atmnil ] then is:= yes
1619               else
1620               if mt [ list ] <> std [ atmdot ] then is:= no
1621               else begin
1622                           if ischar ( argument ( list, env, car ), c ) then
1623                                                         buildname ( c )
1624                           else is:= no;
1625                           list:= argument ( list, env, cdr )     (*tail*)
1626               end
1627       until is <> dontknow;
1628       if is = no then c:top:= builtname           (* restore dictionary state *)
1629       else atom:= findatom ( wrapname, 0 );
```

309

(continued)

```
1630                  trycharseq := is := yes
1631       end;
1632
1633    procedure pname ( var success : boolean );
1634    (* implement pname( functor, charlist ) *)
1635    var list : mtx;  atom : atx;
1636    begin   if not isvar ( spar [ 1 ] ) then              (* explode *)
1637                 if not isargless ( spar [ 1 ] ) then syserror:= true
1638                 else begin
1639                       list:= nameexplode ( at [ mt [ spar [ 1 ] ] . name ] );
1640                       success:= unify ( spar [ 2 ], ancenv, list, vtop )
1641                 end
1642            else           (* construct after checking for non-empty list *)
1643                 if not isnormal ( spar [ 2 ] ) then syserror:= true
1644            else
1645                 if mt [ spar [ 2 ] [ [ ] ] <> std [atmdot then syserror:= true
1646            else
1647                 if trycharseq( spar[2], ancenv, atom ) then bindpar( 1, sterm( atom ))
1648            else syserror:= true
1649    end (*pname*);
1650
1651    procedure pnamei ( var success : boolean );
1652    (* implement pnamei( integer, digitlist ) *)
1653    var num : integer;
1654    begin   if not isvar ( spar [ 1 ] ) then              (* explode *)
1655                 if not isint ( spar [ 1 ] ) then syserror:= true
1656                 else success:= unify ( spar [ 2 ], ancenv,
1657                                        intexplode ( sparv [ 1 ] ), vtop )
1658            else
1659                 if trydigseq ( spar [ 2 ], ancenv, num ) then
1660                       bindpar ( 1, heapint ( num ) )
1661            else syserror:= true
1662    end (*pnamei*);
1663
```

```
        (*----------- clause/assert/retract ------------*)

        (* assert uses free stack storage for temporary data *)


function varconvert ( v : stackx ) : varnumb;
(* v is a variable instance. return its number in temporary
   variable dictionary, inserting it there if missing.           *)
var  p : stackx;  found : boolean;
begin  p:= vardictbot;  found:= false;
       while ( p <> vtop ) and not found do
             if mt [ p ] = -v then found:= true
             else p:= p + 1;
       if not found then begin
             pushvars ( 1 );      mt [ p ]:= - v            (* p = vtop *)
       end;
       varconvert:= p - vardictbot
end;

function storeterm ( pt : mtx;  env : stackx ) : protx;
(* used only by storeclause. pt is a non-variable term instance or
   prot in variable environment env. store it as a prototype, using
   temporary variable dictionary to renumber variables.          *)
var  p : protx;  k : argnumb;  args : mtx;
begin  (* check (10, not isndvar ( pt ) ); *)
       if ( pt >= protlow ) and ( pt < ptop ) then storeterm:= pt  (*ground*)
       else                           (* heap integer still possible *)
       if isint ( pt ) then storeterm:= newintprot ( intval. ( pt ) )
```

(continued)

```
1698          else begin
1699                   p:= initprot ( mt [ pt ] );
1700                   for k:= 1 to setarity ( pt ) do begin
1701                           arg:= argument ( pt, env );
1702                           if isndvar ( arg ) then
1703                                   newparvararg( p,k,varconvert( varadr( arg,env)))
1704                           else newpars ( p, k, storeterm ( arg, env ) )
1705                   end (*for*);
1706                   storeterm:= wrapprot ( p )
1707          end
1708  end;
1709
1710  function storeclause ( headpt, bodypt : mtx;  env : stackx )  : procptr;
1711  (* headpt and bodypt are correct terms ( or prots in env) representing
1712     a clause head and body ( cf.assert ).  store this clause.           *)
1713  var  p : procptr;
1714  begin  vardictbot:= vtop;        (* variable dictionary used by storeterm *)
1715         new ( p );
1716         with p @ do begin
1717                 next:= nil;  systemroutine:= false;
1718                 head:= storeterm ( headpt, env ) ;
1719                 body:= storeterm ( bodypt, env ) ;
1720                 nvars:= vtop - vardictbot;       (*no. of vars in dictionary*)
1721         end;
1722         vtop:= vardictbot;  storeclause:= p
1723  end ;
1724
1725  function procok ( headatom : atx )  : boolean;
1726  (* if headatom is associated with a system routine or protected procedure
1727     (but single-letter argless predicates can't be protected!),            *)
1728     yield false & a warning
1729  var  ok, keep : boolean;
1730  begin  with at [ headatom ] do begin
1731          if proc = nil then ok:= true
```

312

```
1732          else
1733          if proc @. systemroutine then ok:= false
1734          else with proc@ do
1735              ok:= ( (head >= sprotected) and (head <= nsprotected) )
1736                  or ((head >= minchprotx) and (head <= maxchprotx)) ;
1737      if not ok then begin
1738          keep:= telling;     telling:= false;    putline;
1739          write ( co, '-------redefinition of system routine ', ' , ' ,
1740                      'or protected procedure ignored :'        ) ;
1741          putline;     putname ( headatom ) ;   putch( '/' ) ;
1742          putint ( arity ) ;     putline;     telling:= keep
1743          end
1744      end (*with*);
1745      procok:= ok
1746  end;
1747
1748  procedure linkclause ( cl : procptr;  n : integer ) ;
1749  (* insert cl after the nth clause in its procedure ( as first if n <= 0 ,
1750      as last if n too large). ** note the effect of redefining ** *)
1751  var  headatom : atx;   p : procptr;
1752  begin   headatom:= mt [ cl @. head ] ;
1753      if procok ( headatom ) then begin
1754          if redefining and ( headatom <> lastasserted ) then begin
1755              lastasserted:= headatom;           at [ headatom ]. proc:= nil
1756          end;
1757          p:= at [ headatom ]. proc;
1758          if ( n <= 0 ) or ( p = nil ) then        (*insert as first*)
1759              with at [ headatom ] do begin
1760                  cl@.next:= proc;     proc:= cl
1761              end
1762          else begin   (* find clause n (or last) to link to *)
1763              while ( n <> 1 ) and ( p@.next <> nil ) do begin
1764                  n:= n - 1;     p:= p@.next
1765              end;
```

(continued)

```
1766                                   cl@.next:= p@.next;    p@.next:= cl
1767                             end
1768                   end
1769         end (*linkclause*);
1770

1771   procedure assert;
1772   (* implement assert( head, body, number ) :
1773        construct a clause and invoke linkclause.        *)
1774   begin  if not isnormal(spar[1]) or not isint(spar[3]) then syserror:= true
1775          else
1776          if not iscallsequence ( spar [ 2 ], ancenv ) then syserror:= true
1777          else linkclause ( storeclause( spar[1],spar[2], ancenv ), spar[3], ancenv ), spar[3] )
1778
1779   end ;
1780
1781   procedure clause ( var success : boolean ) ;
1782   (* implement clause( functor, arity, n, head, body) . the first 3 are
1783        given. find the n'th clause in the procedure associated with functor &
1784        arity (failing if none) and try to unify it with head and body.       *)
1785   var  atom : atx;   p : procptr;  k : integer;  body : protx;
1786   begin  if not isint(spar[3]) then syserror:= true
1787          else atom:= atomspar ( 1, 2 ) ;   (* checks parameters, remember ? *)
1788          if not syserror then begin                            (* call ok *)
1789                   p:= at [ atom ]. proc;  k:= 1;
1790                   while ( p<> nil ) and ( k < spar [ 3 ] ) do begin
1791                            p:= p@.next;    k:= k + 1
1792                   end;
1793                   if ( p = nil ) or ( spar [ 3 ] < 1 ) then success:= false
1794                   else
1795                   if p@.systemroutine then success:= false
1796                   else begin       (* create fresh clause instance and unify *)
1797                            (*check (l1, topenv := vtop );*)   pushvars ( p@.nvars );
                             success:= unify( spar[ 4 ], ancenv, p@.head, topenv ) ;
```

314

```
     if success then          (*heads unified, bodies now *)
         success:= unify ( g.[5,[],ancenv,
                          p@.body, topenv )
 end
end (*call ok*)
end (*clause*);

procedure genproc ( var success : boolean );
(* implement $proc( head ) , an auxiliary of proc( head )  ( which is
   written in prolog ) , try to unify with the most general term instance
   of the atom shown by procindx (cf. proclimit).             *)
begin  success:= unify ( g.[ 1 ], ancenv, sterm ( procindx ), vtop )
end;

procedure proclimit ( var success : boolean );
(* implement $proclimit , a shameful auxiliary of proc( head ) .
   set procindx (which is initialised by $procinit , cf. sysroutcall)
   to the next atom associated with a non-system procedure and f a i l .   *)
   (succeed if no such atoms left).
var found : boolean;
begin  found:= false;
       while ( procindx < athish ) and not found do begin
             procindx:= procindx + 1;
             with at [ procindx ] do
                  if name <> emptyatom then
                     if proc <> nil then
                        found:= not proc@.systemroutine
       end;
       success:= not found
end;

procedure retract ( var success : boolean );
(* implement retract( name, arity, number )  =  retract the number'th
```

315

(continued)

```
1831       clause of those whose head predicate has this name and arity,
1832       fail if none such.                                        *)
1833  var  atom : atx;  p : procptr;   n : integer;
1834  begin  atom:= atomspar ( 1, 2 ) ;
1835       if not syserror then syserror:= not procok ( atom )  or
1836                                        not isint ( spar [ 3 ] ) ;
1837                                                    (* call ok *)
1838       if not syserror then begin
1839            n:= sparv [ 3 ] ;
1840            if n < 1 then success:= false
1841            else
1842            if n = 1 then         (* remove first clause *)
1843                 with at [ atom ] do
1844                      if proc = nil then success:= false
1845                      else proc:= proc@.next
1846            else begin          (* find the preceding clause *)
1847                 p:= at [ atom ]. proc;
1848                 while ( n <> 2 ) and ( p <> nil ) do begin
1849                      n:= n - 1;   p:= p@. next
1850                 end;
1851                 if p = nil then success:= false      (*no (n-1)'th*)
1852                 else with p@ do
1853                      if next <> nil then next:= next @. next
1854            end (*not 1st*)
1855       end (*call ok*)
1856  end (*retract*);
1857
1858  procedure abolish;
1859  (* implement abolish( name, arity )  *)
1860  var  atom : atx;
1861  begin  atom:= atomspar ( 1, 2 ) ;
1862       if not syserror then if procok ( atom ) then at [ atom ]. proc:= nil
1863  end;
1864  procedure redefine;
```

```
1865  (* tag used as nil ( tag can't be redefined ) *)
1866  begin   redefining:= not redefining;
1867          if not redefining then lastasserted:= std [atmtag]
1868  end;
1869
1870  procedure predefined ( var success : boolean );
1871  (* implement predefined( name, arity ) : is this a system routine ? *)
1872  var atom : atx;
1873  begin   atom:= atomspar ( 1, 2 );
1874          if not syserror then
1875                  with at [ atom ] do
1876                          if proc = nil then success:= false
1877                          else success:= proc @. systemroutine
1878
1879
1880  end;
1881
1882  procedure protect;
1883  (* set protected boundaries, so that clauses which are already defined
1884     will be protected by procok                                    *)
1885  begin   sprotect:= stop;  nsprotect:= nsbot
1886  end;
1887
1888
1889
1890  (*--------- h i g h   i n p u t / o u t p u t ---------*)
1891
1892
1893
1894  procedure rdchar;
1895  (* read the next character into cch ( linend returned as chr(eol) ).
1896     non-user file end redirects input stream to user, user file end is fatal.*)
1897
1898  begin   while endoffile do
```

317

(continued)

```
1899              if sysloading or seeing then begin
1900                    closefile ( true );   writeln ( co );
1901                    writeln ( co, ' ------end of file, terminal input now' );
1902                    putline
1903              end
1904           else error ( usereof );
1905        if endofline then begin
1906           setline;   cch:= chr ( eol )
1907        end
1908     else setch ( cch )
1909  end (*rdchar*);
1910
1911  procedure lastch ( var success : boolean );
1912  (* try to unify sysrout parameter with current character.
1913  ( special-case unification coded here for efficiency ) *)
1914  var  c : char;
1915  begin  if isvar ( spar [ 1 ] ) then bindpar ( 1, charprot ( cch ) )
1916         else
1917         if ischar ( spar [ 1 ], c ) then success := cch = c
1918         else success:= false
1919  end;
1920
1921  procedure skipbl;
1922  (* ensure that cch is not filled with a white space character *)
1923  begin  while cch <= ' ' do rdchar              (*** ASCII version ***)
1924  end;
1925
1926  procedure wch;
1927  (* output the sysrout parameter, which should be a character term *)
1928  var  c : char;
1929  begin  if ischar ( spar [ 1 ], c ) then
1930              if c = chr ( eol ) then putline
1931              else putch ( c )
1932         else syserror:= true
```

318

```
1933        end;
1934    procedure newfile ( see : boolean ) ;
1935    (* implement see or tell, according to parameter *)
1936    begin  if not isarsless ( spar [ 1 ] ) then syserror:= true
1937           else
1938           if mt [ spar [ 1 ] ] = std [atmuser] then begin
1939                  closefile ( see ) ;
1940                  if see then seeobj:= userprot
1941                         else tellobj:= userprot
1942           end
1943           else begin
1944
1945                  openfile ( at [ mt [ spar [ 1 ] [ [ . name ,    see ) ] ;
1946                  if see then seeobj:= spar [ 1 ]
1947                         else tellobj:= spar [ 1 ]
1948           end
1949    end (*newfile*);
1950
1951    procedure whatfile ( see : boolean; var success : boolean ) ;
1952    (* implement seeing or telling, according to parameter *)
1953    var  fileterm : mtx;
1954    begin  if see then fileterm:= seeobj
1955           else fileterm:= tellobj;
1956           success:= unify ( spar [ 1 ] , ancenv, fileterm, vtop )
1957    end;
1958
1959
1960
1961
1962    (*-------- s y s t e m  r o u t i n e s  --------*)
1963
1964
1965
1966    procedure haltaction ( var stop : boolean ) ;
```

(continued)

319

```
1967    (* display the sysparam and halt the interpreter *)
1968    begin  putline; display ( spar [ 1 ] , ancenv ) ;    putline;
1969           stop:= true;  terminate:=true
1970    end;
1971
1972    procedure sysroutcall (* ( id : sysroutid;  var success, stop : boolean ) *);
1973    (* perform a system routine call *)
1974    var  k : nsysparam;
1975    begin  syserror:= false;   success:= true;   (* might change yet *)
1976           for k:= 1 to setarity ( ccall ) do begin
1977                   spar [ k ]:= argument ( ccall, ancenv, k );
1978           if isint( spar [ k ] ) then spar [ k ]:= intval( spar [ k ] ( 
1979           end;
1980           case id of
1981    idfail          : success:= false;            (* keep this as first  *)
1982    idtag ,
1983    idcall          : ;                    (* never called ! (cf. control) *)
1984    idslash         : slash;
1985    idtagcut        : tagcut ( success );
1986    idtagfail       : tagfail ( success );
1987    idtagexit       : tagexit ( success );
1988    idancestor      : ancestor ( success );
1989    idhalt          : haltaction ( stop );
1990    idstatus        : status;
1991    iddisplay       : display ( spar [ ], ancenv ) ;
1992    idrch           : rdchar;
1993    idlastch        : lastch ( success );
1994    idskipbl        : skipbl;
1995    idwch           : wch;
1996    idecho          : echo:= true;
1997    idnoecho        : echo:= false;
1998    idsee           : newfile ( true );
1999    idseeing        : whatfile ( true, success );
2000    idseen          : closefile ( true );
2001    idtell          : newfile ( false );
```

2002	idtelling	::	whatfile (false, success) ;
2003	idtold	::	closefile (false) ;
2004	idordchr	::	ordchr (success) ;
2005	idsum	::	sum (success) ;
2006	idprod	::	prod (success) ;
2007	idinf	::	inf (success) ;
2008	idnameinf	::	nameinf (success) ;
2009	idbisletter	::	chiclass (cbisletter, success) ;
2010	idsmalletter	::	chiclass (csmalletter, success) ;
2011	idletter	::	ch2class (csmalletter, success) ;
2012	iddigit	::	chiclass (cdigit, success) ;
2013	idalphanum	::	ch2class (cunderscore, success) ;
2014	idbracket	::	chiclass (cbracket, success) ;
2015	idsolochar	::	chiclass (csolochar, success) ;
2016	idsymch	::	chiclass (csymch, success) ;
2017	ideqvar	::	eqvar (success) ;
2018	idvar	::	success::isvar (spar [1]) ;
2019	idatom	::	success::isargless(spar [1]);
2020	idinteger	::	success::isint (spar [1] ;
2021	idnonvarint	::	success::isnormal (spar[1] [;
2022	idfunctor	::	functor (success) ;
2023	idarg	::	arg (success) ;
2024	idpname	::	pname (success) ;
2025	idpnamei	::	pnamei (success.) ;
2026	idproc	::	genproc (success) ;
2027	idproclimit	::	proclimit (success) ;
2028	idprocinit	::	procindx:: atlow — 1;
2029	idclause	::	clause (success) ;
2030	idretract	::	retract (success) ;
2031	idabolish	::	abolish;
2032	idassert	::	assert;
2033	idredefine	::	redefine;
2034	idpredefined	::	predefined (success) ;
2035	idprotect	::	protect;

(continued)

```
2036              idnonexistent   : shownonexistent:= true;
2037              idnonnonexistent : shownonexistent:= false;
2038              iddebug         : debug:= true;
2039              idnodebug       : debug:= false;
2040              idtrue          : (*no action*)      (* keep this as last *)
2041              end (*case*)
2042    end (*sysroutcall*);
2043
2044
2045
2046
2047
2048    (*-------- r e a d e r --------*)
2049
2050          (* frame variable area is used as an auxiliary argument stack *)
2051
2052
2053
2054    procedure rd;
2055    (* the reader's input routine : like rdchar but skips linends *)
2056    begin  repeat rdchar
2057           until cch <> chr ( eol )
2058    end;
2059
2060    procedure skipcombl;
2061    (* skip white space and comments. a comment is a sequence between a "%"
2062       and a linend ( outside clauses or following dots and head colons )  *)
2063    begin  skipbl;
2064           while cch = "%" do begin
2065                  repeat rdchar
2066                  until cch = chr ( eol ) ;
2067                  rd; skipbl
2068           end
2069    end;
```

```
2070
2071     procedure synterr;

2072     (* produce a syntactic error message and raise recoverable error
2073        ( the reader does not normally process hand-produced code ) *)
2074     var  keep : boolean;
2075     begin  keep:= echo;  echo:= true;
2076            while cch <> chr ( eol ) do rdchar;          (* skip this line *)
2077            echo:= keep;  error ( whaterr )
2078     end;
2079
2080     function rddigits : integer;
2081     (* read a non-empty sequence of digits, return the integer value *)
2082     (* overflow checking as in trydigseq, cf. comment to call in rdterm *)
2083     var v, d : integer;
2084     begin  skipbl;  v:= 0;
2085            if cc [ cch ] <> cdigit then synterr;
2086            repeat  d:= ord ( cch ) - ord ( '0' );  (* value of digit *)
2087                    if v > maxint div 10 then synterr;
2088                    v:= v * 10;
2089                    if v <> 0 then
2090                            if ( maxint div v = 1 ) and ( d > maxint mod v ) then
2091                                                                            synterr;
2092                    v:= v + d;
2093                    rd
2094            until cc [ cch ] <> cdigit;
2095            rddigits:= v
2096     end;
2097
2098     function rdfunctor : atx;
2099     (* read a functor and return name atom pointer *)
2100     const quote = '''';
2101     var  stop : boolean;
2102     begin  skipbl;
```

323

(continued)

APPENDIX A.1 (*Continued*)

```
2103         if cc [ cch ] <= csmalletter then                    (* i.e. a letter *)
2104             repeat buildname ( cch ) ;  rd
2105             until cc [ cch ] > cdigit            (*i.e. not a letter or digit*)
2106         else
2107         if cch = '<' then begin               (* <>, i.e. a "nice" nil *)
2108             rd;  if cch <> '>' then synterr;  rd;
2109             buildname ( '<' ) ;  buildname ( '>' )
2110         end
2111         else
2112         if cch = '!' then begin                    (* a "nice" cut *)
2113             buildname ( cch ) ;  rd
2114         end
2115         else begin
2116             if cch <> quote then synterr;
2117             stop:= false;
2118             repeat rd;
2119                 if cch <> quote then buildname ( cch )
2120                 else begin           (* either last '' or '''',ie. quote*)
2121                     rd;
2122                     if cch = quote then buildname ( quote )
2123                     else stop:= true
2124                 end
2125             until stop
2126         end (*else*);
2127         rdfunctor:= wrapname
2128     end;
2129
2130     function rdterm : integer;  forward;   (*------------------------------*)
2131
2132     procedure mkars ( p : protx;  n, arg : integer ) ;
2133     (* insert arg as n'th in prot p. arg <= 0 encodes variable offset -arg. *)
2134     begin if arg <= 0 then newpvars ( p, n, - arg )
2135         else newpars ( p, n, arg )
2136     end;
```

324

```
function rdnonvarint : protx;
(* read a non-variable & non-integer term, return its prototype *)
var   name : atx;   toplev : stackx;   prot : protx;   k : integer;
begin   toplev:=vtop;                        (* auxiliary stack level *)
        name:= rdfunctor; skipbl;
        if cch = '(' then begin          (* read and stack the arguments *)
                  repeat rd; pushvars ( 1 );
                         mt [ vtop - 1 ] := rdterm; skipbl
                  until cch <> ',';
                  if cch <> ')' then synterr
                  else rd
        end;
        (* number of arguments known now : construct the prototype *)
        prot:= initprot ( findatom ( name, vtop - toplev ) );
        for k:= 1 to vtop - toplev do mkars ( prot, k, mt [ toplev-1+k ] );
        vtop:= toplev;   rdnonvarint:= wrapprot ( prot )
end;

function rdterm (* : integer *);
(* read a term and return a prot for a non-var or a negated offset for a var.
   sequences processed recursively to allow proper ground prot treatment. *)
var   sign : -1..1;   varoff : varnumb;   prot : integer;   dot : protx;
begin   skipbl;
        if cch = '(' then begin          (* eg.  a . (b . c) . d *)
                  rd; prot:= rdterm; skipbl;
                  if cch <> ')' then synterr; rd
        end
        else
        if cch = '.' then begin                  (* a dummy variable *)
                  rd; prot:= dumvarx                (* treated as non-var here *)
        end
        else
        if cch = ';' then begin                  (* a variable *)
                  rd; varoff:= rddigits; prot:= - varoff;
```

(continued)

325

```
2172                    if varoff + 1 > nclvars then nclvars:= varoff + 1
2173                  end
2174                else
2175                if ( cch = '+' ) or ( cch = '-' ) or ( cc [cch] = cdigit ) then begin
2176                    if cch = '-' then sign:= -1 else sign:= 1;
2177                    if cc [ cch ]<> cdigit then rd;
2178                    (* number itself processed as positive : this
2179                     causes loss of smallest integer in two's complement *)
2180                    prot:= newintprot ( sign * rddigits )
2181                  end
2182                else prot:= rdnonvarint;
2183                skipbl;
2184                if cch <> '.' then rdterm:= prot
2185                else begin                (* a sequence, as it turns out *)
2186                    dot:= initprot ( std [atmdot] );  mkarg ( dot, car, prot );
2187                    rd;  skipcombl;
2188                    mkarg ( dot, cdr, rdterm );  rdterm:= wrapprot ( dot )
2189                  end
2190          end (*rdterm*);
2191
2192    procedure rdclause ( var issoal : boolean; var nvars : varnumb;
2193                                     var head, body = protx );
2194    (* read a clause.
2195       ( a goal has an empty head and is terminated by a '#' )    *)
2196    begin  nclvars:= 0;                (* number of variables in this clause *)
2197          vtop:= mtlow;   csbot:= stackhigh;       (*initialise argument stack*)
2198          skipcombl;
2199          if cch = ':' then begin
2200                issoal:= true;    head:= nilprotx
2201              end
2202          else begin
2203                issoal:= false;  head:= rdnonvarint;  skipbl;
2204                if cch <> ':' then synterr
```

```
2205        end;
2206      rd; skipcombl; body:= rdterm; nvars:= nclvars;
2207      if issgoal then begin (*"#" terminates a goal,so resolution can
2208                               begin before more input is requested.    *)
2209        skipbl; if cch <> '#' then synterr;
2210        cch:= ' '  (*std 1st lastch, 1st rch sets char following "#"*)
2211
2212      end
2213  end (*rdclause*);
2214
2215  procedure readtogoal ( var goalsequence : protx;   var nvarsingoal : varnumb ) ;
2216  (* read clauses until nearest goal statement :  return its attributes *)
2217  var issgoal : boolean; locproc: locproc;  p : procptr;
2218  begin locproc.next:= nil;  locproc-systemroutine:=false;
2219    repeat with locproc do begin   (*read clause, iscallsequence checks*)
2220                 rdclause ( issgoal, nvars, head, body );
2221                 vtop:= mtlow;
2222                 pushvars ( nvars );    (*dummy env for iscallsequence*)
2223                 if not iscallsequence ( body, mtlow ) then synterr
2224               end;
2225      if issgoal then begin
2226                 goalsequence:= locproc.body;
2227                 nvarsingoal:= locproc.nvars
2228               end
2229      else begin    (* note that mthigh > no. of clauses *)
2230                 new ( p ); p@:= locproc; linkclause ( p, mthigh )
2231               end
2232    until issgoal
2233  end (*readtogoal*);
2234
2235  function rdatom : atx;
2236  (* read an atom description ( during sysloading ). format : functor/arity *)
2237  var name : atx;
2238  begin skipcombl; name:= rdfunctor;
```

(continued)

327

```
2239            if cch <> '/' then synterr;
2240          rd; rdatom:= findatom ( name, rddigits )
2241      end;
2242
2243
2244
2245
2246
2247   (*-------- i n i t i a l i s a t i o n --------*)
2248
2249
2250
2251   procedure initvars;
2252   (* initialise global variables (cf. startresolution & loadsyskernel) *)
2253   var  a : atx;  c: char;
2254   begin  write( co, ' ' );
2255          colinesize:= 0;    solinesize:= 0;
2256          seeins:= false;    tellins:= false;
2257          ctop:= ctlow;      builtname:= ctlow;
2258          freeatoms:= athish - atlow + 1;
2259          for a:= atlow to athish do at [ a ]. name:= emptyatom;
2260          stackhish:= mtlow - 1 + stacksize;   protlow:= stackhish + 1;
2261          dumvarx:= protlow;    nilprotx:= dumvarx + 1;
2262          minchprotx:= nilprotx + 1;   maxchprotx:= minchprotx + maxchar;
2263          stdintprotx:= maxchprotx + 1;
2264          if stdintprotx+(maxstdint-minstdint) >= mthish then error( sysinit ) ;
2265          mt [ dumvarx ] := varlim;
2266          stop:= stdintprotx;     (* loadsyskernel picks stop up from here *)
2267          nsbot:= mthish;
2268          sprotect:= stop;      nsprotect:= nsbot;
2269          tminfree:= tthish;    bminfree:= bthish;
2270          fminfree:= fthish;    stackminfree:= stackhish - mtlow;
2271          terminate:= false;
2272          redefining:= false;   lastasserted:= std [atmtas];  (*cf. "redefine"*)
```

```
2273      shownonexistent:= false;          (* don't warn on calls to nonexistent *)
2274      cch:= ' '; echo:= false;       debug:= false;
2275      (* character classification, ASCII version.
2276      symch is a non-alphameric freely used to form symbols. *)
2277      for c:= chr ( 0 ) to chr ( maxchar ) do cc [ c ] := cother;
2278      for c:= 'a' to 'z' do cc [ c ] := csmalletter;
2279      for c:= 'A' to 'Z' do cc [ c ] := cbisletter;
2280      for c:= '0' to '9' do cc [ c ] := cdigit;
2281      cc [ '(' ] := cbracket;      cc [ ')' ] := cbracket;
2282      cc [ '[' ] := cbracket;      cc [ ']' ] := cbracket;
2283      cc [ '{' ] := cbracket;      cc [ '}' ] := cbracket;
2284      cc [ '.' ] := csolochar;
2285      cc [ ',' ] := csolochar;     cc [ '!' ] := csolochar;
2286      cc [ '_' ] := cunderscore;
2287      cc [ '+' ] := csymch;        cc [ '-' ] := csymch;
2288      cc [ '*' ] := csymch;        cc [ '/' ] := csymch;
2289      cc [ '#' ] := csymch;        cc [ '@' ] := csymch;
2290      cc [ '%' ] := csymch;        cc [ '$' ] := csymch;
2291      cc [ '&' ] := csymch;        cc [ '?' ] := csymch;
2292      cc [ ':' ] := csymch;        cc [ ';' ] := csymch;
2293      cc [ '<' ] := csymch;        cc [ '>' ] := csymch;
2294      cc [ '=' ] := csymch;        cc [ '\' ] := csymch;
2295      end (*initvars*);
2296
2297      procedure loadsyskernel;
2298      (* create standard objects.
2299      kernel library will be processed in main program loop.   *)
2300      var k : integer;    a : stdatomid;    s : sysroutid;
2301      p : procptr;    prot : protx;
2302      begin sysloading:= true;    whaterr:= loadfile;
2303      (* reset ( mc, 'sysfile','tos','tos', ... ) *)
2304      for a:= atmsemcol to atmuser do std [ a ] := rdatom;
2305      for s:= idfail to idtrue do begin
2306          new ( p );
```

329

(continued)

```
2307              with p@ do begin
2308                  next:= nil;  nvars:= 0;
2309                  systemroutine:= true;  sysid:= s
2310              end;
2311              at [ rdatom ], proc:= p          (* NOTE the function call *)
2312          end (*for*);
2313      whaterr:= syntax;
2314      (* create nil, character & standard integer prototypes *)
2315      mt [ nilprotx ] := std [atmnil];
2316      for k:= 0 to maxchar do begin
2317          buildname ( chr ( k ) );
2318          mt [ minchprotx + k ] := findatom ( wrapname, 0 )
2319      end;
2320      for k:= minstdint to maxstdint do mkint ( k );
2321      (* create error call sequence & user file name prot *)
2322      prot:= initprot ( std [atmerror] );  newpvars ( prot , 1, 0 );
2323      prot:= wrapprot ( prot );
2324      errorcallseq:= initprot ( std [atmdot] );
2325      newpars(errorcallseq,1,prot );  newpars(errorcallseq, 2, nilprotx);
2326      errorcallseq:= wrapprot ( errorcallseq );
2327      userprot:= wrapprot ( initprot ( std [atmuser] ) );
2328      (* mc is a special stream. set default streams for when it ends *)
2329      seeobj:= userprot;         tellobj:= userprot
2330  end (*loadsyskernel*);
2331
2332
2333  begin (*********** toy prolog *************)
2334      initvars;
2335      loadsyskernel;
2336   2: repeat  readtogoal ( goalstmnt, ngoalvars );
2337             resolve ( goalstmnt, ngoalvars )
2338      until terminate;
2339   1: closefile ( true );   closefile ( false )
2340  end.
```

330

Kernel File

```
1    % KERNEL file
2    % standard atoms
3    ';'/2   ','/2   'call'/1   'tag'/1
4    '[]'/0  '.'/2   'error'/1  'user'/0
5
6    % atoms identifying system routines (keep 'fail' 'first and 'true' last)
7    'fail'/0   'tag'/1   'call'/1   '|'/0
8    'tagcut'/1   'tagfail'/1   'tagexit'/1   'ancestor'/1
9    'halt'/1   'status'/0
10   'display'/1   'rch'/0   'lastch'/1   'skipbl'/0   'wch'/1
11   'echo'/0   'noecho'/0
12   'see'/1   'seeing'/1   'seen'/0   'tell'/1   'telling'/1   'told'/0
13   'ordchr'/2   'sum'/3   'prod'/4   'less'/2   '@<'/2
14   'smalletter'/1   'bisletter'/1   'letter'/1   'digit'/1   'alphanum'/1
15   'bracket'/1   'solochar'/1   'symch'/1
16   'eqvar'/2   'var'/1
17   'atom'/1   'integer'/1   'nonvarint'/1
18   'functor'/3   'arg'/3   'pname'/2   'pnamei'/2
19   '$proc'/1   '$proclimit'/0   '$procinit'/0
20   'clause'/5   'retract'/3   'abolish'/2   'assert'/3   'redefine'/0
21   'predefined'/2   'protect'/0
22   'nonexistent'/0   'nonnonexistent'/0
23   'debug'/0   'nodebug'/0
24   'true'/0
25
```

(continued)

```
26   % kernel library
27   error(:0) :- nl , display('+++ System call error: ') , display(:0) ,
28               nl , fail . []
29   :ordchr(10, :0) , assert(iseoln(:0), [], 0) ,
30               assert(nl, wch(:0),[], 0) , [] #
31   '='(:0, :0) :- []
32   ','(:0, :1) :- call(:0) , call(:1) , []
33   ';'(:0, _) :- call(:0) , []
34   ';'(_, :0) :- call(:0) , []
35   not(:0) :- call(:0) , '!' , fail , []
36   not(_) :- []
37   check(:0) :- not(not(:0)) , []
38   'side_effects'(:0) :- not(not(:0)) , []
39
40   once(:0) :- call(:0) , '!' , []
41
42   '@=<'(:0, :1) :- '@<'(:1, :0) , '!' , fail , []
43   '@=<'(_, _) :- []
44   '@>'(:0, :1) :- '@<'(:1, :0) , []
45   '@>='(:0, :1) :- '@=<'(:1, :0) , []
46
47   % - - - - - basic input procedures - - - - -
48   rdchsk(:0) :- rch , skipbl , lastch(:0) , []
49   rdch(:0) :- rch , lastch(:1) , sch(:1, :0) , []
50   % convert nonprintable characters to blanks
51   sch(:0, :0) :- '@<'('/', :0) , '!' , []
```

```
52  sch(::0, ' ') :: []
53
54  repeat :: []
55  repeat :: repeat . []
56  member(::0, ::1) :: []
57  member(::0, _::1) :: member(::0, ::1) . []
58
59  proc() :: '$procinit' . '$pr'(::0) . []
60  '$pr'(::0) :: '$proclimit' . '!' . fail . []
61  '$pr'(::0) :: '$proc'(::0) . []
62  '$pr'(::0) :: '$pr'(::0) . []
63
64  % b a s o f   (preserves order of solutions)
65  basof(::0, ::1, _) :: asserta("BAG"("BAG")) . call(::1) .
66        asserta("BAG"(::0)) . fail . []
67        %% 0 Item, 1 Condition,
68  basof(_, _, ::0) :: "BAG"(::1) . '!' . intobas(::1, [], ::0) . () . []
69        %% 0 Bag, 1 Item,
70  intobas("BAG", ::0, ::0) :: '!' . retract("BAG", 1, 1) . []
71        %% 0 Final_bag,
72  intobas(::0, ::1, ::2) :: retract("BAG", 1, 1) . "BAG"(::3) . '!' .
73        intobas(::3, ::0::1, ::2) . []
74        %% 0 Item, 1 This_bag, 2 Final_bag, 3 Next_item,
75
76  % end of file — txprolog will now read from the terminal
77  :: display("Kernel file loaded.") . nl . see(user) . [] #
```

APPENDIX A.3

"Bootstrapper"

```
1   % % % translator of Prolog-10(mini) into Toy-Prolog % % %
2   translate(::0, ::1) :- see(::0) - tell(::1) - program - seen - told .
3          see(user) - tell(user) - display(translated(::0)) - nl . []
4   % -- -- -- -- -- -- %% 0 from_file, 1 to_file
5
6   % main loop
7   program :- rch - skpb(::0) - tag(transl(::0)) - isendsym(::0) - ';' - puttr(::0) . []
8   program :- program . []
9   transl('@') :- ';' - rch . []
10  transl('%') :- comment('%', ::0, []) - ';' - puttr(::0) . []
11  transl(::0) :- clause(::0, ::1, []) - puttr(::1) - putvarnames(::2, 0) . []
12          %% 0 startch, 1 termrepr, 2 sym_tab
13  isendsym('@') :- []          % otherwise fail, ie loop
14  % --
15  % error handling: skip to the nearest dot
16  err(::0, ::1) :- display('*** error in ') - display(::0) .
17          display(::1) :- unexpected'') - display(::1) - lastch(::2) .
18          display('' - text skipped: '') - skip(::2) - nl - tasfail(transl(_)) . []
19          %% 0 proc_name, 1 bad_item, 2 first_skipped_char
20  skip('.') - wch('.') . []
21  skip(::0) :- wch(::0) . rch - lastch(::1) - skip(::1) . []
22  % --
23  % a comment extends till end_of_line
24  comment(::0, ::0, ::1) :- iseoln(::0) . []
25          %% 0 eoln, 1 rest_of_termrepr
26  comment(::0, ::0, ::1) :- rch - lastch(::3) - comment(::3, ::1, ::2) . []
27          %% 0 char, 1 termrepr, 2 rest_of_termrepr, 3 nextchar
28  % --
29  % read a goal
30  clause('::', '::', ::0, ::1, ::2) :- ';' - ctail('::', ::0, '@', ::1, ::2) . []
```

334

```
31                          %% 0 termrepr, 1 rest_of_termrepr, 2 sym_tab
32  % read an assertion/rule
33  clause(::0, ::1, ::2, ::3) :: fterm(::0, ::4, ::1, ' ', ':', ::5, ::3) .
34      .      ctail(::4, ::5, ::2, ::3) . []
35                 %% 0 fterm_firstch, 1 termrepr, 2 rest_of_termrepr,
36                 %% 3 sym_tab, 4 ctail_firstch, 5 middletermrepr
37  clause(::0, _, _, _) :: err(clause, ::0) . []
38  % _ _ _ _ _ _ _
39  % clause tail
40  ctail(' ', ' ', '[', ']', ::0, _) :: ' ' . []
41                 %% 0 rest_of_termrepr
42  % righthand side of a non-unit clause, or a goal
43  % eoln and blanks inserted to make the output look tidy
44  ctail(' ', ::4, ' ', ' ', ::0, ::1, ::2) :: rdch(' ', _) . ' ' . iseoln(::4) .
45      rdchsk(::3) . ctailaux(::3, ::0, ::1, ::2) . []
46                 %% 0 termrepr, 1 rest_of_termrepr, 2 sym_tab, 3 calls_firstch,
47                 %% 4 eoln
48  ctail(::0, _, _, _) :: err(ctail, ::0) . []
49  % set the righthand side of a clause (embedded comments will not be displaced)
50  ctailaux('%', ::0, ::1, ::2) :: comment('%', ::0, ' ', ' ', ' ', ::5) . ' ' .
51      rdchsk(::3) . ctailaux(::3, ::5, ::1, ::2) . []
52                 %% 0 termrepr, 1 rest_of_termrepr, 2 sym_tab, 3 rest_firstch,
53                 %% 5 middletermrepr
54  ctailaux(::0, ::1, ::2, ::3) :: fterm(::0, ::4, ::1, ' ', ' ', ::5, ::3) .
55      fterms(::4, ::5, ::2, ::3) . []
56                 %% 0 fterm_firstch, 1 termrepr, 2 rest_of_termrepr,
57                 %% 3 sym_tab, 4 fterms_firstch, 5 middletermrepr
58  % a list of functor-terms (ie calls)
59  fterms(' ', ' ', '[', ']', ::0, _) :: ' ' . []
60                 %% 0 rest_of_termrepr
61  % eoln and blanks -- cf ctail/2
62  fterms(' ', ::4, ' ', ' ', ' ', ::0, ::1, ::2) :: ' ' . iseoln(::4) .
63      rdchsk(::3) . ctailaux(::3, ::0, ::1, ::2) . []
64                 %% 0 termrepr, 1 rest_of_termrepr, 2 sym_tab, 3 ctail_firstch,
```

335

(continued)

```
65  fterms(::0, ._, ._, ._) :: err(fterms, ::0) . []        %% 4 eoln
66  X -- -- -- -- :: -- -- -- -- -- --
67  X a functor-term
68  fterm(::0, :1, ._,._, :2, :3, :4) ::
69      ident(::0, :5, :2, ._,._, :6) . ._,._ . args(::5, :1, :6, :3, :4) . []
70      %% 0 id_firstch, 1 terminator, 2 termrepr, 3 rest_of_termrepr,
71      %% 4 sym_tab, 5 id_terminator, 6 middletermrepr
72  X identifiers: words, ._ quoted names, symbols
73  ident(::0, :1, :0.:2, :3) ::
74      wordstart(::0) . rdch(:4) . alphanums(:4, :1, :2, :3) . []
75      %% 0 id_firstch, 1 terminator, 2 termrepr
76      %% 3 rest_of_termrepr 4 nextch
77  ident(._,._, ::0, ._,._, :1) :: rch . skpb(::0) . []
78      %% 0 terminator 1 termrepr
79  ident(._,._, ::0, :1, :2) :: rdch(:3) . aident(::3, ::0, :1, :2) . []
80      %% 0 terminator 1 termrepr 2 rest_of_termrepr 3 nextch
81  ident(::0, :0.:2, :3) ::
82      symch(::0) . rdch(:4) . symbol(:4, :1, :2, :3) . []
83      %% 0 symb_firstch, 1 terminator, 2 termrepr,
84      %% 3 rest_of_termrepr.4 nextch
85  X quoted identifiers
86  aident(._,._, ::0, :1, :2) ::
87      rdch(:3) . aident(:3, ::0, :1, :2) . ._,._ . []
88      %% 0 terminator, 1 termrepr, 2 rest_of_termrepr, 3 nextch
89  aident(::0, :1, ._,._, :3) :: rdch(:4) . aident(:4, :1, :2, :3) . []
90      %% 0.:2, :3) :: rdch(:4) . aident(:4, :1, :2, :3) . []
91      %% 0 char, 1 terminator, 2 termrepr
92      %% 3 rest_of_termrepr.4 nextch
93  aident(._,._, ::0, ._,._,._,.-.:1, :2) ::
94      rdch(:3) . aident(::3, ::0, :1, :2) . []
95      %% 0 terminator, 1 termrepr, 2 rest_of_termrepr, 3 nextch
96  aident(._,._, ::0, :1, :2) :: skpb(::0) . []
97      %% 0 terminator 1 rest_of_termrepr
98  X words and symbols
```

```
 99    alphanums(::0, ::1, ::0,::2, ::3) ::
100         alphanum(::0) . 'i' . rdch(::4) . alphanums(::4, ::1, ::2, ::3) . []
101         %% 0 an_alphanum, 1 terminator, 2 termrepr
102         %% 3 rest_of_termrepr, 4 nextch
103    alphanums(_, ::0, ::1, ::1) :: skpb(::0). []
104         %% 0 terminator, 1 rest_of_termrepr
105    symbol(::0, ::0,::2, ::3) ::
106         symch(::0) . 'i' . rdch(::4) . symbol(::4, ::1, ::2, ::3) . []
107         %% 0 a_symbolchar, 1 terminator, 2 termrepr,
108         %% 3 rest_of_termrepr, 4 nextch
109    symbol(_, ::0, ::1, ::1) :: skpb(::0). []
110         %% 0 terminator, 1 rest_of_termrepr
111    % Set argument list: nothing or a sequence of terms in brackets
112    args('(', '('::1, ::2, ::3) ::
113         'i' . rdchsk(::4) . terms(::4, ::1, ::2, ::3) . rdchsk(::0) . []
114         %% 0 nextch, 1 termrepr, 2 rest_of_termrepr,
115         %% 3 sym_tab, 4 terms_firstch
116    args(::0, ::1, ::1, _) :: []
117         %% 0 nextch, 1 rest_of_termrepr
118    % Set a sequence of terms
119    terms(::0, ::1, ::2, ::3) :: term(::0, ::4, ::1, ::5, inargs, ::3) .
120         termstail(::4, ::5, ::2, ::3) . []
121         %% 0 term_firstch, 1 termrepr, 2 rest_of_termrepr, 3 sym_tab,
122         %% 4 terminator, 5 middletermrepr
123    termstail(')', ')'::0,::0, _) :: ',' . []
124         %% 0 rest_of_termrepr
125    termstail(',', ',', ::0, ::1, ::2) ::
126         ',' . rdchsk(::3) . terms(::3, ::0, ::1, ::2) . []
127         %% 0 middletermrepr, 1 rest_of_termrepr, 2 sym_tab, 3 nextch
128    termstail(::0, _, _, _) :: err(termstail, ::0) . []
129    % — — — — —
130    % Set a term (context used to force brackets around lists within lists)
131    term(::0, ::1, ::2,::3, ::4, ::5) . t(::0,::1, ::2, ::3,::4, ::5) . 'i' . []
132         %% 0 firstch, 1 terminator, 2 termrepr,
```

337

(continued)

```
133  term(::O, _, _, _, _, _) :: err(term, ::0) . []        XX 3 rest_of_termrepr, 4 context, 5 sym_tab
134  t(::0, ::1, ::2, ::3, _, ::4) :: variable(::0, ::1, ::2, ::3, ::4) . []
135  t(::0, ::1, ::2, ::3, inargs, ::4) :: list(::0, ::1, ::2, ::3, ::4) . []
136  t(::0, ::1, '(', ::2, ::3, inlist, ::4) :: list(::0, ::1, ::2, ')', ::3, ::4) . []
137  X a dirty patch for negative numbers
138  t('-', ::0, ::1, ::2, _, ::3) ::
139       rdch(::4) - numberorfterm(::4, ::0, ::1, ::2, ::3) . []
141            XX 0 terminator, 1 termrepr, 2 rest_of_termrepr,
142            XX 3 sym_tab, 4 nextch
143  t(::0, ::1, ::2, ::3, _, :) :: number(::0, ::1, ::2, ::3) . []
144  t(::0, ::1, ::2, ::3, _, ::4) :: fterm(::0, ::1, ::2, ::3, ::4) . []
145  X — — — — —
146  numberorfterm(::0, ::1, _, ::2, ::3, _) ::
147       digit(::0) - number(::0, ::1, ::2, ::3) . []
148            XX 0 nextch, 1 terminator, 2 termrepr, 3 rest_of_termrepr
149  numberorfterm(::0, ::1, ::2, _, ::3, ::4) ::
150  symbol(::0, ::5, ::2, ::6) - args(::5, ::1, ::6, ::3, ::4) . []
151            XX 0 nextch, 1 terminator, 2 termrepr, 3 rest_of_termrepr,
152            XX 4 sym_tab, 5 symbol_terminator, 6 middletermrepr
153  X — — — —
154  X set a variable
155  variable(::0, ::1, ::2, ::3, ::4) :: varstart(::0) - alphanums(::0, ::1, ::5, []) -
156       findv(::5, ::2, ::3, ::4) . '' . []
157            XX 0 firstch, 1 terminator, 2 termrepr
158            XX 3 rest_of_termrepr, 4 sym_tab, 5 name
159  findv('-', '_', ::0, ::0, _) :: []        X no search: an anonymous variable
160            XX 0 rest_of_termrepr
161  findv(::0, ::1, ::2, ::3) :: look(::0, 0, ::4, ::3) - setn(::4, ::1, ::2) . []
162            XX 0 name, 1 termrepr, 2 rest_of_termrepr, 3 sym_tab, 4 num
163  X look always counts from 0 and finds the position of a name in the symtab
164  look(::0, ::1, ::1, ::0-::2) :: []
165            XX 0 name, 1 num, 2 symtabtail
```

```
166  look(::0, ::2, ::1, __::3) :: sum(::2, 1, ::4) . look(::0, ::4, ::1, ::3) . []
167                %% 0 name, 1 num, 2 currnum, 3 symtabtail, 4 currnumplus1
168  % set a number: no more than two digits (should be enough)
169  setn(::0, ::1.::2) :: 'less'(::0, 10) :
170      ordchr(::3, '0') . sum(::3, ::0, ::4) . ordchr(::4, ::1) . []
171                %% 0 num, 1 char, 2 rest_of_termrepr, 3 k, 4 kplusnum
172  setn(::0, ::1, ::2) :: 'less'(::0, 100) . prod(10, ::3, ::4, ::0) .
173      setn(::3, ::1, ::5) . setn(::4, ::5, ::2) . []
174                %% 0 num, 1 termrepr, 2 rest_of_termrepr,
175                %% 3 numby10, 4 nummod10, 5 middletermrepr
176  setn(::0, _, _) :: err(setn, ::0) . []
177  % --
178  % set a list in square brackets
179  list('[', ::0, ::1, ::2, ::3) :: rdchsk(::4) . endlist(::4, ::1, ::2, ::3) .
180      rdchsk(::0) . []
181                %% 0 terminator, 1 termrepr, 2 rest_of_termrepr,
182                %% 3 sym_tab, 4 nextch
183  endlist(']', '[','[','[', _) :: []
184                %% 0 rest_of_termrepr
185  endlist(::0, ::1, ::2, ::3) :
186      term(::0, ::4, ::1, ',', ::5, inlist, ::3) . ltail(::4, ::5, ::2, ::3) . []
187                %% 0 firstch, 1 termrepr, 2 rest_of_termrepr,
188                %% 3 sym_tab, 4 nextch, 5 middletermrepr
189                %% 0 rest_of_termrepr
190
191  ltail(']', ::0, ::1, ::2) :: variable(::3, '[', ::0, ::1, ::2) . []
192                %% 3 nextch
193  ltail(',', ::0, ::1, ::2) :: ',' . rdchsk(::3) .
194      term(::3, ::4, ::0, ',', ::5, inlist, ::2) . ltail(::4, ::5, ::1, ::2) . []
195                %% 0 termrepr, 1 rest_of_termrepr, 2 sym_tab,
196                %% 3 term_firstch, 4 nextch, 5 middletermrepr
197  ltail(::0, _, _) :: err(ltail, ::0) . []
198  % --
```

(continued)

```
199   % numbers: only natural ones
200   number(::0, ::1, ::2, ::3) = digit(::0) . digits(::0, ::1, ::2, ::3) . []
201   digits(::0, ::1, ::2, ::3) = digit(::0)
202       ':', rdch(::4) . digits(::4, ::1, ::2, ::3) . []
203       %% 0 firstch, 1 non_digit, 2 termrepr, 3 rest_of_termrepr
204       %% 0 firstch, 1 non_digit, 2 termrepr, 3 rest_of_termrepr
205       %% 4 nextch
206   digits(_, ::0, ::1, ::1) = skpb(::0) . []
207       %% 0 non_digit, 1 rest_of_termrepr
208   % - - - - - - - - - - - - - -
209   % auxiliary tests
210   wordstart(::0) = smalletter(::0) . []
211   varstart(::0) = bigletter(::0) . []
212   varstart("_") = []
213   % - - - - - - - - - - - - - -
214   skpb(::0) = skipbl . lastch(::0) . []
215   % - - - - - - - - - - - - - -
216   % output the translation
217   puttr([]) = ':' . []
218   puttr(::0.::1) = wch(::0) . puttr(::1) . []
219   putvarnames(::0, _) = var(::0) . ':' . nl . []
220       %% 0 sym_tab_end
221   putvarnames(::0.::1, ::2) = nextline(::2) . wch(' ') . display(::2) . puttr(':', ::0) .
222       wch(',') . sum(::2, 1, ::3) . putvarnames(::1, ::3) . []
223       %% 0 currname, 1 sym_tab_tail, 2 currnum, 3 nextnum
224   nextline(::0) = prod(6, _, 0, ::0) . ':' . nl . display(' %%') . []
225       %% 0 a_multiple_of_line_size
226   nextline(_) = []
227   % % % the end % % %
228   = display("BOOTSTRAPPER loaded.") . nl . see(user) . [] #
229
```

User Interface and Utilities

```
1    %                 Toy - the Prolog part.
2    % (c) COPYRIGHT 1983 - Feliks Kluzniak, Stanislaw Szpakowicz
3    %            Institute of Informatics, Warsaw University
4    % :::::::::::::::::::::::::::::::::::::::::::::::::::::::::: ::
5    % -:-:-:-:-:-       INTERACTIVE DRIVER - TOP LEVEL  -:-:-:- -:-
6    % :::::::::::::::::::::::::::::::::::::::::::::::::::::::::: ::
7    ear :- nl, display("ToyProlog listening:"), nl, tag(loop).
8    ear :- halt("ToyProlog, end of session.").
9
10   loop :- repeat,
11          display(?-), read(Term, Sym_tab), exec(Term, Sym_tab), fail.
12
13   stop :- tagfail(loop).
14
15   exec('e r r', _) :- !.              % this covers variables, too
16   exec(:-(Goals), _) :- !, once(Goals).
17   exec(N, _) :- integer(N), !, num_clause.
18   exec(Goals, Sym_tab) :-
19          call(Goals), numbervars(Goals, 0, _),
20          printvars(Sym_tab), enough, !.
21   exec(_, _) :- display(no), nl.      % if call(Goals) fails
22
23   enough :- rch, skipbl, lastch(Ch), rch, not(=(Ch, '?')).
24
25   printvars(Sym_tab) :- var(Sym_tab), display(yes), nl, !.
26   printvars(Sym_tab) :- prvars(Sym_tab).
27
28   prvars(Sym_tab) :- var(Sym_tab), !.
```

341

(continued)

```
29   prvars(Evar(NameString, Instance) ! Sym_tab_tail]) :-
30        writetext(NameString), display(' = '),
31        side_effects(outt(Instance, fd(_, _), q)),
32             % this is equivalent to writeq(Instance) but we avoid
33             % superfluous calls on numbervars - cf WRITE
34        nl, prvars(Sym_tab_tail).
35
36   num_clause :- display('+++ A number can''t be a clause.'), nl.
37
38   % read a program upto end.    (the only way to define user procedures);
39   % consult/reconsult must be issued from the terminal, and it returns
40   % there ( consult(user) is correct, too )

41   consult(File) :-  seeing(OldF), readpros(File), see(OldF).
42   reconsult(File) :- seeing(OldF), readpros(File), see(OldF), redefine.
43        redefine, :-  !, setpros.
44   readpros(user) :-  !, setpros.
45   readpros(File) :-  see(File), echo, setpros, noecho, seen.
46
47   % the actual job is done by this procedure
48   setpros :- repeat, read(T), assimilate(T), =(T, end), !.
49
50   assimilate('e r r') :-  !, !.
51   assimilate( --->(Left, Right) ) :- !    % a variable is erroneous, too
52        !, tag(transl_rule(Left, Right, Clause)), assertz(Clause).
53   assimilate( :-(Goal) ) :-  !, once(Goal).
54   assimilate(end) :-  !.
55   assimilate(N) :-  integer(N), !, num_clause.
56   % otherwise  store the clause
57   assimilate(Clause) :-  assertz(Clause).
58
59
60
61   % :::::::::::::::::::::::::::::::::::::::::::::::::::::::::::::
62   % - - - - -          READ A TERM           - - - - -
```

342

```
63  % :::::::::::::::::::::::::::::::::::::::::::::::::::::::::::::::::::::::::::::::::
64  read(T) :- read(T, Sym_tab).
65  read(T, Sym_tab) :-
66      gettr(T_internal, Sym_tab), !, maketerm(T_internal, T).
67  % if gettr fails then...
68  read('e r r', _) :-
69      nl, display('+++ Bad term on input. Text skipped: '), skip, nl.
70
71  % skip to the nearest full stop not in quotes or in comment
72  skip :- lastch(Ch), wch(Ch), skip(Ch).
73
74  skip(.)    :-  rch, lastch(Ch), e_skip(Ch), !.
75  skip('%')  :-  skip_comment, !, rch, skip.
76  skip(Q)    :-  isquote(Q), skip_s(Q), !, rch, skip.
77  skip(_)    :-  rch, skip.
78
79  % stop on a "layout" character
80  e_skip(Ch) :- @=<(Ch, ' ').
81  e_skip(Ch) :- wch(Ch), rch, skip.
82
83  skip_comment :- repeat, rch, lastch(Ch), wch(Ch), iseoln(Ch), !.
84
85  isquote('''').                 isquote('"').
86
87  % skip a string
88  skip_s(Quote) :- repeat, rch, lastch(Ch), wch(Ch), =(Ch, Quote), !.
89
90  % :::::::::::::::::::::::::::::::::::::::::::::::::::::::::::::::::::::::::::::::::
91  % -----------------------        P A R S E R        ---------------
92  % :::::::::::::::::::::::::::::::::::::::::::::::::::::::::::::::::::::::::::::::::
93  % This is an operator precedence parser for Prolog-10. gettr
94  % constructs the internal representation of a term. Next, maketerm
95  % constructs the term proper -- see  r e a d. Here is an informal
96  % description of the underlying operator precedence grammar ( each "rule"
```

343

(continued)

```
 97   % corresponds to one clause of  r e d u c e). Sides are separated by ==>
 98   % and multiple righthand sides - by OR.
 99   %   t ==>  variable     OR  integer    OR  string
100   %   t ==>  identifier
101   %   t ==>  identifier ('t')
102   %   t ==>  [] OR {}
103   %   t ==>  ( t ) OR [ t ] OR { t }
104   %   t ==>  [ t : t ]
105   %   t ==>  t postfix_functor
106   %   t ==>  t infix_functor t
107   %   t ==>  prefix_functor t
108   % Sequences of terms separated by commas - in rules 3, 5, 6 - will be recognised
109   % as comma-terms (commas are infix functors covered by rule 8).
110   % There are five types of operators: vns(_), id(_), ff(_, _, _),
111   % br(_, _), bar - see the scanner. The terminal symbol dot never sets onto
112   % the stack. The terminal symbol bottom is never returned by the scanner;
113   % it is only used to initiate and terminate the main loop (p a r s e). The
114   % only nonterminal symbol is t(_).
115   % There are five types of internal representations (Args denotes the represen-
116   % tation of arguments - usually a comma-term):
117   %   tr(Name, Args)    -- for functor-terms,
118   %   arg0(X)           -- for X a variable, an atom, a number, or a string,
119   %   bar(X, Y)         -- for a list with front X and tail Y,
120   %   tr1(Name, X)      -- for prefix and postfix functors,
121   %   tr2(Name, X, Y)   -- for infix functors.
122   % A Name in tr may be a bracket type. See  r e d u c e (clauses 5, 6)
123   % and  m a k e t e r m  for details.
124
125   % -- set the internal representation of a term
126   settr(X, Sym_tab) :-
127       settoken(T, Sym_tab), parse([bottom], T, X, Sym_tab).
128
129   % p a r s e takes four parameters: the current stack, the current token
130   % from input, the variable that drifts down and brings the internal repre-
```

```prolog
% sentation to the surface, and the symbol table (used by gettoken)
parse([t(X), bottom], dot, X, _) :- !.
parse(Stack, Input, X, Sym_tab) :-
    topterminal(Stack, Top, Pos),
    establish_precedence(Top, Input, Pos, Rel, RTop, RInput),
    exch_top(Top, RTop, Stack, RStack),
    step(Rel, RInput, RStack, NewStack, NewInput, Sym_tab),
    parse(NewStack, NewInput, X, Sym_tab).

% the topmost terminal will be covered by at most one nonterminal
% (the third parameter gives Top's position: 1 on the top, 2 covered)
topterminal([t(_), Top : _], Top, 2) :- !.
topterminal([Top : _], Top, 1).

% exchange the topmost terminal (applies only to disambiguated mixed functors)
exch_top(Top, Top, Stack, Stack) :- !.
exch_top(_, RTop, [t(X), _ : S], [t(X), RTop : S]) :- !.
exch_top(_, RTop, [_ : S], [RTop : S]).

% - - perform one step:  shift (stack the current token) or reduce
step(lseq, RInput, Stack, [RInput : Stack], NewInput, Sym_tab) :-
    !, gettoken(NewInput, Sym_tab).
step(gt, RInput, Stack, NewStack, RInput, _) :-
    reduce(Stack, NewStack), !.
% fail if reduction impossible (parse and settr will fail, too -
% this failure will be intercepted by settr's caller)

% reduce top segment of the stack according to the underlying grammar
reduce([ vns(X) : S ], [ t(arg0(X)) : S ]).
reduce([ id(I) : S ], [ t(arg0(I)) : S ]).
reduce([ br(r, ')'), t(X), br(l, '('), id(I)) : S ] ,
        [ t(tr(I, X)) : S ]).
reduce([ br(r, Type), br(l, Type) : S ] ,
        [ t(arg0(Type)) : S ]) :- not(=(Type, '()')).
```

APPENDIX A.4 (Continued)

```prolog
165                                     % '[]' or '{}', see p. 2nd clause
166   reduce([ br(r, Type), t(X), br(l, Type) | S ], E,
167                           [ t(tr(Type, X)) | S ]).
168   reduce([ br(r, '[]'), t(Y), bar, t(X), br(l, '[]') | S ], E,
169                           [ t(bar(X, Y)) | S ]).
170   reduce([ ff(I, Type, _), t(X) | S ], E,
171                           [ t(tr1(I, X)) | S ]) :-
172           ismpostf(Type).
173   reduce([ t(Y), ff(I, Type, _), t(X) | S ], E,
174                           [ t(tr2(I, X, Y)) | S ]) :-
175           isminf(Type).
176   reduce([ t(X), ff(I, Type, _) | S ], E,
177                           [ t(tr1(I, X)) | S ]) :-
178           ismpref(Type).
179   % otherwise fail (cf step p)
180
181   % -- auxiliary tests for the parser
182   ispref(fy) :- ispref(fx).
183
184   ispostf(yf) :- ispostf(xf).
185
186   ismpref([fTUn]) :- ispref(TUn).
187   ismpref([_, TUn]) :- ispref(TUn).
188
189   isminf([fTBin]) :- member(TBin, [xfy, yfx, xfx]).
190   isminf([_, _]).
191
192   ismpostf([fTUn]) :- ispostf(TUn).
193   ismpostf([_, TUn]) :- ispostf(TUn).
194
195   % -- establish precedence relation between the topmost
196   % terminal on the stack and the current input terminal
197   establish_precedence(Top, Input, Pos, Rel, RTop, RInput) :-
198           p(Top, Input, Pos, Rel0),
```

```
199    finalize(Rel0, Top, Input, Rel, RTop, RInput) :- !.

200    finalize(lseq, Top, Input, lseq, Top, Input).
201    finalize(st, Top, Input, st, Top, Input).
202    finalize(lseq(RTop, RInput), _, _, lseq, RTop, RInput).
203    finalize(st(RTop, RInput), _, _, st, RTop, RInput).

204
205    p(id(_), br(l, '()'), l, lseq).
206    p(br(l, Type), br(r, Type) _, lseq).
207    p(br(l, []), bar, 2, lseq).
208    p(bar, br(r, []), 2, lseq).

209
210    p(Top, Input, l, st) :-
211        vns_id_br(Top, r),   br_bar(Input, r).
212    p(Top, ff(N, Types, F), l, st(Top, ff(N, RTypes, F))) :-
213        vns_id_br(Top, r),   restrict(Types, Lfx, fyl, RTypes).

214
215    p(Top, Input, l, lseq) :-
216        br_bar(Top, l),   vns_id_br(Input, l).
217    p(Top, ff(N, Types, F), Fos, lseq(Top, ff(N, RTypes, F))) :-
218        br_bar(Top, l),   pre_inpost(Pos, Types, RTypes).
219    p(ff(N, Types, F), Input, Pos, st(ff(N, RTypes, F), Input)) :-
220        br_bar(Input, r),   post_inpre(Fos, Types, RTypes).
221    p(ff(N, Types, F), Input, l, lseq(ff(N, RTypes, F), Input)) :-
222        vns_id_br(Input, l),   restrict(Types, Lxf, yfl, RTypes).

223
224    % functors with equal priorities
225    p(ff(NTop, TsTop, F), ff(NInp, TsInp, F), Pos, Rel) :-
226        res_confl(TsTop, TsInp, Fos, RTsTop, RTsInp, Rel0),
227        !, do_rel(Rel0, ff(NTop, RTsTop, F), ff(NInp, RTsInp, F), Rel).

228    % different priorities
229    p(ff(NTop, TsTop, FTop), ff(NInp, TsInp, FInp), Pos,
230        st(ff(NTop, RTsTop, FTop), ff(NInp, RTsInp, FInp))) :-
231        stronger(FTop, FInp), !,
232        restrict(TsInp, Lfx, [Lfl, RTsInp),
```

(continued)

347

```
233        post_inpre(Pos, TsTop, RTsTop).
234   p(ff(NTop, TsTop, FTop), ff(NInp, TsInp, FInp), Pos,
235        lseq(ff(NTop, RTsTop, FTop), ff(NInp, RTsInp, FInp))) :-
236        stronger(FInp, FTop), ! ,
237        restrict(TsTop, [xf, yf], RTsTop),
238        pre_inpost(Pos, TsInp, RTsInp).
239
240   p(_, dot, _, gt).
241   p(bottom, _, _, lseq).
242   % otherwise fail (p a r s e  fails, too)
243
244   vns_id_br(vns(_), _).
245   vns_id_br(id(_), _).
246   vns_id_br(br(LeftRight, _), LeftRight).
247
248   br_bar(br(LeftRight, _), LeftRight).
249   br_bar(bar, _).
250
251   stronger(Prior1, Prior2) :- less(Prior1, Prior2).
252
253   pre_inpost(1, Types, RTypes) :-         % the functor must be prefix
254        restrict(Types, [xf, yf], A),
255        restrict(A, [xfy, yfx, yfx], RTypes).
256   pre_inpost(2, Types, RTypes) :- .       % the functor must not be prefix
257        restrict(Types, [fx, fy], RTypes).
258
259   post_inpre(1, Types, RTypes) :-         % the functor must be postfix
260        restrict(Types, [fx, fy], A),
261        restrict(A, [xfy, yfx, yfx], RTypes).
262   post_inpre(2, Types, RTypes) :- .       % the functor must not be postfix
263        restrict(Types, [xf, yf], RTypes).
264
265   % leave only those types that do not belong to RSet,
266   % fail if this would leave no types at all (RSet
```

```
267  % contains only binary types, or only unary types)
268  restrict([T], RSet, [T]) :- ! , not(member(T, RSet)).
269  restrict([TBin, TUn], RSet, [TBin]) :-    member(TUn, RSet), !.
270  restrict([TBin, TUn], RSet, [TUn]) :-     member(TBin, RSet), !.
271  restrict([Types, _, Types).
272
273  % compute relation for two functors with equal priorities, four cases:
274  %  both normal, Top mixed, Input mixed, both mixed
275  res_confl([TTop], [TInp], Pos, [TTop], [TInp], RelO)    :-
276          ! , ff_p(TTop, TInp, Pos, RelO).
277  res_confl([TTopBin, TTopUn], [TInp], Pos, RTsTop, [TInp], RelO)   :-
278          ! , ff_p(TTopBin, TInp, Pos, RelB),
279          ff_p(TTopUn, TInp, Pos, RelU),
280          match_rels(RelB, RelU, RelO,TTopBin, TTopUn, RTsTop).
281  res_confl([TTop], [TInpBin, TInpUn], Pos, [TTop], RTsInp, RelO)   :-
282          ! , ff_p(TTop, TInpBin, Pos, RelB),
283          ff_p(TTop, TInpUn, Pos, RelU),
284          match_rels(RelB, RelU, RelO, TInpBin, TInpUn, RTsInp).
285  res_confl([TTopBin, TTopUn], [TInpBin, TInpUn], Pos, RTsTop, RTsInp, RelO)   :-
286          ff_p(TTopBin, TInpBin, Pos, RelBB),
287          ff_p(TTopBin, TInpUn, Pos, RelBU),
288          ff_p(TTopUn, TInpBin, Pos, RelUB),
289          ff_p(TTopUn, TInpUn, Pos, RelUU),
290          res_mixed(RelBB, RelBU, RelUB, RelUU, RelO,
291                    TTopBin, TTopUn, TInpBin, TInpUn, RTsTop, RTsInp), !.
292
293  do_rel(lseq, TopF, InpF, lseq(TopF, InpF)).
294  do_rel(gt, TopF, InpF, gt(TopF, InpF)).
295  % fail if RelO = err
296
297  match_rels(Rel, Rel, Rel, TBin, TUn, [TBin, TUn]) :- !.          % err included
298  match_rels(err, Rel, Rel, _, TUn, [TUn]) :- !.
299  match_rels(Rel, err, Rel, TBin, _, [TBin]) :- !.
300  match_rels(_, _, err, TBin, TUn, [TBin, TUn]).
```

349

(continued)

APPENDIX A.4 (*Continued*)

```prolog
301  res_mixed(RelO, RelO, RelO, RelO, RelO,
302            TTopBin, TTopUn, TInpBin, TInpUn,
303            [TTopBin, TTopUn], [TInpBin, TInpUn]).
304  res_mixed(err, err, RelUB, RelUU, RelO,
305            _, TTopUn, TInpBin, TInpUn, [TTopUn], RTsInp) :-
306            match_rels(RelUB, RelUU, err, err, RelO,
307            _, TTopUn, TInpBin, TInpUn, TTopBin, RTsInp).
308  res_mixed(RelBB, RelBU, err, err, RelO,
309            TTopBin, _, TInpUn, [TTopBin, RTsInp], RTsInp) :-
310            match_rels(RelBU, RelBB, RelO, TInpUn, RelO,
311            TTopBin, _, TInpUn, RTsTop, [TInpUn]) :-
312            match_rels(RelBU, RelUU, RelO, TTopBin, TTopUn, RTsTop).
313            TTopBin, TTopUn, _, TInpUn, RTsTop, [TInpUn]) :-
314  res_mixed(err, err, RelUB, err, RelO,
315            TTopBin, TTopUn, _, RTsTop, [TInpBin]) :-
316            match_rels(RelBB, RelUB, RelO, TTopBin, TTopUn, RTsTop).
317  res_mixed(_, _, _, _, err, _, _, _, _, _, _).
318
319  % establish precedence relation for two (basic) types
320  ff_p(TTop, TInp, Pos, lseq) :-
321       member(TTop, [xfy, fy]),              % right_associative
322       ff_p_aux1(Pos, TInp), !.
323  ff_p(TTop, TInp, Pos, gt) :-
324       member(TInp, [yfx, yf]),              % left_associative
325       ff_p_aux2(Pos, TTop), !.
326  ff_p(_, _, _, err).
327
328  ff_p_aux1(1, TInp)  :- ispref(TInp).
329  ff_p_aux1(2, TInp)  :- member(TInp, [xfy, xf]).
330
331  ff_p_aux2(1, TTop)  :- ispostf(TTop).
332  ff_p_aux2(2, TTop)  :- member(TTop, [yfx, fx, xfx]).
333
334  % ==================================================
```

```
335   % --  ::  --  |        internal representation ----> term       --  | -- | --  | -- | --  |
336   % ::  ::  ::  ::  ::  ::  ::  ::  ::  ::  ::  ::  ::  ::  ::  ::  ::  ::  ::  ::  ::  ::  ::  ::  ::  ::  ::  ::  ::  ::  ::  ::  ::  ::  ::  ::  ::
337   maketerm(arg0(X), X) :-- | !.           % variable, atom, number, string
338   maketerm(tr('()', RawTerm), T) :--
339          !, maketerm(RawTerm, T).
340   maketerm(bar(RawList, RawTail), T) :--
341          !, maketerm(RawTail, Tail),
342          makelist(RawList, Tail, T).
343   maketerm(tr('[]', RawList), T) :--
344          !, makelist(RawList, '[]', T).
345   maketerm(tr('{}', RawArg), '{}'(Arg)) :--
346          !, maketerm(RawArg, Arg).
347   maketerm(tr(Name, RawArgs), T) :--
348          !, makelist(RawArgs, '[]', Args),
349          =..(T, [Name ! Args]).
350   maketerm(tr2(Name, RawArg1, RawArg2), T) :--
351          !, maketerm(RawArg1, Arg1), maketerm(RawArg2, Arg2),
352          =..(T, [Name, Arg1, Arg2]).
353   maketerm(tr1(Name, RawArg), T) :--
354          maketerm(RawArg, Arg), =..(T, [Name, Arg]).
355
356   % comma-term to dot-list-with-Tail
357   makelist(tr2(',', RawArg, RawArgs), Tail, [Arg ! Args]) :--
358          !, maketerm(RawArg, Arg), makelist(RawArgs, Tail, Args).
359   makelist(RawArg, Tail, [Arg ! Tail]) :--   maketerm(RawArg, Arg).
360
361   % ::  ::  ::  ::  ::  ::  ::  ::  ::  ::  ::  ::  ::  ::  ::  ::  S C A N N E R  ::  ::  ::  ::  ::  ::  ::  ::  ::  ::  ::  ::  ::  ::  ::  ::
362   % --  ::  --  |  --  |  --  |  --  |                                 --  |  -- |  -- |  --  |
363   % ::  ::  ::  ::  ::  ::  ::  ::  ::  ::  ::  ::  ::  ::  ::  ::  ::  ::  ::  ::  ::  ::  ::  ::  ::  ::  ::  ::  ::  ::  ::  ::  ::  ::  ::  ::
364   % this scanner returns six kinds of tokens:
365   % vns(_)                        variables, numbers, strings
366   % id(Name)                      atoms
367   % ff(Name, Types, Prior)        "fix" functors
368   % br(Which, Type)               brackets (left/right, '()' / '[]' / '{}')
```

(continued)

351

```
369   %     bar                      !  (in lists)
370   %     dot                      .  followed by a layout character
371
372   % -- read a token and construct its internal form
373   % the input is supposed to be positioned
374   % over the first character of a token (or preceding "white space")
375   gettoken(Token, Sym_tab) :-
376         skipbl, lastch(Startch), absorbtoken(Startch, Rawtoken), !,
377         maketoken(Rawtoken, Token, Sym_tab), !.
378
379   % -- read in a suitable sequence of characters
380   % a word, ie a regular alphanumeric identifier
381   absorbtoken(Ch, id([Ch : Wordtail]) :-
382         wordstart(Ch), setword(Wordtail).
383   % a variable
384   absorbtoken(Ch, var([Ch : Tail])) :-
385         varstart(Ch), setword(Tail).
386   % a solo character is a comma, a semicolon or an exclamation mark
387   absorbtoken(Ch, id([Ch]) :- solochar(Ch), rch.
388   % a bracket, ie ( ) [ ] { }
389   absorbtoken(Ch, br(Wh, Type)) :-
390         bracket(Ch), bracket(Ch, Wh, Type), rch.
391   absorbtoken('!', bar) :- rch.
392   % a string in quotes or in double quotes
393   absorbtoken('''', aid(Qname)) :-
394         rch(Nextch), setstring('''', Nextch, Qname).
395   absorbtoken('"', str(String)) :-
396         • rch(Nextch), setstring('"', Nextch, String).
397   % a positive number
398   absorbtoken(Ch, num([Ch : Digits])) :-
399         digit(Ch), setdigits(Digits).
400   % a negative number or a dash (possibly starting a symbol, see below)
401   absorbtoken(--, Rawtoken) :- rch(Ch), num_or_sym(Ch, Rawtoken).
402   absorbtoken(., Rawtoken) :- rch(Ch), dot_or_sym(Ch, Rawtoken).
```

```prolog
403    % a symbol, built of . : - < = > + / * ? & @ # ~ \
404    absorbtoken(Ch, id([Ch : Symbs])) :- symch(Ch), getsym(Symbs).
405    % an embedded comment
406    absorbtoken('%', Rawtoken) :-
407        skipcomment, lastch(Ch), absorbtoken(Ch, Rawtoken).
408    % this shouldn't happen:
409    absorbtoken(Ch, _) :- display(errinscan(Ch)), nl, fail.
410
411    num_or_sym(Ch, num([-, Ch : Digits])) :-
412        digit(Ch), getdigits(Digits).
413    num_or_sym(Ch, id([-, Ch : Symbs])) :- symch(Ch), getsym(Symbs).
414    num_or_sym(_, id([-])).
415
416    % layout characters precede ' ' in ASCII
417    dot_or_sym(Ch, dot) :- @=<(Ch, ' '), !.    % no advance
418    dot_or_sym(Ch, id([., Ch : Symbs])) :- symch(Ch), getsym(Symbs).
419    dot_or_sym(_, id([.])).
420
421    skipcomment :- lastch(Ch), iseoln(Ch), skipbl, !.
422    skipcomment :- rch, skipcomment.
423
424    % -- auxiliary input procedures
425    % read an alphanumeric identifier
426    getword([Ch : Word]) :-
427        rdch(Ch), alphanum(Ch), !, getword(Word).
428    getword([]).
429
430    % read a sequence of digits
431    getdigits([Ch : Digits]) :-
432        rdch(Ch), digit(Ch), !, getdigits(Digits).
433    getdigits([]).
434
435    % read a symbol
436    getsym([Ch : Symbs]) :-
```

353

(continued)

```
437            rdch(Ch), symch(Ch), !, getsym(Symbs).
438   getsym([]).
439
440   % read a quoted id or string (Delim is either ' or ")
441   getstring(Delim, Delim, Str) :-
442      !, rdch(Nextch), twodelims(Delim, Nextch, Str).
443   getstring(Delim, Ch, [Ch | Str]) :-
444      rdch(Nextch), getstring(Delim, Nextch, Str).
445   twodelims(Delim, Delim, [Delim | Str]) :-
446      !, rdch(Nextch), getstring(Delim, Nextch, Str).
447   twodelims(_, _, []).    %close the list
448
449   % -- auxiliary tests
450   wordstart(Ch) :- smalletter(Ch).
451   varstart(Ch) :- bigletter(Ch).
452   varstart('_').
453   bracket('(', 1, ')').            bracket(')', r, '()').
454   bracket('[', 1, ']').            bracket(']', r, '[]').
455   bracket('{', 1, '}').            bracket('}', r, '{}').
456
457   % -- transform a raw token into its final form
458   maketoken(var(Namestring), vns(Ptr), Sym_tab) :-
459         makeptr(Namestring, Ptr, Sym_tab).
460   maketoken(id(Namestring), Token, _) :-
461         pname(Name, Namestring), make_ff_or_id(Name, Token).
462   maketoken(qid(Namestring), id(Name), _) :-
463         pname(Name, Namestring).
464   maketoken(num([_ : Digits]), vns(N), _) :-
465         pnamei(N1, Digits), sum(N, N1, 0).
466   maketoken(num(Digits), vns(N), _) :- pnamei(N, Digits).
467   maketoken(str(Chars), vns(Chars), _).
468   maketoken(Token, Token, _).       % br(_,_) and bar and dot

469   % variables are kept in a symbol table (an open list)
```

```
471   makeptr(['*','-',_,_).          %no search - an anonymous variable
472   makeptr(Nmstr, Ptr, Sym_tab) :- look_var(var(Nmstr, Ptr), Sym_tab).
473
474   % look-up
475   look_var(Item, [Item | Sym_tab]).
476   look_var(Item, [_ | Sym_tab]) :- look_var(Item, Sym_tab).
477
478   make_ff_or_id(Name, ff(Name, Types, Prior)) :-
479       'FF'(Name, Types, Prior), !.
480   make_ff_or_id(Name, id(Name)).
481
482   % ::::::::::::::::::::::::::::::::::::::::::::::::::::::::::::::::::::::::
483   % :- ---------------- GRAMMAR RULE PREPROCESSOR ------------------- :-
484   % ::::::::::::::::::::::::::::::::::::::::::::::::::::::::::::::::::::::::
485   transl_rule(Left, Right, Clause) :-
486       two_ok(Left, Right),
487       isolate_lhs_t(Left, Nont, Lhs_t),
488       connect(Lhs_t, Outpar, Finalvar),
489       expand(Nont, Initvar, Outpar, Head),
490       makebody(Right, Initvar, Finalvar, Body, Alt_flag),
491       do_clause(Body, Head, Clause).
492
493   do_clause(true, Head, Head) :- !.
494   do_clause(Body, Head, (Head :- Body)).
495
496   % Lhs_t is a list (possibly empty) of lefthand side terminals
497   isolate_lhs_t(','(Nont, Lhs_t), Nont, Lhs_t) :-
498       ','(nonvarint(Nont), rulerror(varint)),
499       ','(isclosedlist(Lhs_t), rulerror(ter)), !.
500   isolate_lhs_t(Nont, Nont, []).
501
502   % fail if not a closed list
503   isclosedlist(L) :- check(iscll(L)).
504   iscll(L) :- var(L), !, fail.
```

355

(continued)

```
505   iscll([]).
506   iscll([_ : L]) :- iscll(L).
507
508   % connect terminals to the nearest nonterminal's input parameter
509   % (actually, "open" a closed list)
510   connect([], Nextvar, Nextvar) :- !.
511   connect([Tsym : Tsyms], LTsym : Outpar], Nextvar) :-
512          connect(Tsyms, Outpar, Nextvar).
513
514   % -- translate the righthand side (loop over alternatives)
515   % in alternatives, each righthand side is preceded by a dummy
516   % nonterminal, as defined by 'dummy' --> []. (since terminals
517   % are appended to input parameters, the input parameter of a common
518   % lefthand side must be a variable)
519   makebody(';',(Alt, Alts), Initvar, Finalvar,
520          ';'(',',(' dummy'(Initvar, Nextvar), Alt_b), Alt_bs), _) :-
521          !, two_ok(Alt, Alts),
522          makeright(Alt, Nextvar, Finalvar, Alt_b),
523          makebody(Alts, Initvar, Finalvar, Alt_bs, alt).
524   makebody(Right, Initvar, Finalvar, Body, Alt_flag) :-
525          var(Alt_flag), !,             % only one alternative
526          makeright(Right, Initvar, Finalvar, Body).
527   makebody(Right, Initvar, Finalvar,
528          ',',(' dummy'(Initvar, Nextvar), Body), alt) :-
529          makeright(Right, Nextvar, Finalvar, Body).
530
531   % -- translate one alternative
532   makeright(',',(Item, Items), Thispar, Finalvar, T_item_items) :-
533          !, two_ok(Item, Items),
534          transl_item(Item, Thispar, Nextvar, T_item),
535          makeright(Items, Nextvar, Finalvar, T_items),
536          combine(T_item, T_items, T_item_items).
537   makeright(Item, Thispar, Finalvar, T_item) :-
538          transl_item(Item, Thispar, Finalvar, T_item).
```

```
539   combine(true, T_items, T_items) :- !.
540   combine(T_item, true, T_item) :- !.
541   combine(T_item, T_items, ','(T_item, T_items)).
542
543
544   % -- -- translate one item (sure to be a functor-term)
545   transl_item(Terminals, Thispar, Nextvar, true) :-
546           isclosedlist(Terminals),
547           !, connect(Terminals, Thispar, Nextvar).
548   % conditions (the cut and others)
549   transl_item(!, Thispar, Thispar, !) :- !.
550   transl_item('{}'(Cond), Thispar, Thispar, call(Cond)) :- !.
551   % bad list of terminals (missed the first clause)
552   transl_item([_ : _], _, _) :- rulerror(ter).
553   % a nested alternative
554   transl_item(';'(X, Y), Thispar, Nextvar, Transl) :-
555           !, makebody(';'(X, Y), Thispar, Nextvar, Transl, _).
556   % finally, a regular nonterminal
557   transl_item(Nont, Thispar, Nextvar, Transl) :-
558           expand(Nont, Thispar, Nextvar, Transl).
559
560   % add input parameter and output parameter
561   expand(Nont, In_par, Out_par, Call) :-
562           =..(Nont, [Fun : Args]),
563           =..(Call, [Fun, In_par, Out_par : Args]).
564
565   % -- -- error handling
566   two_ok(X, Y) :- nonvarint(X), nonvarint(Y), !.
567   two_ok(_, _) :- rulerror(varint).
568
569   rulerror(Message) :-
570           nl, display('+++ Error in this rule: '), mes(Message), nl,
571           tasfail(transl_rule(_, _, _)).
572   % diagnostics are only very brief (and not too informative ...)
```

```
573    mes(varint)    :-   display("variable or integer item.").
574    mes(ter)       :-   display("terminals not on a closed list.").
575
576    % -- initiate grammar processing
577    phrase(Nont, Terminals)  :-
578         nonvarint(Nont), !,
579         expand(Nont, Terminals, []), Init_call),
580         call(Init_call).
581
582    phrase(N, T)   :-   error(phrase(N, T)).
583
584    , dummy"(X, X).
585
586              % *****************************************
587              % ***********************************************
588              % ***     L I B R A R Y    ***
589              % ***********************************************
590              % *****************************************
591    %================================================
592    % - : - : - : - : - : - : - : - : -    (read as "univ")
593    % = : - : - : - : - : - : - : - : - : - : - : - : -
594    % =..(X, Y)  :- var(X), var(Y), !, error(=..(X, Y)).
595    % =..(Num, [Num])  :- integer(Num), !.
596    % =..(Term, [Fun | Args])  :-
597         setarity(Term, Args, N),
598         functor(Term, Fun, N),        % this works both ways
599         not(integer(Fun)),            % we don't want eg 17(X)
600         setargs(Term, Args, 0, N).    % this works both ways, too
601
602    setarity(Term, Args, N)   :- var(Term), !, length(Args, N).
603         % notice that bad Args give an error in length
604    setarity(_, _, _).        % Arity will be set by functor in =..
605
606    % both numeric parameters are given
607    % the loop stops when the third reaches the fourth
```

358

```
607   % (works both ways because a r g  does)
608   setargs(_, [], N) :- !.
609   setargs(Term, [Arg : Args], K, N) :-
610              sum(K, 1, K1), arg(K1, Term, Arg),
611              setargs(Term, Args, K1, N).
612
613   % find the length of a closed list; error if not closed
614   length(List, N) :- length(List, 0, N).
615
616   % this is a tail-recursive formulation of length
617   length(L, _, _) :- var(L), !, error(length(L, ...)).
618   length([], N, N) :- !.
619   length(L.._ : List, K, N) :-
620              !, sum(K, 1, K1), length(List, K1, N).
621   length(Bizarre, _, _) :- error(length(Bizarre, ...)).
622
623   % bind every variable to a distinct 'V'(N)
624   numbervars('V'(N), N, NextN) :- !, sum(N, 1, NextN).
625   numbervars('V'(_), N, N) :- !.
626   numbervars(X, N, N) :- integer(X), !.
627   numbervars(X, N, NextN) :- numbervars(X, 1, N, NextN).
628
629   numbervars(X, K, N, NextN) :-
630              arg(K, X, A), !, numbervars(A, N, MidN),
631              sum(K, 1, K1), numbervars(X, K1, MidN, NextN).
632   numbervars(_, _, N, N) :- !.
633
634   % ::::::::::::::::::::::::::::::::::::::::::::::::::::::::::::::::::::::::::::::::
635   % :::::::::::::::::::: PREDEFINED "FIX" FUNCTORS AND O P ::::: | : | : | : |
636   % ::::::::::::::::::::::::::::::::::::::::::::::::::::::::::::::::::::::::::::::::
637   % (ordered according to probable frequency)
638   'FF'('.', '.') := [xfx] fx^[, 1000).
639   'FF'(':-') := [ xfx, fx^x, 1200).
640   'FF'('?', '?') := [fg], 1100).
```

(continued)

359

```
641   'FF' (not, Cfy], 900).
642   'FF' (\=, Cxfx], 700).
643   'FF' (is, Cxfx], 700).
644   'FF' (---->, Cxfx], 1200).
645   'FF' (+, Cyfx, fx], 500).             'FF' (--, Cyfx, fx], 500).
646   'FF' (*, Cyfx, fx], 400).             'FF' (/, Cxfx, fx], 400).
647   'FF' (mod, Cxfx], 300).
648   'FF' (<, Cxfx], 700).                 'FF' (=<, Cxfx], 700).
649   'FF' (>, Cxfx], 700).                 'FF' (>=, Cxfx], 700).
650   'FF' (=:=, Cxfx], 700).               'FF' (=\=, Cxfx], 700).
651   'FF' (@<, Cxfx], 700).                'FF' (@=<, Cxfx], 700).
652   'FF' (@>, Cxfx], 700).                'FF' (@>=, Cxfx], 700).
653   'FF' (==, Cxfx], 700).
654   'FF' (\==, Cxfx], 700).               'FF' (=.., Cxfx], 700).
655
656   % this implementation of op takes care of redefinitions
657   % and of mixed functors
658   op(Prior, Type, Name) :-
659         atom(Name), pname(Name, String), noq(String),
660                           % noq -- see WRITE
661         integer(Prior), less(O, Prior), less(Prior, 1201),
662         set_kind(Type, Kind), !,
663         do_op(Prior, Type, Name, Kind).
664   % if not all parameters are OK --
665   op(P, T, N) :- error(op( P, T, N )).
666
667   % set Kind to bin or un
668   set_kind(Type, bin) :-  binary(Type, _), !.
669   set_kind(Type, un) :-  unary(Type, _, _), !.
670
671   % test for binary and instantiate Assoc
672   binary(xfy, a(r)).      % right associative
673   binary(yfx, a(l)).      % left associative
674   binary(xfx, na(_)).     % non-associative
```

360

```
675   % test for unary; instantiate Kind and Assoc
676   unary(fy,  pre,  a(r)).        % right associative
677   unary(fx,  pre,  na(r)).       % right non-associative
678   unary(yf,  post, a(l)).        % left associative
679   unary(xf,  post, na(l)).       % left non-associative
680
681   do_op(F, T, N, Kind)   :-
682         'FF'(N, Oldtypes, Oldprior), !,
683         addff(Oldtypes, Oldprior, F, T, N, Kind).
684   do_op(F, T, N, _) :- assertz('FF'(N, [T], F)).
685
686   % add or redefine a functor
687   % for mixed functors, keep the binary type before the unary
688
689   % the same priority: redefine or make mixed
690   addff([Oldtype], F, F, T, N, Kind) :-
691         !, set_kind(Oldtype, Oldkind),
692         addff1(Oldkind, Kind, Oldtype, T, N, F).
693   addff([Oldtype1, Oldtype2], F, F, T, N, Kind) :-
694         !, addff2(Kind, Oldtype1, Oldtype2, T, F, N).
695   % otherwise the priorities were different: redefine
696   addff(_, _, F, T, N, _) :- redeff(N, [T], F).
697
698   % make a mixed functor or change type
699   addff1(bin, un, Oldtype, T, N, F)  :-          mk_mixed(N, [Oldtype, T], F).
700   addff1(un, bin, Oldtype, T, N, F)  :-          mk_mixed(N, [T, Oldtype], F).
701   addff1(Kind, Kind, _, T, N, F) :- redeff(N, [T], F).
702
703   % adjust a mixed functor by changing one of its types
704   addff2(bin, _, Oldtype2, T, F, N) :- mk_mixed(N, [T, Oldtype2], F).
705   addff2(un, Oldtype1, _, T, F, N) :- mk_mixed(N, [Oldtype1, T], F).
706
707   mk_mixed(N, Types, F) :-
708         retract('FF'(N, _, _)), !, assertz('FF'(N, Types, F)).
```

361

(continued)

```
709    % redefine and issue a warning
710    redeff(N, T, P) :-
711        nl, display("functor "), display(N),
712        display(" redefined"), nl,
713        retract('FF'(N, _, _)), !, asserta('FF'(N, T, P)).
714
715
716    % remove a declaration
717    delop(Name) :- atom(Name), retract('FF'(Name, _, _)), !.
718    delop(Name) :- error(delop(Name)).
719
720
721    % ::::::::::::::::::::::::::::::::::::::::::::::::::::::::::::::::::::::
722    % -- -- -- -- --    EVALUATE AN ARITHMETIC EXPRESSION    -- -- -- --
723    % ::::::::::::::::::::::::::::::::::::::::::::::::::::::::::::::::::::::
724    is(N, N) :- integer(N), !.
725    is(Val, +(A, B)) :-
726        !, is(Av, A), is(Bv, B), sum(Av, Bv, Val).
727    is(Val, -(A, B)) :-
728        !, is(Av, A), is(Bv, B), sum(Bv, Val, Av).
729    is(Val, *(A, B)) :-
730        !, is(Av, A), is(Bv, B), prod(Av, Bv, O, Val).
731    is(Val, /(A, B)) :-
732        !, is(Av, A), is(Bv, B), prod(Bv, Val, _, Av).
733    is(Val, mod(A, B)) :-
734        !, is(Av, A), is(Bv, B), prod(Bv, _, Val, Av).
735    is(Val, +(A)) :- !, is(Val, A).
736    is(Val, -(A)) :- !, is(Av, A), sum(Val, Av, O).
737    is(N, [N]) :- integer(N).
738    % otherwise fail
739
740    % -- -- -- -- --    EVALUATE AN ARITHMETIC RELATION    -- -- -- --
741    =:=(X, Y) :- is(XV, X), is(XV, Y).
742    <(X, Y) :- is(XV, X), is(YV, Y), less(XV, YV).
```

```
743  =<(X, Y) :-      is(XV, X), is(YV, Y), not(less(YV, XV)).
744  >(X, Y) :-       is(XV, X), is(YV, Y), less(YV, XV).
745  >=(X, Y) :-      is(XV, X), is(YV, Y), not(less(XV, YV)).
746  =\=(X, Y) :-     not(=:=(X, Y)).
747
748  % ::::::::::::::::::::::::::::::::::::::::::::::::::::::::::::::
749  % - - - - - - - -       PERFECT EQUALITY OF TERMS      - - - - -
750  % ::::::::::::::::::::::::::::::::::::::::::::::::::::::::::::::
751  ==(T1, T2) :-    var(T1), var(T2), !, eqvar(T1, T2).
752  ==(T1, T2) :-    check(==?(T1, T2)).
753
754  \==(T1, T2) :-   not(==?(T1, T2)).
755
756  ==?(T1, T2) :-
757          integer(T1), integer(T2), !, =(T1, T2).
758  ==?(T1, T2) :-
759          nonvarint(T1), nonvarint(T2),
760          functor(T1, Fun, Arity), functor(T2, Fun, Arity),
761          equalargs(T1, T2, 1).
762
763  equalargs(T1, T2, Argnumber),
764          arg(Argnumber, T1, Arg1), arg(Argnumber, T2, Arg2),
765          % arg fails given too large a number
766          !, ==(Arg1, Arg2), sum(Argnumber, 1, Nextnumber),
767          equalargs(T1, T2, Nextnumber).
768  equalargs(_, _, _).
769
770  % ::::::::::::::::::::::::::::::::::::::::::::::::::::::::::::::
771  % - - - - - -  assert, asserta, assertz, retract, clause  - - - - -
772  % ::::::::::::::::::::::::::::::::::::::::::::::::::::::::::::::
773  % - - add a clause (using built-in assert(_, _, _))
774  assert(Cl) :-    asserta(Cl).
775  asserta(Cl) :-
776          nonvarint(Cl), convert(Cl, Head, Body), !,
```

(continued)

363

```
777          assert(Head, Body, 0).
778    asserta(Cl) :-    error(asserta(Cl)).
779
780    assertz(Cl) :-
781       nonvarint(Cl), convert(Cl, Head, Body), !,
782       assert(Head, Body, 32767).       % ie 2 to 15th minus 1
783    assertz(Cl) :-    error(assertz(Cl)).
784
785    % convert the external form of a Body into a dotted list
786    convert(:-(Head, B), Head, Body) :-    conv_body(B, Body).
787    convert(Unit_cl, Unit_cl, []).
788
789    % this procedure works both ways
790    conv_body(B, [call(B)|B]) :-    var(B), !.
791    conv_body(true, []).
792    conv_body(B, Body) :-    conv_b(B, Body).
793
794    conv_b(B, [Body]) :-    var(B), !, conv_call(B, Body).
795    conv_b(','(C, B), [Call | Body]) :-
796       !, conv_call(C, Call), conv_b(B, Body).
797    conv_b(Call, [Call]).    % not a variable
798
799    % interpreter can process variable calls only within call
800    conv_call(C, call(C)) :-    var(C), !.
801    conv_call(C, C).
802
803    % :- remove a clause (this procedure is backtrackable)
804    retract(Cl) :-
805       nonvarint(Cl), convert(Cl, Head, Body), !,
806       functor(Head, Fun, Arity), remcls(Fun, Arity, 1, Head, Body).
807    retract(Cl) :-    error(retract(Cl)).
808
809    % ultimate failure if N too big (retract/3 fails)
810    remcls(Fun, Arity, N, Head, Body) :-
811       clause(Fun, Arity, N, N_head, N_body),
```

```
812         remcls(Fun, Arity, N, N_head, Head, N_body, Body).
813
814    remcls(Fun, Arity, N, Head, Head, Body, Body) :-
815        retract(Fun, Arity, N).
816    % user's backtracking resumes  r e t r a c t  here
817    % (after removing the Nth clause the next becomes Nth)
818    remcls(Fun, Arity, N, N_head, Head, N_body, Body) :-
819        check(=(N_head, Head)), check(=(N_body, Body)),
820        !, remcls(Fun, Arity, N, Head, _, Body).
821    remcls(Fun, Arity, N, _, Head, _, Body) :-
822        sum(N, 1, N1), remcls(Fun, Arity, N1, Head, Body).
823
824    % - - generate nondeterministically all clauses whose head
825    %     and body match the parameters of  c l a u s e
826    clause(Head, Body) :-
827        nonvarint(Head), !, functor(Head, Fun, Arity),
828        gencls(Fun, Arity, 1, Head, Body).
829    clause(Head, Body) :- error(clause(Head, Body)).
830
831    % generate; ultimate failure if N too big (clause/5 fails)
832    gencls(Fun, Arity, N, Head, Body) :-
833        clause(Fun, Arity, N, N_head, N_body),
834        gencls(Fun, Arity, N, N_head, Head, N_body, Body).
835
836    % fail if N_head does not match Head,
837    %     or if N_body converted does not match Body
838    gencls(_, _, _, N_head, N_head, N_body, Body) :-
839        conv_body(Body, N_body).
840    % user's backtracking resumes  c l a u s e  here
841    gencls(Fun, Arity, N, _, Head, _, Body) :-
842        sum(N, 1, N1), gencls(Fun, Arity, N1, Head, Body).
843
844    % ::::::::::::::::::::::::::::::::::::::::::::::::::::::
845    % - - - - - - -          LISTING
846    % ::::::::::::::::::::::::::::::::::::::::::::::::::::::
```

(continued)

```prolog
847   % list procedures determined by the parameter ( listing(_) )
848   % or all user's procedures ( listing )
849   listing :-
850        proc(Head), listproc(Head), nl, fail.
851   listing.           % catch the final fail from proc
852
853   listing(Fun) :- atom(Fun), !, listbyname(Fun).
854   listing(/(Fun,Arity)) :-
855        atom(Fun), integer(Arity), =<(0, Arity), !,
856        functor(Head, Fun, Arity), listproc(Head).
857   listing(L) :-
858        isclosedlist(L), listseveral(L), !.
859   listing(X) :- error(listing(X)).
860        % isclosedlist -- of grammar rule preprocessor
861
862   listseveral([]).
863   listseveral([Item | Items]) :-
864        listing(Item), listseveral(Items).
865
866   % all procedures with this name
867   listbyname(Fun) :-
868        proc(Head), functor(Head, Fun, _),
869        listproc(Head), nl, fail.
870   listbyname(_).          % succeed
871
872   % one procedure
873   listproc(Head)    :-
874        clause(Head, Body),
875        writeclause(Head, Body), wch(_), nl, fail.
876   listproc(_).          % succeed
877
878   writeclause(Head, Body)  :-
879        not(var(Body)), =(Body, true), !, writeq(Head).
880   writeclause(Head, Body)  :-  writeq(:-(Head, Body)).
881
```

```
%  :::::::::::::::::::::::::::::::::::::::::::::::::::::::::::::::::::
%% :::: -- ---- - --- -          W R I T E          -- --- --- -- -
%  :::::::::::::::::::::::::::::::::::::::::::::::::::::::::::::::::::
write(Term)  :--  side_effects(outterm(Term, noq)).

%  writeq encloses in quotes all identifiers except words,
%  symbols and solochars (not coinciding with "fix" functors)
writeq(Term)  :--  side_effects(outterm(Term, q)).

writetext([Ch | Chs])  :-  !,  wch(Ch),  writetext(Chs).
writetext([]).

outterm(T, Q)  :--  numbervars(T, 1, _),  outt(T, fd(_,_), Q).

%  the real job is done here
outt('V'(N), _, _)  :--  integer(N),  !,  wch('X'),  display(N).
                   %  C A U T I O N :  outt is unable to write 'V'(Integer)
outt(Term, _, _)  :--  integer(Term),  display(Term),  !.
%  the second parameter specifies a context for "fix" functors::
%  the nearest external functor and Term's position
%  (to the left or to the right of the external functor)
outt(Term, Context, Q)  :--
        =..(Term, [Name | Args]),
        outfun(Name, Args, Context, Q).

%  -- -- output a functor-term
%  -- as a "fix" term
outfun(Name, Args, Context, Q)  :--
        isfix(Name, Args, This_ff, Kind),  !,
        outff(Kind, This_ff, [Name : Args], Context, Q).
%  -- as a list
outfun(., [Larg, Rarg], _, Q)  :--
        !,  outlist([Larg : Rarg], Q).
%  -- as a normal functor-term
outfun(Name, Args, _, Q)  :--
```

882
883
884
885
886
887
888
889
890
891
892
893
894
895
896
897
898
899
900
901
902
903
904
905
906
907
908
909
910
911
912
913
914
915
916

367

(continued)

```
917          outname(Name, Q), outargs(Args, Q).
918
919  % isfix constructs a pair  ff(Prior, Associativity), and
920  % 'in' or 'pre' or 'post' (fails if not a "fix" functor)
921  isfix(Name, L_, _], ff(Prior, Assoc), in) :--
922      'FF'(Name, Types, Prior), mk_bin(Types, Assoc).
923  isfix(Name, L_], ff(Prior, Assoc), Kind) :--
924      'FF'(Name, Types, Prior), mk_un(Types, Kind, Assoc).
925
926  % Bintype (if any) is before Untype (if_any)
927  mk_bin(LBintype : _], Assoc) :-- binary(Bintype, Assoc).
928  mk_un(LUntype], Kind, Assoc) :-- unary(Untype, Kind, Assoc).
929  mk_un(L_, Untype], Kind, Assoc) :-- unary(Untype, Kind, Assoc).
930  % tests -- see o p
931
932  % -- output a "fix" term (this outff has 5 parameters)
933  outff(Kind, This_ff, NameArgs, Context, Q) :--
934      agree(This_ff, Context), !,
935      outff(Kind, This_ff, NameArgs, Q).
936  outff(Kind, This_ff, NameArgs, _, Q) :--
937      wch('('), outff(Kind, This_ff, NameArgs, Q), wch(')').
938
939  % agree helps avoid (some) unnecessary brackets around the term
940  agree(_, fd(Ext_ff, _)) :-- var(Ext_ff).
941  agree(ff(Prior1, _), fd(ff(Prior2, _), _)) :--
942      stronger(Prior1, Prior2).           % cf the parser
943  agree(ff(Prior, a(Dir)), fd(ff(Prior, a(Dir)), Dir)).
944
945  % output the functor and the arguments (this outff has 4 parameters)
946  outff(in, This_ff, LName, LArgs, RArgs], Q) :--
947      outt(Largs, fd(This_ff, l), Q),
948      outfn(Name, ' '), outt(Rargs, fd(This_ff, r), Q).
949      outff(pre, This_ff, LName, Args], Q) :--
950      outfn(Name, ' '), outt(Args, fd(This_ff, r), Q).
951      outff(post, This_ff, LName, Args], Q) :--
```

```
952       outt(Args, fd(This_ff, 1), Q), outfn(Name, ' ').
953
954 % output functor's name enclosed in Encl
955 outfn(Name, Encl) :-  wch(Encl), display(Name), wch(Encl).
956
957 % -- -- print a name (in quotes, if necessary)
958 outname(Name, noq) :-  !, display(Name).
959 outname(Name, q) :-
960       'FF'(Name, -, -, -), !, outfn(Name, '''').
961 outname(Name, q) :-
962       pname(Name, Namestring),
963       check(noq(Namestring)), !, display(Name).
964 outname(Name, q) :-  outfn(Name, '''').
965
966 noq([Ch : String]) :-  wordstart(Ch), isword(String).
967 noq([Ch]) :-  solochar(Ch).
968 noq(['.','.',.']).
969 noq([Ch : String]) :-  symch(Ch), issym(String).
970
971 isword([]).
972 isword([Ch : String]) :-  alphanum(Ch), isword(String).
973 issym([]).
974 issym([Ch : String]) :-  symch(Ch), issym(String).
975
976 % -- -- output a list of arguments (cf outfun)
977 outargs([], -) :-  !.
978 outargs(Args, Q) :-
979       fake(Context), wch('('), outargs(Args, Context, Q), wch(')').
980
981 outargs([Last], Context, Q) :-  !, outt(Last, Context, Q).
982 outargs([Arg : Args], Context, Q) :-
983       outt(Arg, Context, Q), display(','), outargs(Args, Context, Q).
984
985 % commas are used to delimit list items, so we must bracket commas
986 % within items (it's a trick: we depend on ',' having
```

(continued)

369

```
987    %    the priority 1000 and being associative)
988    fake(fd(ff(1000, na(_))_, _)).
989
990    %  --  --  output a list in square brackets (cf outfun -- the main
991    %        functor is the dot, and the list cannot be empty)
992    outlist([First : Tail], Q) :-
993        fake(Context), wch('['), outt(First, Context, Q),
994        outlist(Tail, Context, Q), wch(']').
995
996    outlist([], _, _) :- !.
997    outlist([Item : Items], Context, Q) :-
998        !, display(', '), outt(Item, Context, Q),
999        outlist(Items, Context, Q).
1000   %  the bar and the closing item (still bracketed if it contains commas)
1001   outlist(Closing, Context, Q) :-
1002       display(' : '), outt(Closing, Context, Q).
1003
1004   %  **************************************************
1005   %  *****                                       *****
1006   %  ***        T R A N S L A T O R           ***
1007   %  *****                                       *****
1008   %  **************************************************
1009   %  read a program upto end. and translate it into "kernel" form
1010   translate(Infile, Outfile)  :-
1011       see(Infile), tell(Outfile),
1012       nl, repeat,
1013       read(Clause), put(Clause), nl,  =(Clause, end),  !,
1014       seen, told, see(user), tell(user).
1015
1016   %  --  produce and output the translation of one clause
1017   put(:-(Head, Body)) . :-
1018       !, puthead(Head, Sym_tab), putbody(Body, Sym_tab).
1019   put(-->(Left, Right), :-(Head, Body))) :-
1020       !, tag(transl_rule(Left, Right, :-(Head, Body))),
```

370

```
1021            puthead(Head, Sym_tab), putbody(Body, Sym_tab).
1022    put((:-(Goal)) :-
1023            !, putbody(Goal, Sym_tab), wch($), nl,
1024            once(Goal).    % a failure here wouldn't matter (cf translate)
1025    put(end) :- !.
1026    put('e r r') :- !.
1027    put(Unitclause)   :- puthead(Unitclause, Sym_tab), putbody(true, _).
1028
1029    % -- put a head call (it must be a functor-term)
1030    puthead(Head, Sym_tab) :-
1031            nonvarint(Head), !, putterm(Head, Sym_tab).
1032    puthead(Head, _) :- transl_err(Head).
1033
1034    % -- put a list of calls and [] at the end
1035    putbody(Body, Sym_tab) :-
1036            punct((:-), conv_body(Body, B), !, putbody_c(B, Sym_tab).
1037            % see assert etc for c o n v _ b o d y
1038
1039    putbody_c([], _) :- !, display([]).
1040    putbody_c([Term : Terms], Sym_tab) :-
1041            not(integer(Term)), !, putterm(Term, Sym_tab),
1042            punct(.), putbody_c(Terms, Sym_tab).
1043    putbody_c([Term : _], _) :-  transl_err(Term).
1044
1045    punct(Ch)   :- wch(' '), wch(Ch), nl, display(' ').
1046
1047    % -- put a term (with infix dots, and canonical otherwise)
1048    putterm(Term, Sym_tab) :-
1049            var(Term), !, lookup(Term, Sym_tab, -1, N),
1050            wch(:-), display(N).
1051    putterm(Term, _) :- integer(Term), !, display(Term).
1052    putterm([Head : Tail], Sym_tab) :-
1053            !, putterm_inlist(Head, Sym_tab),
1054            display(' . '), putterm(Tail, Sym_tab).
```

(continued)

371

```
1055   putterm(Term, Sym_tab) :-
1056          =..(Term, [Name : Args]), outfn(Name, ''''),      % cf WRITE
1057          putargs(Args, Sym_tab).
1058
1059   % Sym_tab is an open list of pairs  vn(Variable, Number)
1060   % (this formulation helps avoid too many additions)
1061   lookup(V, S_t_end, PreviousN, N) :-
1062          var(S_t_end), !, sum(PreviousN, 1, N),
1063          =(S_t_end, [vn(V, N) : New_s_t_end]).
1064   lookup(V, [vn(CurrV, CurrN) : _], _, CurrN) :-
1065          eqvar(V, CurrV), !.
1066   lookup(V, [vn(_, CurrN) : S_t_tail], _, N) :-
1067          lookup(V, S_t_tail, CurrN, N).
1068
1069   % arguments -- nothing, or a list of terms in parentheses
1070   putargs([], _) :- !.
1071   putargs(Args, Sym_tab) :-
1072          wch('('), putarglist(Args, Sym_tab), wch(')').
1073
1074   putarglist([Arg], Sym_tab) :- !, putterm(Arg, Sym_tab).
1075   putarglist([Arg : Args], Sym_tab) :-
1076          putterm(Arg, Sym_tab), display(', '),
1077          putarglist(Args, Sym_tab).
1078
1079   % -- a list within a list must be enclosed in parentheses
1080   putterm_inlist(Term, Sym_tab) :-
1081          nonvarint(Term), =(Term, [_ : _]), !,
1082          wch('('), putterm(Term, Sym_tab), wch(')').
1083   putterm_inlist(Term, Sym_tab) :- putterm(Term, Sym_tab).
1084
1085   % -- error handling (only one error is discovered by translate)
1086   transl_err(X) :-
1087          nl, display('+++ Bad head or call: '), display(X), nl, fail.
1088
1089   :- protect, seen, ear.
```

372

APPENDIX A.5

Three Useful Programs

A simple editor

```
1    X  A simple interactive clause editor.
2    X  Watch for name conflicts with its procedures !
3    X  Note that this version has no safeguards against Prolog's crash
4    X  (eg. due to stack overflow).
5    X  Call  edit( name/arity )  to edit the procedure of this name and arity.
6    X  Each invocation of edit is associated with a cursor, which is the number of
7    X  a clause. Initially the cursor is at clause 0, i.e. before the first clause
8    X  in this procedure. The cursor's value and its associated clause is usually
9    X  displayed between commands.
10   X  Commands are listed below. Terminate the line immediately after typing
11   X  last character. Don't use blanks where not shown and only one where shown.
12   X
13   X  Commands ::
14   X  ----------
15   X
16   X  e Name/Arity      ::  invoke a nested instance to edit another procedure.
17   X                        The current cursor stays in place unless you happen
18   X                        to modify this procedure within a nested instance.
19   X  x                 ::  exit from the current editor instance.
20   X  +                 ::  move the cursor to the next clause, no action if none.
21   X  <cr>              ::  an empty line is an alternative form of +.
22   X  -                 ::  move the cursor to the previous clause, no action if at 0.
23   X  t                 ::  top :: move the cursor to 0.
24   X  b                 ::  bottom :: move the cursor to the bottom clause
25   X                        (0 for empty procedures).
26   X  l                 ::  list the whole procedure.
27   X  d                 ::  delete the current clause and move the cursor to
28   X                        the next (or to the new bottom if bottom is deleted).
```

(continued)

373

```
29   % i                          :- insert after the current clause. In the following
30   %                                lines write clauses as you would after consult(user)
31   %                                (terminate the sequence with end.). The cursor is
32   %                                positioned at the last inserted clause.
33   % f Filename                  :- like i, but read the clauses from a file.
34   %                                Take care! filename correctness is not checked.
35   % p                           :- invoke a nested instance of Prolog. If there is
36   %                                no memory overflow, invoking stop will return
37   %                                control to the editor.
38   %---------------------------------------------------------------------------
39
40
41   edit( Name/Arity ) :-  not ( atom( Name ), integer( Arity ) ), !,
42                          write( 'Bad parameters " ' ), !,
43                          write( edit( Name/Arity ) ), nl, fail.
44   edit ( Name/Arity ) :-  predefined( Name, Arity ), !,
45                          write( "Can''t edit system routine " " ),
46                          write( Name/Arity ), nl, fail.
47   edit( NameArity ) :-  tag( ed( NameArity, 0 ) ).
48
49   ed( NameArity, Cursor ) :-  show( NameArity, Cursor ), !,
50                          docmd( NameArity, Cursor, NewCursor ),
51                          ed( NameArity, NewCursor ).
52   ed ( NameArity, Cursor ) :-  display( 'Cursor out of range " ' ),
53                          display( Cursor ), nl, ed( NameArity, 0 ).
54
55
56   docmd( NameArity, Cursor, NewCursor ) :-
57                          repeat, % repeat over incorrect commands
58                          setline( Line ), cmd( Line, NameArity, Cursor, NewCursor ),
59                          !.
60
61   setline( [] ) :- rch, lastch( C ), iseoln( C ), !.
```

374

```
62   getline( [ C : L ] ) :- lastch( C ), getline( L ).
63
64   % cmd fails for incorrect commands.
65   cmd( [], NmAr, Cur, NCur ) :- next_cursor( NmAr, Cur, NCur ).
66   cmd( ['+'], NmAr, Cur, NCur ) :- next_cursor( NmAr ,Cur, NCur ).
67   cmd( ['-'], _, Cur, NCur ) :- prev_cursor( Cur, NCur ).
68   cmd( [t], NmAr, _, 0 ).
69   cmd( [b], NmAr, Cur, NCur ) :- bottom_cursor( NmAr, Cur, NCur ).
70   cmd( [l], NmAr, Cur, Cur ) :- listing( NmAr).
71   cmd( [d], NmAr, Cur, NCur ) :- delete( NmAr, Cur, NCur ).
72   cmd( [i], NmAr, Cur, NCur ) :- insert( NmAr, Cur, NCur ).
73   cmd( [f,'',' ' : NameString], NmAr, Cur, NCur ) :-
74          file_insert( NameString, NmAr, Cur, NCur ).
75   cmd( [e,'',' ' : Args], NmAr, Cur, Cur ) :-
76          append( NameString, ['/' : ArityString], Args ),
77          call_edit( NameString, ArityString ).
78   cmd( [x], _, _, _ ) :- tagexit( ed( _, _ ) ).
79   cmd( [p], NmAr, Cur, Cur ) :- invoke_Prolog.
80   cmd( String, _, _, _ ) :- display( '---incorrect command = ' ),
81          writetext( String ), nl, fail.
82
83
84
85   % check is provided with the standard library ( check(C) :- not not C )
86   next_cursor( Name/Arity, Cursor, Next ) :-
87          Next is Cursor + 1, check( clause( Name, Arity, Next, _, _ ) ), !.
88   next_cursor( _, Cursor, Cursor ).        % cursor at last clause
89
90
91   prev_cursor( 0, 0 ).
92   prev_cursor( Cursor, Prev ) :-  Cursor > 0, Prev is Cursor - 1.
93
94
```

375

(continued)

APPENDIX A.5 *(Continued)*

```prolog
95    bottom_cursor( Name/Arity, Cursor, Bottom ) :-
96       Next is Cursor + 1, check( clause( Name, Arity, Next, _, _ )), !,
97       bottom_cursor( Name/Arity, Next, Bottom ).
98    bottom_cursor( _, Cursor, Cursor ).
99
100
101   delete( _, 0, 0 ) :- !, display( 'Can''t delete clause 0' ), nl.
102   delete( Name/Arity, Cursor, NewCursor ) :-
103      retract( Name, Arity, Cursor ),
104      cursor_in_range( Name, Arity, Cursor, NewCursor ).
105
106   cursor_in_range( Nm, Ar, Cur, Cur ) :- check( clause( Nm, Ar, Cur, _, _ )), !.
107   cursor_in_range( _, _, Cur, Prev ) :- Prev is Cur - 1.
108
109
110   % convert is defined in the standard library
111   insert( NameArity, Cursor, NewCursor ) :-
112      repeat, % set end. or a clause of Name/Arity, skip others
113      read( Clause ), convert( Clause, Head, Body ),
114      accept( Head, NameArity, Clause ),
115      !,
116      end_or_proceed( Head, Body, NameArity, Cursor, NewCursor ).
117
118   end_or_proceed( end, [], _, Cursor, Cursor ) :- !.
119   end_or_proceed( Head, Body, NameArity, Cursor, NewCursor ) :-
120      Next is Cursor + 1, assert( Head, Body, Cursor ),
121      insert( NameArity, Next, NewCursor ).
122
123   accept( _, _, end ).
124   accept( Head, Name/Arity, _ ) :- functor( Head, Name, Arity ).
125   accept( _, _, Clause ) :-
126      display( '------clause not in edited procedure -- ignored' ),
127      nl, write( Clause ), fail.
```

376

```
128   file_insert( FNameString, NameArity, Cursor, NewCursor ) :-
129       pname( FileName, FNameString ),
130       see( FileName ), insert( NameArity, Cursor, NewCursor ),
131       seen, see( user ).
132
133
134
135   call_edit( NameString, ArityString ) :-
136       pname( Name, NameString ), pnamei( Arity, ArityString ),
137       edit( Name/Arity ).
138
139
140   invoke_Prolog :- tag( loop ).      % this works only for the Toy-Prolog monitor
141   invoke_Prolog.                     % ( loop terminated by tagfail )
142
143
144   %conv_body is defined in the standard library (asserta etc.), so is writeclause.
145   show( NameArity, 0 ) :- !, write( "[0] (" ), write( NameArity ),
146       write( ")" ), nl.
147
148   show( Name/Arity, Cursor ) :-
149       side_effects( ( clause( Name, Arity, Cursor, Head, Body ),
150           conv_body( NiceBody, Body ),
151           display( "[" ), display( Cursor ),
152           display( "] " ),
153           writeclause( Head, NiceBody ),
154           display( ".", nl ) )        ).
155
156
157   append( [], L, L ).
158   append( [ E | L ], L2, [ E | LL2 ] ) :- append( L, L2, LL2 ).
159   %
```

(continued)

377

A primitive tracing tool

```prolog
 1   % A primitive tracing package.
 2   % Watch for name conflicts with its procedures !
 3   % Use spy( Pattern ) to trace calls matching Pattern,
 4   %     nospy( Pattern ) to stop tracing.
 5   % To trace, execute trace( Goal ) instead of Goal.
 6   % Successful calls are displayed with a plus, failing calls with a minus.
 7   % Note : tagcut, tagexit, tagfail and ancestor will not be executed properly !
 8   %     trace is slow : if you wish to have the insides of a correct and
 9   %                     costly procedure executed at normal speed, add
10   %                     a predefined(...) assertion for its call.
11
12   spy( All ) :- var( All ), !, assert( spied( All ) ).
13   spy( Pattern ) :- spied( Pattern ), !.           % spied already
14   spy( Pattern ) :- assert( spied( Pattern ) ).
15
16   nospy( Pattern ) :- retract( spied( Pattern ) ), fail.
17   nospy( _ ).
18
19   trace( Goal ) :- tag( runbody( Goal ) ).
20
21
22   runbody( (A , B) ) :- !, runbody( A ), runbody( B ).
23   runbody( (A ; B) ) :- !, ( runbody( A ) ; runbody( B ) ).
24   runbody( call( Call ) ) :- var( Call ), !, runbody( Call ).
25   runbody( call( Call ) ) :- !, runbody( Call ), !, showfailure( call( Call ) ), fail.
26   runbody( tag( Call ) ) :- !, runbody( call( Call ) ).
27   runbody( Call ) :- predefined( Call ), !, runbody( call( Call ) ).
28   runbody( Call ) :- tag( runuser( Call ) ), !, runsystem( Call ).
29   runbody( Call ) :- tag( runuser( Call ) ).
```

```
30   runsystem( ! ) :- runcut.
31   runsystem( Forbidden ) :- isforbidden( Forbidden ), !, nl,
32                             display( 'FORBIDDEN CALL ' ), write( Forbidden ),
33                             display( ' FAILS !' ), nl, fail.

34   runsystem( Call ) :- not spied( Call ), !, Call.
35   runsystem( Call ) :- Call, !, showsuccess( Call ).
36   runsystem( Call ) :- showfailure( Call ), fail.

37
38   runuser( Call ) :- not spied( Call ), !,
39                      clause( Call, Body ), runbody( Body ).
40   runuser( Call ) :- clause( Call, Body ), showsuccess( Call ),
41                      runbody( Body ).
42   runuser( Call ) :- showfailure( Call ), fail.

43
44   runcut :- spied( ! ), simulatecut, showsuccess( ! ).
45   runcut :- simulatecut.

46
47   simulatecut :- tascut( runuser( _ ) ).
48   simulatecut :- tascut( runbody( _ ) ).       % cut in initial goal

49
50   showsuccess( Call ) :- display( ' + ' ), write( Call ), nl.
51   showfailure( Call ) :- display( ' - ' ), write( Call ), nl.

52
53
54   isforbidden( tasexit( _ ) ).
55   isforbidden( tasfail( _ ) ).
56   isforbidden( tascut( _ ) ).
57   isforbidden( ancestor( _ ) ).

58
59   predefined( Call ) :- check( ( functor( Call, F, N ), predefined( F, N ) ) ).
60   %----------------------------------------------------
```

379

(continued)

APPENDIX A.5 (Continued)

A program structure analyser with analyser analysed

```
1    % Given a procedure name and arity, print its call tree.
2    % The main data structure is a queue of procedures whose tail contains
3    % calls which were not yet seen. Each element of the queue contains a list
4    % of calls (references to main queue elements) and a variable to hold its
5    % ordinal number in the listed tree.
6    % Queues are searched linearly : the algorithm is costly for large trees.
7    % CAUTION : don't attempt to list a trace of this program — cyclic structures
8    % are formed as a rule.
9
10
11   calltree( Name/Arity ) :-   add( proc( Name, Arity, Ord, Calls ), Queue ),
12                               fill( Queue, Queue ),
13                               print_calls([proc(Name,Arity,Ord,Calls)],3,1,_).
14
15   % add finds (inserts) an element in ( to ) an open list
16   add( El, [El ! Tail] ) :- !.
17   add( El, [_ ! Tail] ) :- add( El, Tail ).
18
19   % fill walks the queue and expands procedures, inserting their calls into
20   % the queue if not yet seen. Queue beginning is passed along to allow search.
21   fill( [], _ ) :- !.                % evidently reached the terminating variable
22   fill( [proc(Name,Arity,_,[]) !QTail], Q ) :-  predefined( Name, Arity ), !,
23                                                 fill( QTail, Q ).
24   fill( [proc(Name,Arity,_,undefined) !QTail], Q ) :-
25                      not clause( Name, Arity, _, _ ), !, fill( QTail, Q ).
26   fill( [proc(Name,Arity,_,Calls) !QTail], Q) :-
27                      add_calls( Name, Arity, 1, Calls, Q ), fill( QTail, Q ).
28
29   % add_calls processes the clauses of a procedure, adding calls to its list
30   % of calls and to the queue (only finding in the queue if already there)
```

```prolog
31    add_calls( Name, Arity, N, Calls, Q ) :-
32        clause( Name, Arity, N, _, Body ), !,
33        body_calls( Body, Calls, Q ), N1 is N + 1,
34        add_calls( Name, Arity, N1, Calls, Q ).
35    add_calls( _, _, _, [], _ ) :- !.       % close the list if empty
36                                            % ( only unit clauses )
37                                            % non-empty list left open
38    add_calls( _, _, _, _, _ ).
39    body_calls( [], _, _ ) :- !.
40    body_calls( [Call : BodyTail], Calls, Q ) :-
41        functor( Call, Name, Arity ),
42        add( proc(Name,Arity,Ord,Callees), Calls ),
43        add( proc(Name,Arity,Ord,Callees), Q ),
44        add_insides( Call, Calls, Q ),
45        body_calls( BodyTail, Calls, Q ).
46    % add_insides unpacks metalogical calls: if their arguments are not variable
47    % or integer, they are added to the queues.
48    add_insides( Call, Q1, Q2 ) :- meta_call_1( Call, Arg ), !,
49        add_insides( Arg, Q1, Q2 ).
50    add_insides( Call, Q1, Q2 ) :-
51        meta_call_2( Call, Arg1, Arg2 ), !,
52        add_insides( Arg1, Q1, Q2 ),
53        add_insides( Arg2, Q1, Q2 ).
54    add_insides( _, _, _ ).
55
56    add_inside( V, _, _ ) :- ( var( V ) ; integer( V ) ), !.
57    add_inside( Call, Q1, Q2 ) :- functor( Call, Name, Arity ),
58        add( proc(Name,Arity,Ord,Callees), Q1 ),
59        add( proc(Name,Arity,Ord,Callees), Q2 ),
60        add_insides( Call, Q1, Q2 ).
61
62
63    meta_call_1( call( Call ), Call ).
```

(continued)

381

```
64    meta_call_1( tag( Call ) , Call ).
65    meta_call_1( not Call, Call ).
66    meta_call_1( check( Call ), Call ).
67    meta_call_1( side_effects( Call ), Call ).
68    meta_call_1( once( Call ), Call ).
69
70    meta_call_2( ( A , B ) , A, B ).
71    meta_call_2( ( A ; B ) , A, B ).
72
73    % Print calls, starting at given tab setting and ordinal, returning next ordinal
74    % number. Third clause fails if ordinal numbers don't match i.e. proc
75    % was already printed in another line.
76    print_calls( [], _, Ord, Ord ) :- !.    % this matches the terminating var
77                                              % of a call list.
78    print_calls( [proc(Name,Arity,Ord,undefined)!Calls], Tab, Ord, NOrd ) :-
79                !, start_undefined( Ord, Tab ),
80                writeq( Name/Arity ), display( '  **undefined**' ), nl,
81                'Ord is Ord + 1, print_calls( Calls, Tab, TOrd, NOrd ).
82    print_calls( [proc(Name,Arity,Ord,Callees)!Calls], Tab, Ord, NOrd ) :-
83                !, start_line( Ord, Tab ), writeq( Name/Arity ), nl,
84                InnerTab is Tab + 3, writeq( Name/Arity ), nl,
85                print_calls( Callees, InnerTab, InnerOrd, TOrd ),
86                print_calls( Calls, Tab, TOrd, NOrd ).
87    print_calls( [proc(Name,Arity,AnotherOrd,_)!Calls], Tab, Ord, NOrd ) :-
88                start_unnumbered_line( Tab ), writeq( Name/Arity ),
89                repetition( Name, Arity, AnotherOrd ), nl,
90                print_calls( Calls, Tab, Ord, NOrd ).
91
92    repetition( Name, Arity, _ ) :- predefined( Name, Arity ), !.
93    repetition( _, _, Ord ) :- display( ' (see ' ), display( Ord ),
94                                display( ')' ).
95
96    % Ord numbers are printed in 4 columns, right justified
97    start_line( Ord, Tab ) :- number_line( Ord ), !, tab( Tab, ' ' ).
```

```
 98
 99
100   number_line( N ) :- N lt 10, display( ' ' ), display( N ).
101   number_line( N ) :- N lt 100, display( ' ' ), display( N ).
102   number_line( N ) :- N lt 1000, display( ' ' ), display( N ).
103   number_line( N ) :- display( N ).
104
105   start_unnumbered_line( Tab ) :- display( ' ' ), tab( Tab , ' ' ).
106
107   start_undefined( Ord, Tab ) :- number_line( Ord ), tab( Tab , '.' ).
108
109
110   tab( 0, _ ) :- !.
111   tab( N, Ch ) :- wch( Ch ), N1 is N - 1, tab( N1, Ch ).
112   %------------

 1    calltree / 1
 2      add / 2
 3        ! / 0 (see 2)
 4      fill / 2
          ! / 0
 5      predefined / 2
        fill / 2 (see 4)
 6      'not' / 1
 7        call / 1
          ! / 0
 8        fail / 0
 9      clause / 5
10      add_calls / 5
        clause / 5
          ! / 0
11      body_calls / 3
          ; / 0
```

(continued)

```
12        functor / 3
          add / 2 (see 2)
13        add_insides / 3
14          meta_call_1 / 2
            ! / 0
15          add_inside / 3
16            ';' / 2
              call / 1
17            var / 1
18            integer / 1
            ! / 0
            functor / 3
            add / 2 (see 2)
            add_insides / 3 (see 13)
19          meta_call_2 / 3
            body_calls / 3 (see 11)
20        'is' / 2
          integer / 1
            ! / 0
          'is' / 2 (see 20)
21          sum / 3
22          prod / 4
23        add_calls / 5 (see 10)
          print_calls / 4
            ! / 0
24          start_undefined / 2
25          number_line / 1
26          '<' / 2
            'is' / 2 (see 20)
27            less / 2
28            display / 1
29          tab / 2
            ! / 0
```

```
30      wch / 1
        'is' / 2 (see 20)
        tab / 2 (see 29)
31      writeq / 1
        display / 1
32      nl / 0
        wch / 1
        'is' / 2 (see 20)
        print_calls / 4 (see 23)
33      start_line / 2
        number_line / 1 (see 25)
        ! / 0
        tab / 2 (see 29)
34      start_unnumbered_line / 1
        display / 1
        tab / 2 (see 29)
35      repetition / 3
        predefined / 2
        ! / 0
        display / 1
```

REFERENCES

Aho, A. V. and Ullman, J. D. (1977). "Principles of Compiler Design." Addison-Wesley, Reading, Massachusetts.

Astrahan, A. M. (1976). System R: Relational Approach to Database Management. *ACM Trans. Data Base Systems* **1**(2), pp. 97–137.

Ballieu, G. (1983). A Virtual Machine to Implement Prolog. In Pereira *et al.* 1983, pp. 40–52.

Battani, G. and Méloni, H. (1973). Interpréteur du langage de programmation PROLOG. Groupe d'Intelligence Artificielle, Université d'Aix-Marseille.

Battani, G. and Méloni, H. (1975). Mise en oeuvre des constraintes phonologiques, syntaxiques et sémantiques dans un système de compréhension automatique de la parole. Ph.D. thesis, Université d'Aix-Marseille.

Bendl, J., Köves, P. and Szeredi, P. (1980). The MPROLOG System. In Tärnlund 1980, pp. 201–209.

Bergman, M. and Kanoui, H. (1973). Application of Mechanical Theorem-Proving to Symbolic Calculus. In "Proceedings of the 3rd Colloquium on Advanced Computing Methods in Theoretical Physics," Marseille.

Bergman, M. and Kanoui, H. (1975). Sycophante: Système de calcul formel et d'intégration symbolique sur ordinateur. Groupe d'Intelligence Artificielle, Université d'Aix-Marseille.

Bobrow, D. G. and Wegbreit, B. (1973). A Model and Stack Implementation of Multiple Environments. *Commun. ACM* **16**(10), 591–603.

Bowen, D. L. (1981). DECSystem-10 Prolog User's Manual. Department of Artificial Intelligence, University of Edinburgh.

Bowen, D., Byrd, L. and Clocksin, W. (1983). A Portable Prolog Compiler. In Pereira *et al.* 1983, pp. 74–83.

Boyer, R. S. and Moore, J. S. (1972). The Sharing of Structure in Theorem Proving Programs. In "Machine Intelligence 7" (B. Meltzer and D. Michie, eds.), pp. 101–116. Edinburgh University Press.

Bruynooghe, M. (1976). An Interpreter for Predicate Programs: Part 1. Report CW16, Katholieke Universiteit Leuven.

Bruynooghe, M. (1978). Intelligent Backtracking for an Interpreter of Horn Clause Logic Programs. Report CW16, Katholieke Universiteit Leuven. Also in "Mathematical Logic in Computer Science" (B. Dömölki and T. Gergely, eds.), pp. 215–258. North-Holland Publ., Amsterdam.

Bruynooghe, M. (1982a). Adding Redundancy to Obtain More Reliable and More Readable Prolog Programs. In Van Caneghem 1982a, pp. 52–55.

Bruynooghe, M. (1982b). The Memory Management of PROLOG Implementations. In Clark and Tärnlund 1982, pp. 83–98.

Bruynooghe, M. and Pereira, L. M. (1981). Revison of Top-Down Logical Reasoning through Intelligent Backtracking. Report CIUNL-8/81, Universidade Nova de Lisboa.

Bundy, A., ed. (1983). "Proceedings of the 8th International Joint Conference on Artificial Intelligence", 8–12 August 1983, Karslruhe. William Kaufmann, Inc., Los Altos, California.

Burstall, R. M. and Darlington, J. (1977). Transformation for Developing Recursive Programs. *J. ACM* **24**(1), 44–67.

Campbell, J. A., ed. (1984). "Implementations of PROLOG". Ellis Horwood Ltd., Chichester.

Chamberlin, D. D., Astrahan, M. M., Eswaran, K. P., Griffith, P. P., Lorie, R. A., Mehl, J. W., Reisner, P. and Wade, B. W. (1976). SEQUEL2: A Unified Approach to Data Definition, Manipulation and Control. *IBM. Res. Dev.* **20**(6), pp. 560–575.

Chomicki, J. and Grudziński, W. (1983). A Database Support System for Prolog. In Pereira *et al.* 1983, pp. 290–303.

Clark, K. L. (1978). Negation as Failure. In Gallaire and Minker 1978, pp. 293–322.

Clark, K. L. and Gregory, S. (1983). PARLOG: A Parallel Logic Programming Language. Research Report DOC 83/5, Imperial College, London.

Clark, K. L. and McCabe, F. G. (1980a). IC-PROLOG—Aspects of Its Implementation. In Tärnlund 1980, pp. 190–197.

Clark, K. L. and McCabe, F. G. (1980b). IC-PROLOG—Language Features. In Tärnlund 1980, pp. 45–52.

Clark, K. L. and McCabe, F. G. (1984). "micro-PROLOG. Programming in Logic". Prentice-Hall, Englewood Cliffs, New Jersey.

Clark, K. L. and Tärnlund, S.-Å. (1977). A First Order Theory of Data and Programs. In "Information Processing 77" (B. Gilchrist, ed.), pp. 939–944. North-Holland, Amsterdam.

Clark, K. L. and Tärnlund, S.-Å., eds. (1982). "Logic Programming". Academic Press, New York and London.

Clark, K. L., McCabe, F. G. and Gregory, S. (1979). The Control Facilities of IC-PROLOG. In "Expert Systems in Micro-Electronic Age" (D. Michie, ed.), pp. 129–149. Edinburgh University Press.

Clark, K. L., Ennals, J. R. and McCabe, F. G. (1982a). "A micro-PROLOG Primer". Logic Programming Associates Ltd., London.

Clark, K. L., McCabe, F. G. and Gregory, S. (1982b). IC-PROLOG—Language Features. In Clark and Tärnlund 1982, pp. 253–266.

Clocksin, W. F. and Mellish, C. S. (1981). "Programming in Prolog". Springer-Verlag, Berlin and Heidelberg.

Codd, E. F. (1970). A Relational Model of Data for Large Shared Data Banks. *Commun. ACM* **13**(6), 377–387.

Codd, E. F. (1979). Extending the Relational Data Base Model to Capture More Meaning. *ACM Trans. Data Base Systems* **4**(4), pp. 397–434.

Coelho, H. (1982). Man-Machine Communication in Portuguese—A Friendly Library Service System. *Information Systems* **7**(2), 163–181.

Coelho, H., Cotta, J. C. and Pereira, L. M. (1980). How to Solve It in Prolog. Laboratório Nacional de Engenharia Civil, Lisboa.

Colmerauer, A. (1975). Le grammaires de métamorphose. Groupe d'Intelligence Artificielle, Université d'Aix-Marseille.

Colmerauer, A. (1978). Metamorphosis Grammars. In "Natural Language Communication with Computer" (L. Bolc, ed.), pp. 133–189. Springer-Verlag, Berlin and Heidelberg.

Colmerauer, A. (1979). Prolog and Infinite Trees. Groupe d'Intelligence Artificielle, Université d'Aix-Marseille. Also in Clark and Tärnlund 1982, pp. 45–66.

Colmerauer, A. (1982). PROLOG II. Manuel de référence et modèle théorique. Groupe
d'Intelligence Artificielle, Université Marseille II.

Colmerauer, A. (1983). Prolog in Ten Figures. In Bundy 1983, pp. 487–499.

Colmerauer, A., Kanoui, H., Roussel, P. and Pasero, R. (1972). Un système de communication homme-machine en français. Rapport preliminaire. Groupe d'Intelligence Artificielle, Université d'Aix-Marseille.

Colmerauer, A., Kanoui, H., Roussel, P. and Pasero, R. (1973). Un système de communication homme-machine en français. Rapport de rechereche sur le contrat CRI no 72-18 de
février 72 a juin 73. Groupe d'Intelligence Artificielle, Université d'Aix-Marseille.

Colmerauer, A., Kanoui, H. and Van Caneghem, M. (1979). Etude et réalisation d'un
système Prolog. Groupe d'Intelligence Artificielle, Université d'Aix-Marseille.

Colmerauer, A., Kanoui, H. and Van Caneghem, M. (1981). Last Steps toward an Ultimate
Prolog. In "Proceedings of the 7th International Joint Conference on Artificial Intelligence" (R. Schank, ed.), Vancouver, Canada, pp. 947–948.

Colmerauer, A., Kanoui, H. and Van Caneghem, M. (1983). Prolog, bases théoriques et
développements actuels. *Techniques et Science Informatiques* 2(4), 271–311. English
translation in *Technology and Science of Informatics* 2(4).

Conery, J. S. and Kibler, D. F. (1983). AND Parallelism in Logic Programs. In Bundy 1983,
pp. 539–543.

Dahl, V. (1977). Un système déductif d'interrogation de banques de données en espagnol.
Ph.D. thesis, Université d'Aix-Marseille.

Dahl, V. (1980). Two Solutions for the Negation Problem. In Tärnlund 1980, pp. 61–72.

Date, C. J. (1982). "An Introduction to Database Systems", 3rd. ed., Vol. 1. Addison-
Wesley, Reading, Massachusetts.

Dijkstra, E. W. (1975). Guarded Commands, Nondeterminacy and Formal Derivation of
Programs. *Commun. ACM* 18, 453–457.

Donz, P. (1979). Une méthode de transformation et d'optimisation de programmes Prolog:
définition et implémentation. Ph.D. thesis, Université d'Aix-Marseille.

Eisinger, N., Kasif, B. and Minker, J. (1982). Logic Programming—a Parallel Approach. In
Van Caneghem 1982a, pp. 71–77.

Emden, M.H.van (1981).AVL-Tree Insertion: A Benchmark Program Biased towards Prolog.
Logic Programming Newslett. 2, 4.

Emden, M.H. van (1982). An Interpreting Algorithm for Prolog Programs. In Van Caneghem
1982a, pp. 56–64. Also in Campbell 1984, pp. 93–110.

Emden, M. H. van and Kowalski, R. A. (1979). The Semantics of Predicate Logic as a
Programming Language. *J. ACM* 23(4), 733–744.

Ennals, J. R. (1983). "Beginning Micro-Prolog". Ellis Horwood, Chichester, U.K.

Fikes, R. E. and Nilsson, N. J. (1971). STRIPS: A New Approach to the Application of
Theorem-Proving to Problem Solving. *Artif. Intell.* 2, 235–246.

Filgueiras, M. (1982). A Prolog Interpreter Working with Infinite Terms. Report FCT/UNL-
20/82, Universidade Nova de Lisboa. Also in Campbell 1984, pp. 250–258.

Filgueiras, M. and Pereira, L. M. (1983). Relational Databases a La Carte. In Pereira *et al.*
1983, pp. 389–407.

Gallaire, H. (1983). Logic Databases versus Deductive Databases. In Pereira *et al.* 1983, pp.
608–622.

Gallaire, H. and Minker, J., eds. (1978). "Logic and Databases". Plenum Press, New York.

Gallaire, H., Minker, J. and Nicolas, J.-H., eds. (1981). "Advances in Database Theory", vol. I. Plenum Press, New York.

Gregory, S. (1980). Towards the Compilation of Annotated Logic Programs. Research Report DOC 80/16, Imperial College, London.

Gries, D. (1971). "Compiler Construction for Digital Computers". Wiley and Sons, New York.

Guizol, J. (1975). Synthèse du français à partir d'une représentation en logique du premier ordre. Ph.D. thesis, Université d'Aix-Marseille.

Guizol, J. and Méloni, H. (1976). Prolog modulaire. Groupe d'Intelligence Artificielle, Université d'Aix-Marseille.

Hill, R. (1974). LUSH Resolution and Its Completeness. DCL Memo 78, University of Edinburgh.

Hoare, C. A. D. (1962). Quicksort. *Comput. J.* **5**(1), 10–15.

Hogger, C. J. (1979). Derivation of Logic Programs. Ph.D. thesis, Imperial College, London.

Joubert, M. (1974). Un système de résolution de problèmes a tendance naturelle. Ph.D. thesis, Université d'Aix-Marseille.

Kanoui, H. (1973). Application de la démonstration automatique aux manipulations algébrique et à l'intégration formelle sur ordinateur. Ph.D. thesis, Université d'Aix-Marseille.

Kanoui, H. (1982). PROLOG II. Manuel d'exemples. Groupe d'Intelligence Artificielle, Université d'Aix-Marseille II.

Kanoui, H. and Van Caneghem, M. (1980). Implementing a Very High Level Language on a Very Low Cost Computer. In "Information Processing 80" (S. Lavington, ed.), pp. 349–354. North-Holland, Amsterdam.

Kluźniak, F. (1981). Remarks on Coroutines in Prolog. In Szpakowicz 1981, pp. 19–29.

Kluźniak, F. (1984). The "Marseille Interpreter"—a Personal Perspective. In Campbell 1984, pp. 65–70.

Kluźniak, F. and Szpakowicz, S. (1983). "Prolog" WNT (Wydawnictwa Naukowo-Techniczne), Warsaw.

Kluźniak, F. and Szpakowicz, S. (1984). Prolog—a Panacea? In Campbell 1984, pp. 71–84.

Knuth, D. E. (1968). Semantics of Context-Free Languages. *Math. Syst. Theory* **2**, 127–145.

Komorowski, H. J. (1982). QLOG—The Programming Environment for Prolog in LISP. In Clark and Tärnlund 1982, pp. 315–322.

Koster, C. H. A. (1974). Using the CDL Compiler–Compiler. In "Compiler Construction. An Advanced Course" (F. J. Bauer and J. Eickel, eds.), pp. 366–426. Lecture Notes in Computer Science 21, Springer-Verlag, Berlin and Heidelberg.

Kowalski, R. A. (1972). The Predicate Calculus as a Programming Language. In "Proceedings of the International Symposium and Summer School on Mathematical Foundations of Computer Science", Jabłonna near Warsaw, Poland.

Kowalski, R. A. (1974). Predicate Logic as Programming Language. In *"Proceedings of the IFIP Congress"*, pp. 569–574. North-Holland, Amsterdam.

Kowalski, R. A. (1978). Logic for Data Description. In Gallaire and Minker 1978, pp. 77–103.

Kowalski, R. A. (1979a). Algorithm = Logic + Control. *Commun. ACM* **22**, 424–431.

Kowalski, R. A. (1979b). "Logic for Problem Solving". North-Holland, Amsterdam.

Kowalski, R. A. and Kuehner, D. (1971). Linear Resolution with Selection Function. *Artificial Intelligence* **2**(3/4), 227–260. Also in "The Automation of Reasoning II" (J. H. Siekmann and G. Wrightson, eds.) Springer-Verlag, Berlin and Heidelberg, 1983.

Lloyd, J. W. (1982). An Introduction to Deductive Database Systems. Department of Computer Science Report TR 81/3, University of Melbourne.

McCabe, F. G. (1981). "Micro PROLOG Programmer's Reference Manual". Logic Programming Associates Ltd., London.

Mellish, C. S. (1981). Automatic Generation of Mode Declarations in Prolog Programs. Paper presented at Workshop on Logic Programming, Long Beach, Los Angeles, California.

Mellish, C. S. (1982). An Alternative to Structure Sharing in the Implementation of a Prolog Interpreter. In Clark and Tärnlund 1982, pp. 99–106.

Mellish, C. and Hardy, S. (1983). Integrating Prolog into the Poplog Environment. In Bundy 1983, pp. 533–535. Also in Campbell 1984, pp. 147–162.

Moss, C. D. S. (1979). A New Grammar for Algol 68. Department of Computing report 79/6, Imperial College, London.

Mycroft, A. and O'Keefe, R. (1983). A Polymorphic Type System for Prolog. In Pereira *et al*. 1983, pp. 107–122.

Neves, J. and Williams, M. (1983). Towards a Co-operative Data Base Management System. In Pereira *et al*. 1983, pp. 341–370.

Neves, J., Anderson, S. and Williams, M. (1983). Security and Integrity in Logic Data Bases using QBE. In Pereira *et al*. 1983, pp. 304–340.

Pasero, R. (1973). Représentation du français en logique du 1er ordre en vue de dialoguer avec un ordinateur. Ph.D. thesis, Université d'Aix-Marseille.

Pereira, L. M. and Porto, A. (1980a). An Interpreter for Logic Programs using Selective Backtracking. Report 3/80, Centro de Informatica da Universidade Nova de Lisboa.

Pereira, L. M. and Porto, A. (1980b). Selective Backtracking for Logic Programs. In "Proceedings of the 5th Conference on Automated Deduction" (W. Bibel and R. Kowalski, eds.), pp. 306–317. Springer-Verlag, Berlin and Heidelberg.

Pereira, L. M. and Porto, A. (1981). All Solutions. *Logic Programming Newslett*. **2**, 9–10.

Pereira, L. M. and Porto, A. (1982). Selective Backtracking. In Clark and Tärnlund 1982, pp. 107–114.

Pereira, F. C. N. and Warren, D. H. D. (1980). Definite Clause Grammars for Language Analysis—a Survey of the Formalism and a Comparison with Augmented Transition Networks. *Artif. Intell.* **13**(3), 231–278.

Pereira, L. M., Pereira, F. C. N. and Warren, D. H. D. (1978). User's Guide to DECSystem-10 Prolog (Provisional Version). Department of Artificial Intelligence, University of Edinburgh.

Pereira, L. M., Porto, A., Monteiro, L. and Filgueiras, M., eds. (1983). "Logic Programming Workshop '83 Proceedings", Praia da Falésia, Algarve, Portugal, 26 June to 1 July, 1983, Universidade Novade Lisboa.

Porto, A. (1982). EPILOG: A Language for Extended Programming in Logic. In Van Caneghem 1982a, pp. 31–37.

Robinson, J. A. (1965). A Machine-oriented Logic Based on the Resolution Principle. *J. ACM* **12**(1), pp. 23–41.

Robinson, J. A. (1979). "Logic: Form and Function—the Mechanization of Deductive Reasoning". North-Holland, Amsterdam.

Roussel, P. (1975). PROLOG, manuel de référence et d'utilisation. Groupe d'Intelligence Artificielle, Université d'Aix-Marseille.

Sedgewick, R. (1983). "Algorithms". Addison-Wesley, Reading, Massachusetts.

Sergot, M. (1982). A Query-the-User Facility for Logic Programming. Research report DOC 82/18, Imperial College, London.

Shapiro, E. Y. (1983a). "Algorithmic Program Debugging". MIT Press, Cambridge, Massachusetts.

Shapiro, E. Y. (1983b). A Subset of Concurrent Prolog and Its Interpreter. ICOT (Institute for New Generation Computer Technology) Technical Report TR-003, Tokyo.

Stonebraker, M., Wong, E., Kreps, P. and Held, G. (1976). The Design and Implementation of INGRES, *ACM Trans. Data Base Systems* **1**(3), pp. 189–222.

Szeredi, P. (1977). PROLOG—a Very High Level Language Based on Predicate Logic. Preprints of 2nd Hungarian Computer Science Conference, Budapest.

Szeredi, P. (1982). Module Concept for Prolog. Paper presented at the Prolog Programming Environments Workshop, Linköping.

SzKI (1982). MPROLOG User's Manual. Szamistastechnikai Koordinacios Intezet, Budapest.

Szpakowicz, S., ed. (1981). Papers in Logic Programming I. IInfUW Report No. 104, Warsaw University.

Tärnlund, S.-Å., ed. (1980). Preprints of: Logic Programming Workshop, 14–16 July 1980, Debrecen, Hungary.

Ullman, J. D. (1982). "Principles of Database Systems", 2nd ed. Computer Science Press, Rockville, Maryland.

Van Caneghem, M., ed. (1982a). "Proceedings of the 1st International Logic Programming Conference", 14–17 September 1982, Faculté de Sciences de Luminy, Marseille, France.

Van Caneghem, M. (1982b). PROLOG II. Manuel d'utilisation. Groupe d'Intelligence Artificielle, Université Marseille II.

Vasey, P. (1982). AVL-Tree Insertion Revisited. *Logic Programing Newslett.* **3**, 11.

Warren, D. H. D. (1974). WARPLAN—a System for Generating Plans. DGL Memo 76, University of Edinburgh.

Warren, D. H. D. (1976). Generating Conditional Plans and Programs. In "Proceedings of the AISB Summer Conference", Edinburgh, pp. 344–354.

Warren, D. H. D. (1977a). Implementing Prolog—Compiling Predicate Logic Programs. DAI Report Nos. 39 and 40, University of Edinburgh.

Warren, D. H. D. (1977b). Logic Programming and Compiler Writing. DAI Report No. 44, University of Edinburgh.

Warren, D. H. D. (1980a). An Improved Prolog Implementation Which Optimises Tail Recursion. In Tärnlund 1980, pp. 1–11.

Warren, D. H. D. (1980b). Logic Programming and Compiler Writing. *Software—Practice and Experience* **10**(2), 97–125.

Warren, D. H. D. (1981). Efficient Processing of Interactive Relational Database Queries Expressed in Logic. In "Proceedings of the 7th International Conference on Very Large Data Bases", Cannes, pp. 272–281.

Warren, D. H. D. and Pereira, F. C. N. (1982). An Efficient Easily Adaptable System for Interpreting Natural Language Queries. *Am. J. Computational Linguistics* **8**(3–4), 110–119.

Warren, D. H. D., Pereira, L. M. and Pereira, F. C. N. (1977). Prolog—the Language and Its Implementation Compared with Lisp. Presented at the ACM Symposium on Artificial Intelligence and Programming Languages, Rochester, New York. SIGART Newsletter No. 64, *SIGPLAN Notices* **12**(8), 1977, pp. 109–115.

Wijngaarden, van A., ed. (1976). "Revised Report on the Algorithmic Language Algol 68". Springer-Verlag, Berlin and Heidelberg.

Wirth, N. (1976), "Algorithms + Data Structures = Programs". Prentice-Hall, Englewood Cliffs, New Jersey.

Wise, M. J. (1984). EPILOG: Re-interpreting and Extending Prolog for a Multiprocessor Environment. In Campbell 1984, pp. 341–351.

Zloof, M. M. (1977). Query-by-Example: A Data Base Language. *IBM Syst. J.* **16**(4), 324–342.

INDEX

Page numbers in italics indicate material referring to implementation issues; page numbers followed by n indicate material in footnotes.

C

A.P.I.C. Studies in Data Processing
General Editors: Fraser Duncan and M. J. R. Shave

(continued)

*Out of print.